# SOCIALISM TODAY AND TOMORROW

# SOCIALISM
# TODAY AND TOMORROW

**Michael Albert and Robin Hahnel**

**SOUTH END PRESS**

I discovered that...I should need to do battle with a certain phantom. And the phantom was a woman...she was intensely sympathetic. She was immensely charming. She was utterly unselfish. She excelled in the difficult arts of family life. She sacrificed herself daily. If there was chicken, she took the leg; if there was a draught, she sat in it—in short she was so constituted that she never had a mind or wish of her own, but preferred to sympathise always with the minds and wishes of others. Above all—I need not say it—she was pure....And when I came to write I encountered her with the very first words. The shadow of her wings fell on my page; I heard the rustling of her skirts in the room...she slipped behind me and whispered: '...Be sympathetic; be tender; flatter, deceive; use all the arts and wiles of your sex. Never let anybody guess that you have a mind of your own. Above all, be pure.' And she made as if to guide my pen. I now record the one act for which I take some credit to myself...I turned upon her and caught her by the throat. I did my best to kill her. My excuse, if I were to be had up in a court of law, would be that I acted in self-defence. Had I not killed her, she would have killed me.

Virginia Woolf


A century ago, when the workers were a small class of downtrodden, helpless individuals, the call was heard: workers of the world unite! You have nothing to lose but your chains; you have a world to win. Since then they have become the largest class; and they have united; but only imperfectly. At that time no clear goal could be depicted around which to unite; so their organizations in the end became tools of capitalism. Now the goal becomes distinct; against the stronger domination of the state-direct planned economy of the new capitalism stands what Marx called the association of free and equal producers. So the call for unity must be supplemented by an indication of the goal: take the factories and machines; assert your mastery over the productive apparatus; organize production by means of workers' councils.

Anton Pannekoek

# Acknowledgements

A number of people have read all or part of this volume in draft form and made various editorial and contextual suggestions. To enumerate their singular contributions would accomplish little and be quite impossible. For their advice has been instrumental in determining the ideas and the presentation of every chapter. Although it is also true that conversations with many people have greatly influenced this work, we would like to take this space to give special thanks to those who made direct contributions as a result of reading a part or all of the manuscript at some stage of its development: Robert Berko, Carl Boggs, Peter Bohmer, Sandy Carter, Ward Churchill, Herb Gintis, Jean Hahnel, Micaela di Leonardo, David Plotke, Lydia Sargent, John Schall, Steve Shalom, Sheila Walsh, and John Willoughby.

We would also like to thank Michael Prokosch for his design and preparation of the front cover.

SOUTH END PRESS
302 COLUMBUS AVE
BOSTON MA 02116

Library of Congress Card Catalog Number: 81-50138
ISBN   0-89608-077-3
ISBN   0-89608-078-1
Cover by Michael Prokosch; Typeset by Carrier Pigeon and South End Press; Design and Paste Up by South End Press.

# Dedication

For workers on the line, bored, tired, and robbed of their creative days;

For women raped, pinched, door-opened, decultured, feminized, beaten, married;

For Blacks, Latinos, Native Americans, Asians... nameless, robbed of dignity, lynched, harassed, low-paid, running, jailed;

For the drunks and addicts, the worn-out and the never lively, for the old and ill who should be long-lived and wise;

For the young, schooled and unschooled, enduring boredom, sniffing glue, stealing sex and losing love, trying to escape or trying to find a way in:

For those on welfare or off, looking in or looking out, employed or unemployed alone or in pairs, hiding their sex or flaunting it, angry, sad, mad;

For all those who feel less than they could feel, for those who are less than they could be in this rich land, the United States; and,

For the Chilean, Paraguayan, Argentinian, South African, Liberian, Iranian, Thai, and Pakistani exploited, robbed, starved, cheated, tortured, ambushed, kidnapped, death squadded;

For all the world's citizens suffering brutality and indignity—the electric shocks and murdered relatives, the starvation and the working for pennies, the military boot and the cultural stamp—

For the empire's citizens; and,

For the empire's enemies:

For the strikers, the saboteurs, the feminists and anarchists, the Marxists and nationalists, for those with no ideology but liberty;

For the memory of Che and the Cuban freedom fighters;

For the memory of Cabral and the liberation of Africa;

For the memory of Kollontai and the Russians in revolt, for Luxemburg and the German left, for Ho and the Vietnamese—the Vietnamese who yesterday taught us all—

For the New Leftists, Panthers, Women's Liberationists, Farm Workers, Puerto Rican Nationalists, for those of AIM and their relatives who resisted and died in the past and who nonetheless live on:

For the ones who dodged the draft, for those who went and disrupted, and for those who went and died—or lived;

For the French in the streets in May and the Italians in Autumn, for the Mexicans in the summer and the Czechs and Chinese...

For everyone who has fought, fights, or will fight for a better world than they were, are, or are going to be bequeathed;

and at the same time, necessarily:

Against the Rockefellers, the Somozas and Pinochets, the elite Savaki of the world, and the Kissingers all;

Against the doctors who deal in dollars but not in dignity, the landlords, the lawyers, and the politicians with eyes closed to injustice;

Against the owners, administrators, bosses, rapists and racists, those on top and those who aspire only to be there; against the dealers of bad hands;

Against the social ties and unties that breed the good and the bad, that breed the pain and we who grow ugly by inevitably "benefitting" from its continuance; and last, for after all this is to be a book;

Against the intellectuals who keep knowledge as if it were their private property, who enshrine their own ignorance under false halos, who can justify barbarism or technically dissect it as their interests require—but who never show a tear;

Against the media-liars, the news-pimps, the career thinkers, the academics who propagate propaganda to preserve this system or the other, the academics who call themselves socialists and always do nothing, the ones who succeed but don't stay angry, the ones that don't really care;

it is time for all of us on the outs to talk of what a better world could—will—really be like, that we might together make it so.

Till when there will be fewer acquaintances and many more friends, lovers and first and last;

To those who have yet to live under socialism though they have certainly seen the last of capitalism—we dedicate this book.

# Table of Contents

# Part One

# Preparation

The weapon of criticism, of course, cannot supplant the criticism of weapons, material force must be overthrown by material force. But theory too, will become a material force as soon as it seizes the masses. Theory is capable of seizing the masses as soon as its proofs are ad hominem and its proofs are ad hominem as soon as it is radical. To be radical is to grasp the matter by the root. But for people the root is people themselves.

Karl Marx

# INTRODUCTION

It is necessary, with bold spirit and in good conscience, to save civilization.... We must halt the dissolution that corrupts the roots of human society. The bare and barren tree can be made green again. Are we not ready?

Antonio Gramsci

Whether you talk to an optimist or a pessimist, a futurist or a person who would welcome a reversion to the past, one thing is certain. In the United States few are content with what is. Double digit stagflation, disintegration of the family and threat of World War have us on the run. The resurgence of the Ku Klux Klan, the rebirth of HUAC under a new name, and a "born again" CIA free of restriction, all argue that something is deeply wrong—our society is not growing more humane, but less. And at the same time patchwork approaches to solving social problems are losing supporters. The middle is eroding. Election, reform, and business as usual awaken only cynicism. If the usual metaphor is employed—the country is ill—almost no one believes that soup and aspirin will do the trick. A few are willing to consider radical surgery but have little idea what needs amputation. Most worry that the patient is terminal and would rather avoid the matter entirely.

Though a host of factors govern where one stands on this matter—whether all is hopeless, reform can rejuvenate us, or radical change is required—surprisingly the extent one is horrified by current ills is not one of them. For example there are reformists and even cynics who are as deeply horrified by many current ailments as are radicals. A different concern separates the "reformer" from the "socialist." However horrified by current injustices, the reformer feels they are an outgrowth of unnecessary social flaws which can be corrected without disturbing society's most basic institutions. On

1

the contrary, the socialist feels that as the source of current injustices our basic institutions must and can be changed. Yet if we imagine a reformist and a socialist taking turns on a soap box, how will each try to win our allegiance? The reformist must make us believe that many of the hardships we endure and that our country imposes on other parts of the world are a product of relatively minor institutional flaws, bad people, ignorance, and other similar problems which can be remedied without major restructuring. The reformist must therefore overcome popular suspicions that these problems run far deeper, into the very definition and foundations of our society, and must also counter immense popular cynicism about the possibility of making even minor changes through our present system.

The socialist, on the contrary, must convince people that our basic institutions are oppressive and that an alternative structure for society could be more just and conducive to human development. Moreover, the socialist must also demonstrate that the road from where we are to this new society is passable.

Though this book isn't the place to make the case, the reformist's task is ultimately impossible. The growing popular consciousness that our society's institutions aren't geared to change and that they are horribly flawed and responsible for many of our ills is correct. The economy breeds inequality and alienation. It robs our lives of meaning at work and subjects us to shoddy and dangerous goods in consumption. As a gritty reminder of its omnipotence and ugliness, from dawn to dusk it dumps toxic waste in our air, rivers, streets, and playgrounds. Haven from this economic denigration that they might be, our families are nonetheless fraught with recrimination, tension between the generations, and especially psychological and all too often physical abuse of women. In the United States there is a rape every six minutes and this has nothing to do with genetics but is a product of basic social relations which must be changed. The potential for racial conflict and even race war grows continually greater as the degradation and denial of minorities persists. The government imposes upon us in all aspects of our lives, yet is entirely beyond our influence. The politicians lie with regularity and it no longer even bothers us—it is a normal part of what has become a kind of Kafkaesque existence. Our petitions for improvement have yielded so little that the reformist's pleas now land on deaf ears. Fewer of us go to the polls each November. Fewer of us pay attention to events beyond the perimeter of our own homes and jobs. Feeling that the basic contours of society make real change a hopeless pipedream, we become cynical in our wisdom.

But the socialist on the soapbox who would have us cast aside this cynicism and become activists obviously has a hard road to hoe as well. We might easily accept the logic of the impassioned speech: "If there is a better way to organize society than we should work to bring it about." But this "if" is a big one. A hand goes up in the audience facing the soapbox: "What is this better society to look like? You call it socialism but we know that socialism is no good—they have it in Russia and what did it get them?" The crowd thins. The socialist ranks never grow beyond a few diehards.

Other factors certainly influence our attitudes about calls for minor or major social change, but one factor which is exceptionally important is our view of what alternative is possible. Is the system we have the best one imaginable, even with all its flaws, or is a socialist alternative superior? But if we are to believe the latter, how does one explain the countries that call themselves "socialist"? Certainly they have little to offer us.

By and large, in the public imagination and even in the minds of many who favor socialism, socialist change in the U.S. is thought of in terms of revolutions that have occured elsewhere, principally in the Soviet Union, China, and Cuba. As a result people look at these countries to see if they have basic social institutions superior to those we have here in the West. No doubt the popular understanding of what goes on in these countries is jaundiced by the media, yet nonetheless when people draw the lesson that little there is superior to what we have known, they are hardly leaping to unwarranted, ill-informed, or ignorant conclusions. In many ways, they are right. Risking the uncertainties of social strife to try to transform our country into some version of what we see in the East just isn't worth it. And though the soapbox socialist might counter this reasonable doubt by arguing that these so called socialist societies are deficient and claiming that what he or she suggests is different, too often no compelling criticism or viable alternative are offered.

Is it any wonder there is skepticism? Beyond doubts about "treatment" remarkably this "soapbox socialist surgeon" doesn't even know what good health is. What is the value of scathing criticism of capitalism without a workable vision of how things might be better? This soapboxer is just depressing.

This is the situation we want to address in this book. Elsewhere, we and many other socialists who have grown horrified by the ills of our society have made a case against "aspirin and soup" palliatives. Here we want to make a case that there *is* a workable and desireable model to aim for that differs substantially from the Soviet Union, China or Cuba.

In a companion volume, *Marxism and Socialist Theory*, we have addressed the concepts usually used to understand history and especially post-capitalist societies—not only those of various Marxists, but also those of feminists, nationalists, and other schools of thought. We have also tried to evolve an alternative totalist framework better suited to contemporary socialist needs. In the first chapter of this book we *summarize* positive results of that discussion in a highly accessible way. Those who read this book and wish to know more about the theoretical approach that lies behind it and its relation to other theories and analyses of socialism might want to consult *Marxism and Socialist Theory*.

In chapter two, three, and four of this book, we present discussions of the historical experiences of the Russian, Chinese, and Cuban revolutions. In each case we discuss politics, economics, kinship, and community (race and cultural) dynamics. Obviously these discussions aren't comprehensive histories. There are innumerable books on each of these revolutionary experiences, each addressing only one, or perhaps two of these four spheres of daily life. We seek the insights that can be gained from seeing the "whole forest" not because we think more detailed but narrow studies are useless, but 1) because we think they should be informed by a totalist overview, 2) because we think there has been far too little attention paid to the non-economic side of these revolutionary experiences, 3) because we think most analyses of socialist economies have been based on a seriously flawed theory of the class dynamics at work, 4) because we feel the study of each sphere can enlighten the study of the others, and 5) because we are concerned with developing some positive images of socialism and we believe these images must touch all sides of social life rather than being confined to only one or two.

Therefore, after assessing these three historical experiences in an unusual way, and after arriving at an unusual set of judgements about them, we will propose a positive vision as an alternative. We will discuss political, economic, kinship, and community relations in sufficient detail to provide clarity about what socialism can be. Finally, we will also discuss certain problems that will plague efforts to attain socialism. In the chapters on vision we will focus primarily on a society that is well established and functioning smoothly, but we will also discuss problems of transition that might arise in the earlier days of new socialist relations. And in our last chapter we will address the lessons of our vision for problems of how we should act in the present. If, as we will argue, neither social democracy nor Leninism are viable paths to attaining socialism, then what allegiances are we to form? This will be the subject of the concluding chapter.

At a time when cynicism is rampant and people are clearly perceiving just how limited our current social institutions are, those who wish to foster basic change have a responsibility to clarify what they want. Of course a blueprint with detailed instructions is impossible. Futures are a product of immense social forces, they cannot be prescribed in advance as one might design one's room down to the last detail before moving any furniture. At the same time, to beg off the task of being specific about socialism fearing that specificity would be "utopian" or "unscientific" is ridiculous. There is more than one possible future. Which one we will enjoy or endure will depend on how clever we can be in understanding not only the present and its forces fostering different kinds of change, but also the future and the institutions it might encompass. To get someplace desirable we must have a compelling idea of what that place will be like. Otherwise, either we won't move at all—not many people will rise out of cynicism till a compelling vision convinces them their action is worthwhile—or we'll arrive someplace we'd rather not.

There is a big market for books about self-help, making it through the crises to come in the eighties, how to win friends, and other individualist approaches to improving one's life. These do not deserve scorn. They are a sign that the normal operation and the normal allegiances and beliefs of our society are crumbling. This is a book about what might be done in the large about these problems we all face daily. It first addresses experiences other than our own—for the post-capitalist experiences of others stand as an immense barrier to believing in socialism. We must understand them before we can make headway with something new ourselves. For only then will we be able to address what our own situation can and should be in the future. Hopefully our vision will be compelling enough to convince others to make it still richer, more detailed, more practical, and easier to communicate to a broad audience. Then perhaps together we can all work to replace the contemporary spectre of a roller skater with earphones escaping just about everything that is social with a picture of people concerned about their worldly lot and collectively intent upon overcoming all obstacles to make it better. For if we don't make that transition before too long the lonely disco rollerskater is going to need a gas mask to accompany his or her earphones, and then a knife or gun for protection. Will it be socialism in the decades ahead or portable bomb shelters, laser wars, and general moral degradation? That is the question we must all answer.

# 1
# GENERAL METHODOLOGY

An hour's listening disclosed the fanatical intolerance of
minds sealed against new ideas, new facts, new feelings,
new attitudes, new hints at ways to live. They denounced
books they had never read, people they had never known,
ideas they could never understand, and doctines whose
names they could not pronounce. Communism, instead of
making them leap forward with fire in their hearts to
become masters of ideas and life, had frozen them at an
even lower level of ignorance than had been theirs before
they met Communism.

Richard Wright

Imagine attending a session of Congress. To understand what
was going on, what data would you collect? Would it be best to
bring a camera, tape recorder, or simply take notes? Should the emphasis be on *who* talks, on *how long* people talk, or the order of
events; on just the speakers or on how people react; on topics, agenda, or the ideology and social pressures behind these? Could one
understand the events without prior analysis of Congress's place in
history and in society? What kinds of information? How should it be
perceived? How should it be interpreted?

The most critical determinant of answers to these three questions is one's purpose. If the person studying Congress was interested in decision-making the list of possible investigative topics
mentioned above is relevant. But, if the analyst was concerned with
effects of the heating and air conditioning systems, then none of the
information mentioned above would have been relevant. Instead,
the proper focus would have been air currents and temperature gradients.

7

To make an "abstraction" is to leave out what is presumably inessential to one's main purposes while focusing on what is most critical. To abstract is inevitable and essential. We are never capable of assembling all possible information about anything and assessing it in its entirety. To try to do everything would be to achieve nothing. In the Congressional example, the political analyst wouldn't bother with temperature gradients, the air conditioning engineer wouldn't bother with debates on the floor, and the structural engineer would have still another agenda. In short, one's purpose always limits one's attention to certain critical features. If this abstracting is done properly, what is salient will be emphasized and what is peripheral or irrelevant will be left for later treatment or ignored entirely.

But there is a problem in this. For which comes first, understanding or abstracting? Each seems a prerequisite for the other. A) To understand a set of events we must focus on only some aspects, not the whole in all its infinite facets. Thus to even begin our analysis, we must more or less know how to abstract, that is, what to leave out and what to pay close attention to. But B) to abstract intelligently we must have some idea what is important and unimportant. That is, we must understand the phenomena we are seeking to divide into focused and peripheral aspects enough to discern what is critical and what isn't. This contradiction is real. "A" requires "B" and "B" requires "A". The conundrum is overcome only by an on-going process which theoretically assesses events, reaches an understanding, tests the understanding, improves the theory that allowed one to define what aspects to focus on, uses the improved theory to reach a new understanding, and so on. The processes of "making good abstractions" and of "reaching an overall understanding" therefore progress in sequence and complementarity.

It might strike the reader, however, that if one starts with a poor understanding which leads to poor abstractions, the sequence may become bogged down. Someone goes to Congress seeking to understand how decisions are arrived at. The individual starts with a tentative theory which suggests that the body language of Representatives is the real determinant of voting patterns. He takes that insight with him to his analysis and therefore to avoid distraction uses soundless movie cameras to record people's gestures during debates. He finds that indeed, one can tell from these gestures how votes are going to be cast. He decides that his theory was correct. Yet it is clear his theory is false. Yes, body language correlates with voting patterns but as an effect not a cause. For even though gestures precede votes, they follow the decision on how to vote, and that decision is obviously not a function of body movements but of complex social processes encompassing vested interests, lobbying, ideology, electoral concerns, economic relations, and so on. Another example would be an individual who looks at only one of many real causes of Congressional decision-making, say economic interests, seeking thereby to explain the entire process of congressional governing. This analyst collects information which abstracts non-economic factors. Like the body linguist, he or she may ignore precisely the evidence that could show his or her understanding to be incomplete. The resulting economistic analysis may thereby defend itself against criticism to persist even in face of its own failures. This could indicate an honest but mistaken over-confidence or a self-interested attachment to a self-serving viewpoint. Political analysts in the United States who talk about state power without paying any attention to economic interests, and male theorists who never notice the obvious patriarchal component of political interactions provide good examples of the not so benign version of this failing.

In this book we assess complex historical processes to propose a vision of a future we might share here in the United States. But we can't look at every historical event in the Soviet Union since their revolution. We can't span China's geography assessing all communes, all sides of daily life, and all changes in philosophy. Even Cuba, small though it is, is infinitely too big to be examined in complete detail. We must abstract. Anyone attempting to write intelligently about what has occurred in these countries or about what might occur in the future in the U.S., has no choice but to abstract from most events and details so as to focus on others. We must make an initial choice about what is most important, and to make this choice we need guidance from a general social theory.

### Social Theories and Socialism

The left theory most often employed to understand socialist history and potentials is orthodox Marxism. The focus is on economic relations. A society is understood principally in terms of class relations on the one hand, and the forces and social relations of production on the other. When a society's "mode of production" is sufficiently understood, and when the character of class definitions and struggles is also well understood, then it is fitting to go on to analyze other sides of life. For these will be explicable largely in terms of the economic or material "base." However, this orthodox Marxist orientation is far from monolithic. There are different schools of thought about how to abstract and then, as one lowers the level of abstraction by going beyond economics into areas of family life, culture, or politics, about how to understand the interrelations of these different aspects of society with each other and with the more critical economic base. But no matter how many differences there may be among orthodox Marxists, they all consider economics basic and define socialism *only* in terms of new economic relations including public ownership of the means of production and (most often) economic coordination by a central plan.

Another approach has been advanced by radical feminists who say the first priority is to understand the "kinship relations" central to sexual interaction, childbirth, and the socialization of each new generation. For a feminist, relations between women, men, and children rather than between economic classes primarily determine the character of any society. When radical feminists envision a revolutionized society, their attention goes first to eliminating oppressive relations between men and women. Their theory says that if this is accomplished negative features of economic and other social spheres will also pass. This belief informs the radical feminist's choice of what to abstract when looking at social events and is analogous to the orthodox Marxist notion that economic change fuels change in all spheres of social life.

For an anarchist, on the contrary, the focus is political relations. The state is now the central institution of society and relations between people in political and bureaucratic hierarchies are most critical to daily life. As the orthodox Marxist and the radical feminist each see society as a kind of split level structure—for one the economy is the foundation, for the other it is kinship relations—the anarchist also has a split-level conceptualization, but now political relations are fundamental.

Finally, cultural nationalists feel the essential underpinings of all social phenomena reside in the cultures of religious, ethnic, racial or national communities. In this view, one should focus on community divisions and on the institutional and ideological relations that define them. Through this cultural analysis, one can develop not only an understanding of the primary causes of most community events, but also the deepest causes of all other phenomena—for example, the different kinds of political, kinship, and economic relations we find in different societies. Sexism, for example, or different approaches to economic organization, become outgrowths of different community cultures.

Despite obvious differences these orientations do have much in common. For example, within each orientation there are differences about how strongly to assert the primacy of the *one* favored sphere of social life and how to understand the influence of other spheres. At one extreme, the orthodox member of each camp is fixated on one sphere as a primary focus of attention and explains all other phenomena only from that single cause be it economic, kinship, political, or community relations. When analyzing Cuban history, for example, an orthodox Marxist might write a book of hundreds of pages with no mention of anything other than economic phenomena claiming not only to have explained the economy—a dubious claim in itself—but also, at least implicitly, the whole rest of the society as well. Similarly, the radical feminist will minimize the relevance of economic differences where basic kinship similarities exist and, if she is orthodox enough, analyze history in terms of kinship relations and little else. In this extreme, each of these four schools instructs adherents to analyze historical phenomena—the history of a school system, the art works of a particular country, or even the post-revolutionary history of China—by paying strict attention to *one* set of social relations and human struggles and only peripheral attention to others.

But in each of the four orientations there are other more flexible schools in which the analysis raises the level of importance of one or more *other* spheres while not questioning the centrality of the favorite. For example, a flexible Marxist might continue to deem economics primary, but recognize that other spheres also have independent dynamics which deserve separate analysis. Then, of course, there are different views about how these separate analyses should be undertaken and especially about how the interrelations between spheres should be understood. The anarchist might go so far as to become an anarcho-Marxist or anarcho-feminist allowing for two first rank spheres; and likewise the feminist could become a feminist-Marxist, and so on.

However we diverge from all four of these orientations and their simple amalgamation, two or more at a time, even while recognizing many insights each orientation has fostered. For we believe that *all four of these spheres* of social life are critical to social definitions and that one can't say a priori that any is necessarily more important than the others. Furthermore, rather than seeing these four spheres as a multi-storied formation, we view them as *integrated* with one another wholistically. For some purposes we can understand each in turn, but in truth they only operate interactively. Each influences the character and sometimes even the definition of the others. We are therefore suggesting a transition from *monistic* theories that treat different spheres of social life hierarchically and as exterior to one another to a more *totalist* theory which treats the four key spheres as equally important, entwined, and mutually defining. The new approach sees the whole *and* each sphere in a new way, and it also instructs us to abstract and to organize information in new ways. In the companion to this volume, *Marxism and Socialist Theory*, we focus almost exclusively on theory, develop our new approach more rigorously than we will here, and carefully contrast it to other schools of Marxist and radical thought. But what is most important here is a summary of the positive theoretical results that can inform how we should abstract information about post capitalist societies.

### A Broad Theoretical Overview

The evolution of a star, a particular species, or a society are all historical, yet quite different from one another. Physical history is governed by the processes of physics, biological history by the processes of natural evolution, and human history by social processes as yet only partially known and about which there is much controversy. Whether the laws of natural evolution or human history are reducible to complex instances of the known laws of physical interaction is also a hotly contested question. What we are confident of, however, is that to be understood, the biological realm involving natural selection requires a qualitatively different kind of abstraction and theoretization than the world of atomic particles, and that in turn the social world involving conscious decision-making and planning requires still another kind of abstraction and theoretization. Since at the social level, the innovation is the unique character of human nature, to understand human history we should begin by assessing human nature itself.

Beyond the need for sustenance, the capacity to reproduce, and similar life-defining attributes, human nature also includes a highly developed sociality, a capacity for empathy, and needs for freedom, love, and community. Furthermore, we have unique capacities for conceptualization and communication and these allow us to envision future possibilities before enacting them, and to thereby consciously change our environments and ourselves.

We are *social beings*. To meet many of our needs we must consciously interact with other people. We feel empathy and can share in other people's pains and pleasures. Many of our capacities cannot be employed save in concert with other people. Complex language, for example, as one of the distinguishing features of humans vis-a-vis other organisms, is a paradigm "social capacity." But in addition, we are also beings of *praxis*. When we use our capacities to consciously change our environment, we also change ourselves. On top of our genetic human nature, our personalities, skills, and consciousness are functions of our daily practice. The history of our surroundings and our own history are therefore inextricably entwined.

### Four Spheres of Human Activity

Nearly all our activity involves either the creation or use of material objects, and this production and consumption is central to *economic activity*. Likewise people must give birth if the species is to continue and reproduction and socialization centrally characterize what we call *kinship activity*. Further, as social beings we must enter relations with other people to form groups sharing similar cultural conceptions. This constitutes *community activity*. Finally, since people are social beings of praxis, our pasts and futures both impact upon our present plans. The regulation of differences to allow smooth interactions of many actors constitutes *political activity*.

Each of these four kinds of activity are everpresent in human behavior and human interaction involves all four types to at least some degree. For example, in households there is certainly a predominance of kinship activity but material things are also being produced and consumed, cultures are elaborated and learned, and general social coordination occurs. We can say household activity is primarily kinship activity, yet it also has an economic, political, and community aspect or *moment*. Likewise, in a factory economics is the predominant feature. Yet there are also sexual dynamics involving different roles for men and women, community dynamics among, say, Appalachians, Blacks, Hispanics, Irish, etc., and a political moment of broader coordination as well.

But not only can all human activity be thought of as composed of four moments, with one frequently dominant, but each type of activity is of such importance that it comes to constitute a "sphere" of institutional and social relations. That is, as people inevitably have economic needs and capacities, in all societies they will necessarily enter social relationships with one another to act economically. The resulting "economy" becomes a basic social sphere and includes a network of institutions and various human attributes. Likewise, in all societies people enter relationships in pursuit of sexual partners, and procreating and socializing the next generation. These relations characterize the kinship sphere. Similarly, political institutions and human characteristics come into being in the process of people coordinating their various plans for society's future and together these come to constitute society's political sphere. And finally, as people enter social groups that have common cultural attributes regarding matters of communication, philosophies of life, and ways of thinking about celebration, art, and ethics, the community sphere emerges including ethnic, religious, racial, and national institutional and consciousness relations.

Every society has each of these four spheres, but the form of each sphere varies from one society to another and even within a society from one epoch to another. For example, a society may have feudal, capitalist, or socialist economic relations. And similarly there are many different kinds of political, kinship, and community relationships that may hold from society to society. And while any society is more than the complex amalgamation of these four spheres in one social system, we feel the proper way to approach a society for purposes of understanding its impact upon daily life and its potentials for stability and change is to initially abstract the rest and focus on exactly these relationships.

The orthodox Marxist focuses first on the economy. The feminist chooses to emphasize the kinship sphere. We argue that it is necessary to pay attention to *all four spheres and their subtle interrelations*. But first, why these four spheres in particular? Each of these spheres organizes the parameters for important aspects of social life. Each creates a context which governs how we engage in activities essential to expressing and developing ourselves as people. Furthermore, each has historically shown itself capable of causing people to group together along lines of difference and contradiction. For example, economic relations have led to the formation of class divisions among people. In feudalism nobles had one role in society, serfs another. In capitalism, there are capitalists, workers, and other classes as well. These divisions cause differences in people's ways of thinking about their situations, in their economic opportunities, and in their needs. Moreover these differences are usually of a contradictory character. Ultimately, that is, what was good for nobility was bad for serfs, what is good for capitalists is bad for workers, and vice versa. Similarly, political relations have led to differences according to party affiliation, between actors at different levels in bureaucracies, and in different political institutions, for example social service or the military. Kinship activity has led to differences between men and women, adults and children, and often along lines of sexual preference. And community activity has led to differentiation by race, religion, ethnic group, and nationality. Each sphere has an inexorable impact on life in any particular society. Each helps determine the different life options, limits upon accomplishment, and forms of pleasure and oppression people endure. Together we think these four spheres constitute enough of what makes any society distinct and of how any society will affect human possibilities so that by focusing on them we are making a useful abstraction. On the other hand, we feel that to ignore any of these spheres is to risk not only error by deletion, but also misunderstanding of what one does address. For example, ignoring kinship, as we shall see, one may well fail to fully understand economics or community as well.

Every society has people and institutions, four main kinds of activity, and four main spheres of social interaction. But what makes a society truly complex is that these components all exist in the exact same space, rather than side by side. A society is a social formation of particular kinds of economic, political, kinship, and community institutions and of people with innate characteristics and historical personalities and consciousness all fused together in one entwined totality. For convenience we call the human aspects the *center* and the institutional aspects the *boundary* and the fact that they exist together and that the four spheres intertwine in one space and time has very important implications for what is possible in history and for how societies evolve and sometimes change drastically.

The economic network certainly includes the places of production and consumption and also institutions of allocation, but we have also seen that the family has an economic aspect and is therefore part of this network. And surely the state also has economic functions as well as political ones. For example in modern societies it is often the state which takes responsibility for producing means of defense and roads and for ameliorating ecological problems as well. Likewise, community dynamics often entail economic production and consumption. And this analysis applies to each case in turn—the kinship sphere includes the family, daycare centers, and schools for example, yet each of these institutions has non-kinship moments. The factory is economic but also has a kinship moment and must be considered part of the kinship network. Similarly community activity has a kinship moment and so does politics. In fact, viewed broadly, each of the four spheres encompasses the entirety of any society's boundary and one facet of its center. The economic sphere is all of society viewed in terms of the economic moment of human activity. The kinship sphere is all of society viewed in terms of kinship activity. Yet there are four aspects, and when we view society in turn from each of these four angles, with each shift of orientation new institutions become central. For the polity the state achieves centrality. For kinship, the family gains predominance.

What is most crucial to understand is that when we analyze the features of one sphere, say kinship, we must remember that it will always exist within a social formation and that therefore any particular kind of kinship relations will be different if they "share" their space with a feudal *or* a capitalist economy; a monarchy, parliamentary or socialist democracy; a slave, racist, or pluralist community sphere. It is often desirable to assess each sphere in turn, but to gain a full understanding of any one sphere or of any whole society, it is also necessary to understand how the four spheres influence and even define one another's main contours.

The "monist" theorists assume we know the character of this inter-sphere influence in advance. Their favorite sphere—for the orthodox Marxist the economy, for the feminist the kinship sphere, etc.—will determine the main attributes of the rest. In our approach, while such a predominance of one or two spheres over others isn't inexorably ruled out, it is considered unlikely. The situation we expect to be more common is *co-definition* wherein each sphere helps to create the context and the contours of every other.

For example, if community relations in a particular society embody racist definitions and cultural norms, then the fact that the community and other spheres overlap suggests that racism will permeate other sides of social life as well. Likewise, class differentiations elaborated primarily within the economy will not become mute and irrelevent in kinship, political, and community occurances. One possibility is simply that each sphere will accomodate with the core features elaborated in the others. And indeed, this much is necessary. For if a *core characteristic* elaborated in one sphere were contradicted in another, the fact that the spheres overlap and that but one set of people feels these opposite pressures means that this contradiction will create severe problems within society and that in time it will be resolved via some accommodation between the spheres. For example, if kinship deems men superior to women and entitled to great advantages but community cultures or economic relations create equity between men and women or even female dominance, something will have to give. Even more complex than this necessary level of accommodation, however, different spheres might "co-define" one another. In this case, not only would economic relations not severely contradict central attributes engendered by kinship dynamics, but they might help define kinship roles. What it is to be a man or a woman, or what it is to be a worker or consumer may vary not only because of kinship and economic requirements respectively, but also economic roles might be in part defined and enforced by kinship requirements, and kinship roles in part defined and enforced by economic requirements. In the companion volume, *Marxism and Socialist Theory*, we have elaborated these ideas in detail and also clarified the many differences between our approach and other more familiar alternatives. Here we would rather focus on the minimum of necessary concepts for the tasks we will undertake in this book and since those tasks constitute *only the first steps* of a totalist analysis of certain historical experiences and possibilities, many complex theoretical ideas needn't be emphasized here, though to take the historical and programmatic studies of this volume further than we have, such emphasis will prove necessary.

### Evolution and Revolution

In the normal daily life of any society there is constant change. There is on-going production and consumption. People are born, personalities alter and skills are enhanced or lost. Decisions are made, laws passed or broken, and sometimes new bureaucracies come into being or old ones are eliminated. Cultures evolve and frictions between communities become more or less intense. Most often, however, these and multitudes of other daily changes are such that we don't think of society itself as fundamentally altered. Although there are changes, the basic defining features of society are reproduced in tact. It is a process of "evolution." Changes occur, but only in context of the maintenance of the contours of society's core characteristics. The four spheres maintain their defining features. For example, within an economy, new industries evolve, technologies are transformed, and people develop new skills or lose ones they had previously possessed. But the basic social relationships defining class divisions remain in place. Or in the political sphere, perhaps a new bureaucratic layer is elaborated, there is a change in leadership, or new laws are refined and enacted. But the basic core defining relations are preserved. This is societal *evolution.*

In contrast, basic defining features may change. Private ownership might be eliminated in the economy. Family structure may alter or the role of women and men be substantially transformed in the kinship sphere. Politically, there could be a change from monarchy to parliamentary forms, or from parliamentary forms to dictatorship. And within the community sphere, a transition from slave to segregationist relations or from segregationist to equal relations could occur. In each case, people's options and group struggles within society change. This is what we mean by *revolution.*

In an evolutionary period there will be accommodation and perhaps co-definition between spheres and also a relatively smooth fit between people's expectations and capacities in the human center and the institutional role structures of society's boundary. For if two spheres were out of synchronization regarding characteristics critical to daily life, there would be accommodating changes in one sphere or the other. And likewise, a misfit between people at society's center and institutional possibilities at its boundary would also create pressures propelling realignment. Imagine, for example, a situation of economic roles requiring a certain level of skill or passivity and people not having the skill or being too aggressive. The contradiction would create pressure for change—perhaps a slight redefinition of work roles, an alteration of school curricula or the number of trade as compared to liberal arts colleges. The normal course of events within any society would continually create such misfitting and then refitting in an on-going evolutionary process. And this would occur in all four spheres and between them as well. For example, the above intra-sphere economic contradiction could lead to a change first in schooling and then in household relations as well finally provoking another round of changes in the economy.

The likelihood of revolution hinges on the same kind of misfitting/refitting dynamics as the steady evolutionary process, though in highly exaggerated ways. For example, within a sphere a contradiction could lead to very severe conflict between different social groups—classes, gender groups, communities, or political groups—which might in turn lead to a new alignment of forces and definition of structures within society. Class struggle between workers and capitalists could engender a redefinition of property relations and therefore a revolutionary rather than merely an evolutionary change of economic relations. Or gender struggle between men and women could dissolve old family norms and relations revolutionizing the kinship sphere. It is important to realize, however, that after the "dust settles" there will again be a (rough, flexible) mutual fitting of different spheres and of center and boundary. As a result, if an upheaval tends to initially affect only one sphere, or only institutions *or* consciousness, it becomes problematic. It may persist, eventually causing further accommodating alterations throughout the rest of society—in a sense dragging the rest along—or it may itself dissipate, "dragged back" by the lack of change in other parts of society. These possibilities become very important when we think about revolutionary strategies that focus almost entirely on one or two spheres and when we try to evaluate the dynamic pressures on post-revolutionary societies of this type.

As a revolution is basic change in one or more of the four defining spheres of any society, the most crucial agents of revolutionary change are the social groups demarcated by each sphere—classes, gender groups, communities, and political groups. Therefore, to effectively study a revolutionary process one needs to assess the division of society into these agents of history, their struggles and how these affect social processes. Similarly, to propose a compelling socialist vision, one should address each of the four spheres including institutional and human attributes. Yet to follow this course we will need a deeper understanding of some of the characteristics of each specific sphere, and we now therefore turn to a discussion of some theoretical issues concerning first politics, then economics, kinship, and community in turn.

### The Political Sphere
Unlike for other animals, the coordination of human behavior is neither genetic nor unnecessary. Due to our consciousness and sociality, we need both to interact and to develop a context where our expectations about each other's behavior will be met. Politics is the art of creating this conformity. Political activity aims at organizing disparate desires into shared plans of action and rules of behavior.

### The Political Sphere Within Society
The main political institution—the hub of the political network—is most often the state. It can take a variety of forms and its extension through local branches and even into chiefly economic or kinship institutions is inevitable precisely as there is a political moment to all kinds of social activity. Different kinds of state are characterized by different requirements for citizens, different role structures for poltical activity, and different ideologies of legitima-

tion and rationalization. A monarchy, dictatorship, parliamentary democracy and socialist democracy all share certain features but obviously diverge at many points as well. Their differences are responsible for creating political environments that have different impact upon people working within and outside the state, and on the whole trajectory of social coodination, aims, and interests the state will serve.

Political institutions are not simply neutral governing vehicles. Rather they have intrinsic features which imply certain kinds of outcome and tend to rule out other kinds. That is, politics has a kind of "life of its own." Political relations of a particular type will have their own characteristic features and these will set limits on social possibilities, propel some kinds of social results and hinder others. One set of political relations might be authoritarian, another might elicit collective self-management. One might serve only the interests of a narrow elite, another those of all citizens equally. Finally, one set of political institutions might produce passive behavior and a disposition to obedience and cynicism, while another set fosters critical insight and a disposition to initiative.

However, political activity and the state always exist *within* a whole social formation. Whatever particular type of state a society has, it also has particular kinds of economic, kinship, and community relations. These latter spheres help establish the environment within which the state exists. For example, in many cases the economy elaborates a hierarchy of class relations, the kinship sphere elaborates a hierarchy of kinship relations, and the community sphere elaborates a hierarchy of cultural/community relations. Minimally the state must respect these hierarchies, if they exist, or else there will be serious instability leading to possible revolution on the one hand, or back toward some sort of accommodation on the other.

One possibility, for example, is that the state will merely be a political representation of the power of one or more of the groups which dominate these other social hierarchies. But in our view this is unlikely. For example, the theory that the state is just the ruling economic class's means of administering extra-economic coordination ignores the explicitly political roots of the state and the (sometimes fundamental) explicitly political character of the state's *own* social relations and hierarchies as well as the impact of kinship and community. In our view, it is more likely that in a particular society the state will have its own political elite which will in turn be composed primarily of elements common to the elites of other spheres or acting as agents of those elites. Insofar as the state seeks a stable context for social planning, while also accommodating to existing hierarchies, naturally it seeks to reproduce the defining contours of all four social spheres. Insofar as it must at least accommodate, the exertion of authority in the state will rest in the hands of people who by their class, kin, and community affiliations also dominate other spheres. But this in no way denies that the state will have a dynamic of its own.

There are many ways accommodation can come about and furthermore, as we discussed earlier, the state may also be in a co-defining relation with other spheres of any particular society. The operation of the state might help to reproduce sexism, for example, insofar as its governing method is "male," its laws enforce male dominance, and its power obstructs womens' liberation. And likewise, the family's socialization procedures could instill certain political beliefs and habits in us as we grow up, critical to reproduction of the political activity of the state. The state is a mechanism for social coordination and whatever its specific type, during socially stable periods it will at least accommodate with and perhaps co-define relations in other spheres of social life. Moreover, the state's own social relations may have structural implications that affect people differently depending upon their positions in society. For example, people who staff the state and people outside the state may develop different desires, powers, skills, personalities and ways of understanding social interaction. Likewise, even within the state itself, people operating at different levels of bureaucracies or in different bureaucracies could also evolve different world views, interests, and powers. For the first kind of demarcation, think of the gap between rulers and ruled in a dictatorship; for the second, think in terms of the different perspectives of members of the U.S. Department of Health, Energy, or Defense.

## Legitimation of the State

Insofar as the state sets limits on acceptable (or sometimes mandatory) behavior, how does it guarantee obedience? Where does the state's authority come from? One obvious answer is that the state is society's main coercive institution. It is the institution which has a monopoly on the legitimate use of force and even violence. Yet this alone is insufficient to explain the coordinative power of all but the most blatantly military state. Rather, most states benefit from a legitimacy which elicits obedience not only out of fear but also out of respect or habit.

This legitimacy is gained in a number of ways. First, as we have taken pains to emphasize, the state exists within a whole society and at least accommodates to the hierarchies of authority created in other spheres. This alone insures a certain legitimacy. That is, if kinship, for example, inculcates a view that men are superior to women and the state staffs its uppermost decision-making bodies primarily with men and operates primarily in "male-defined" ways, then its leadership has a familiar character legitimated elsewhere. But it is also possible, and usually necessary, for the state to win allegiance through "serving the populace" in a variety of ways. That is, the state wins popular favor by providing the populace with many services ranging from defense to public transportation, to providing medical care, welfare and pollution safeguards. The state is therefore to be respected and obeyed in part because it delivers certain benefits in return. Finally, beyond coercion, the borrowing of legitimacy by employing familiar authority figures, and "serving the people," the state also wins legitimacy and rationalizes its own authority by amassing to itself a mantle of expertise and often, if possible, a monopoly of political knowledge and capability. The state apparatus evolves such that only the politician can navigate its intricacies. A cult of expertise evolves to enshroud political decision-making with an aura of difficulty such that it must be entrusted only to the state's experts. Think of the secrecy of foreign policy, mystification of law making, and denial of the public's "right to know," or capacity to understand, judge, and decide. Even if one doesn't like a political directive, what alternative to obedience exists in a context where no one but the state functionaries have the capability of coordinating social outcomes? With these parameters, the choice is obedience or chaos.

To study the political sphere of a particular social formation, the above discussion suggests we would need to first assess the particular political relations, dominant institutions, their role characteristics and associated implications for different members of society. Then it would be necessary to examine the means by which different social elites—political, economic, kin, and community—manifest their powers within the political network and also vice versa: how the state influences the evolution of other spheres. What would be a mistake, however, would be to assume *a priori* that the state was only a neutral vehicle for ruling class dominance, for this would neglect the fact that state structures have implications of their own, that other agents of history besides classes compete for power over state institutions, and that dominance of any group is seldom complete.

## Marxist Leninist Political Forms and Socialism

Within Marxism Leninism, which is the currently dominant school of thought about the nature of socialism, two political forms are extolled—vanguard leadership and democratic centralism. Each rests on the same general hypothesis regarding the means of emergence of expertise and the best way to employ it once it exists. The idea is that expertise, both theoretical and practical, results from "professionalism." That is, one becomes progressively better at any particular kind of thinking or acting primarily by sustained study and practice and the ensuing accumulation of the lessons of experience. Since the creation of socialism involves a bitter stuggle against intransigent and very powerful capitalist foes, Leninists argue that it is essential that socialists should be led by the most able leaders that can be assembled. Moreover, since Marxism Leninism assumes that any state is only a means of ruling class power, what is most essential about the socialist state is that it should be a) as effective as possible in its leadership functions, and b) expressive of the will of the working class, who for Leninists are the presumed rulers of the new society. What is not so important, however, is to worry about the particular *form* of new state relations as purely political institutions. To compromise operational efficiency or leadership by working class representatives because of concerns about the social effects of state relations themselves would be folly. For in the Leninist view, the evolution of the state is subservient to the evolution of the economy and therefore all that is crucial is that the state be able to enhance the socialization of the economy in the workers' interests.

The idea of the "vanguard" follows directly. There is no need for a plurality of socialist parties because it is only the working class which is to become the new ruling class and therefore only the most able party representing the working class should exercise political leadership. Furthermore, since this leadership is rationalized and legitimated by the party's possession of "Marxist Leninist Science," politics becomes the mechanical application of objective theory to the problems of socialist construction. The vanguard party is simply a mass of individuals who are political experts due to their professional attention to matters of political theory and their devotion to political practice. There is no need for a plurality of leadership because there is no need for a plurality of options to be expressed and debated. One program will suffice, for it has the power of science behind it. All other programs, for example that of an autonomous women's or national movement, of an opposition political group, or even of workers organizing in factories or communities or as a faction within the party itself, will necessarily be "non-scientific," and therefore mere ideology representing the interests of some recalcitrant class—the usual label being "bourgeois" or "petty bourgeois."

Within the party "democratic centralism" is the main organizing principle. There is nothing complex about this. The idea is to promote and take maximum advantage of expertise within the party. Democratic centralism means that the party will be arranged in a hierarchy much like what exists in most military apparatuses. This engenders levels of functionaries each with different powers and interests. At the pinnacle of the hierarchy is the politbureau or even sometimes a single absolute dictator. As one moves down there are levels of policy-makers, advisers, functionaries, and finally the base of party cadre. Directives move from the top down and after brief debate they are implemented without question. Votes are rare and promotion within the hierarchy is almost always by decision of higher authorities. Experience at bending the party apparatus and applying its might to social problems is progressively monopolized by a small elite whose skill in these matters—whatever their other qualifications or attributes—steadily grows. Obedience becomes rewarded as a means of gaining favor from superiors and criticism from below becomes a lost art. Even more important, authority figures at the highest levels accrue what becomes a responsibility to monopolize decision-making and to view their own ideas as sacrosanct. For they have greatest experience. Why else would they be at the top of a party which employs scientific Marxism Leninism to guide its practice were they not the most intelligent and successful interpretors and employers of this theory? That being so, they should exercize their will forcefully—to do otherwise would be to make insufficient use of the immense insight their experience has bequeathed them. And going down the hierarchy each lower level should regard superiors as one might a learned teacher, and those on lower levels as one might an aspiring pupil.

In our view, democratic centralism and the vanguard approach to leadership are antithetical to the possibility of the creation of socialism. These forms only masquerade as efficient and socially neutral vehicles by which a party supposedly representing workers' interests can manifest its preferences. Rather, democratic centralism and vanguard forms have their own inherent dynamics which affect both political practice and the broader character of society as a whole. As we argued in detail in the companion volume, *Marxism and Socialist Theory*, and much more briefly above, democratic centralism breeds authoritarianism—a division among people along lines of giving and taking orders—a political elite within the party, a diminution of critical faculties, a disposition to obedience, and a trend toward dictatorial dominance by a few often pursuing very narrowly defined interests. Likewise, adherence to a vanguard one party approach militates against autonomous movements that can struggle around kinship, community, and economic issues and prepares the way for a philosophy of "one right way" and "scientific government" consistent with the most anti-democratic conceptions of leadership imaginable. The cult of the expert is itself antithetical to the idea of socialist self-management. For it not only emphasizes the importance of expertise, a fact in itself relatively unobjectionable, but it also relegates all authority to experts as if one cannot make decisions unless one has the fullest possible technical understanding of all intricacies of a situation. But this is ridiculous. For example, one needn't know the chemical reasons why lead based paint is harmful to be in favor of a law against its use in painting the walls of public schools. One can trust the expert's chemical analysis and then make the social decision oneself. The notion that narrow expertise in a particular field yields a special wisdom applicable to social planning is suspect to the point of being transparently bankrupt. Yet if "science" is to justify state power, just such a notion inevitably comes to dominance.

Our theory tells us that political practice, no less than economic practice, can yield elites and subordinate groups who vie for power and influence in society. Political institutions, no less than kinship institutions, can influence the development of interests, and consciousness of different groups of people differently. Vanguard leadership makes an immediate demarcation between professional political leaders and citizens at large. Democratic centralism further delineates the professional politicians along a host of hierarchical lines, most party members relatively powerless, and a few at the top accruing most power to themselves. The rationalization of these forms of organization by appeal to expertise and science only further aggravates these differentiations, shrouding them in obscure language which only the initiated can understand. The overall structure of these political forms is conducive not to the most creative possible leadership but instead to a steady divorce of leaders from touch with those who are led, an accumulation of independent interests among leaders, and a tendency to bend reality to fit theory rather than vice versa. For if the party and its higher echelons are led by science, then their decisions always carry the weight of objectivity. When they actually do prove incorrect, rather than recognize this and call the entire "scientific apparatus" into question, it is better either to blame poor implementation by purgeable functionaries or an intransigent but disciplinable population.

The outcome of the application of these forms of political organization is bureaucracy on a grand scale: a multi-tiered state within which each individual is subordinate to some others, superior to many, and primarily motivated by the desire to preserve or increase personal status and power by positively impressing superiors. Such bureaucracy structurally requires a diminution of one's critical faculties and honesty, and a willingness to toady to those above and enforce the greatest possible obedience from those below. Far from efficiency, in this apparatus we have the seeds of Kafkaesque degeneracy. The whole state may move with uniform purpose, but the likelihood that that purpose will reflect other than myopic political interests diminishes as the system becomes ever more refined and entrenched.

This bureaucratic, vanguard, democratic centralist apparatus, characterized briefly above, exists within a whole social formation and this fact tends to aggravate and complicate the picture considerably. As this state's activity will significantly impact not only on political relations in society, but on economic, kinship, and community relations as well, interest groups demarcated in each of these sectors will struggle to influence state decision-making. Thus, in addition to a bureaucratic political dynamic, pressures from other spheres also operate within the political network. We might expect, for example, that elements within the vanguard party would come to represent interests of groups in these other spheres and that they might therefore act to defend their "other sphere" interests against the self-interested extremism of the political elite. In one context the elite might totally dominate, deciding all aspects of political activity according to its own whims and interests. In another situation, however, this elite might have to compete—perhaps even from a position of relative weakness—with groups demarcated in other spheres. Stalinism would be an example of the first situation. Struggles in China wherein a political elite was overruled by representatives of classes within the state, would be an example of the second.

In any case, in studying the Soviet, Chinese, and Cuban experiences we should pay attention both to the elaboration of political forms and groups and to the interface between the political sphere and the evolution of the economic, kinship, and community spheres. As succinct and general as the above abstract discussion was, it will nonetheless help guide our investigation assisting us in finding and interpreting important information regarding the political sphere.

### The Economic Sphere

Workers in a factory produce various goods; individuals in households consume them. This is the hard core but far from the totality of the subject matter of economic analysis. For when workers enter the factory, do their labor, and then leave through one door while the finished goods are transported away through another, more has occurred than simply the production of cars or razor blades and the using up of rubber, steel, or natural resources. On the one hand pollution and other side products may be "outputs" as well. More subtly, however, there will also be human and social inputs and outputs. In the morning as the work process begins, the workers with their own particular needs, skills, and personalities, as well as the social relations between them constituting the social relations of the workplace also enter the production process. And as the day ends, although it is conceivable these workers and the relations between them have acted only as catalysts being reproduced unchanged, it is more than likely that they will have been altered as well. Social divisions and hostilities may have been aggravated or lessened, lines of authority legitimated or challenged, and the skill levels, needs, dispositions, consciousness and even personalities of workers transformed. The worker too leaves the plant as an "output" and whether the effects of the day's work are obvious—exhaustion, irritability, or even physical pain or debilitation—or more subtle and only visible as they accumulate over long periods as a change in personality or skill, they are nonetheless present. And similarly for consumption: we use the razor blade, car, or other product, but we do so only by bringing ourselves and our social relations to the act, and so not only might the product disappear, but our characteristics and relations to others might alter as well. The negative effects of consuming pornographic literature on our personality and relations to others are evident. The consumption of T.V. shows, more subtly, may allow us to pass otherwise tedious time enjoyably, yet simultaneously diminish our faculties for critical thought, creativity, or social interchange. The consumption of movies at downtown movie theatres on the one hand, or via home video casettes on the other, may have markedly different implications for individual and social outcomes. It is one thing to consume energy via cutting one's own wood, another thing to get electricity from an Edison generator, and still another thing to get it from a nuclear plant located but a short distance from one's home. And who knows what the effects of computer games may turn out to be?

The economic sphere principally includes such institutions as production units, consumption units, and the mechanisms which allow for coordination between these, the allocation units. In the United States, for example, there are private corporations, households, and the competitive and monopolistic markets that connect them.

The impact of the economic network on our lives is profound including determining how we exchange labor and goods, the distribution of income and economic decision-making power, and the way our skills and personalities are constrained by the requirements of economic role structures. A study of economic relations entails an investigation of these attributes. An economic theory must address them and an economic vision must discuss how they will be fulfilled.

But before proceeding to basic definitions we should clarify that our break with the usual socialist approach to economic analysis—orthodox Marxist theory—occurs along two primary axes. First, we pay more attention to the impact of economic relations on consciousness and on the determination of all kinds of human characteristics rather than on only material fulfillment. Our focus on the material *and also* the human and social "inputs" and "outputs" of economic activity is indicative of this difference and we'll shortly see how it leads to substantial innovations in our overall economic theory. Second, we make a clean break with two types of "economism": we do not *a priori* claim that the economy imposes a structure upon the rest of society such that an understanding of the economy leads directly to an understanding of society as a whole. And we do not make the mistake of overlooking the impact of other spheres of social life within the economy itself.

### Basic Definitions

One of the most fundamental characteristics of any economy is the manner in which it establishes a division of labor. Every individual cannot simultaneously do all economic tasks. A *division of labor* and then an exchange of the products of labor is necessary to attain development—if we each had to produce everything we consume our diets would be sparse and our wardrobes, bare. Another critical aspect of any economy is the set of rules which determine the *ownership relations* of existing tools and workplaces, and also of the products of peoples' labor. Finally, the *allocation mechanisms* which determine how exchange is to occur are also critical to establishing the basic characteristics of any economy.

All economists use the concept *use-value* to refer to things people desire or have a taste for. But what determines whether a particular good or service has use-value for different people? Most economists including orthodox Marxists refer this question to studies of "taste" and "psychology" denying that economic factors per se really have any significant impact upon this determination. But we have a very different view. We recognize that use-value is in part affected by economic circumstances in at least two important respects. First, if we know that in the future one type of good will be readily available and another hard to obtain it is likely we will mold our taste to enhance the use value of the available good relative to the inaccessible one. For example, we might mold our tastes and desires to be pleased with different qualities of food, stereo reproduction, or living quarters. Even more important, perceiving the wide availability of certain types of entertainment emphasizing spectating or private consumption and the relative scarcity of opportunity for participatory entertainment or collective consumption, again we might slowly mold our tastes to accord. In a society with football constantly on the tube it makes sense to develop a taste for watching it. In a society with playing fields in easy access, with sports equipment plentiful, and with an ethos that makes it likely that one has many friends all in good shape and with time to play ball, one might spend more time on the field than in the easy chair. There are many other ramifications of this set of ideas and we have pursued them in some detail in other places, but the point here is simply that economic institutions are not neutral vis-a-vis our "tastes." If they tend to make some things plentiful and cheap while making other things virtually inaccessible, we will alter our tastes in accord. As a result, the fact that an economy delivers what people "want" at a particular moment in time may or may not be a positive accomplishment. It will all depend on whether this is really indicative of the economy meeting peoples' freely expressed, varied, and rich desires, or whether it is indicative of the economy's having successfully molded peoples' tastes such that they have become narrow enough to be easily met even in the face of the relative paucity of things the economy makes available. The relevant point for coming discussions is that if a particular set of economic institutions has an oppressive bias in the kinds of opportunities it makes available to people, it is likely that people working and consuming in context of these institutions will progressively alter themselves to gain the greatest *possible* fulfillment in context of these oppressive biases, even if it means mutilating their own tastes and personalities to do so.

The second issue that distinguishes us for purposes of this volume is our understanding of class relations. For the orthodox Marxist, though there are other classes besides the capitalist and the workers, these two are most crucial because they are the only ones with the capacity to be ruling classes in whose interests economic arrangements are structured. For us, however, there is another class which shares this lofty distinction. The orthodox understanding of class is largely limited—at the level of determining the existence of classes—to noting the differences in ownership relations and direct material interests. We feel, however, that while these relations are important, the actual work situation of people within the economy can be crucial as well. For the type of activity people engage in is, as we have argued, a prime determinant of who we become, our personalities, consciousness, etc. The capitalist occupies a position, due primarily to owning the means of production, which gives him an interest in maximizing profit and thus a certain orientation to economic events and life in general. The worker, on the other hand, sells his or her labor power in order to get a wage with which to consume and survive and possibly gain some enjoyment and personal pleasures. As a result of occupying this different position within the economy, he or she has different interests and sees economic events from still another perspective. And while we agree in general with this orthodox analysis, we think it obscures the importance of the actual activity—not just the relation to its product and to income and profit—of economic agents on their outlook. Consider for example, the high paid electrical engineer who designs automated assembly equipment on the one hand, and the assembly line worker on the other—or the high paid lawyer and cop on the beat, the editor of a major newsweekly and the typesetter for the same paper, the tenured professor at a major university and the secretary of his or her department, the union bureaucrat and the day laborer, the plant manager and the workers who are managed. In both cases, the individuals sell their abilities to work for a wage and own no means of production. Should we just lump them together as workers and leave it at that? In our view the answer has to be no, but it is not primarily because of the income differentials, though that is part of it. More important, however, (and also the basis of those differentials), is the fact that the former person in each set has more control over their work, has authority over other workers, and has work which is of a primarily conceptual type. It often involves figuring out plans others will implement or creating equipment other workers will use. In our view, the different character of the work day of these two types of economic agents, workers and *coordinators,* leads to different dispositions, personality types, and economic interests. The coordinator, like the worker, wants better work conditions and higher income, but his or her bargaining position is much better and he or she also not only has conflicts with capitalists, but with workers as well. For the coordinator wants to preserve a relative monopoly of conceptual skills and expertise giving him or her an interest in preventing the widespread intellectual advance of workers, as well as a paternal, elitist attitude toward them. In response, the worker is likely to develop an ambivalent feeling of admiration for the coordinator's knowledge and also contempt for his or her arrogance, elitism, and isolation from real work. Again, we have dealt elsewhere with these relations as they bear on the character of life and class relations within capitalism. What is particularly relevant for this volume is the simple idea that this conceptually oriented class of coordinators might become a ruling class within an economy in which they were no longer subservient to capitalists but at the same time managed to maintain their virtual monopoly on managerial and technical expertise. Just as private ownership and market relations create an economic context in which capitalists dominate, perhaps another set of economic relations might create a context in which coordinators would dominate. This is a possibility that is simply overlooked in the orthodox Marxist analysis.

### Alternative Socialist Economic Forms

All socialists, ourselves included, agree that one precondition of socialism is the elimination of the distinction between capitalists and workers based upon private ownership of the means of production by the capitalists. However, beyond "socialization of the means of production" which is simply the creation of public ownership, there is considerable disagreement about what constitutes a socialist economic system. In one view, what is necessary is to retain a market structure and have worker's management within economic units. Another more prevalent approach calls for a system of central planning under the leadership of a planning board subordinate to the "worker's state." Here we would like to briefly assess these two types of economic form—markets and central planning—in a way that will provide the necessary theoretical tools to conduct our historical analyses of the Soviet, Chinese, and Cuban economies.

### Markets and Socialist Economics

Markets are one possible means by which each unit within an economy can determine its inputs and outputs so that what is produced will be consumed and what is needed for production will be available.

But markets are not neutral. They are not like a truck delivering this item here, that item there, and never influencing the character of economic outcomes other than by their capacity to make efficient deliveries and to ensure that there will be neither surpluses nor deficits when each period ends. Rather, markets have inherent structures which have profound implications for how economic actors think and behave, and for the types of production and consumption that will come to dominate economic activity.

In the first place, markets are competitive. Each participant seeks personal advance with no eye to the well-being of other participants. This is what makes markets work—to the extent they do—and cannot be easily dispensed with. The competitive ethic that ensues is one price we pay for using markets as a means of allocation. But markets are also individualistic. We consume by purchasing items individually. There is no account taken of what the effects of our purchase will be on others and others have no say in what we will buy. If our neighbors, for example, would benefit by a particular purchase this is not often expressed through our market behavior. And for people at a greater distance there is even less communication. Markets compel us to make consumption decisions only in light of our own feelings and desires even when others will be affected by our choices. We have insufficient information to take into account the desires of others, or to express their interests, nor would markets work effectively if we were to try to do so. Moreover, we cannot take into account the situation of the people who produce what we consume. Markets are impersonal and asocial. They reduce economic calculation to a confrontation between one individual and one object of possible consumption. The commodities become everything, the human labor and social relations that brought them into being are entirely lost. Markets provide no knowledge of how rock and roll records are made, of who picked the vegetables in our salad, nor of the impact of work on the workers themselves.

On the production side, markets mean that each firm must be concerned with the competitive threat posed by every other firm. Markets ensure a vicious struggle to survive in a competitive context. Market exchange also guarantees that workers will be ignorant of the impact of their efforts on consumers—all that the worker can know is how much consumers will pay for the product they create and how much of it they will buy. The market communicates nothing social or personal to producers any more than it did to consumers—only prices and quantities. Markets tend to foster a division between work itself on the one hand, and a set of technical calculations about how work should be organized and what techniques should be employed on the other.

Remember, we have already argued that people create themselves through their activities—individualist behavior does not yield empathetic individuals—and that people's use-values are partially socially determined by the availabilities of different goods. In a system which over supplies impersonal relations and under supplies personal ones, and over supplies private goods, under supplying public ones, we mold our tastes and dispositions accordingly. Thus markets tend to create actors who have historically been called "homo-economus" rather than vice versa.

The disposition to choose markets in context of public ownership is a response to the ills of central planning that we will discuss in a moment. But it is an ill-conceived response. Though markets can foster a certain liberalization vis-a-vis central planning, and though they will enhance the relative power of workplace managers as compared to central planners—therefore being in the interest of the former as opposed to the latter—they are not a vehicle to truly socialist outcomes. Rather than fostering solidarity between economic actors, they retard it. We should anticipate that their use in "socialist societies" will reflect the interests of managers in factories rather than workers and that their impact won't be to foster socialist outcomes but to hinder them.

### Central Planning and Socialism

Most orthodox Marxists favor central planning as the proper allocation mechanism for socialist economies. The idea is that central planners decide each unit's inputs and outputs in the interests of society's workers and citizenry as a whole. The procedures for accomplishing this are quite varied and are assessed in detail in the companion volume, *Marxism and Socialist Theory*. There are certain things that all central planning systems have in common, however, whatever their particular detailed means of operation.

In the first place, central planning is inherently incapable of offering self-management. Even if every member of society exercised an equal opportunity to express their desires about the different possible outcomes of economic activity, even if the central planners did nothing more than take these goals as givens and calculate the most efficient means for their achievement in light of society's resources and available technology; this system in which every citizen would have an equal say in every aspect of society's production plan would not be characterized by self-management. For self-management is choosing in proportion to the extent you are affected by the outcome of the choice. It is workers having more say over what will be done in their factory than in other factories, but having some say over what goes on in all parts of the economy that affect them to some degree. Even in its ideal form central planning would fall far short of this.

But central planning is intrinsically authoritarian as well. No matter how democratically the priorities of the central planners are set, and no matter how altruistic the central planners might be in carrying those directives out, the relations between the center and the production units of the economy are those of order-giver to order-takers. As we analyzed in detail in *Marxism and Socialist Theory*, all the different conceivable forms of back and forth communication between center and units in a centrally planned economy are means of transfering information from the units to the center so the center can accumulate knowledge, or means of communicating instructions from the center to the units by which the center exercises its authority. Hence, even when given every benefit of the doubt, central planning creates an undersupply of self-managed work situations, denies production units and workers information about how their activities are related to those of others in the economy, and reduces workers to a passive role. If one accepts this situation as a given, the only rational response by workers is to become increasingly apathetic.

But in realistic versions central planning has additional weaknesses. Planners occupy a different position in the economy than other workers. Their labor is conceptual and they have great authority over determination of economic outcomes. As they dispense orders and accumulate information they have an interest in placing people in each unit who share their overall attitudes and can be held accountable for plant performance. These managers also do primarily conceptual work and though they may have less power and status than the central planners, they have considerably more power and status than the workers they coordinate. There is therefore a tendency in central planning to divide workers, conceptual on one side, executionary on the other. As a result of this differentiation into classes the benign character of planning disappears. For far from being altruistic, the planners now have interests that are not always parallel to those of workers and other members of society. First, they are concerned to retain their positions of status and power. It is in their interest to always pursue plans which maximally elaborate the distinction between experts and workers, intellectuals and laborers, and to avoid plans which might enhance the relative knowledge workers have of the economy and their place in it. Second, the planners have an interest in skewing outcomes to their own material advantage, either by bonuses, extra-plan perks, or direct salary differentials. Finally, there is the problem of incentives and worker organizations.

At first, in a revolutionized economy workers might be motivated out of feelings of solidarity and a desire to build a new kind of equitable society. But as class divisions become entrenched and it becomes plain that the basic character of work remains an alienated process in which one has little say, motivation lags. At this point, planners must either coerce their workforce or provide it with material incentives. The latter can be accomplished by tying salaries to output, piece rates, etc., but will only have impact if the salaries can be put to good use. In a context where everything is equitably distributed and many needs accommodated by wide availability of free public goods the motivation to endure draining and alienating work to get extra income will be relatively low. The planners, therefore, have no interest in creating a social environment that is too fulfilling, secure, or collective. Rather, workers must have plenty of aroused needs and few collective ways of addressing them. Only then, will the pursuit of higher wages and bonuses make good sense. So ironically, after the period of revolutionary elan passes, central planning isn't much better than markets at generating solidarity. Instead, as class divisions grow, central planning also has a tendency to promote individualism and consumerism. Our picture of central planning is not a pleasant one. Individual initiative, democracy and self-management are sacrificed. A strict class stratification is preserved. And ultimately there is little gain in collectivity. Central planning does not embody norms consistent with socialist values.

Quite the contrary, it has intrinsic characteristics which are conducive to a drift away from socialist possibilities and toward something else entirely.


## Coordinator Mode of Production and Consumption

It is our view that what has till now gone under the name "socialist economy" is actually an economic system in which not workers but coordinators are the ruling class. The workplace is structured to disempower workers, deny conscious collective self-management, divide conceptual and executionary labor, and compel individualist values. The main economic struggles are over the way society's surplus is distributed between classes, the pace and timing of work, and especially the degree of power different sectors of the coordinator class will have—the local managers versus the central planners versus the party political elite. Insofar as this economic structure is embedded within a social formation that has particular political, kinship, and community forms naturally the economic contours alter. Workplace definitions may embody certain gender and cultural norms and income distribution may also be skewed to accord with extra-economic hierarchies. The ebb and flow of economic life will evidence the impact of dynamics in all four spheres, but we can nonetheless reasonably predict certain likely economic tendencies: a drift away from moral incentives toward material incentives and coercion, a growing struggle between the coordinator class and the political elite, especially if the elite began by dominating all aspects of the economy in the absence of a fully evolved coordinator class, and periodic struggles between the managerial and central fractions of the coordinator class over what emphasis to place on market versus planning mechanisms. We will use our understanding of the market and central planning institutions and of the coordinator class as a dominant economic agent to inform our choice of data from the wealth of information available about the Soviet, Chinese, and Cuban economies and also to interpret and explain that data and evaluate those economies. Furthermore, when we later envision a new economic system consistent with workers' self-management, solidarity, and the eventual elimination of all class differences, our criticisms of the coordinator mode of production and consumption will provide a guiding conceptual framework.

## The Kinship Sphere

We are born male or female children but grow up to be men or women adults. This is far more than a biological process of natural aging. Rather, to be a man or a woman is different in different societies and different epochs. Becoming a man or woman, developing a particular sexual preference, and becoming a mother, father, aunt, uncle, or other kin-person, is as social and historical a process as developing a particular political affiliation, or becoming a member of an economic class. The process involved from procreation to maturation into a particular kinship group is called socialization and along with the various behaviors associated with sexual pairing and courting, it constitutes what we mean by "kinship activity." The kinship network is those institutions which are involved in this activity: centrally the family and the roles associated with sexual preference, "dating," etc., and peripherally all the other institutions of society in their kinship moment.

We are unable to demarcate different kinship systems with the same confidence that we distinguish feudalism and capitalism, monarchy and parliamentarism. But, one attempt to find particular characteristics that can help distinguish different sets of kinship systems has been anthropological analysis of the place of women as objects of exchange in marriage and other forms of pairing. But as we discuss in *Marxism and Socialist Theory*, while this analysis yields a great deal, it nonetheless seems to us too narrow. It misses many of the social and psychological dimensions of the kinship network and even of the exchange of women just as an analysis of the flow of income for labor power and commodities misses the qualitative side of economic exchange and obscures the importance of certain power relationships.

The psychological analysis of kinship, on the other hand, often veers too far in the opposite direction. Focusing on interpersonal dynamics, human nature, and family roles it frequently misses the extent to which sexism is a product of a whole social framework of institutions and relations and not solely of one or two.

Yet whatever weaknesses still exist in our means of understanding the ultimate roots and tenacity of kinship forms and in our capacity to distinguish between forms, we still can make certain judgements with confidence.

Almost universally, just as economic relations have been class divided, kinship relations have been sex role divided, and as there has always been a ruling class so too has there always been a dominant gender, to date, men. *Patriarchy* is the name given to any kinship network characterized by male supremacy. Little children are socialized to become men and women where the social roles of the genders are different, their opportunities in life different, and their personalities and consciousnesses different all in ways that give men a position of relative advantage and power over women. The advantages to men and restrictions placed upon women can be more or less beneficial toward the former and rigid and oppressive toward the latter in different systems, but for all patriarchal systems, by definition the order of the hierarchy is the same.

One of the principle features of kinship about which there is wide agreement is the importance of the fact that in almost all systems women "mother." That is, women take primary responsibility for nurturing, dressing, tending, teaching, cleaning, loving, and disciplining children. Men, on the other hand, only father, a practice which requires only a short period of each day, is generally non-nurturant, and takes little attention and responsibility. As a result of this division, not only does the woman do much more of the *housework* which is socially undervalued, but children form very asymmetrical relations to their parents learning through emulation and through their daily perceptions just what it means to be a woman or a man.

However, this division of tasks within the kinship sphere is not the only division of labor along gender lines. For the kinship sphere overlaps other social spheres and so the hierarchy elaborated between men and women within kinship is at least respected and often reproduced elsewhere as well. Within the economy, women are generally excluded from positions of relative material advantage and influence and usually consigned to tasks which have been expressly defined as female. For example, being a nurse, a secretary, teacher, designer, model, garment worker, or prostitute all embody female norms—nurturance, cleaning, dressing and sexual service. Likewise, within the political sphere women are generally excluded from the most important positions, if not all political activity, political life is defined in male ways, political concerns are deemed a male province, and almost all political skills are reserved for males, while political activity is textured in ways which emphasize traits toward which men are socialized but women are not. And finally cultures of communities and within society generally also relegate women to positions of inferior status and power and enforce male supremacist attitudes and social relationships.

Moreover, as other spheres intersect and reproduce kinship relations they are also partially defined by kinship requirements. And since not only men and women but members of classes, political sectors, and castes are "created" in the family out of the raw material of little children, non-kin moments are present in kinship institutions as well. Kinship activity is therefore different for people who are of the same gender but different economic, community, and political background, just as economics for members of a particular class varies with gender, age, and sexual preference.

In the orthodox Marxist and dominant "socialist" analysis, the key to creating equal relations between men and women is the elimination of a male monopoly on participation in the broader economic system. The idea is to incorporate women into the public economy thereby diminishing their dependence, developing their class consciousness, and giving them new confidence in the process. The effects of this advance will then presumably percolate throughout other sides of social life. There are a number of different theories that generate this approach, and we needn't treat each here to see the reason why this strategy is ill-conceived in all its guises. In the absence of a direct effort to change kinship relations per se, especially those in the family, but also all the more subtle dimensions of non-familial male supremacist relations, patriarchy is not likely to be overthrown. Yes, women may be incorporated into the economy in large numbers and this may have significant effects perhaps even including a major change in kinship relations as a whole. But the question is whether such changes are likely to lead to an end to patriarchy itself, and here our answer has to be no.

For insofar as patriarchy is a phenomenon with roots in the family, in social relations between men and women, in sexual divisions of kinship activity as well as labor, and in the dynamics of mothering, socialization, and the psychological formation of adults, the simple act of incorporating women into the economy in large numbers is not likely to overcome male supremacy. For the women who are welcomed to the factory will still have been brought up by women-mothers. They will still be responsible for mothering and thus for the great bulk of household work—on top of their economic tasks in the factory. The cultural and political inequalities which cement the male/female hierarchy won't have been addressed. The many attitudes regarding sexuality, sexual preference, and what it is to be a male or female won't have been confronted directly nor will community cultural differentiations that reinforce male supremacy. Finally, it is even likely that the presence of patriarchal characteristics within the economy itself will have escaped notice and criticism. For focusing primarily on the "material relations" of economic activity, the orthodox Marxist is not likely to have implemented a program to degenderize the norms of the workplace, the definition of jobs, the expectations of men and women at work, and so on. As a result, though women will be welcomed into the workplace, the jobs they receive and treatment they encounter will just be economic versions of the male supremacy they encounter in the home and elsewhere in society. And even if some attempt were made to prevent this, in the absence of alterations in other spheres, in time these attempts would dissipate and patriarchy would come to characterize the situation of women in the economy again.

Feminist analyses of the tasks necessary to overcome male supremacy take us further, however, focusing on the need for a redefinition of relations in the central kinship institutions as well as in the economy. It will be necessary to redefine the ways in which men, women, and children interrelate in all matters. When we envision socialist kinship alternatives we will elaborate on these feminist concerns. However, it is important to note that many feminists underestimate the need for comparably basic alterations in political, economic, and community relations if kinship changes are to have meaning and permanence. They fail to note that male supremacy is reproduced by relations in other spheres and that a full revolution within kinship would be incompatible with the maintenance of class, political, and community oppressions as these in turn require familial socialization of oppressive sorts. Therefore, to liberate gender definitions, it will also be necessary—a parallel requirement, not an inevitable by-product—to liberate other spheres of social life.

Our analysis of the Soviet, Chinese, and Cuban experiences must be sensitive both to revolutionary alterations of kinship and on-going reproduction of patriarchy. The attention given in these countries to alteration of women's roles in the economy should be assessed, but the attention given to the familial and psychological side of kinship relations must also be judged. For if our theoretical framework is correct, if changes in the family and basic kinship roles are limited, we would expect that though economic changes might affect the well-being of women, they would do little to undermine the basic patriarchal asymmetry between men and women. Finally, envisioning a socialist kinship alternative, we will have to address all sides of kinship activity and especially those associated with motherhood, fatherhood, and socialization in general.

## The Community Sphere

By "community" we mean a group of people who share a common culture and approach to the basic problems of personal identity, ethics, celebration, and approach to life and death. There is no single list of determinants for all possible communities. Rather a group becomes a community when enough of their consciousness and ways of behaving are held in common for members to identify with one another as "the same" as compared to "others." There are religious communities, racial communities, national and even regional and geographical communities like southerners in the United States or countryfolk as compared to cityfolk. People are social beings and communities form in the process of people developing and sharing a culture as a means of forging personal and collective identities and of dealing with difficult philosophical conundrums of life—the questions of the place of humanity in the universe, morality, identity, etc. But communities do not exist in isolation from one another and not only are there internal factors in the development of communities due to their evolving intra-community characteristics, but there are also external factors as a result of their relations with other communities, their inter-community context.

In studying community it is necessary to pay attention to both intra- and inter-community characteristics for each separate type of community. For example, a religious community may develop in relative isolation from other religious communities, in a tranquil mutually respectful relation to other communities, or in dire competition or even a military rivalry with other communities. Which occurs will have an immense impact not only on the relations between the religious communities but also on the character of each internally. And the same might be said for ethnic groups and nations. Certainly the development of the Jewish community in Israel has been mightily affected in its outward and in its inward posture by its relations to the Moslem majorities in the area, and vice versa. The evolution of nationalism in a country like the United States has been quite different than the evolution of nationalism in Poland, again not least because of the different inter-community setting. However, the impact of inter-community relations is most significant with respect to the development of racial communities. For it is inter-group dynamics that actually define racial lines of demarcation whereas in each of the other inter-community instances, the communities are defined internally previous to their interaction.

To understand this, however, it is necessary to understand something more about what it means to become a member of a community. One is not born Turkish, Moslem, Jewish, Chinese, white or Black, any more than one is born a capitalist, a communist, party bureaucrat, or a woman. One may well be born into a setting highly likely to lead to a particular community affiliation, but developing that affiliation in more than a purely formal sense, is nonetheless a process which takes time to evolve. Obviously, and it is therefore a good place to start, religious affiliation is a matter of belief, custom, behavior patterns, and discipline—not of genetic inheritance. One becomes a member of a religious community by adopting its defining personal features and giving that community one's respect. And similarly with ethnic and national affiliations: Although one is formally born a U.S. citizen, a Turkish citizen, or an Italian American, one *develops* the culture of these communities and only thereby becomes a member.

But can this also be true of race? Isn't one born black, red, or white? Occidental or oriental? There are two issues here: what constitutes criteria for membership in a race, and what determines the lines of physical demarcation between races. It is easier to start with the second.

When we say that a child grows up to be a member of a community we mean that there is a sphere of community life with its own intricate social relations and consciousness and that as children grow up in different positions with respect to that network of community relations, they adopt views and traits that certify them as members of one or another community. It is really a phenomenon much like the process of filling a particular place within the network of kinship, class, or political relations. Some demarcations in other spheres of social life have no physical definitions. For example, becoming a member of one class or another is not generally a function of or even correlated with some particular set of physical attributes. But on the other hand, becoming a man or woman is almost always determined by an initial physical sex-endowment, even if to be a ''man'' or a ''woman'' is a social phenomenon rather than a purely biological one.

What is it that makes the demarcation male/female as compared to the demarcation tall/short or heavy/light critical for the evolution of kinship groups? Obviously, the difference in gender plays a crucial role in determining one's position in the kinship network. Being a girl or a boy does not genetically give one the traits common to women and men in one's particular society, but it does give one an immediate head start toward acquiring those traits including motherliness, fatherliness, and heterosexual preferences. The socialization doesn't always work out as it is supposed to, but it does in the vast majority of instances. And when it does fail and a grown male person has the personality and disposition of a woman or vice-versa, we see the social character of kinship definitions most graphically.

Now returning to the question of race, what is it that makes *certain* physical characteristics determine what race one is a member of? Again, we may ask, why skin color (for example) and not height? Height is arbitrary, you might say. There is no line to cut off tall from short. But this is no less true with regard to skin color or any other physical demarcation between races. For in regard to community traits used in racial definitions there is always a continuum with a fuzzy dividing line arbitrarily placed here or there, according to some social convention. With respect to kinship, the biological differences between boys and girls are in fact genetically based and not at all fuzzy, and yet we can understand readily enough that "male" and "female" are social determinations. Why not recognize that though skin color, facial structure, and many other aspects of racial definition are largely genetic, they are only indices that earmark races, not biological determinants of race and therefore of culture?

But unlike religious communities, races are almost entirely a product of inter-community relations. A race comes into being precisely because one community—originally defined in other than a racial way—looks outward and encounters another community which is deemed inferior, a different type of human or subhuman group, and therefore a different race. When German Nazis grew to hate Jews they did not do so solely on the grounds of religious disagreement. One could not escape hate and death by a simple disavowal of the Torah. Rather, Jews were demarcated as an inferior race, from which there is no escape. Similarly, Blacks as ghetto dwellers are seen as inferior in much of the "western world." They become a race apart. Algerians colonized and subjugated by the French are seen as inferior. They become a race apart. And in the act of labeling "the other" a race, of course the Germans, whites in the U.S., and French must also deem theselves a race. But what about a Jew who takes up the beliefs of the Nazis, a Black who comes to feel and believe white history and hold white cultural attitudes, or an Algerian brought up in Paris?

To preserve the consciousness that race is a genetic product, each of these individuals may at some point become subject to racial separation and abuse. But in fact, this is purely a matter of preserving mystical beliefs. For a person with Jewish parents can be as deeply a Christian as a person with Christian parents if he or she grows up in a Christian context, adopts Christian beliefs, mannerisms, and celebrations, etc. Likewise, a person with Black skin (to the sight of a white in the U.S.) if brought up isolated from Black culture and immersed in white culture, could easily become white in beliefs, style, and so on, just as a white individual could become Black. In a time of racial hostility such crossings would be disavowed by each community if not by the individuals involved, but that doesn't alter the fact of the sociality of racial designation, nor of its inter-community basis. The terms "oreo" and "apple" used respectively by Blacks and Native Americans to refer to people Black or Red on the outside, but white on the inside, give evidence of community knowlege of the possibility of crossing we are speaking of.

In this analysis we can also find the answer to the first questions raised above. Except at the most formal level, membership in a race is not a biological affair. Rather, to be of a race, means to share certain cultural norms just as being in any other community does—and this is an eminently social phenomenon. In the Soviet Union one is *formally* of whatever ethnic group it says one is on one's passport. But this doesn't fool anyone. A person brought up by Georgian parents and living his or her whole life as a Georgian doesn't become an Estonian just because his or her passport has "Estonian" embossed on it, even if nine out of ten times what it says on the passport and one's actual culture correlate. The same applies to one's looks and one's real racial affiliation—however high a correlation there might be, the physical characteristics are effect and not cause.

The different kinds of inter-community relations that exist are vast in number. For example, there are colonial and slave relations, relations of bigotry, segregation, racism, or even positive relations between communities. The prevalence of hostile and even genocidal relations between communities, however, cannot be denied. More than anything else it reflects the difficulty of attaining a pluralist attitude about culture and ethics, and therefore of having a live-and-let-live attitude toward other communities, or of believing that other neighboring communities will adopt this type of attitude toward yours. For as soon as a community starts to extoll its own definitions of how to live as the only correct and ethical path, then of course that community must begin to view others with disdain and to assume that they in turn, viewing themselves as correct, will have a similarly disdainful attitude in return. The problem of survival rears its head. Each community feels threatened by others—not only might the other's beliefs call one's own definitions into question, but their policies might raid one's membership or even enslave it for purposes of gain. In a context of mutual hostility and disdain, of scarcity, and of a generalized familiarity with instances of war and domination throughout history, it is not hard to fathom why members of existing communities adopt defensive and sometimes aggressively offensive stances toward one another.

But how do we understand the tenacity of community relations, their roots, and their impact on human possibilities? For the orthodox Marxist community formations are manifestations of ignorance and/or manipulation. Religions, for example, are called "the opiate of the people" and deemed to arise as a result of fears and ignorance and as a false drug to lessen the pains of class oppression. Racial divisions, on the other hand, are felt to be primarily products of the machinations of dominant classes. A ruling capitalist class might divide workers by creating antagonisms between different races or ethnic groups. Or capitalists might promote national antagonisms to become racial hostilities through the process of colonization of one country by another. In this view, the tenacity of community divisions resides in their "use-value" for dominant economic classes. Their primary impact upon human possibilities, even beyond the way racism—for example—oppresses those deemed "inferior," and the way religion mystifies and often oppresses its adherents, is the fact that community consciousness impedes the formation of class consciousness by dividing workers amongst themselves, thereby also impeding the struggle for socialism.

Opposed to this extreme economic materialist analysis, cultural nationalists take the view that community definitions are tenacious because they have roots in people's very beings, in our genetic make-up and our approaches to life options. Not only is racism a white man's disease, but so do sexism and class division emerge from certain cultural relationships and the dominance of certain community groups—both religious and racial. The tenacity of these definitions in dominating historical relations resides in the fact that they provide great power and wealth to their holders who in turn use the power and wealth to maintain the definitions.

In our own view, both of these analyses are incomplete. The orthodox Marxist is correct to notice that class and community relations are linked and that often times class relations impose upon the definitions of communities, sometimes perhaps even causing the emergence of racial definitions as by the processes of colonization. The nationalist, on the other hand, is right to stress that there is a non-economic dimension to the formation of communities and that community relations often impact determinatively upon economic and class realities. Class stratification often bends significantly to fit the parameters of pre-existent community definitions, for example.

But what both views miss is the totalist character of community definition in context of its cultural roots, and its breadth of effectivity throughout society. For in our view, the sphere of community life is one of four defining spheres within society. Its basis is the evolution of cultural affiliations among groups of people. But it shares the same space, ideological, and institutional context with economic, kinship, and political relations and is therefore both defined by and defines those relations. Taking racism between whites and Blacks in the U.S. as an example, we can understand some of the implications of community forms for the definition of social life.

The fact that there is a racial demarcation between whites and Blacks means that on both sides of this divide there is a community. The fact that the inter-community relations are hostile to the point of overt on-going violence means that the impact of the racism directed by whites toward Blacks is pervasive. The definition of the Black community and thus of the cultural attitudes of Blacks is affected by the defensive posture Blacks must take within the broader society, by the denial of Black history, culture, dignity and intelligence within that society, and by the denial of access to knowledge and wealth for Blacks within society. The consciousness and culture of whites is also impinged by the existence of an interface with another community which is deemed inferior, denied access to full citizenship, and exploited as servants, entertainers, and subordinates of all kinds. Both groups cannot freely evolve a fulfilling community definition according to intra-community needs alone, as each must operate in context of the impact of racism. Of course, this is not a relation that is equally or similarly debilitating to both communities. Rather the impact is very different on each. Moreover, the relations of inequality and racial hostility are not confined to a cultural interface. Since economic, kinship, and political spheres overlap the community sphere and its inter-community interfaces, they too embody at least the hierarchicalization of these two communities of people, and more often they even have built-in features which tend to reproduce racism and further it. Jobs in the economy not only segregate whites and Blacks, the former largely in higher paid work with more authority, but even the definition of workplace norms and expectations is encrusted with racial suppositions that denigrate Blacks and simultaneously reproduce the contours of racism.

In *Marxism and Socialist Theory* we address the dynamics of racism, of cultural determinations, and of intra- and inter-community relations in greater detail. Here, what is essential is to move to the question of the relation between community aims and dynamics and the goal of creating a socialist society.

What should be the trajectory of change in community relations as a society undergoes a socialist transformation? In the Orthodox Marxist view, community affiliations are primarily a function of economic forces and have fundamentally disruptive and negative impact upon people's life options. Therefore, in the transition to socialism, what is desired is for an end to all the various negative kinds of inter-community relations, and all the obfuscations and mystifications associated with community definitions, especially religion. The means to this end is fairly straightforward. It is not that people should be cultureless, but that all citizens should share a single "proletarian culture." Religion should disappear, for there is no longer need of opiates for the masses. Community hostilities can be overcome most simply by having but one large community. We call the vision "cultural homogenization." The result is a shared culture that is deemed right by its adherants but which does not cause those adherents to denigrate any other community's culture—for there is no other community in existence to denigrate.

The means to this end is also straightforward, at least according to the orthodox theory. For by overcoming class divisions the roots of cultural hostility are extirpated as are the causes of mystification in people's approaches to the problems of daily life. There is no longer a ruling class creating inter-community hostilities. Defensiveness between communities lessens and each begins to recognize the superiority of certain features of "socialist culture" which slowly spreads, non-coercively, till it encompasses all members of society. For culture, like everything else, must respect the requirements of the economic base, and with a socialist economic base, there will come to be a single shared socialist culture.

But of course this analysis is incorrect. The roots of community affiliation extend well beyond class manipulation. The disposition toward religious study and belief, even though it often has led in horribly oppressive directions, is not itself intrinsically inhuman and but a search for mystical salves for economic woes. Rather, a search for identity and philosophical clarity is likely one of the most profound distinguishing traits of humanity and is not going to pass away simply because many inequities of life are eliminated. To the contrary, as people are freed from many oppressions and indignities they now endure, the time they have available and interest they express in philosophical questions is likely to increase, though certainly with many alterations in form.

To try to reduce community affiliations to unity along all axes is not even a positive aim, much less one that can be accomplished in a simple and equitable way. For it denies variety, eliminates the possibility of each community learning from others, denies the religious impulse, and robs much of the creativity of human relations. Moreover, however, in practice, since the roots of community affiliation run deep and wide, any attempt to eliminate community boundaries simply by changing economic relations is foolish. If the aim is really to be fully achieved, coercion will inevitably be necessary. For community does not simply reflect economics, and so even in a society with a revolutionized economy if all communities are to be reduced to one, this will have to be coerced and even then it will remain only formal. Moreover, the favored community will not be "socialist," but simply the community of prior dominance in the old society. Similarly, the idea that culture in all its forms is a simple manifestation of economic realities at the level of art and social life, is equally flawed. Thus the attempt to make artistic expression a tool of "socialist construction" and no more, would equally require an act of coercion and a denial of human possibilities and interests.

A true socialism concerned to ensure the greatest variety of human creativity would not seek to reduce inter-community violence by eliminating community distinctions but by eliminating the causes of tension between communities. In the United States, it is easy to contrast the two views. On the one hand, racism between whites and Blacks is seen as an economic product. The culture of Blacks and of whites are both infected with racism and false, and each should be altered to reflect the dictates of "socialist economic relations." Without even bothering to criticize the definition of "socialism" and "socialist economic relations" that back up this perspective one can still dispense with it with ease. For Black people would know for sure that racism won't just disappear because people earn their keep in a new way or because some laws about the roles of Blacks in the economy are passed (no matter how important such changes could be if enacted in concert with others). And they would also know that the "new culture" wouldn't contain anything of *their* old culture—it would be white. They are asked to peacefully rush to deny their own roots and their community heritage to avoid the threat that the same end will be forced upon them coercively by a racist offensive. This is not a very promising program. And if, as we believe, racism is intimately connected to all basic oppressive relationships in our society, it is not a program which stands much chance of fully confronting these other relations either. Rather, it is a program reasonably well suited to the accrual of power to new elites reproducing both racism and patriarchy, even if in altered forms, and also creating new forms of class and political stratification. In our alternative formulation, Black culture (as well as various others) must persist. No doubt it will alter somewhat as a result of alterations in other spheres of daily life and of changes in the interface between Black and white communities. But there will be no attempt to homogenize all communities into one, nor to eliminate religion. Rather, the aim will be to create what we call "intercommunalism," a concept we will describe later after we have discussed the practical community experiences of the Soviet, Chinese, and Cuban revolutions as well as available information allows.

### Conclusion

In this chapter we have summarized our overall theoretical orientation and a number of theoretical analyses of alternative institutional relations in different spheres of social life. In the companion volume, *Marxism and Socialist Theory*, all of the material presented here is argued in greater detail, with greater analytic precision, and with more attention to a clarification of differences between our approach and others that are currently better known. Our purpose here has been to summarize an intellectual framework suitable for the historical and visionary analyses we are about to undertake.

We can briefly summarize the program of study that emerges from the theory of this chapter: We need to assess all four spheres in each of the countries we are discussing and to envision possible relations in all four spheres in our proposed alternative socialist model. While we can't be comprehensive for any one sphere nor for the intricate interrelations between them, we can illuminate main tendencies and interactive dynamics. With regard to the polity we should examine political relations, supporting ideology, and the impact of each on people occupying different places in the state. We should assess how elites from each sphere influence state decision-making and see how the dynamics of democratic centralism and vanguard organization manifest themselves on political outcomes and consciousness development and on dynamics in other spheres. Does our theoretization of bureaucratic forms apply, how far has bureaucratization progressed and what has been the impact of the scientific rationalization of power? With regard to the economy, we must examine the history to see the influence of different conceptions of economic development and particularly we must assess the use of planning and market forms, the role of incentives, the development of the coordinator class, its rise to ruling class status, the ebb and flow of intra- and inter-class struggles, and the impact of economic elites on other social spheres and vice versa. Similarly, regarding kinship, we must seek to assess whether womens' situations have dramatically altered and to what extent this alteration indicates a full liberation of women or only the elimination of the most barbaric patriarchal forms. Likewise, it would be desirable to understand the historical ebb and flow of kinship relations alongside the ebb and flow of dynamics in other spheres to see how the relative rise and fall of power of different elites accommodates across social spheres. Last, with regard to community history, despite the relative paucity of information available about this, again it would be desirable to see the extent to which cultural homogenization has been achieved, the resistance to it, and its implications for daily life.

If our study of the history of these countries allows us to explain phenomena which other theories ignore, overlook, or can't comprehend and if it allows us to envision a socialist future that is simultaneously implementable and also consistent with our most profound socialist desires and needs, then the theoretical synopsis in this chapter will have shown its worth.

# Part Two

# "Socialism" Today

Descartes used to say that a clock out of order is not an exception to the laws governing clocks, but a different mechanism obeying its own laws; in the same way we should regard the Stalin regime, not as a workers' state out of order, but as a different social mechanism, whose definition is to be found in the wheels of which it is composed and which functions according to the nature of those wheels. And, the wheels of...the Stalin regime consist exclusively of the various parts of a centralized administrative system on which the whole economic, political and intellectual life of the entire country is entirely dependent.

Simone Weil

# 2
# THE SOVIET EXPERIENCE

To present the Russian regime as "socialist" or as a
"workers' state," as do both the "left" and the "right" in
an almost universal complicity, or even to discuss its
nature in reference to socialism to determine at what
points and to what degree it deviates from it, represents
one of the most horrendous enterprises of mystification
known in history.

Cornelius Castoriadis

The Russian revolution was an epoch event of the twentieth
century. Not only did it awaken Russia from a deep and oppressive
slumber, and initiate the period of conflict between East and West,
it also laid claim to the mantle of being the first practical
implementation of the schemes of Karl Marx. Whether this last
claim was reasonable or not, people all over the world at the time
agreed that this was a socialist revolution. As a result, ironically, the
Soviet Union has represented a great impediment to socialist
alterations in the industrialized countries Marx himself pinpointed
as the most likely sites for socialism. As much as the material success
of capitalism, the power of the bourgeois state and media, and the
bullets of national guard or police, the Soviet Union's failure to
achieve freedom and democracy has hindered socialism from
gaining significant following in the United States. And even in
Europe where the socialist heritage is older than the fear of the
Russian catastrophe, that catastrophe has nonetheless hung like an
ugly skeleton to hinder socialist efforts. When socialist movements
advance, the closet door is opened. The skeleton lumbers forth to
scare away growing constituencies, and not without reason.

In this chapter we will address in brief the central
developments of the Soviet political, economic, kinship, and
community spheres. Hopefully, this overall analysis will help clarify
not only how this revolution became other than what many of its
adherants hoped for, but also in what ways modern revolutionary
efforts might hope to prevent similar results from occurring again.

### The Soviet Political Experience

Last chapter in our discussion of political theory we traced the roots of post-capitalist political elitism and authoritarianism to the contours of Leninist theory itself and especially to Leninism's adherence to democratic centralist and vanguardist political forms. We also argued briefly that the ideological basis of these organizational beliefs rests squarely in certain orthodox Marxist formulations which are succinctly stated in a famous passage from Lenin:

> The history of all countries shows that the working class, exclusively by its own efforts, is able to develop only trade union consciousness, i.e., the conviction that it is necessary to combine in unions, fight the employers, and strive to compel the government to pass necessary labor legislation, etc. The theory of socialism, however, grew out of the philosophic, historical, and economic theories elaborated by educated representatives of the propertied classes, by intellectuals...[2]

And it has been these intellectuals who have occupied positions of dominant influence in Bolshevik parties that have fought for "socialism" around the world, and who have therefore occupied the social positions which, if we are correct in our analysis, continually further their elitism, narrow perspective, and self-interested pursuit of power. That some communist leaders were devoted to nothing other than revolution in the name of all oppressed people should come as no surprise. That some may have maintained such a desire through long years of elite practice is less likely, but of course not at all impossible. But the idea that anyone occupying a post of power in a hierarchical organization that is in turn situated hierarchically above the rest of the population would not have had their consciousness adversely affected by these relations seems to us preposterous *and quite unMarxist*. In Soviet history we find the instance in which the negative potentials of Leninist political themes regrettably ran the authoritarian course to its ultimate conclusion.

The fact that the centralism, secrecy, and organizational discipline of the early Bolsheviks was largely a function of the repressive apparatus of the Czar does not excuse us from analyzing *the effects* of these policies. One can but wonder over the stories related by Isaac Deutscher of Lenin sending secret messages from underground to party meetings in the spring and summer of 1917 telling them to "listen to Trotsky" since only Trotsky understood the urgency of insurrection, chiding the other members of the Bolshevik Central Committee for vacillating, and threatening that if they didn't act he would dissolve the central committee, and unilaterally form a new one that would declare for an insurrection.[3] Apparently the necessity for discipline extended to all but Lenin, just as in the past Marx and Engels had always felt themselves above party requirements, and as Stalin would feel again in the future.

But before pursuing the intricacies of internal Bolshevik social relations, it will be helpful to review the entire spectrum of political opposition to the Czar so we can recapture an important but frequently overlooked sense of the political elements involved. At the time of the overthrow of the Czar there were four major opposition political groups: 1) the bourgeois republican opposition whose major party was the Cadets, 2) the Marxist opposition including both the Mensheviks and Bolsheviks, 3) the Social Revolutionary Party (henceforth, S.R.s) established in 1901 as an outgrowth of the earlier revolutionary Narodniki movement and representing a base of peasants, and 4) the Anarchists including both rural and urban groups. The S.R.s were the largest party by far, the Cadets were next, and the Marxists and Anarchists were tied for third, with the Bolsheviks the smaller of the two Marxist groups.

All four opposition political groups participated in the February revolution which overthrew the Czar. The Cadets, Mensheviks, and right wing of the Social Revolutionary Party supported the parliamentary based government (called the *DUMA*) headed by Kerensky that officially replaced the Czar. However, between February and October, the Bolsheviks, Anarchists, and left wing of the S.R.s intensified their opposition to the policies of the Kerensky regime and built the urban and rural Soviets as an increasingly powerful shadow government. The October revolution overthrew the Kerensky Duma and established a revolutionary government based on the Soviets, thus ending the period of "dual power" in the Russian revolution. This revolution was fought under the slogans of "Land" (sanctioning the radical agrarian reform that was actually proceeding in the villages rather than the hesitant agrarian policy of the Kerensky regime), "Peace" (Russian withdrawal from World War I rather than Kerensky's backing of continued hostilities), "Bread" (a wishful commitment that the

Soviet government would be more serious and effective at stopping the mass starvation that was occurring), and "All Power to the Soviets" (a reference to the institutional basis of the new regime supported by the Bolsheviks, Anarchists, and Left S.R.s alike).

Since much of the political history of the Soviet Union is textured by the relationship between the Bolshevik party and the peasantry, it is important to pay attention to this interface from the beginning. At the time of the overthrow of the Czar, the Social Revolutionary Party had a mass base among the peasantry. In addition, some rural Anarchist groups had regional peasant bases. Neither the Mensheviks nor Bolsheviks had any significant peasant backing, the Bolsheviks least of all. During the period of dual power, the Social Revolutionary Party divided.

As Maurice Dobb, an author with few sympathies toward the Social Revolutionaries reported:

> But the events of 1917 progressively widened the rift *in the party of the peasantry*, the Social Revolutionary Party itself. As so often happens with peasant parties in agricultural countries, the right-wing tended to adapt its policies to the interests of the more prosperous peasants, and to become a party of the rural bourgeoisie. * But as the actual currents among the peasantry which we have described [land seizures and landlord lynchings] gathered momentum in the summer and autumn of the year, it was the left wing section of the party, favoring a revolutionary solution to the agrarian problem which won adherants in the countryside and became *the political spokesman* of the mass of peasantry in the rural Soviets and in other local bodies. [emphasis added][4]

As Dobb goes on to relate, shortly after the Bolsheviks attained power it was actually the left S.R.s who had a clear majority at the

---

*It is of more than passing interest, perhaps reflecting the thread of anti-peasant elitism running through almost all of non-Maoist Marxism, that Dobb doesn't take the same almost disdainful "as so often happens" view with respect to splits in the Marxist workers' party, splits which didn't even wait until the issue was at hand but which instead caused sectarian infighting for a full 15 years before Czarism was overthrown!

first peasants' Congress, and thus in negotiations with the Bolsheviks it was agreed that representatives of the left S.R.s would be welcomed in the new government. In addition to being the main representative of the peasantry and to taking part in the new government, the left S.R.s were leading the agrarian reform movement in the countryside long before Lenin signed a decree sanctioning this activity. Moreover, the radical agrarian struggle was the force most responsible for toppling both the Czar and the Kerensky regime. There is also reasonable evidence that the left S.R.s were generally supportive of *left* Bolsheviks on the issues of nationalization, treatment of old managers, and workers' control—views which often took them to the left of Lenin himself. Although we will leave issues of economic policy and organization to the next section, it is still useful to quote Dobb on the point here. For the dominant leftist view of the banning of the left S.R.s has been that this peasant party was naive or reactionary or at least an impediment to thorough-going revolution. In fact, quite the contrary was the case.

> But apart from spontaneous tendencies among the workers to force the pace (of nationalizations) born of the sharpened tension of class relations, there was a good deal of conscious opposition at the time to the policy which Lenin was advocating (a go slow on nationalizations): opposition not only from among the ranks of the Bolsheviks who were influenced by the ideas of the left S.R.s but from inside the party itself among the so-called 'left communists.' The latter at one time constituted a separate faction within the party, ran its own newspaper, *The Communist*, and cooperated with the left S.R.s.
> Many of them (the left communists) seemed to have looked askance at Lenin's generous treatment of 'specialists' unless this was to be offset by greater powers of direct control over production by factory committees. Karelin, the left S.R., however, at the Fourth Session of the Soviet Executive Committee openly spoke of Lenin's employment of bourgeois engineers and economists as 'coalition with the bourgeoisie.'[5]

That the left S.R.'s were among those who showed sensitivity to the problem of the emergence of a coordinator class should be kept in mind throughout this chapter's later economic discussions. But the visible conflict which led to the eventual banning of the left S.R.'s and of the anarchists as well had to do not with the above matters, but with food requisitioning and especially the "Committees of the Village Poor."

Even *before the Civil War,* in May of 1918, requisitioning was common, and a May 14th government executive decree declared that "in any district the laboring peasants, not employing other citizen's labor, must see that all peasants who have surplus grain stores and refuse to deliver them up at the fixed prices be declared enemies of the people, and be deprived of their rights as citizens of the Republic and be brought before a Revolutionary tribunal."[6] It is perhaps worthwhile to hypothesize about the kinds of attitudes which may well have existed among the urban, largely intellectual leadership of the party toward the rural peasantry such as to allow such severe formulations regarding their motives and how they should be treated. That there was already a considerable schism between the party leadership and the peasants in the countryside seems clear; that unless countered it would grow seems predictable; but that it would reach the proportions which underlay the later almost genocidal Stalinist approach to the peasants was certainly not evident nor inevitable. In any case, the left S.R.'s were outraged by the decree.

Moreover, shortly after, in June 1918, the "Committees of the Village Poor" were established. The idea was to gain allies within the villages who could help the Bolsheviks implement the requisitioning policy against the more well-to-do peasants who held the surplus. In a complimentary interpretation Dobb suggests that "in this way the supply policy would not be something imposed upon the village from without but carried through by the poorer strata of peasants themselves."[7] But the left Social Revolutionaries were horrified, interpreting the Committees of Village Poor as attempt to encroach the region of left S.R. support, rather than as an attempt at decentralized, mass control of food requisitioning which, in fact, they would have had little reason to oppose. And even according to Dobb himself, "in May the left S.R.s opposed a Bolshevik motion for more centralized control of food supply, and in particular for empowering the Commissariat of Supply to remove local supply commissars and to countermand the orders of local Soviets."[8] Certainly the SR's skepticism was as plausible as Dobb's complimentary interpretation, especially given the general drift of Bolshevik policy toward the enlargement of their own power over the executive branch and increasing deemphasis of the Soviet legislative organs in whose name the revolution was made. In any case, the left S.R. opposition to the Committee's policy was beaten back at the 5th Soviet Congress in July, and the S.R. party itself was outlawed along with most Anarchist organizations who were also until this point largely allies of the Bolskeviks.[9] After an abortive S.R. attempt to overthrow the Bolshevik executive branch in the name of the peasant Soviets, all opposition newspapers and offices were closed down and leading members arrested or driven into hiding. From a broad anti-Czarist opposition in February, to a broad revolutionary political front in October, the revolution had now "progressed" to a single party in command by July, all *before* the Civil War began in earnest.

This seems an immense price to pay for a policy which was in fact reversed by Lenin himself after only six months because of its ineffectiveness and negative impact on class relations:

> Lenin was quick to see the danger to the worker/peasant alliance latent in this fanning of the class struggle in the village. At the end of the year, accordingly, the Committees of the Village Poor was dissolved, and at the 8th Party Congress in March he (Lenin) urged the need to heal the breach with the middle peasantry and to win them as allies in the fight against counter revolution.[10]

It is not unreasonable, therefore, to hypothesize that the drift toward Bolshevik repression of the S.R.'s and other political organizations stemmed not only from momentary disagreements over policies, but also from tendencies inherent in the Bolshevik's self-conception as *the* vanguard organization of the revolution.

Not surprisingly, the years of Civil War led to a further intensification of centralization and hierarchicalization, even to militarization of the party hierarchy and of its conception of itself vis-a-vis the population. As this trend is documented elsewhere, and in any case attributable to wartime exigencies rather than the functioning of democratic centralism, we will not spend time on it. *

---

*The fact that wartime regimentation may be unavoidable makes it no less disruptive of democratic possibilities which of course suggests that it should be countered in every way possible. A quotation from Maurice

What is important is that after the Civil War Soviet revolutionaries had a great "second chance" to address the development of a
repressive political apparatus by instituting a serious democratization. Regrettably, precisely the opposite occurred. Most of the
history of the centralization of power by the Bolshevik apparatus
revolves around struggles over the role of workers, managers and
unions in the economy and will be taken up shortly. But there are
three particular post-war "occurrences" that we would like briefly
to address before moving on to consider the Stalinist extention of
the Bolshevik revolution. The first relates to the further consolidation of the party as the sole ruling agency of the revolution, the
latter two relate to the party's own internal elaboration as an
anti-democratic and eventually dictatorial bureaucratic apparatus.

Two of many militant stuggles between the Bolshevik apparatus and movements of people in protest against political centralization stand out by their magnitude and by the strange historical
treatment they have received. In the Ukraine, workers and
peasants organized in a guerilla force under the military leadership of "comrade Makhno."[11] They fought fiercely against the
anti-Bolshevik "White armies" during the Civil War and evolved
a position in favor of the freest possible evolution of the local
Soviets. They called for "the free election of workers' councils
which will not rule by arbitrary laws because no true soviet system
can be authoritarian."[12] They felt that the soviets should be "the
executive organs of, and not over the workers."[13] This movement
was far from naive or ill-organized. It was a vital pro-Soviet force
in the Civil War and, given official rhetoric about "power to the
Soviets," one would think it might have been left alone to

Dobb's work is relevant to this matter and also provides background for
coming discussions of popular resistance:
    "Soviet officials in the country districts, still carrying over the
    traditions of the Civil War period, too frequently adopted
    sargent/major methods to get things done, ordering things by
    command and bullying those who would not be regimented....
    Arbitary appointments from above, which had been in force
    in the special circumstances of the Civil War, continued in
    many cases; so that village soviets, often lacking democratic
    character and influence, became dead wood and of little
    interest to the peasantry, in some cases being boycotted by
    them. A story was told of a peasant remarking at a congress:
    'If they ordered us to elect a horse to the village soviet, we
    should be compelled to do so.'"

evolve its own democratic experiment in the Ukraine. Had this worked, and there was every reason to believe it might have, the experiment could have been emulated elsewhere. Had it failed, on the other hand, that would have been the time to institute some central controls peacefully, and without destroying the indigenous basis for direct democracy which could be used later, as conditions would allow.

But no, under Trotsky's leadership the Makhnovites were treated as enemies of the state and militarily destroyed by the Red Army. And though one of the contested issues was the matter of local versus national political power, another was the question of community diversity which we will leave for later discussion.[14]

In any case, no community clashes fueled the incidents surrounding the more noted Kronstadt uprising and its repression. An anarchist commentator, Paul Avrich, writes that resentment in the workplace and cities against the reinstatement of former factory bosses and harsh discipline was the soil from which the resistance grew:

> For the rank-and-file workman, the restoration of the class enemy to a dominant place in the factory meant a betrayal of the ideals of the revolution. As they saw it, their dream of a proletarian democracy, momentarily realized in 1917, had been snatched away and replaced by the coercive and bureaucratic methods of capitalism. The Bolsheviks had imposed 'iron discipline' in their factories, established armed squads to enforce the will of management, and contemplated using such odious efficiency methods as the 'Taylor system.' That this should be done by a government which they had trusted and which professed to rule in their name was a bitter pill for the workers to swallow.[15]

With the conclusion of the Civil War, rationales for the coercive excesses became lame, and workers grew more restive. It was the Petrograd workers, the most militant and advanced fighters of the revolution, who struck in 1921 demanding economic relief, free soviets, and an end to repression in and out of the factories. The Bolsheviks broke the strike via a state-of-seige and the introduction of government troops, but not before the neighboring Kronstadt sailors sent representatives who saw the repression and returned to their ships with descriptions. The sailors passed a fifteen-point resolution demanding free elections to new free soviets with secret ballot and free electioneering; freedom of speech and press for workers, peasants, anarchists and all other left socialist parties; right of assembly for trade unions and peasant organizations; freeing of all left political prisoners; organization of a Petrograd non-Party conference; review of cases of those held in prison camps; no special Party detachments in factories and other public institutions; equalization of rations except in special cases; wide press coverage for the resolution itself; and freedom of action for peasants who don't employ others on their own land as well as rights to handicraft production by individuals.[16] The economic demands posed no real problem for the Bolsheviks as Lenin had already decided to embark on a similar set of actions to alleviate national tensions. But the demands aimed at institutional democratization were another matter. The bureaucracy saw these as antithetical to the spirit and direction of *their revolution*, as well they may have been. For the dynamics of centralization which spring from the fruits of a vanguard self-conception had already progressed well past the point of this sort of liberalization. The Kronstadt sailors were subjected to ridicule and portrayed as counter revolutionaries, not as the militant stalwarts they had always been who were now seeking precisely *to extend the revolution* according to its own rhetoric toward direct and free soviet power. From the Bolskevik center came one perspective:

> Struggle against the White Guard plot... Just like other White Guard insurrections the mutiny of ex-General Kozlovsky (who actually had nothing significant to do with the insurrection) and the crew of the Battleship Petropavlovosk has been organized by entente spies... [17]*

*This is likely the first really clear instance of the kind of "blaming it on the capitalist spies" obfuscation common to later military actions in Hungary, Czechoslavakia, and now even perhaps Poland. It is not dissimilar to earlier attempts to link Lenin with German financiers because he passed through that country or, even more clearly, to Western and especially U.S. efforts to "prove" that both internal dissent and third world rebellions are manipulated by a Communist conspiracy. The Cold War, seen at Kronstadt in its infancy, is serviceable for both sides.

And from the sailors themselves came another:

Our cause is just. We stand for the power of the soviets not for that of the party. We stand for freely elected representatives of the toiling masses. Deformed soviets, dominated by the party, have remained deaf to our pleas. Our appeals have been answered with bullets.[18]

And indeed the insurrection "was drowned in blood. Trotsky took charge of operations, promising the insurgents he would 'shoot them down like rabbits,' and making good on the threat."[19] Their response was prophetic: "Be careful Trotsky. You may escape the judgment of the people, you may shoot down innocent men and women by the score, but even you cannot kill the truth."[20]

Remarkably, however, the Bolsheviks came quite close to succeeding in not only the military but also the propagandistic task. For in writing the history of the events they defamed the Petrograd workers and Kronstadt sailors by every means at their disposal. Perhaps that alone is enough to explain why many modern commentators pay so little attention to these events, but perhaps a level of subjectivity and obfuscation is also at work. Consider Charles Bettleheim's skewed account:

The very fact that the revolt could occur confirms that discontent among a section of the masses, especially the peasants (or those who were of peasant origin like the young recruits in Kronstadt), had then reached the pitch of explosion in some places, so that some of the peasantry were wide open to the petty bourgeois propaganda of the SR's, Mensheviks, and anarchists...  [21]

It would seem that the workers, peasants, and militants at the base, though imbued with insight and courage when they fight on the side of the Bolsheviks, are somehow infused with class collaboration when they rise in opposition even though at both times they expressed the same desires and aims. Contrast their supposedly collaborationist and counterrevolutionary demands to the presumably insightful and revolutionary analysis put forth below by Trotsky, their most fierce opponent, during the same period:

It has been said more than once that we have substituted the dictatotship of the Party for the dictatorship of the

Soviets. However, we can claim without fear of contradiction that the dictatorship of the soviets was only made possible by the dictatorship of the Party... In fact, there has been no substitution at all, since the Communists express the fundamental interests of the working class... the Communists become true representatives of the working class as a whole.[22]

This is the acme of vanguard consciousness in action. That the people the vanguard "represents" are excluded from power is irrelevant. That they are distressed is perhaps regrettable but no more. That they express a desire for change is counterrevolutionary. The Party is, by definition, the embodiment of revolution. No wonder it can righteously mete out punishment to even its own former allies. Was it the sailors who were enemies of socialism?

Yet the centralization of political power did not end with the elimination of all extra-Party opposition, including both grass-roots organizations at the base of society and also all parties other than the Bolsheviks. Rather it extended into the party as well. At the Tenth Party Congress in 1920, after the Civil War was effectively over, party factions were banned and an end was put to public discussions of Party matters. According to Bettleheim, "The Tenth Congress was the last to have been preceded by a broad, open, discussion. At subsequent Congresses, the various oppositions would not be allowed to express themselves with such freedom.... Increasingly the means of expression were to be withdrawn from opposition tendencies, in the end disappearing altogether."[23] Here we see the dynamics of hierarchicalization methodically undermining the democratic part of democratic centralism. "The Tenth Congress... passed a resolution laying down new rules which prohibited factions. In principle this rule forbade the formation within the party of groups organized on the basis of a platform and having their own internal discipline, that is, tending to constitute a sort of party within the party."[24] Bettleheim goes on to say that "the ban was adopted as a temporary measure justified by exceptionally difficult circumstances."[25] But what were these circumstances? The war had been won. Perhaps it was that many within the Party were still sympathetic to calls for democracy from workers and peasants at the base of society. This would indeed have been a problem and so we see how the logic of the "vanguard" and of internal centralism are effectively the same and also interlinked. It should therefore come as no surprise that in practice there was nothing "temporary" about the measure. As Bettleheim goes on to describe it in more detail, "Any party member, including any member of the Central Committee, who acted in violation of this resolution, could be expelled by decision of the Central Committee."[26] With parties other than the Bolsheviks outlawed; with movements of workers, peasants, and soldiers subject to military repression; with factions outlawed even within the party; effectively, collective expression of any dissent against the will of the center became impossible. This was the basis for the rise of Stalinism. And the logic of the evolution was clear even at the Tenth Congress. For if the rank-and-file of the Party and even its central committee is itself denied the ability to organize in support of policies, all power to set policy must reside in a still more central or higher organ, the politbureau.

Again, as Bettleheim reports:

> In another way too, the Tenth Congress limited the possibility of open ideological debate, for it considerably reduced the authority of the Central Committee, which was precisely where extensive and thorough discussion took place [that is, the situation was already, before the Congress, hardly a testimony to the widest possible involvement even in party debate]. From this time onward, in fact, the C.C. ceased to be the Party's supreme body between Congresses. The interval between its meetings were made longer: henceforth it was to meet only once every two months, and its powers were in practice delegated to the Political Bureau which beginning in 1921, had only seven members. Inside the Political Bureau itself the dominant position was increasingly held by representatives of the Party's administrative apparatus, those who headed the secretariat, the assignments office, and so on.[25]

The bureaucracy with its own logic was formalized, its pinnacle given almost unlimited power. That Stalinism *in all its extremes* was not an inevitable outgrowth of this on-going dynamic seems sure. That it was one possible outcome, one possible development consistent with the prior processes, is proved by history. As the above discussion has been only cursory, providing both exemplification of what we mean by our analysis of the non-neutrality of political institutions and also evidence in favor of our particular analysis of tendencies intrinsic to vanguardism and democratic centralism, so the following discussion of Stalinism is also a bare sketch meant to show only the magnitude of the crimes of the period and to thereby further motivate the importance of an independent understanding of political relationships and their impact on social history.

### Stalinism

For Trotsky, Stalinism represented a complete break with the Leninist heritage and its reading of Marx. It was a reaction which distorted the revolution laying a political dictatorship on top of a socialized mode of production.* For many other analysts, in particular of late the French "new philosophers," Stalinism was simply the natural and inevitable outgrowth of the application of Marxism Leninism, not an abberation at all. Our view, like that of Alvin Gouldner in his essay from which we draw, "Stalinism: A Study of Internal Colonialism,"[25] lies somewhere in between. The ground had certainly been paved for Stalin. His means and aims were but an extension of earlier Bolshevik means and aims. Yet in their exceptional extremism and violence they went beyond anything that was "inevitable." This however, does not alibi away the responsibility of the Leninists, who went before. The seeds they sowed could and did bring forth the gargoyle that was Stalinism. To have a theoretical orientation which minimizes the importance of political institutions in favor of emphasizing the economy alone and to

*We will assess the assertion that production relations in the Soviet Union are now or ever were socialist shortly. What is theoretically interesting about this Trotskyist assertion, however, is its strangely unMarxist logic. How could a socialist economic apparatus exist as the foundation for (or, in our view, in context of) a grossly authoritarian political sphere? Shouldn't the presumed socialist base transform the political superstructure (or vice versa) in something less than sixty years and shouldn't the liberating dynamics of presumed socialist economic relations create a populace unwilling to submit to the arbitrary rule of a totalitarian maniac? Obviously. And so one would expect the Trotskyists to admit that either Stalin and the political institutions were not so bad—an unlikely leap for them to make and an unwarranted one as well—or that the economy itself must not have been socialist, a case we will make shortly. That many Trotskyists do not follow this logic is testimony to the fact that like their namesake they confine Marxist analysis to matters on which the results of such analysis bear out their interests and expectations.

espouse a political practice which extols authoritarian and centralizing forms with little understanding of their intrinsic dangers, is to travel a path which may yield the horrors of Stalinism and certainly won't lead to democratic and participatory socialism.

In 1929, Stalin began the forced collectivization of Soviet agriculture. In ten years "about twenty million Soviet citizens were killed. They were shot, or died of famine, disease, or exposure, directly resulting from the punitive actions of the Soviet government."[28] This cannot be dismissed as an aberration. A historical monstrosity, it must be understood, not dodged. According to the last available census, taken in 1897, there had been "2.5 million industrial workers, 1.25 million soldiers, 1 million bureaucrats, 17,000 students, and 100 million peasants."[74] The fact that the revolution was centralized by a Party which claimed dictatorial powers *in the name of the workers alone* explains much about how a consciousness could evolve among the leadership which would lead to harsh denial of the well-being and even existence of much of the peasantry. That the leadership was an urban elite which evolved into a kind of isolated cultural community seeing itself as superior to the lowly rural peasants was likely also a considerable factor. With regard to the decision of the Party to use force and attempt the quickest possible collectivization of the countryside as well as the most forceful and extreme forms of requisitioning, Gouldner says, "The decision to be ruthless was legitimated by a siege mentality but was made possible by the system of internal colonialism (the urban elite colonizing the—to their eyes—culturally inferior rural poor) within which the most extreme sanctions could be inflicted upon the peasantry with impunity."[30]

In 1929 Stalin called for the liquidation of the kulaks as a class. The land-owning peasants were to be forced off their land into collective farms. With the ensuing organizational structure of huge state controlled farms, the Stalinists had much easier access to the agricultural product so as to make more of it a surplus to be redistributed away from the producers for use in financing industrialization. Did the need for rapid industrialization justify the cost? Did it require this extreme level and form of appropriation? It is impossible to answer this question affirmatively. The camps in Artic areas known as the Gulag Archipelago were established, cadres were militarized, and according to the contemporary Nobel laureate dissident, Andre Sakharov, "at least 10 to 15 million people perished...by torture or execution in camps for exiled kulaks..."[31] No matter the enlargement of "forces of production," this is not the way to a sane, much less an ideal society.

This was a period of armed cadre bursting into village homes and confiscating what was of value while herding the citizens off to camps. One is reminded of the precision of Nazi terror and likely the associated rationalizations and derivative effects on social relations must have been somewhat similar. As Gouldner argues: "The infrastructure of rational terror consists of committee meetings, of clerical computations, bookkeeping, inventories, personnel and budgetary appropriations. The collectivizers came with guns in one hand, and pencil and paper in the other. In short, collectivization meant an immediate massive expansion of the secret police and of the entire state bureaucracy."[32] It was this latter development that allowed the eventual extension of the terror beyond treatment of the kulaks to treatment of Party members themselves.

Stalin was aberrant enough in the level of his violence and self-infatuation that resistance did begin forming within the ranks of the Party itself. But having elaborated an effective form for dealing with opposition from those in the countryside, Stalin was able to re-aim his apparatus not only toward the small remaining non-Stalinist factions, but most incredibly even toward a majority of his own increasingly disillusioned faction.

According to Krushchev's revelations, the repression of the Party itself was almost complete.[33] The 17th Congress elected a Central Committee whose 1937 plenum challenged some of the charges that Stalin was bringing against previously loyal Party members. According to Krushchev, "of the 139 members and candidates of the Party's Central Committee who were elected at the 17th Congress, 98 persons, i.e., 70 percent, were arrested and shot mostly in 1937-38... of 1,966 delegates (to the Congress) with either voting or advisory rights, 1,108 were arrested on charges of anti-revolutionary crimes... "[34] According to Sakharov between 1936 and 1939 "more than 1.2 million party members, half the total membership, were arrested. Only 500,000 regained freedom. The others... were shot (600,000) or died in camps."[35] The opposition within the ranks was obviously considerable—"Stalin killed and tortured more Communists than any other dictator in the 20th century, whether Hitler, the Czar, the Shah of Iran, or the Chilean Junta,"[36] but the fact still remains that the apparatus of Soviet political relations was such that resistance was fated to fail, for it could never be brought to bear in an effective form. And this was traceable to the centralization of the Party in earlier years and to the banning of other parties and movements.

The terror was not confined to the Party but also extended to the infrastructure of the Red Army, thus putting the lie to any notion that Stalin was only acting as he must to prepare the Soviet Union for an inevitable war with Nazi Germany. Thirteen of 15 generals were killed. "80 percent of all colonels were killed or removed, as were 30,000 officers below the rank of colonel. Between 35 to 50 percent of the entire officer corps was eliminated. More senior officers were killed during the purges than during the entire war with the Nazis."[37] In the war itself, the Soviet rate of desertion was tremendous. The fact that a Soviet officer Vlasov, after being captured by the Nazis organized 200,000 disillusioned Red Army troops to fight against their own country is indicative of the opposition to Stalin. It seems plausible that had it not been for the almost unlimited racial barbarism of the Nazis against the Soviet population, they may well have been able to tame the country largely to their will much as they had with France. However, in light of that racism, the Soviets did mount a nationalist defense and were then largely responsible for breaking and reversing the momentum of the fascist armies. That Stalin often receives credit for this, instead of the Russian people, is just one more ugly irony of history.

A last characteristic of the Stalinist horror Gouldner graphically addresses is that it was directed against "members of groups" for the very fact of their group membership, rather than against individuals for the actuality of their behavior. "In most cases, then, persons were jailed, shot, or exiled not because of what they had done but because of their supposed readiness to do injury to Soviet society inferred on the basis of their social category: social origin, nationality, or group membership."[38] The trials were for show. Guilt was a function of social position as individuals were considered ciphers for the expression of social relationships. The lesson about the danger of the orthodox (and now structuralist) Marxist underemphasis of the human subject in history is obvious.[39]

There has yet to be a serious accounting of Stalinism in the Soviet Union which truly addresses the crimes and their meaning for the institutions, and for the validity or vapidity of certain theoretical commonplaces of Soviet life. Perhaps one can understand the hesitancy to undergo such a self-critical assessment in a society where so many were implicated and so many suffered as well. But a considerable part of the socialist movement in the West still hesitates to sharply condemn the Stalinist heritage or the authoritarian character of the current Soviet State. A still broader segment refuses to even consider the possible links between Leninism and Stalinism. And a tiny segment even continues to espouse Stalin as a mentor. This is a travesty.* Hopefully by telescoping some of the horrendous detail of the period into this brief discussion we will have made more leftists aware of the historic crime that was committed in the name of Socialism, and the need to categorically reject all manner of rationalizations and excuses that have been offered in its defense.


## THE SOVIET ECONOMIC EXPERIENCE

The use of both central planning *and* markets at different times in Soviet history have contributed to the consolidation of coordinator rule in the first country to overthrow capitalism. During the first eight months after the October revolution, during the Civil War that followed, and during the heart of the Stalinist period of collectivization of agriculture and rapid industrialization it was the institutions of central planning that—whatever else may or may not have been their merits—formed the structural environment in the economy that facilitated the rise of coordinators' power. During the New Economic Policy of the 1920's the market relations among the state-owned industrial "Trusts" and private peasant farming—whether or not they were necessary for the material survival of the society and the political survival of the regime—also contributed to the momentum building toward a coordinator rather than socialist society.

### The First Eight Months

The struggle over workers' control was joined in the very first months after the October Revolution. Anarchists, independent

---

*There are still many radical bookshops in the U.S. that would sooner use their sparse cash to stock Stalin's tome "On Handling the Opposition" than anarchist or councilist critiques of the Soviet experience; Stalin's essays on "the national question" than nationalist critiques of Communist racism; Stalin's comments on art than Tom Robinson or The Clash as art, etc. Does this serve developing movements, does it increase sales, or does it simply fulfill some strange and distorted notion of responsibility to a heritage that is largely misunderstood and in any case deserving of only our most emphatic repudiation?

leftists, left Social Revolutionaries and Left-Communists disagreed with governmental authorities and Lenin on the proper interpretation of the admittedly ambiguous Decree on Workers' Control of November 14th, 1917. While this Decree "gave the workers' committees in each enterprise 'the right to supervise the management' and 'to determine a minimum of production,' and the right to have access to all correspondence and accounts... the General Instructions appended to the Decree expressly reserved to the proprietor the executive right of giving orders as to the conduct of the enterprise and forbade the factory committee to interfere in this or to countermand such orders; while Article 9 forbade committees 'to take possession of the enterprise or direct it' except with the sanction of the higher authorities." Dobb informs us that "many factory committees went beyond the legal powers awarded to them in the decree on workers' control, and eventually took the administration of factories into their own hands."[40] As a matter of fact, "of individual firms that had been nationalized prior to July 1918 only about 100 were nationalised by decree of the centre, while over 400 had been nationalised on the initiative of local organisations."[41] The following provides a revealing picture of the dynamic involved:

> The case of a group of factories in the Urals which the central authorities had decided to leave in private hands was not untypical. The local factory committee, declaring that the attitude of the owners was provocative, announced their intention of taking over the factory. The Central Council of Trade Unions sent a delegation from Moscow to dissuade them, but without avail; and followed this by telegraphing instructions forbidding any action to be taken by the factory committee. To this telegram the only reply was a laconic report announcing the date on which the factory had been taken over on the authority of the local Soviet.[42]

While the first conflict centered around how much industry to nationalize how fast—this debate was largely resolved by the autonomous action of the working class itself—the same political forces proceeded quickly to struggle over who should direct the administration of nationalized enterprises. The Supreme Economic Council, or Vesenkha, was established in December of 1917 to assume the management of enterprises that had been nationalized in fact, whether with or without government approval. Vesenkha was to organize the financing of nationalized enterprises and appoint the factory managers "or managing 'collegiates', whose authority was in theory supreme in technical questions, but which were subject in practice on most matters to another body called a 'factory collegiate', composed of representatives of the workers in the factory."[43] Although the most thorough description of the struggle between Vesenkha and the factory committees is provided by Maurice Brinton in *The Bolsheviks and Workers' Control, 1917-1921*, Brinton is an avowed sympathizer with the factory committees' point of view. Since Dobb explicitly supported the Leninist view in this matter, his testimony is even more telling:

> At the third Congress of Trade Unions which opened on April 20th (1918) some strong opposition was expressed to proposals by the Government to introduce the principle of individual management into industry and to apply methods of payment by results and scientific management. The latter were particularly denounced as 'relics of capitalist exploitation' by Riazanov (a Bolshevik who had recently resigned from his Party owing to disagreement on this point); and both the Alliance of Workers' Representatives and Maxim Gorky's Novaya Ahizn group allied themselves with the opposition. . . .
> The counter-proposal was made that the factory committees and trade unions should be entrusted with 'collective responsibility' for a certain minimum programme of production, to be fixed in joint consultation between Vesenkha and the union representatives. The government spokesmen on the other hand argued that there was a wide gulf fixed between piece-rates and scientific management as used in the old days and under the new regime. There was now no question of using such methods to extort larger profits for shareholders and no fear of their being used to the detriment of the workers' class interests, seeing that a Workers' State was in being and the trade unions were strongly represented on the Supreme Economic Council.

On the contrary, such methods were an essential instrument for increasing production, which would serve to raise the workers' standard of life and strengthen socialist industry. The majority policy of the Bolshevik Central Committee eventually carried the day, although not without some concessions to the objectors. Individual management of factories by managers responsible to the higher economic bodies which appointed them was accepted in principle, and was applied forthwith in cases where the requirements of production made it urgently necessary; but the principle was not generally applied in industry until 1920 following the discussions at the 9th Party Congress.... The first round, at least, of the battle of Bolshevism against syndicalist tendencies had been won.[44]

There is no disagreement among scholars that the two central issues of industrial policy during the first eight months of the new regime were how much to nationalize and how to administer whatever was nationalized. Moreover, there is no denying that the majority position of the Bolshevik party backed Lenin's position that a slower nationalization than favored by significant portions of the workers themselves was desirable, and that a strong centralized administration of nationalized enterprises exercised through a team of managers appointed by and responsible to Vesenkha rather than the workers they managed was essential. Finally, it is obvious that among Lenin's reasons for holding both these positions was a low estimation of the Russian workers' abilities to direct their own economic activities:

'When workers' delegations came to me with complaints against the factory owners,' Lenin once said, 'I always said to them: 'You want your factory nationalised. Well and good. We have the decree ready and can sign it in a moment. But tell me, can you take the organization into your own hands? Do you know how and what you produce? And do you know the relations between your product and the Russian and international market? And inevitably it transpired that they knew nothing. There was nothing written about such matters in the Bolshevik text books, or even in those of the Mensheviks.'[45]

What we wish to point out is that whether or not Lenin's estimation of the workers' abilities was correct, the decisions to retard nationalization, and to press for control of nationalized production through central planning mechanisms, tended to undermine the power of the "direct producers" and their factory committees to the eventual benefit of former owners and their supervisory staffs in one case and new central planners and managers recruited from the higher ranks of the Bolshevik party in the other. Furthermore, we have argued that the continued practice of central planning can be expected to have a series of long term effects that undermine the capabilities, determination, and power of the executors of economic activities and enhance the power of a small group of conceptualizers and coordinators in a variety of more subtle ways. So at a minimum, we suggest that the Bolshevik policy on these economic issues had a number of "costs" that have gone little noticed by most left historians of the period, and appear not to have been considered by Lenin and the majority of his party at the time. This would be true, and important in explaining subsequent developments, even if Lenin's judgment of the workers' capabilities at that time was essentially accurate and the "benefits" outweighed all the "costs" including those we have pointed out.[46]

A somewhat more controversial suggestion is that Lenin's judgment on these matters might well have been in error. In this view the costs and benefits would come out differently when formulated in accord with the theoretical framework we are suggesting. The additional costs our theory highlights, as well as the historical results of Soviet development we can observe with the benefit of hindsight, lead one to the conclusion that a policy more oriented toward developing the capabilities and power of the workers and their direct organizations rather than ridiculing their lack of knowledge and systematically destroying their organizations would have been more suitable.[47]

The most controversial interpretation of the events of this period would be to suggest that the policies were not so much "mistaken" policies that emanated from a sincerely "socialist" point of view, but policies consistent with a different view of the nature of at least the medium-term societal goal—consolidation of economic power in the hands of a group of anti-capitalist administrators who would "rationalize" the economy to better provide for the well being of "the masses."[48]

We feel confident that certain kinds of costs and consequences have gone generally unnoticed. We tend to believe that some of the policies in this early period *preceding* the outbreak of the Civil War arose from overestimating the economic dislocation that would have resulted from whatever organizational and managerial deficiencies may have characterized the factory committees. After all, if one re-reads the "counter proposal" calling for factory committee and trade union collective responsibility for a minimum production program to be determined in consultation with Vesenkha, it appears quite modest. On the other hand, we are well aware that the degree of maturity of the factory committees as well as the reasonableness of the different opposition political groups are factors that are difficult, if not impossible, to judge at a distance. And particularly in judging a period of history so surrounded by controversy and whose very facts have been so frequently distorted by competing political interests, we are resigned to the likelihood that it may be impossible for leftists of our generation to come to an incontestable opinion. Finally, with hindsight about the kind of people who flocked into the Bolshevik party in the aftermath of the Civil War, and the view of "socialism" that came to dominate the Soviet Communist Party during Stalin's rule, we are willing to entertain the last interpretation that views these policies and events as the first round in a long battle between the workers and peasants and a bureaucratic elite that was to eventually dominate not only the political and military aspects of Soviet life, but day to day economic activity as well. In this view, whether Lenin and other heroic figures of the revolution were in some sense conscious collaborators or merely unwitting accomplices in the early phases of this process, becomes a rather unimportant matter.

### "War Communism"

The approach of the Civil War brought two major changes in industry: a tremendous increase in the pace of nationalization as former owners were deemed completely untrustworthy in a situation of armed conflict against the new regime, and a simultaneous almost total consolidation of central administrative control over industrial production. Dobb describes the latter process as follows:

> There was some simplification of the personnel of the central controlling bodies, and at the factory level a

substitution of one-man management, or at least of small directorates of about three, for the earlier committee-management, against which Lenin in particular had inveighed so forcibly. The representative boards or councils of which the Centres had consisted were abolished in favour of a smaller Presidium, which now tended to lose its representative character and to be appointed wholly by Vesenkha, even though the latter generally acted in consultation with the trade unions in making these appointments.[49]

Kritsman estimated that by 1920 eighty-five percent of industrial enterprises were under individual management and no longer under committees.[50] And by the end of the Civil War the factory committees—far and away the leading mass organizations of workers and shock-troops of the revolution itself—had been so shattered that all opposition to one-man management and central administrative authority rallied around the unions as a counter-weight to administrative bureaucracy. The irony of this is only apparent when one recalls that in the first eight months the Bolshevik leadership had championed the unions *against* the factory committees since the unions were more open to Bolshevik leadership, less insistent on decision-making input about production, and willing to settle for consultation only with regard to remuneration and working conditions.

In many left defenses of Lenin's industrial policies during the early years, the Civil War is cited as the principal reason justifying authoritarian practices.* Even were this the case, we would argue that the consequences have been grossly underestimated in most accounts. But the fact that the authoritarian policies were proposed and pushed by the Bolshevik government long before the outbreak of the Civil War, and the fact that the advent of the Civil War was really only what helped the Bolsheviks complete and consolidate their victory over more democratic counter-proposals for managing industry, tend to belie these interpretations. Furthermore, in the face of tremendous popular demands for revitalizing the soviets as political institutions and allowing workers' organizations more

*Maurice Dobb and Charles Bettleheim both make arguments of this sort.

influence over industrial policy in the aftermath of the war, the Bolshevik government refused to move in a more democratic direction on either front.


## The New Economic Policy

We have already discussed the refusal to reconstitute the soviets and to legalize non-Bolshevik socialist organizations, the suppression of the Kronstadt uprising, the suppression of various regional guerrilla armies who were successful in battling the White armies in their native areas but unsuccessful in demanding regional and ethnic autonomy from the Bolshevik government, and the "unity resolution" banning factions within the Bolshevik party itself which all occurred after the Civil War was won. But the post Civil War debate on industrial policy, which fit the pattern of pragmatic yet undemocratic choices made in other spheres of society, is what concerns us here.

Dobb admits that during the war there was a "growing suspicion of the trade unions as an apparatus designed to secure acquiescence by the workers in the Government's designs, rather than an organ of the rank and file upholding the interests of the masses in State counsels."[51] And that "the position of trade unions under war conditions—their co-operation with industry to maintain labour discipline and to recruit labour armies and the fairly general practice of substituting appointment for election to offices—powerfully contributed to this attitude."[52] Yet a tendency, within what might be considered the relatively "safe" confines of the Bolshevik party itself, "opposed to the principle of one-man management in industry" was dubbed a 'syndicalist group' and vilified for "virtually advocating the handing over of industrial administration to the trade unions."[53] Rather than democratize both the work place and the choice of national economic priorities *after* the Civil War was over, the government instituted Lenin's New Economic Policy of 1) dismantling the central planning apparatus and re-instituting free markets, and 2) organizing production units into massive "trusts" whose "one-man managers" were appointed by a Board of Directors who were in turn appointed by Vesenkha. This policy was certainly aimed at achieving a drastic "decentralization" from the system that had become rather intriguingly known as "War Communism." But it was a decentralization aimed at ameliorating certain practical, economic inefficiencies, getting industrial production back to pre-World War One levels of output, and providing incentives for the peasantry who were not only refusing to sell grain to state purchasing agencies at offical prices but even refusing to plant beyond their own needs. The NEP was in no way a decentralization aimed at incorporating the workers themselves into economic decision making, as even the most modest "syndicalist proposals, advocating the restoration of internal democracy within the unions"[54] were soundly defeated at the Tenth Party Congress held in March of 1921.

According to Charles Bettleheim, no sympathizer of the Workers' Opposition:

> The Workers' Opposition pointed to the grave dangers threatening Russia's socialist future as a result of the increased powers enjoyed by bourgeois specialists and administrators. It fought for the granting of broad rights of initiative to the workers and for greater trust to be shown in relation to them, with the establishment of forms of organization such as would allow the workers really to develop their own initiative. It called for an effective struggle against the tendencies for the administrative apparatuses to acquire independence and to dominate the masses. It declared for freedom of criticism in the party, and for the working people as a whole, especially for the workers and their trade unions. It demanded that all party members engage regularly in productive manual labor and that inequality in wage levels, which had been intensified during 'war communism,' be reduced.[55]

The most concrete manifestation of the overall difference between the Workers' Opposition and the majority of the Bolshevik Central Committee concerned "the mode of appointment of the leading personnel in the political, administrative, and economic spheres."

> As the CC majority saw it, the party could not really carry out its leading role unless a substantial proportion of the leading personnel, in trade unions as elsewhere, were appointed by the party. As the Workers' Opposition saw it, only the election of such personnel was in conformity

with socialist principles and would guarantee the confidence of the masses in the leaders they had chosen.[56]

But not only did the Workers' Opposition Platform get soundly defeated at the Congress (receiving 18 votes, to 50 votes for the position of "The Eight" to 336 votes for the majority position of the Central Committee, also known as the position of "The Ten") the dangers they pointed to were ignored by the majority in their arguments during the debate and only further aggravated by the NEP policies.

According to Lenin:

> All these outcries against appointees, all this old and dangerous rubbish which finds its way into various resolutions and conversations must be swept away. Otherwise *we* cannot succeed. If we have failed to master this lesson in these two years, we are lagging, and those who lag get beaten.[57]

Zinoviev argued against the Workers' Opposition call for convening an All-Russia Supreme Congress of Producers by pointing out that at such a congress "the majority at this grave moment will be non-party people, a good many of them Social Revolutionaries and Mensheviks."[58]

Bettleheim summarizes the majority critique of the Workers' Opposition Platform and adds his concurrence that the Opposition "forget"... "the fundamental problem, that of power, which requires that maximum attention be paid to what Lenin rightly called 'the revolutionary interest' to which 'formal democracy must be subordinate'."[59]

As a final indication of the complete failure of the majority position to respond with anything other than double-talk to the concerns of the Opposition we offer the following from Point 7 of the resolution on the role and tasks of the trade unions adopted by the Tenth Congress:

> The Russian Communist Party continues unconditionally to direct, through its central and local organisations, all the ideological side of trade-union work... Selection of the leading personnel of the trade-union movement must take place under the Party's guiding supervision. However, the Party organisation must be especially

attentive to the applying of normal methods of proletarian democracy in the trade unions, where the selection of leaders must, above all, be made by the organised masses themselves.[60]

We have been at such great pains to demonstrate that the NEP should not be considered a concession to the demands for more industrial democracy in the aftermath of the Civil War because what leftist criticisms there have been of the damaging effects of the NEP have tended to focus entirely on the negative social effects of the stimulation of private enterprise agriculture, and in a few exceptional cases on the negative effects of markets in general. Before agreeing that our analysis bolsters the criticisms of markets others have made, we wished to also make clear that the NEP made no change with regard to one-man management, central appointment of managers, nor Party appointment of trade union officials. The NEP initiated no change in the authoritarian relations between the coordinator class and the industrial workers; instead it marked a drastic shift in the relative power of managers of individual production units on the one hand and the central economic authorities on the other, in other words a shift in power between fractions of the coordinator class.

The dominant focus of those critical of the effects of the NEP on socialist development has been that it re-established "capitalist social relations" in the countryside thereby stimulating the growth of a "rural bourgeoisie" otherwise known as the kulaks. Although a variety of Maoist theoreticians have been the newest wave of left scholars to emphasize the importance of this process (in their attempts to provide some historical backdrop for their claim that the Soviet Union is now a particularly dangerous capitalist society), the argument dates back to the "Left Opposition" within the Bolshevik party during the NEP period itself. At the Thirteenth Party Congress in early 1924 it was Piatokov, Preobrazhensky, and Ossinsky—all long time members of the Bolshevik Central Committee—who emphasized "the large role played by the private trader, especially in village retail trade, and the need to counter his growth."

Preobrazhensky estimated that between one third and one half of the net profits of trade and industry in the previous year had gone into the hands of Nepmen or capitalists, and claimed that the question of whether the Nepmen would strengthen his influence with the peasant and form an economic alliance to stem the drift to Socialism, or whether the Workers' State would be strong enough to break such an alliance and convert the private trader into a dependent agent of State industry, was a pressing one.[61]

By 1925 prominent Bolshevik leaders such as Trotsky, Zinoviev, and Kamenev had joined the Left opposition at the Fourteenth Party Conference and Congress where a comprehensive "consistent line of policy"[62] combining a shift in the terms of trade between agricultural and industrial products designed to weaken the "NEP-men," and a return to central planning with emphasis on the development of heavy industry was presented as an alternative to continuation of the NEP.

Ossinsky blamed "the lack of a plan uniting the work of all the branches of State economy," and "the attempt, instead of aiming at a general economic plan, to regulate economy from the financial centre."[63] Trotsky warned that "if nationalization was not to become 'an obstacle to economic development' rather than an aid, and if private capital was not 'to undermine the foundations of socialism,' there must be a comprehensive economic plan in the application of which Gosplan (the organizational descendant of Vesenkha) must become the dominant organ."[64] Trotsky went on to state:

> In the struggle of State industry for conquest of the market, the plan is our principle weapon... Gosplan should control all fundamental factors of State economy, to co-ordinate them with one another and with peasant economy. Its central work should be to develop State industry. Precisely in this sense I have had occasion to say that 'dictatorship' ought to belong, not to finance, but to industry.[65]

However our analysis of market institutions would suggest that the major negative effects of the NEP were perhaps other than what the Left opposition focused on at the time or Maoists have emphasized more recently. Rather than the problems of increasing the financial resources of the kulaks and reducing the "material surplus" available for expansion of the State owned industrial sector, our evaluation of markets would emphasize the individualistic effects of entering into market exchanges on the consciousness of the average citizen, and the strategic leverage gained by the managers and directors of the State owned Trusts. In this light the principal "costs" of the NEP—whatever may have been its "benefits"—were that it helped erode whatever little revolutionary solidarity among the citizenry might have survived the Civil War, and it fortified the position of an important fraction of the coordinator class—the technocrats within the Trusts, not the NEP-men and kulaks.

## Collectivization and the Five Year Plans

After the Left Opposition had been soundly defeated and the old guard Bolshevik leaders in its ranks had been effectively removed from positions of political leadership at the Party Congress of 1927, Stalin was free to implement their program virtually intact. In the "spinal year" of 1929 "the policy toward the kulak was abruptly changed from one of 'encircling the kulak' and limiting his influence to one of 'eliminating as a class' the upper 5 or 6 per cent labour employing, land-leasing, grain-trading and money-lending stratum of petty-capitalist farmers"[66]; and the pace of industrialization was wrenched all the way from first to fourth gear under the direction of Gosplan. Forced collectivization, forced industrialization, central economic administration, massive repression against the great majority of the rural population and national minorities, violent purges within the Party, and the foundation of a modern industrial economy in a time period ten times shorter than had ever before occurred in history, are among the hallmarks of the period from 1929 to 1939. But this is not the place to offer our analysis and critique of Bolshevik policy toward the peasantry and minority nationalities. Nor is it the place to decry the dictatorial culmination of a lengthy authoritarian trend within the political sphere. Here we wish merely to point out that the incredibly centralized planning procedures used during the remainder of Stalin's rule both complemented the authoritarian dynamics running rampant in all other social spheres and further consolidated the coordinator class's hold on economic power, even if it was primarily the central faction of this class which exercised the dominance at the suffrance of the political elite.

In our view, to speak of the Soviet Union as a "deformed workers' state" by the mid-1930's—as Trotskyists do—or to harken back to the 1930's as the "golden age of heroic Russian socialism"—as Maoists do—is such a gross misrepresentation as to be difficult for an honest investigator to make. Yet we do not doubt the honesty nor socialist convictions of the great majority of leftist historians who have done just that. Vilification of every aspect of the Russian revolution by "scholars" in hostile capitalist countries made negative information difficult to believe. Fundamental misconceptions in Marxist theory concerning the issues of socialist development blinded many.[67] A fervent wish that revolutionary efforts always bear positive fruit, along with a host of other ameliorating factors, have led to the misinterpretations above. But for all these difficulties it is even more important than usual to detach oneself from the complicated reasonings about negative objective circumstances and disputes about who and what are to blame, and recognize 1) that by this point in Soviet history a tiny ruling group was firmly in power over Soviet society; 2) that a part of that ruling group, consisting of high level central planning technocrats and enterprise managers and their immediate subordinates, was firmly in control of the industrial working class's economic activities; and 3) that opposition to this domination in the form of independent and effective workers' organizations, as well as the consciousness and resolve of the workers themselves, had reached a nadir.

The extreme central planning of those years provides a case study of negative trends toward bureaucratic political and coordinator class rule. Moreover, we suggest that the argument we offered earlier about "institutionally produced apathy" among the workers in a centrally planned economy is an important addition to explanations emphasizing political repression alone. Major economic priorities were settled by the Politburo alone—about whose selection process there can be no democratic illusions at this point. Calculation of a national production plan to carry out those priorities was done by Gosplan, subject only to direct interference from the highest political authorities. Production orders were sent to directors of units who served at the pleasure of central authorities alone. Failures to meet quotas met with political reprisals. There was not even the semblance of any "up-down, down-up" exchange of information or opinions between the workers and planners. There was not even much of this kind of communication between the plant managers and the central planners, the latter having greatly increased their power at the expense of the former.

The coordinator class was not to wait long before it saw its consolidation of economic power translated into greater material reward.

In Stalin's famous Six Point Speech of June 23rd, 1931...
he noted 'definite signs of a change of attitude towards the Soviet Government on the part of a certain section of the intelligentsia who formerly sympathised with the wreckers', which imposed upon the government and the working class the need 'to change our attitude towards engineers and technicians of the old school, to show them greater attention and solicitude, to display more boldness in enlisting their co-operation.'

To give encouragement to the growth both in quantity and quality of the higher technical grades, as well as to improve their morale and win their whole-hearted co-operation, serious measures were taken in the early '30's to improve their terms of employment and their living conditions. Enterprises were encouraged to assign them special dining-rooms and living quarters. A government order of March 25, 1932, instructed Gosplan to arrange for the provision of special housing facilities for engineers and technicians over the next two years, in addition to those that were already being provided on new industrial sites. For example, it was stipulated in some detail that there should be ten blocks of flats, each containing 200 apartments, in Moscow, five in Leningrad, and two each in Kharov and Stalingrad; the standard to be three or four rooms in each flat, in addition to kitchen and bathroom. Smaller blocks, having 100 flats a piece, were also to be built in 27 other towns, and blocks of 50 flats in a further 67 towns. [Dobb refers to V.V. Prokofiev, Industrial and Technical Intelligentsia in the USSR, p. 67-8.] In all negotiations about wages and working conditions the special sections formed by engineering and technical staffs in the trade unions (the E.T.S.) were accorded the right of separate representation. Generally, with regard to remuneration, there was a reaction against the *'wage-levelling' tendencies of the second half of the '20's.*[68]

And similarly, this class' growth was also steady and rapid. As Daniel Singer recounts, for example, ''Among the people employed in Russia on the eve of the October Revolution barely 190,000 specialists had graduated from university or a technical college. By 1976 their number had grown to 24 million.''[69]

### Lieberman Cycles in the Post-Stalin Period

There is one remaining aspect of Soviet economic history we believe our theory of central planning and markets sheds light on. The post-Stalin period of Kruschev and Breshnev has been characterized by a discernible repeated fluctuation between "market reforms" and "retrenching centralization" in the economy. The impulse toward greater use of markets and reliance on some sort of profit incentives for individual units—dubbed the "liberal" trend—has been more forceful in various Eastern European countries in the soviet Bloc than in the Soviet Union itself, but discernable in the "Great Socialist Fatherland" nonetheless. The view of many radical economists sensitive to the technical problems of both central planning and markets, that the solution lies in the correct mixture and balancing of the two forms, can be interpreted to confer a progressive status to this "cyclical" phenomenon. There are also some Western European radicals who discern the rumblings of working class struggle in a push for "liberalization" in the economy. Unfortunately, we believe that both these interpretations are misreadings of the phenonenon named after a minor Soviet economist, Lieberman, who wrote a very unremarkable essay on reforms.

It is true that both central planning and markets have certain "practical" deficiencies that we can ignore in theoretical discussions, but real world economists cannot. Markets don't reach equilibrium in the real world even if we assume they do in theory, and particularly with respect to finding long-term globally optimal development patterns, market systems can be dreadfully short sighted. On the other hand, central planners cannot accumulate perfect knowledge of all the resource availabilities and production capabilities of units in the economy, and frequently bureaucracies have been known to adjust less rapidly to changes in information than markets. These deficiencies have led numerous socialist economists, and particularly the managers of individual production units, to suggest that enterprise profit incentives responding to the immediate information received from market prices can avoid some of the economic inefficiencies accompanying a cumbersome central planning bureaucracy.

We would be the last to deny the possibility that some artful combination of planning and markets might eliminate some of these "practical" deficiencies. But concluding that this means that the problems of central planning and market systems can be solved by mixing the two in the right proportion is making the critical mistake of identifying only the "practical" deficiencies of the two systems and ignoring the "social" and "human" deficiencies each contains. A mixture of two different forms which serve to prevent worker rule is not likely to increase "working class domination over the production process." Nor is a mixture of one form that enhances individualism and another that generates authoritarianism likely to develop solidarity and self-management in the citizenry.

Instead of interpreting the Lieberman cycles as either a progressive groping for the correct mixture of planning and markets for socialist development, or as a sign of working class unrest, we would interpret them as symptoms of continued struggle between two fractions of the coordinators class—central planners and unit managers, or the central and local technocracies. When the inefficiencies of the central planners have accumulated to the point where they could potentially stimulate working class opposition to coordinator rule in general—or, more likely, in the ease of the Soviet Union itself, when the inefficiencies threaten Soviet economic and military competition with the West—the plant managers and local bureaucracies seize the time to push for a relaxation of central controls *over them,* and an increase in their authority with regard to hiring and dismissing workers. If unit management can arrange for their own supplies and deliveries among themselves, without having to rely on central administration, the position of their class fraction is greatly enhanced. Similarly, a political liberalization which might accompany "market growth" could improve the status of the broad class of coordinators as against that of the political elite. On the other hand, when plant managers use their new leeway to bully workers to the point of unrest—or, more likely for the Soviet Union, when markets lead to a drift away from investment in heavy industry and the military sector toward consumer goods, or when the highest ranking Party officials see some of their power shifting toward a broad segment of the coordinator class they have historically not been tightly allied with—the rubber band snaps back on "liberalization" trends in the economy.

We hope this discussion is interpreted as it is offered—as a broad brush stroke analysis of one aspect of Soviet economic struggle. We do not wish to deny that the working class can enter into such a struggle allying itself with either fraction of the coordinator class in efforts to protect and/or expand its own interests. Indeed, political liberalization—as a kind of by-product —does allow workers more room to communicate and express their own interests. Presumably, however, this impetus to class expression is offset by the fragmenting effect of the turn to markets on worker relations with one another. Likewise, the turn to markets can be disruptive for the workers and thus for the whole system by threatening job security—the local managers will certainly employ their enhanced hiring and firing power and it is the workers who will pay. Indeed, it may be this factor that has historically limited the extension of Lieberman-type reforms in the Soviet Union.[70] In any case, having mixed attitudes to the give-and-take struggle between fractions of the coordinators and middle strata, though the workers may take sides on some occasions, on others they may well exclude themselves. As Daniel Singer suggests, for them "a battle over civil rights without social content, seemingly a conflict over the right to write or to paint freely, may well look to the ordinary Russian as *their* quarrel, a settling of accounts among the privileged," as indeed it largely is.[71]

The Soviet economy can not stimulate work via an appeal to loyalty to the revolution. Whether the central plan is in full swing or being ameliorated by market reforms has little effect on this reality. In the former case, job security and coercion enforce productivity; in the later, the desire for personal advance. In both cases, the underlying motivation to work is to eke out the best possible personal existence; and for most people this is a matter of immediate survival and hopes for a better future. The economic project necessarily becomes—though the ideological scaffolding is rhetoric about increasing productive forces—a "Russian version of the American dream...durable consumer goods—the telly, the washing machine, tomorrow the car—[these] were gradually supposed to replace the *knout* and the *gulag* as the means of social control."[72] Kruschev called it "goulash socialism." That increasingly available material incentives have yet to allow a full slackening of Gulag tactics is evidenced by the following story relayed at a conference on "already existing socialist societies":

> Last year in Leningrad, a group of artists wrote some slogans on a number of public buildings including the Peter-Paul Fortress which, once a Tsarist prison, is now a museum. On the fortress walls they wrote: 'You are crushing freedom, but its spirit is ever-lasting,' or something like that. They were arrested and brought before the city court nót, as you might think, for anti-Soviet propaganda, but for defacing a historic monument. Now I would really like to meet someone who writes on public buildings and gives a thought to the fact that he is defacing historical monuments. Anyway, these 'defilers' got off with a 'light' sentence: only three or four years in a camp, plus a huge fine of about 20,000 rubles. The paper *Evening Leningrad* wrote: 'Our beautiful city has such splendid historical monuments, and yet there are vandals who come and spoil them...' However, the paper did not say a word about what they had written: it spoke only of hooligans defacing public buildings.[73]

That this has nothing whatsoever to do with socialism and could not happen in a socialist society should be transparent. Hopefully we have made at least the beginnings of a compelling case that such occurrences would be rather natural in a coordinator economy, especially one coupled with a dictatorical political formation, and that these are the relations that prevail in the Soviet Union and that have prevailed there for many many decades, indeed since very early in the revolutionary process.

## Women, Kinship, and Soviet Socialism

Two analysts of an open society about which hard statistical data is easily available and subjective impressions easily compared need not agree in their evaluations. They may address different data and organize their perceptions into different conceptual molds and arrive at different interpretations and evaluations. If this is possible in a relatively "open society" how much more likely is it when credible data is scarce and subjective impressions hard to compare? Analyses of the situation of women in the Soviet Union are an excellent case in point.

### Revolution or Stagnation

An orthodox Marxist who deems the Soviet Union socialist proclaims a tremendous advance in the situation of Soviet women since the October revolution. Far from being patriarchal, it is argued, the country is now egalitarian. Women are treated equally. They are becoming more independent as the vestiges of presocialist sexism steadily erode.[74]

But the radical feminist is horrified by the same society. What revolution is this? Certainly not one for women. The country is still patriarchal. The changes are only cosmetic. They are motivated solely by desires to increase production; there is no self-conscious revolution in the relations between men and women.[75]

The optimist offers some evidence: before the revolution women were chattel, often considered less than human. A few popular sayings indicate the degree of degradation. "A chicken is not a bird and a peasant woman is not a human being." "Beat your wife for breakfast and for dinner too." Peasant women were like sexual livestock. They were often sold to the highest bidder and treated like farm implements by their husbands.[76] In the cities, on the other hand, many women worked in the home and also in the newly opened factories. Childbirth was a horror with women working in dangerous environments until the very last minute. Infant mortality was extremely high and contraception almost unknown. Though better protected and materially more comfortable, even upper class women had no real power or dignity.[77]

Then came the revolution and liberation. Within a brief time the state wrenched control of marriage from the church. Complete equality of rights between men and women became the law. Divorce became simple and women were not bound to follow their husbands. As economic development allowed, child care was greatly enlarged and maternity benefits improved. And the material basis for all of this was clear. Women were welcomed into the public workforce. There was even a move, for a time, to "abolish the family." This extremism passed, to be sure, but the guiding sentiment—that women should be free and able to contribute to society through productive work—persisted. Now over fifty percent of the workforce is female. Many are doctors and educators, as well as productive workers in all sorts of factories and on farms.[78] "The following occupations [as of 1976] in particular have higher proportions of female workers than in Western countries: engineers 40%, designers and draughtsmen 57%, scientific research personnel 40%, librarians 95%, teachers in higher education 43%, doctors and dentists 77%, and medical administrators 53%."[79] How can this be called patriarchy? Of course there is room for improvement. Old ways die hard. In the household, for example, men still shirk equal responsibility and women carry too much of the load. But this will pass too since the material conditions insure progress.

The radical feminist is not so sanguine. Women were drafted into the workforce to increase output and strengthen the state, not for their own benefit. Soviet jobs are still segregated into "men's" and "women's" work. Moreover, "when one looks at the data, the existence of an inverse relationship is self evident—the higher the proportion of women, the lower the average wage."[80] And just because a particular occupation enjoys relatively high status and remuneration outside the Soviet Union where it is dominated by men, the same benefits need not be accorded that occupation inside the Soviet Union where it is dominated by women. Medicine is the obvious example: Russian women doctors enjoy nothing like the status of their male counterparts in the West. In sum, most women work but so what? This doesn't make them independent, nor skillful, nor respected. In many cases women continue to perform the most physically monotonous and debilitating tasks such as digging on collective farms while men drive tractors, and removing snow and ice off the streets by hand.[81] In 1970, for example, "98% of milkmaids, 74% of workers in livestock feeding, and 72% of orchard, vineyard, vegetable and melon workers were women,"[82] not to mention that "over 90% of trade and public catering workers (sales assistants, managers of sales stands and buffets, and cooks) are women and almost 85% of all postal workers.''[83] Yes, women were drafted into the labor force, but not in positions of power. ''They were employed as supervisors, shop chiefs, and in comparable leadership positions only one-sixth to one-seventh as frequently as men.''[84] The male doctors, for example, without domestic responsibility, rise to positions of greater influence and power than the women. In politics, the presence of women falls off as one progresses up the hierarchy until there are only 4% in the party central committee and none in the Politbureau.[85]

Income per family is so low that while women are free in theory to take time off for childbirth, economic restrictions prevent this in practice. In the home the man still rules. ''In the factory we work like our husbands, often in the same shop. But in the house the duties are unequally divided...And when you ask a husband to help the answer is always the same, 'Do you want me to do a woman's work? Why, the neighbors would laugh at me.' It is the wife, the grandmother, or maybe the children who do the housework. If the man helps at all it is marginal.''[86] Similarly, ''childcare in the Soviet Union has remained a woman's responsibility—children are looked after by their mothers and grandmothers as well as by women teachers in nurseries and kindergartens. There seems to have been no effort to recruit men into fields in which they would be dealing with small children.''[87]

So which view is correct? Could both be partially right? Sheila Rowbotham points out that ''passivity and fatalism were particularly close to Russian women; their subordination was so absolute and so bound up with the backwardness of the country, and their poverty was so extreme, they rose from such a long and deep sense of nothing, of knowing no hope for change.''[88] Is there really any doubt that they did rise, that the revolution has meant a considerable improvement in the life of women? The orthodox analysis correctly points out this gain, and the radical feminist in search of continuing patriarchy is wrong to dismiss these meaningful changes. On the other hand, the orthodox Marxist's fixation on statistical participation in the workforce and on formal marriage laws is myopic. The radical feminist is right to insist that control over one's body and life is decided by more than laws, and entry into women's work in the public economy coupled with a full work load in the home hardly indicates an end to patriarchy.

With a totalist approach the riddle in the contrasting views disappears. Just because we discover that kinship relations in the Soviet Union are still patriarchal, we can't assume they are not different and less oppressive than those before the revolution. And just because we see that the situation of Russian women has improved qualitatively, we can't leap to the assertion that they are not oppressed at all and that the Soviet Union is no longer patriarchal. A totalist analysis would begin by expecting that changes in political and economic spheres would be accompanied by changes in kinship relations. But a totalist would also expect to find non-socialist dynamics at work within the kinship sphere if some form of non-socialist consolidation were taking place in other spheres of social life. In any case, for a totalist the task is to evaluate the form of patriarchal kinship relations that exist in the Soviet Union today, to understand their relations with characteristics of other spheres, and to understand the process by which this all came about. Of course, all we can do here is sketch in some parts of the whole picture.

### The Historical Experience

Sheila Rowbotham, Kate Millett, and Wilhelm Reich all chronicle a similar story, however sparse the details.[89] Emma Goldman and Alexandra Kollantai add first hand reports with collaborative data.[90] In the immediacy of the revolution there was an impressive outpouring of "sexual change" that augured a kinship revolution that might have eliminated sex-role divisions and created liberating socialization processes for future generations. However, these early experiments were quickly suppressed. Modes of consciousness that were difficult to combat—jealousy, desires for sexual privilege, are deep historical psychological dispositions among men and women—represented a far greater obstacle than those seeking revolutionary transformations of kinship relations had anticipated.[91] But more important, the will to overcome these unexpected obstacles was quite weak, at least among men and the revolutionary leadership. Where the rhetoric was progressive—bringing countless women into the revolutionary struggle—the practice left much to be desired. Consider the following Bolshevik woman's lament:

> And in those very meetings which he forbids me to attend because he is afraid I will become a real person—what he

needs is a cook and mistress wife—in those very meetings where I have to slip in secretly, he makes thunderous speeches about the role of women in the revolution, calls women to a more active role.[92]

And when women attempted to bring the rhetoric of revolution to reality they were forcefully opposed. Reich relates numerous incidents:

In 1928, a twenty-year-old girl, Zarial Haliliva, escaped from her parental home and began to call meetings for the sexual emancipation of women; she went unveiled to the theatre and wore a bathing costume on the beach. Her father and brothers sat in judgment over her, condemned her to death, and cut her up alive.[93]

Apparently this was not so uncommon as one would hope. In Uzbekistan, for example, "in 1928 there were 203 cases of anti-feminist murder. Girls were also beaten and punished severely simply for attending the meetings of the women's clubs."[94] Since most of these acts were most likely committed by Islamic fanatics, the Bolsheviks can justifiably deny that they represented any direct revolutionary betrayal on their own part. However, the fact that the Bolsheviks were less willing to intervene against (criminal) anti-feminist attacks than against the justifiable movement for religious and ethnic autonomy of eastern Moslems is indication of their complicity in anti-feminism.

In any case, an unwillingness to confront sexism did not reside only among the "masses." Discussion of sexuality was taboo within the party itself. The theory of scientific socialism had little time for such concerns. Wilhelm Reich quotes Koltsov, a communist party functionary, complaining that "these questions are never discussed; it was as if for some reason they were being avoided. I myself have never given them a serious thought. They are new to me. They are extremely important and should be discussed."[95] And another comrade, Tseitlin, as exclaiming:

In the literature, the problems of marriage and the family, of the relations between man and woman, are not discussed at all. Nevertheless these are exactly the questions that interest workers, male and female alike. When are such questions going to be the topic of our meetings? The masses feel that we hush up these problems and in fact we do hush them up.[96]

But this openness among a minority of party cadre was not reciprocated throughout the party, or even in its upper echelons. Batya Weinbaum relates how Lenin saw socialist revolution and not feminism as the "antidote to women's oppression."[97] She also addresses a critical turnabout in revolutionary analysis: "Before the revolution, socialists reasoned that the problem was economic; after the revolution it suddenly became a matter of 'prejudice' to be eradicated."[98] Weinbaum goes on to dissect a conversation between Lenin and Clara Zetkin in a way which reveals the narrowness intrinsic to his analysis and motives. He decries the organization of prostitutes as a "morbid deviation," fails to see that the situation of women is in part a result of the desires of men, criticizes the establishment of meetings to discuss marriage and sex, and so on.[99] No wonder, decades later a noted Russian woman doctor could assert in an important essay, "girls should learn self-respect, then there won't be any need to pass a law prohibiting hugging and kissing on the street. Women's modesty increases man's sexual energy but lack of it repels men and brings about total fiasco in their intimate relations."[100]

Most recently, in a Reuters by-lined *Washington Post* article dated January 5, 1981, Ralph Boulton reported that on "Jan. 1, new regulations came into effect banning women from 460 occupations, including exceptionally heavy or dangerous work in the construction, chemical and metals industries." As Boulton put it, "with the start of the new year, women throughout the Soviet Union have laid down their pickaxes, turned in their coveralls and parked their bulldozers for the last time." An indication of whether women's participation in various types of work is considered normal or exceptional, only to be encouraged when it serves economic ends which otherwise cannot be met, is provided by a comment of Leonid Sharikov, "a specialist in work conditions at the State Committee for Labor who compiled the list of restricted occupations...'I am frankly astonished by the work our women are prepared to put in. They're willing to take on any task. I tell you, sometimes I gasp." In the same interview Sharikov goes on to report, "recently we had a letter from a woman who drove a tractor trailer and didn't want to give up her job, but what can you do?" Boulton's article goes on to elaborate a possible reason for the turn around in policy—concern over a decline in population growth. Quoting a Soviet specialist in family affairs, Boulton notes, "A husband's work week, including domestic and professional labor, comprises 50 hours, while a wife's work week is 80 hours." Apparently Soviet experts believe that the immense burden women are bearing is a significant factor in the increase of divorce rates to one in three marriages and the decline in birthrates as well. The solution: rescind prior economic reforms which were never really meant to challenge partriarchy in the first place.[101]

Weinbaum does an excellent job of showing how the Bolshevik "stage theory" of revolution effectively postpones the emancipation of women to a future that never arrives. Moreover, she explains the opportunistic use of progressive rhetoric alongside reactionary policies in terms of deep-seated psychological needs and dispositions of male revolutionaries and male-dominated women.[102] Whatever the ultimate cause, at the Third Congress of the Comintern "the basic proposition that there is no 'specific woman question' and 'no specific women's movement' was reaffirmed." According to Alena Heitlinger, "Women were therefore urged to concentrate on the general struggle for socialism, which supposedly included the struggle for women's liberation. Cultural, psychological, and other similar components of female oppression were not mentioned in the communist resolutions dealing with women. Any statement of the need for self-transformation of personal relationships was also lacking. The main task of the women's section of the Communist Party was to awaken the class consciousness of women workers and then recruit them to the party, the agent of the forthcoming revolution. It was assumed, rather naively, that women's emancipation would follow automatically after the socialist revolution." Naturally one must assess the deeper roots of such "naivete" coming from such "enlightened vanguard elements."[103]

In agreement with Weinbaum's critique of the Bolshevik "stage theory" of revolution our own analysis shows that the Bolsheviks' myopic focus on class as the sole critical category for analyzing people in struggle doomed their understanding of the post revolutionary struggle against patriarchy to inadequacy. The Bolshevik's ability to combat the psychic structures of patriarchy and to recognize its institutional roots in kinship relations was almost nil. In addition a totalist analysis helps explain why the motivation to combat patriarchy diminished as new political and economic hierarchies hardened in Russia. The coordinator economy requires both subservience in the face of expertise and also easy acclimation to rote work roles. Bureaucratic political forces require acceptance of authoritarian norms. Patriarchal relations are well suited to a kind of socialization compatible with these requirements, whereas more egalitarian kin relations might not be.[104]

The history of the Russian revolution and its aftermath is full of information relevant to the study of the interrelationships between kinship and other spheres of social life. However, short of a full analysis, it is patently obvious that whatever advances have taken place in the lives of women, sexism has not been eliminated and patriarchy has not been erased. Just as a coordinator class dominates the Soviet economy and a single bureaucratic party is politically supreme, men dominate women in Soviet kinship activity. Since we cannot yet fully differentiate patriarchal kinship modes from one another, we are not yet able to clarify the alterations in kinship structure produced by the Soviet revolution. But the following summary of Alena Heitlinger's excellent study, *Women and State Socialism* is sufficient to indicate that, at best, Soviet kinship relations are some new form of patriarchy:

> Despite the effects of almost universal employment, the overwhelming majority of [Soviet] women do, in fact, accept a role involving less autonomy and initiative than men. This is marked not only in relation to their sexuality but also in the many areas of behavior bearing on family and work relations between men and women. Women occupy a disproportionately small number of positions of authority, both in the economy and in political institutions. The regime, led almost exclusively by men, has had few advocates within the innermost circles who would fight the broader battle to liberate women from the 'tyranny' of husbands and the home. The resources allocated to the consumer sphere, and to the socialization of housework have been wholly insufficient.[105]

Moreover, Heitlinger also draws the relevant conclusion as far as Western socialism is concerned:

> The experience of Eastern Europe clearly shows that a state-socialist transformation is insufficient to bring about the liberation of women. Women have entered the pro-

ductive labor force in large numbers, yet still suffer from inequality...Thus, one cannot but agree with the position taken by many socialist feminists in the West today that the struggle for women's liberation has its own specificity. It is related to the class struggle, but it is at the same time independent of it.[106]

## Community Interrelations in the Soviet Union

The history of Bolshevik interactions with workers and peasants have been widely discussed, though of course with different biases. Lately many socialist women have reinvestigated the experiences of women under Bolshevism, and this history too has become better known. But the history of Bolshevik interactions with minority movements and religious groups within the Soviet Union is much less studied. Here we are only able to present just enough information to give some weight to our criticisms of the orthodox socialist program of cultural homogenization, and to help motivate the positive discussion of our own approach that will follow.

A little known aspect of Soviet "socialism" is the history of Soviet policy toward the Moslem minority within its own borders. Not only is this a story that deserves to be told along with the better known histories of Soviet policy toward various white, Christian nationalities such as the Ukrainians, Lithuanians, Estonians, and Latvians; it is interesting because it reveals a general consistency of policy regarding "internal communities" dating from the Bolshevik Party under Lenin beyond Stalin's long rule into the reign of Nikita Khrushchev. It is also an increasingly relevant history in light of the Islamic resurgence in Iran along the Soviet southern border and the Soviet invasion of Afghanistan.

As the Bolsheviks attempted to consolidate their revolution in the early years they encountered serious resistance in the southern and eastern regions of the old Russian empire. The population of these regions was primarily composed of a variety of Islamic ethnic groups with a long history of anti-imperialist struggle and hostility to the minority population of Russian "colonizers," and with a tradition of indigenous forms of non-capitalist collectivism quite different from those of European Russia.[107] These Moslems were afraid of Great Russian hegemony and strongly inclined against statist tendencies in general. The conflict resulting from Bolshevik efforts to impose strong central authority administered by Russians was severe. There were hundreds of uprisings and armed struggles of different durations. The case of one Moslem leader, Sultan-Galiev, is illustrative.

Sultan-Galiev became a Communist in 1917 and organized the Musulman Communist Party. He fought against Kolchak in the Civil War, and received promises from central Bolshevik authorities—over the opposition of local Russian leaders—that he would be permitted to establish a Musulman State at the war's conclusion. But Stalin, who was in charge of national matters for the Party even in Lenin's time, withdrew the promise and ordered the merging of the Musulman Communist Party with the Russian Communist Party. Stalin opposed what he termed "indigenous nationalism." Sultan-Galiev urged that policies be adopted which preserved the progressive features of Islam, but when his protestations were ignored he came to the conclusion that the Eastern proletariat (Russians) were not interested in liberating the Eastern peasants (Moslems) but in exploiting them, and led uprisings against the Russians. Sultan-Galiev feared the continuation of Russian imperialism under Bolshevik auspices and became what we would today call a "revolutionary nationalist." He was finally put on trial and removed from the Party by Stalin in 1923. (In retrospect Sultan-Galiev was lucky to live in that his experience was one of the earliest episodes in Stalin's progression toward absolute power.)

During the mid-twenties "the influence of Islam was pared down by gradual changes in the law," but "in 1928 a general assault on Islam was begun. It was conducted by the Party, the schools, the Komosol, and especially the League of the Militantly Godless (disbanded in 1937), and continued until 1941."[108] After the war, in 1947, the anti-Islamic campaign was revived. "The alphabet was made Cyrillic, the language 'cleansed,' and history re-written in a way favorable to the Russians; much of the traditional literature was condemned."[109]

After Stalin died Beria argued for relaxing the drive for cultural homogenization while Khrushchev opposed any "liberalization." When Khrushchev came to power in 1956 he stressed that a period of cultural "rapproachment" (presumably what had taken place under Stalin!) should be followed by a period of cultural "amalgamation." Khrushchev "hailed the Soviet Union as a new type of ethnic community higher than the nation,"[110] and pushed policies aimed at "complete unity"—"a future single worldwide culture of communist society"[111] in which all indigenous cultures would be assimilated.

The point is simply this: The democratic rights of national minorities, so championed in Lenin's writings while the Czarist Empire still lived, were never upheld in the practice of Soviet "socialism." The point could have been illustrated by a number of cases other than that of the Moslem minority, but in our opinion, the fact that orthodox theory inevitably consigns these rights to a liberal and tactical status was a contributing cause for the insufficient defense of national minority rights in the face of the strenuous exigencies of economic development and geo-political survival in the Soviet Union. Certainly a Marxist theory of "community" upholding the central value of diverse cultures would have provided a *more* effective obstacle to the reactionary policies pursued in this sphere by the Soviets, whether or not it would have proved able to withstand the powerful legacy of racism and authoritarianism in the end. *

In any case, it is clear that the "national question" is far from resolved in the Soviet Union. The positive attributes of nationalism associated with the development of culture and the assertion of

---

*A contrary interpretation was put forward by Earl Ofari in the *Black Scholar*, September, 1972 article, "Marxism Leninism, The Key to Black Liberation." He argued that the Bolsheviks were eager for national diversity but also had to develop indigenous communist leadership, thus: "The next step was to build up local communist leadership. In the case of the Muslims, the emphasis was on suppressing the bourgeois-feudalist Mullahs who steered the Muslim movement toward narrow nationalism and accommodation with reactionary pro-imperialist forces." (p. 36) In our view, however, this sort of argument reveals merely the ease with which any crime can be swept away under the rhetoric of "defending or enlarging the revolution." For as Ofari himself says later in the same article, tending to substantiate our view of "homogenization": "Marxists were opposed to any division along racial, cultural or religious lines which did not lead to workers' solidarity." (p. 37) According to Ofari this meant that with respect to movements of all kinds one had to apply a "rigid class analysis of the movement to determine its progressive content" and he then claims that nationalism has never succeeded in creating a socialist state and exaggerates by claiming it also hasn't ever overthrown imperialism, but he neglects to mention that Leninism has never created socialism either.

dignity and power are quite incompatible with the existing set of social relations of Soviet society, and the various nationalist movements within the Soviet empire have a revolutionary potential beyond what we usually hear about in the West. We close with a quotation from a Ukrainian, Valentyn Moroz, who was tried in 1970 and sentenced to 14 years of imprisonment and exile. He had this to say at his trial:

> The awakening of a national consciousness is the deepest of all spiritual processes. . . . Your dams are strong, but now they stand on dry land, bypassed by the spring streams, whch have found other channels. Your drawgates are closed, but they stop no one. . . . You stubbornly insist that all those you place behind bars are dangerous criminals. . . . You can pursue this absurd policy for, let us say, ten more years. But then what? These movements in the Ukraine and in the whole country are only the beginning.[112]

The Soviet Union was the first country to proclaim itself socialist and as such became for many generations either a beacon of left potential or a benchmark of left failure. What we are arguing is that neither interpretation of the Soviet experience is correct precisely since the Soviet Union is not a socialist country and therefore its experience is not a test of socialist values or ideas. What is true, is that we can learn much from the revolutionary experience of the Soviet Union, even if that experience is in no sense a blueprint of what socialists should hope to accomplish in the future. And though the main purpose of this book is to approach the positive problem of socialist visions as they might really be

More, he goes on to argue reasonably that all Black groups, for example a Black party, would be divided along class lines with Black elites possibly gaining control because of their advantages and then manifesting their own interests. He fails to consider, however, that in mixed working class organizations whites might dominate due to their advantages and orient policy toward interests that are again not universal, to say the least. The hole in the reasoning is blatant and stems from a theoretical framework which itself suffers from the same flaw: class demarcation is deemed critical but race demarcation only secondary. That one might have something other than an either/or approach is seemingly ruled out a priori.

applicable in the present, the differences between the Soviet Union and China and Cuba are more than great enough so that an analysis of the latter experiences will reward us greatly before going on to those positive problems.

# 3
# THE CHINESE EXPERIENCE

Women, women limping on the edges of the
   History of Man
Crippled for centuries and dragging the heavy emptiness
Past submission and sorrow to forgotten
   and unknown selves.
It's time to break and run.

                         Rita Mae Brown

The Chinese revolution is immensely complicated. Its roots date from the first opposition to Chinese feudalism over a century ago. The main turning points include founding the Chinese Communist Party in 1921, victory over Chiang Kai-chek in 1949, and the final stabilization of a non-socialist regime in the late 1970s. To understand this vast historical process including civil war, periods of foreign occupation, revolutionary warfare and mobilization, development of a modern nation state, the great cultural revolution of the sixties, and the strange purges and vacillations characterizing the whole post-1949 period and especially the recent decade with its show trials is obviously an immense task. It is made all the more difficult by the relatively sparse information we have about China and the controversial and potentially unreliable character of even what we do think we know. Other works have treated the whole revolutionary period in a manner aimed to be as comprehensive as possible. Few of these, however, have addressed more than one or two spheres of social life. As we are going to discuss Chinese experiences in all four spheres in only one chapter of one volume, it would be foolhardy to claim comprehensiveness. Quite the contrary, our study is very fragmentary. We have highlighted main trends to see underlying forces which governed vacillations in the Chinese revolution as a whole. At a time when the Chinese government is enacting a show trial of many former leaders including Mao Tse-tung's wife, Madame Chiang Ching, we feel our analysis will serve two important purposes. First, it will allow people to make some sense of Chinese revolutionary history in a way which will neither roman-

ticize successes nor obscure failures. This is critical if the Chinese experience and its current horrible manifestations are to lead to more
than cynicism in the West. Second, our focus on main trends and
tendencies of Chinese history will enable us to draw useful insights
regarding socialist possibilities in general, and will provide a
backdrop for our later discussion of what socialism could be like in
the United States. As in the last chapter on the Soviet Union, we
will treat Chinese history four times, so to speak, first addressing
politics, then economics, kinship, and finally community relations.
This is not ideal for two reasons. First, the sections are uneven due to
differential availability of information. Second, and more fundamental, though a full totalist approach might begin with a parti-
tioned analysis, it would proceed to treat all the processes in their interaction. But as this level of "totalism" is beyond our current
means, this chapter should be seen as only a beginning that may
hopefully serve to introduce and situate other work that must still be
done.


## An Overview of Chinese Revolutionary History

Prerevolutionary China was hell for most Chinese. The conditions described, for example, in the early pages of William Hinton's
*Fanshen*, cannot be subsumed by any other metaphor.[1] The human
degradation and corruption, the warlordism, poverty, famine,
slavery, infanticide, footbinding and other violence against women
were of such humiliating magnitude that there is likely no way for
an outsider who did not experience these conditions to understand
their impact. The transition to a well organized, agriculturally self
sufficient, industrializing nation in a few decades of revolutionary
leadership is an accomplishment that ranks with any other social
achievement we know of. At the same time, it is *not* the establishment of socialism.

The revolutionary struggle for power in China was not a brief
affair punctuated by a few major encounters and finally a
cataclysmic victory. Instead, it was a protracted struggle with many
complex phases. During this struggle the Chinese Communist Party
was molded into an efficient fighting *and* administrative vehicle.
For it ruled liberated zones which it won control over in the course of
its many battles for long periods prior to final victory in 1949. The
Red Army became a unique military force, schooled in politics as

well as war, able to initiate agricultural campaigns as well as guerrilla offensives and classic military campaigns.[2]

When the Communists took over the country in 1949 the orders of the day were regularizing the economy, eliminating the most barbaric and decadent feudal practices, and establishing organs of leadership and means of educating the populace as quickly as possible. The Communists succeeded at all these important tasks.

The first period of consolidation saw the completion of agrarian reform throughout the nation and the emergence of an efficient state apparatus. Practices like foot binding and other barbarisms were ended. Structures of economic planning were established and international relations that could benefit industrialization were opened. Next, the first five year plan began the long process of modernizing the country. That famine was overcome and agricultural self-sufficiency attained is itself a minor miracle. That light industry and the infrastructure for much modern heavy industry was also established is that much more remarkable. But at the same time there were important social costs.

During the whole period of revolutionary struggle Maoism had included a priority concern for the ills of bureaucracy and "commandism." Mao's commitments to fighting these ills even in context of commanding an immense and highly centralized and bureaucratic party and army were legion. And these Maoist priorities did not disappear with victory. But the consolidation period and first five year plan led to bureaucratic entrenchment and the evolution of economic and social divisions which the Maoist faction of the party found antithetical to the aims of socialism. The Maoist faction felt that these efforts had successfully created a socialist economic foundation in China, but concomitant development of bureaucracy and social divisions were an obstacle that needed to be forcibly removed. As a result the Maoists initiated a series of movements culminating in the massive Great Leap Forward of the late 1950s. This ebb and flow of bureaucratic trends and anti-bureaucratic campaigns, of periods of growing class stratification and campaigns attacking elitism and class advantages, characterized not only the period of stuggle for power in China and the early days of consolidation, but the entire post-revolutionary experience.

For the Great Leap Forward ended in bitter failure. A combination of opposition by entrenched interests, limitations posed by China's human center, ideological and strategic failings within the Maoist faction itself, and a series of natural catastrophes brought the Great Leap Forward to an abortive close. Mao was suddenly isolated within the ruling group, no longer in position to dominate its every decision. A new period of retrenchment followed under the leadership of Liu Shao-chi and Teng Hsiao-ping, two long-standing members of the central committee and respected communists who disagreed with Mao fundamentally.

However, the cycle of struggle did not end at this point. Mao had managed to get a disciple, Lin Piao, into position as head of the People's Liberation Army as his last major victory before he resigned as head of state. He used the following period of the New Economic Policies of Liu Shao-chi to garner support and to mobilize the army under Lin Piao and develop his personal cult. Then, after all these preparations, he finally unleashed an immense movement of criticism against the party leaders and even the whole party itself: The Great Proletarian Cultural Revolution.

This movement was often chaotic and undisciplined. It began with vast student mobilizations and spread through major cities to worker organizations but less so to peasants. It often went to extremes of ideological purism and unnecessary violence. But, at the same time, it showed the existence of an immense popular sentiment against bureaucracy, commandism, social stratification, and the general relegation of workers and students to positions of powerlessness over their own lives. The same individuals who loved the revolution for what it had accomplished (once the leadership said it was right to rebel) had plenty of grievances. The movement demobilized and virtually toppled the Communist Party apparatus. It knocked out of office not only university faculty and administrators but also city mayors and regional governors forcing these individuals to admit errors and parade in disgrace. It was as if the anti-war movement in the U.S. had grown fifty times and focused on all sides of life. Tactics included marches, millions of posters, meetings, building occupations, physical confrontations and battles of all kinds, regional and sometimes nationwide school and work stoppages, and so on. At its most impressive the movement spawned what was called the Shanghai Commune, an accomplishment that may yet become a model for successful socialist upheaval not only in China but in other parts of the world as well. But in the end the Cultural Revolution failed. The left was repressed. Maoism, in part at the hands of Mao himself, was denuded of its anti-bureaucratic thrust. Mao's own heir designate, Lin Piao, once undeniably the second most powerful individual in China, was accused not only of having plotted Mao's death, but of having been a tyrant and a "bourgeois spy" from the beginning of the revolution. He turned up dead and major purges removed those who had attained positions of authority during the Cultural Revolution. Those who had been unmasked as "capitalist roaders" were now welcomed back to dominate local, regional, and national government institutions. Finally, immediately following Mao's death, his widow Chiang Ching and other leaders of the Cultural Revolution were rounded up, accused of all manner of heinous crimes, and kept under house arrest until late 1980 when they were brought to public trial in a manner reminiscent of Stalin's show trials.[3]

How does one understand a process with so many turning points? How can one understand a country being in immense upheaval, hundreds of millions of people participating in processes deemed critical to the salvation of their country, and then but a few years later this is all called a "great mistake" or even a "great crime?" What is the meaning of Maoism and of the opposition Mao confronted? What were the virtues of his own view and what were its weaknesses—for surely there must have been serious weaknesses given the ultimate outcome? What were the real forces contending in these Chinese struggles? These are the questions we intend to address while examining some of the history of the Chinese political, economic, kinship, and community spheres. Organizing this chapter, however, presented many problems. The desire to parallel the structure of the Soviet and Cuban discussions meant we would do each sphere in turn. But the intricacy of the Chinese zigzags meant that the political discussion would be hard to understand for readers who hadn't a good familiarity with Chinese history. Our compromise was this brief introduction and a relatively short political discussion which can be read quickly and then reread after the economics section, if the reader so desires. We hope the results will be worth the slight inconveniences.[4]

## The Chinese Political Experience

When the Chinese Communist Party achieved state power in 1949 they confronted a very different situation than their Bolshevik brethren had three decades earlier. In the first place their party had been steeled by decades of struggle. Having administered liberated zones for many years in the further reaches of China the Chinese revolutionaries were practiced at the art of governing. There was no hostile peasantry to confront. On the contrary, it was the peasantry that provided a mass base of support for the new leaders. The new state was neither isolated nor immediately threatened from without. But most important, 1) the poverty of China was even more intense than that which had characterized Russia, 2) the old state was literally gone—there was no danger of being too liberal about using its infrastructure as no such infrastructure prevailed—and finally, 3) there was no real opposition to the development of a strong centralizing and authoritarian state among the populace and there were no significant political parties competing with the Communist Party led by Mao Tse-tung. Unlike in Russia, there were no Soviets, and there would be no workers' opposition to deal with. The initial political task would be the construction of a powerful government apparatus premised on the central authority of the Party itself.[5] Even in the absence of significant opposition, it is remarkable that the Communists were able to carry out such an immense undertaking in so large and poor a country in so short a time, roughly in the period between 1949 and 1952. The Party boasted approximately five million members at the outset of this project. It was tightly knit and centrally disciplined, and having undergone two decades of armed struggle it was more than prepared for the act of constructing a new state bureaucracy.[6] But as history was to show, the party was not itself monolithic. Mao was certainly the dominant figure among many prestigious and competent leaders and Maoism as a doctrine was to largely define the peculiarly unique attributes of the Chinese experience. But there were other ideological trends present within the Party as well and these reflected the existence of factions which had different aims and conceptions than the Maoists.

The principal informal factions within the party were 1) the Maoists, devoted more or less to elaborating socialist outcomes even in the context of having to use institutional forms that had built-in anti-socialist attributes; 2) a broad spectrum of rightists concerned primarily with the party's own place in society, that is, with the elaboration of the party bureaucracy and with the statification of China; and finally, sometimes overlapping with the rightists, 3) there was also a faction aligned with the coordinator class seeking not so much the party's advance as that of either the central fraction of coordinators—the elite planners, expert but not too red—or of the coordinators as a whole, including managers and intellectual workers in general. We will look more at the history of the conflict between class fractions when we discuss the economic history of the Chinese experience. In this section, however, we will confine our attention to assessing the importance of the commitment to democratic centralism and the one-party state for Chinese political developments, even in context of the existence of a party faction concerned to struggle against the negative aspects of these forms.

The Chinese Communist Party was organized according to the dictates of democratic centralism and saw itself as the sole and unique vanguard representative of the Chinese workers and peasants.[7] In this it was distinctly of the Leninist mold. Perhaps the simplest evidence for this assertion is the continuity of the pool of people from whom the leadership of the Chinese state has always been drawn—the post 1927 party's first cadre. In fact, the leading cadre in 1949 are only now being replaced by younger disciples and that is only occurring because they are literally dying out, not because there is any break in the slow but steady accrual of power that generally betokens the rise to governmental authority of communist party members. More significantly this rise of party cadre over the years is in no way subject to any interference from outside the party, nor to any question by the party's lower membership. The leadership itself is responsible for the moving of individuals both upward and downward and even out of the party. There is no democracy in this, either within the party, nor certainly with respect to the population as a whole.[8] Moreover, the party comes out of the long Leninist tradition of "never being wrong." It is only individuals who are found wrong, and as we shall see, their error is always a reactionary adherence to "capitalist" aims concealed more or less cleverly during their entire stay in the party. Thus the individual's weakness is not deemed a result of his or her place in the party nor of some weakness intrinsic to the party itself.

Leadership purges, therefore, are a remarkable phenomenon in China. The individual—even veterans of the Long March such as Liu Shao-chi or Lin Piao—is accused of having been a reactionary capitalist roader from their earliest days of participation in the revolution. Apparently, it is less destructive of the principles of the party to admit that it was infiltrated at the highest level, and that the whole bureaucracy was taken in by die-hard reactionaries, than to simply admit that there are real differences of opinion about what should be done among people who are all anti-capitalist and seeking establishment of one or another new type of society. For this last view would open up vistas of political discussion and evaluation amongst the populace which apparently the whole party, at least until the Cultural Revolution, preferred closed.

K.S. Karol relates his personal reaction to this practice: "I simply had a feeling that I was confronted with two Chinas. There was the China of the People, which I was warmly invited to see—as I shall describe, and which on the whole gave me pleasant surprises. And there was the China of the summit from which rumors emanated of unprecedented conflicts that were hard to interpret but by which one was bound to be fascinated."[9] The population becomes something of a mass voyeur. This is no way to politicize and raise the consciousness of a people so they might enter onto the course of socialist self-management. On the contrary, feeding the population stories about conspiracies of "capitalist roaders" and plots with little basis in history and insisting this be taken as reality, is horribly destructive of any potential for the development of critical thinking and politicization. These phenomena can only magnify an outside observer's worry about the depth of totalitarian relationships in the Chinese polity.

But let us assume for a moment that the situation in China and the world made it necessary for the Chinese revolutionaries to adopt centralized and strictly disciplined forms of organization and to create "myths" of the absolutely socialist character of these organizations, at least at the very outset. What then should have been the role of factions truly committed to the eventual enactment of socialist institutional alterations under these circumstances?

Presumably, conscious of the authoritarian implications of the vanguard relationship between the party and the population on the one hand, and of bureaucratic relations within the party on the other, such a faction would have tried to elaborate political rhetoric, ideology, and strategy suited to countering these trends. Ideally one might look for the construction of extra-party institutions aimed toward socialist political relations and made to grow as the authoritarian vehicles become less necessary, as well as for emphasis on the fallibility of the party—not just because it could become corrupt, but because it inevitably must if not eventually replaced. Short of this, however, one would hope for policies aimed to minimize and counter the elitism of cadre, to challenge the growing bureaucracy, and question material inequalities between party and non-party members.

Although the Maoists and Mao himself didn't follow the "ideal course," they certainly did follow the more modest one of combatting negative tendencies. Yet they did this while championing the very institutions that were yielding the problems. Thus we find Mao constantly admonishing the communist cadre concerning their relations to the masses and constantly pronouncing upon "correct" relations within the party as well. One can find numerous passages with this sort of intent, for example:

> To link oneself with the masses one must act in accordance with the needs and wishes of the masses. All the work done for the masses must start from their needs and not from the desires of any individual, however well intentioned.... There are two principles here: One is the actual needs of the masses rather than what we fancy they need, and the other is the wishes of the masses, who must make up their own minds rather than our making up their minds for them.[10]

> Two principles must be observed: 1-Say all you know and say it without reserve; 2-Don't blame the speaker but take his words as a warning. Unless the principle of 'Don't blame the speaker' is observed genuinely and not falsely, the result will not be 'say all you know and say it without reserve.'[11]

Yet, at the same time, the authoritarian content of the social relations existing between the cadre and the peasants and between the party leaders and the party masses, was never structurally challenged by the elaboration of any lasting alternatives. Similarly, the Maoist effort to prevent elaboration of material inequalities between the party and the people and within the party itself was only an injunction: the seeds for these inequities were always present in the social relations, and no other social relations were ever proposed—at least not until the crisis stage of the Cultural Revolution. Thus, as Karol notes, "Still all this (the entreaties to modest behavior, etc.) did not answer my question about the decision-making power of the masses. The reality was that these modest cadre, devoted to the people and engaging in manual work, nevertheless made all the decisions and were accountable only to their superiors in the party."[12] One is reminded of Lenin's presumed insight in the last stages of his life that perhaps the party's authoritarianism and hierarchy were going too far and had to be countered. But Lenin was neither able to suggest institutional alternatives nor offer a penetrating critique of "Leninist" political forms that would permit their temporary use in full cognizance of their limitations. Instead he could only propose ethical injunctions and bureaucratic counters to bureaucracy.[13] It is almost as if Mao took up where Lenin left off, though in a new setting and with the considerable benefit of hindsight regarding the Soviet experience. For again, it was pressure from within the party that was brought against the inevitable implications of the party's own operation. Moreover, insofar as Mao would have to use the party apparatus as a vehicle for his efforts at rectification, he would simultaneously be furthering and opposing the same trends. No doubt his own understanding of the situation, and that of other Maoists as well, vacillated tremendously as a result.[14]

The Maoists did not formulate the struggle in China as the socialist road versus the road of the bureaucrats and/or coordinators, but instead as the socialist road versus the capitalist road. This description avoided calling into question the actual institutions the revolution had established including the party and planning apparatus. This was a desirable formulation for the two non-socialist party factions. The roots of their interests were obfuscated, making it all the more difficult for them to be effectively challenged within the party, and virtually impossible for anyone outside the party to understand what was going on. Opponents of Mao, or even the Maoists themselves when they were challenged by those on the right, were to be charged always and only with having residual capitalist attitudes and aims. Leaders might therefore come and go, but as their policies' real roots were never properly named much less fully addressed, the actual nature of the struggle in post-capitalist China remained mysterious. "This or that individual or political fragment falls from time to time, to be sure, but the complex bureaucractic infrastructure lives on."[15] What was the basis for the Maoists' participation in the obfuscation which seems at least in part not to have been in their own interest? One possibility is that many of them knew the real nature of the battle, but felt it had to be kept secret for fear that if the public was let in on the fallibility of the central political and economic institutions dominating post-capitalist China, loyalty, order, and all chance for socialist progress would dissipate. This presumed cynicism could have been an accurate assessment, or it could have underestimated the possibility of political sophistication among the populace because of the effects of bureaucratic elitism on the Maoists themselves. We certainly don't have sufficient evidence to judge, although both our theory and historical hindsight push us toward the view that if the Maoists knew the score, they would have done much better to reveal it from the outset.

Another possible interpretation of the Maoist participation in this sort of obfuscation and secrecy would be that they simply believed the incorrect analysis that the roots of non-socialist tendencies were all in the past, in residual interests and thoughts held over from capitalism. This misperception would have been less threatening to their own beliefs and behavior concerning the viability and importance of the party, easier to hold in context of participating in the party and continually asserting the importance of Leninism, etc.* Most likely, parts of all these explanations are applicable to different groups and individuals in the Maoist faction. A careful study may even show that Mao himself wavered on many occasions. Regrettably the nearly complete secrecy shrouding high level Chinese politics makes conclusive determinations impossible.

---

*An interesting formulation is found in Maurice Meisner, *The China Quarterly*, January-March, 1971, p. 29 and quoted in *What Is to Be Undone*, Michael Albert, Porter Sargent Publisher, Boston, 1974: "Whether Mao is consciously aware of the bureaucratic limitations of Leninist organizational principles is problematic; even if he has arrived at such a conclusion, it would be impossible for him to acknowledge it without renouncing the entire Leninist heritage to which he lays claim, and within which he claims to have made creative innovations." However, whether this analysis holds is thrown into doubt by the wild fluctuations in Chinese lines which have, in fact, yet to significantly disturb the party's hegemony. Perhaps even Mao himself will be criticized before long, and certainly if his views can be reinterpreted and even rewritten or rejected, Lenin's could have been similarly treated without disastrous repercussions.

But it is hard to believe that during the Cultural Revolution when Mao urged youthful non-party revolutionaries to attack the bulk of the party membership, openly called into question the idea of one party and of no organized party factions, and even proposed the Paris Commune as a viable alternative organizational model he was unaware of the basic institutional problems of the Chinese polity.

Another peculiar Chinese ideological approach that deserves comment has also emerged due to the over-arching desire to label all failings as "capitalistic." In the post-Cultural Revolutionary period it became necessary for the Chinese bureaucrats to develop a way of criticizing the Maoists and other leftists they wished to purge from the party so as to reassert their own complete hegemony. These individuals would have to be called "leftists," and yet one also had to assert that they were "capitalistic." Otherwise, there was the problem of assessing "left trends" as real possibilities, a problem better left inside the party.* The result was to eliminate all content from the distinction between "left errors" and "right errors." For the Chinese contend that all errors are essentially right and that they all lead one way or another "back" to capitalism. Left errors are therefore "left in form but right in essence." That Mao too went along with this can be explained, by those interested in the details, with either assumption above about the basis for Maoist beliefs and their scope. Either he was compromising with a hostile reality, or he was confused by the same dynamics that led to the "capitalist versus socialist road" polarity in many people's analyses. In any case, it might be useful to take time to notice that the conceptualization of "institutional boundary" and "human center" which we have been using provides an excellent framework for better interpreting the meaning and difference between left and right errors. A left error is pushing for progressive changes in the institutional

---

*In Meisner's detailed account of the period Mao holds great responsibility—whatever the motives—for retrenchment. Indeed, the existence of a struggle between Mao moving rightward, and Ch'en Po-ta, Lin Piao and others still committed to preventing the resurgence of a reconstituted Leninist party and bureaucracy is clearly indicated. No doubt Lin Piao was also horrified at the reactionary trend in foreign policy. "...the policy of 'peaceful coexistence between countries with different social systems' was practiced with a vengeance elsewhere. Entirely 'peaceful

boundary that are inappropriate to the real state of and possibilities inherent in the human center. To be instituted they would therefore have to be imposed in a top-down, authoritarian way (*a la* the Gang of Four, if we are to believe that there was significant popular peasant and worker resentment of their policies). Right errors would be failing to push for changes in the human center through consciousness raising and failing to make progressive changes in the institutional boundary for which the human center is prepared. Both kinds of mistakes obviously take place in pre- as well as post-revolutionary practice. Furthermore, this interpretation allows both for legitimate mistakes motivated by honest misperceptions of social possibilities, as well as for conscious impositions of right or left policies to attain non-socialist, "self-serving" ends. The rhetoric propounded in China by all factions has had the regrettable impact

relations' were maintained with the government of Pakistan during the Bengali revolt and with Madame Bandaranaike during the revolutionary uprising in Ceylon in 1971. The notorious 'Christmas bombings' of North Vietnam in 1972 brought forth verbal protests from Peking, but they were sufficiently restrained to preserve cordial relations with Henry Kissinger and Richard Nixon. All manner of feudal monarchs and military dictators (many formerly denounced as fascist or worse) embarked upon pilgrimages to Peking and were received with all due honors. Normal diplomatic and trade relations were established with the Franco regime in Spain and the fascist military junta in Greece. In recent years China has emerged as one of the great champions of the North Atlantic Treaty Organization and is one of the few countries in what was once known as 'the socialist bloc' to maintain formal relations with the Chilean militarists who so brutally overthrew the Marxist goverment of Allende. And in early 1976 China was to find itself involved in Angola on the same side as the United States and South Africa." (Maurice Meisner, *Mao's China*, Free Press, 1977, p. 371-372).

In any case, the initial criticisms of Lin Piao and Ch'en Po-ta as ultra-leftists at least placed them in the proper *relative* position on the political spectrum—though the view and practice they were trying to preserve was only that which Mao had elaborated in concert with them during the Cultural Revolution. The later reversal to label these men rightists was merely another nail in the coffin of the legitimacy of serious criticism of any kind: "The most difficult matter confronting the congress was to explain—and explain away—the demise of Lin Piao. In 1972 Lin and Ch'en Po-ta had been depicted as 'ultra-leftists.' It was soon realized,

of masking honest differences, as well as obscuring the real roots of potential class differences over aims. In our own approach one might try to discern these two aspects as well. On the one hand there is a conceptualization of agents of history—classes, kin groups, political elements, and community groups—and on the other the conceptualization of center and boundary and of networks of institutional and human relations. The former set of concepts is useful for discerning differences of interest and aim, while the latter is helpful in understanding reasons for honest disagreement over policy even given agreement over aims. Both must be employed to get a full picture.

On balance, as we will see in the coming historical discussion, certainly the structure which has been at the center of the Chinese

however, that such accusations against two of the most prominent leaders of the Cultural Revolution might create doubts about the validity of the whole enterprise or doubts about whether the present leaders truly represented its now canonized principles and spirit. Thus Lin and Ch'en were hastily converted into 'ultra-rightists,' and both formally expelled from the party—Lin, posthumously, as a 'bourgeois careerist, conspirator, counter revolutionary double dealer, renegade, and traitor,' and Ch'en as a 'principle member of the Lin Piao anti-Party clique, anti-Communist Kuomintang element, Trotskyite, renegade, enemy agent and revisionist.' Chou En-lai went to fantastic lengths to connect Lin with Liu Shao-ch'i.'' According to Chou, as quoted by Meisner, Lin's "aim was no less than to turn the CCP into 'a revisionist, fascist party....subvert the dictatorship of the proletariat and restore capitalism,...institute a feudal compradore fascist dictatorship,...[and] capitulate to Soviet revisionism and social imperialism.' As if that was not enough, Chou (in good Stalinist fashion) charged that Lin's crimes were not only of recent vintage but could be traced back to his earliest days as a Communist. Mao, it was claimed, had been 'trying seriously and patiently to educate' Lin since 1929, but, as matters turned out, 'Lin Piao's bourgeois idealist world outlook was not at all remolded. At important junctures of the revolution he invariably committed Right opportunist errors and invariably played double-faced tricks, putting up a false front to deceive the Party and the people.' Why it took more than forty years for Mao to uncover this false front was not explained.'' This comes from a Party that ostensibly "puts its faith in the masses,'' "trusts the masses,'' and so on, but apparently, as Meisner concludes, "the masses were not to be trusted with the truth about their leaders.'' (p. 373-74)

political network has been authoritarian and intrinsically conducive to anti-socialist outcomes. Perhaps its presence was an absolute necessity, given the initial restrictive conditions in both center and boundary confronted by the Chinese revolutionaries. It is less likely, however, that it was necessary to extol the institution as much as was done, or to preclude the development of organized factions within its limits, or to have never fostered the development of alternative political forms that could eventually embody democratic participatory principles outside of the party. Perhaps, had this latter course been taken, when the time for struggle against the party as a whole came during the Cultural Revolution the heritage of extra-party institutions and relationships would have made the transition to "commune politics" a real possibility. Certainly the secrecy attendant to the Chinese party, as well as the concrete authoritarianism of its organizational structure were conducive instead to bureaucratic and coordinator outcomes. The Maoists' willingness to foster rebellion, to fight non-socialist factions, and even to attack the party apparatus itself were all signs of the longevity and tenacity of the struggle to institute socialist forms. Yet however much the Maoists countered selfishness and power-seeking among the cadre with calls to "serve the people," this is still not championing programs promoting "power to the people." As we shall see shortly, when efforts in this direction were finally made, whether at the Maoists' behest or as an extension of their more modest intentions, it proved to be too little too late as far as offsetting the bureaucratic and coordinator implications of the main institutional forms of the Chinese revolution.

> The legacy of Mao is thus an ambiguous one, for it is marked and scarred by a deep incongruity between its progressive socio-economic accomplishments and its retrogressive political features. On the one hand, Maoism has thrown off Stalinist orthodoxies and methods in forging a new pattern of economic development which has, on balance, moved Chinese society in a socialist direction. On the other hand, it has retained essentially Stalinist methods of bureaucratic political rule, generated its own cults, orthodoxies, and dogmas, and consistently suppressed all forms of intellectual and political dissent Mao, to be sure, regarded bureaucracy as the greatest of evils, but his weapon to combat the phenomenon was to

rely on his personal prestige and the forces he could rally under his own banner. Neither in theory nor in practice does the Maoist legacy include institutional safeguards against bureaucratic dominance.[16]

Before moving on to discuss economics we should like to make something of a major caveat. The Chinese revolution is an exceptionally murky affair in large part because of the great secrecy enshrouding the history of the Chinese Communist Party itself. The materials we presented in this section and the more detailed historical outline we will present in our discussion of economics, even together constitute only the most sketchy evidence for our interpretation. Naturally, they are also not the whole basis of it, rather only some substantiation presented here as an overview. Yet the whole basis is still little more than the writings of a number of other analysts, some of whom certainly travelled in China—but only at the behest of the Chinese—and a few writings of Chinese critics of the revolution, as well as of course Mao's own writings and certain documents of the party. This is far from enough to warrant great confidence in the analysis. Even given the conceptual approach we are employing there are a considerable number of ways to interpret the Chinese experience, only one of which we will put forward in this chapter. When one considers the strange stories about Liu Shao chi, Lin Piao, the Gang of Four and perhaps soon even Mao that the people are called upon to believe, memorize, and even endlessly repeat, one has to wonder at the level of regimentation. The facts that there is no extra-party opposition in China and never has been, that the media is all party controlled, that there is no non-state news apparatus, etc., must all be sifted alongside what we emphasize. It is distinctly possible that beyond all the struggles of factions in the party, the level of indoctrination and authoritarianism and of sheer regimentation within China may have been so great as to significantly call into question our interpretation of the materials we have studied. What remains, even in light of this need to be cautious about assessing the history and analysis presented here is that *even the most positive interpretations of Maoism* support our overall analysis of the ill-effects intrinsic to certain political forms and methods and of their intrinsically anti-socialist character. What the Chinese experience says to us, quite softly due to our concern over the reliability of our understanding of what actually took place, is that while authoritarian political forms sometimes may be unavoidable as a means to attain power and even as tools of development, they must be contested clearly and publicly and democratic alternatives must be nourished from the outset. Otherwise the authoritarian attributes will prove too much to overcome, even for the most accomplished, talented, and committed of revolutionaries. This point should gain credence as we discuss more of the history itself.

### The Chinese Economic Experience

Maoism revolutionized the traditional Marxist view of the "socialist transition period" by declaring it a period dominated first and foremost by class struggle. Mao further scandalized the official communist world by eventually pointing straight to the party as the location of the greatest threat to progress toward communism in this period. Finally, Mao presided over a Communist Party and government which not only tolerated, but to a point encouraged, a popular mass upheaval against itself—an event that is to our knowledge unprecedented in the history of "statist" societies. Yet we have also already argued that as positive as the above breakthroughs have been, Maoism has, for whatever reasons, seriously mistaken the nature of the struggle between different agents of history that dominates post-capitalist societies by 1) downplaying the importance of agents of history other than economic classes, and 2) treating the class struggle as fundamentally between workers and capitalists, rather than between workers and peasants on the one hand, and the coordinator class whose position is greatly strengthened by the capitalists' exit on the other. We have also argued that the way in which Maoism points an accusatory finger at the party is both destructive in its conspiratorial over-simplicity and obfuscation, and also imcomplete in its refusal to fully break with traditional communist support for democratic centralism and the single party state.[17]

Here we wish to offer an interpretation of the various swings that have occurred in Chinese economic policy since 1949, an evaluation of the different economic mechanisms that have been used, and a sobering view of the most recent trends. Whereas we argued that active struggle between the coordinator and working class in the Soviet Union had been largely confined to an early period, and that the politically demarcated central fraction of coordinators had emerged economically dominant by the 1930s and been only mildly challenged by the managerial fraction since, we find considerable evidence that the struggle between coordinators and workers and peasants in China has been more continuous and evenly matched and that the medium-term outcome remained in relative balance until recently. In the discussion to follow we will speak of the workers and peasants and of two fractions of the coordinator class, the managerial fraction and the central or central planning fraction. The coordinator class also has representatives operating within the party pursuing coordinator interests alongside other party factions seeking primarily bureaucratic party dominance, and, in the case of the Maoists, a development toward socialist social relationships.

## The Period of Rehabilitation

The years from 1949 to 1952, which the Chinese call the period of Rehabilitation, effectively completed the defeat of the capitalists and landlords. Radical land reform, which had always been the first priority whenever an area was firmly behind Red Army lines during the previous years of guerrilla warfare, was now carried out in the newly liberated areas of Southern and Eastern China as well, thereby eliminating the basis for landlords and rich peasants throughout the country. Though it is true that the policy explicitly exempted "middle peasants" from expropriation, and that these middle peasants in all likelihood formed the bulk of the opposition to later collectivization efforts (no doubt urged on by former rich peasants), we see no useful purpose nor truth in referring to later struggles between small scale family farming and collective agriculture as a continuing threat of landlord, much less capitalist, rule in the countryside. In industry, the immediate policy called for nationalization of only the "international bourgeoisie" and elements of the "national bourgeoisie" who had been closely allied with the Kuomintang. But nonetheless, by 1952 only 22 percent of industrial production remained in private hands, and most of this was under contract to the state. For both landlords and capitalists the handwriting was clear on the wall: short of a U.S. backed reconquest of the mainland by Chiang Kai-chek's armies, they were through as economic classes unto themselves. Yet there were still plenty of reactionary reasons for not braving the chilly swim to Hong Kong—for individuals of these former classes or their children could certainly still hope to become important members of the new coordinator class and thereby retain at least a segment of their economic and other social advantages. We shall see how this process unfolded shortly.

But as much as these early developments marked the defeat of the capitalists and landlords as classes the fact that the revolution had to be "exported" to two other segments of Chinese society contributed to the later development of coordinator power over the peasants and workers. In the newly liberated rural areas the land reform was a relatively top-down operation, brought about by an army composed of peasants from far distant villages and administered by party officials and cadre from other regions. We would suspect, therefore, that the indigenous, democratic style of agrarian reform described so powerfully by William Hinton in *Fanshen* was largely compromised in the villages which underwent reform in the wake of the Civil War rather than during the guerrilla resistance—that is, in the majority of Chinese Villages.[18] An even more serious problem was that no communist had been seen by urban inhabitants since 1927 when the party had fled the coastal cities for the countryside in the aftermath of Chiang Kai-chek's brutal repression of the urban uprisings of that year. With virtually no working class organizations and little leftist tradition within the class, there was little alternative to administering the cities surrounded by the sea of Mao's peasant army, and also the nationalized firms, with party overseers and with the old technical and supervisory personel.

### Learn from the Soviets

The next period, 1953 to 1957, had the slogan "Learn from the Soviets" and was generally marked by a consolidation of centrally planned administration in industry, a five-year plan emphasizing investment in heavy industry, and a gradual collectivization of agriculture through the formation of "mutual aid teams" (five or so families), "lower coops" (20 to 40 families), and "higher coops" (100 to 200 families).[19] Though there is no evidence, only rhetorical flourish, to support the idea of a tendency toward the restoration of capitalism in this period, there was certainly a powerful tendency toward the elaboration of the dominance of the coordinator class, and in particular of the central fraction of it allied with and as a part of the elite of the Communist Party. For in industry, all important production targets were set by the central ministries in Peking—in Chinese parlance one might say that it was a period of emphasis on "expert" rather than "red" in factory management, and that there was also a relative emphasis on "material" as opposed to "moral" incentives.

However, the red versus expert formulation, like many others the Maoists have provided to explain their own experience, is sometimes almost as obfuscatory as it is revealing. Yes, "expert" does connote rather clearly a set of characteristics and dimensions of behavior that would be in the interest of coordinator dominance. What meaning does "red" have? Insofar as the party is referred to, what faction within the party? Similarly, when experts are on the rise, is it the central fraction of the coordinator class, in parallel with the most bureaucratic elements of the party, or is it the managerial fraction of the class in concert with more liberal factions within the party? The reason for the incapacity of the red versus expert conceptualization to clearly address the real issues is simple: it was not designed to do so. Rather, like the idea of a capitalist road versus a socialist road, which we shall address in detail shortly, it was instead meant to simplify the diverse possibilities into a simple polarity.

There is another set of axes along which a rather similar oversimplification takes place, and we might just as well make note of it now too. One usually notes the left or right content of a policy by considering its likely impact upon social relations as an implemented line. In this way we can arrange a set of policies along gradations from left to right, more or less, on the basis of the ends they seem to envision. Yet there is also the issue of the means of implementation of particular policies—on the one hand administrative or top-down, and on the other more participatory and democratic. No matter the content of the aims, this question of means also bears on the outcome which is actually achieved. Thus, the administrative approach, even to the implementation of a relatively lefist policy has implications which can serve the reactionary process of bureaucratic and coordinator development. And similarly, even a relatively rightist policy, were it to be implemented by participatory means, could have progressive implications for politicizing the working class and peasants.

So, in this "Soviet period" we would argue that both the aims (economic centralization, political centralization, industrialization via traditionalist efficiency requirements) and the means (top-down administrative rather than participatory) made socialist outcomes less likely. Where the Chinese say there was a threat of capitalist restoration in this period, we would argue that there were significant tendencies toward a coordinator bureaucratic stabilization.

## The Great Leap Forward

In 1958 and 1959 China underwent what was called The Great Leap Forward. The characteristics of this period are leftist when assessed according to traditional socialist criteria: 1) an incredible spurt of collectivization in agriculture, 2) a further increase in the rate of industrialization 3) a deemphasis on expert as compared to red, and 4) a drastic shift in direction toward egalitarianism with regard to both industrial wages and commune remuneration for agricultural labor.[20] It is interesting to note, however, that the period was foreshadowed by a late policy of the prior five year plan called "Let a Hundred Flowers Bloom." Presumably the party faction concerned about the trend toward political bureaucracy and coordinator economic hegemony, the Maoists, were eager to begin developing support for their upcoming efforts to induce a turn around through the Great Leap Forward. They enacted (perhaps in coalition with the managerial coordinator fraction) an opening up of critical avenues of debate and publication in hopes of a popular criticism of the policies of the Soviet period. This democracy, proving primarily useful to the managerial elements of the coordinator class, seems to have led to a howl for ever greater coordinator democracy and managerial coordinator economic power at the expense not only of the bureaucratic political elite, but also of the Maoists themselves who were presumably championing the interests of workers and peasants. It was thus rapidly brought to a conclusion.* In the West this was seen as a move toward liberalization crushed by the authoritarian party. In our view, it was something more complex: an attempt to use popular criticism to garner support for the Maoist plan to "leap forward" as opposed to the bureaucratic and central coordinator desires to continue with Soviet style policies. But as the democratization was primarily employed by coordinators to attack party dominance—including that of the Maoist faction—over their prerogatives, it had to be suspended. We can see here the top-down quality of efforts at "leftist" policy, the complexity of forces, and the tenuousness of aims and outcomes which will all reappear in even more extreme forms as we address the period of the Cultural Revolution and its aftermath.

A few statistical facts are worth noting about the Great Leap: first, as Wheelwright and MacFarlane report, between 1957 and '59 the percentage of industry controlled by central authorities declined from 46 percent to 26 percent as the percentage controlled by local authorities rose from 54 percent to 74 percent.[21] In agriculture, again, according to Wheelwright and MacFarlane, by Sept. 1958 90 percent of peasant holdings were in communes as 750,000 coops were merged first into 23,000 communes which were then quickly reduced in size and split into 70,000 communes.[22] Accompanying this institutional change there was also a change in the locus of power and status among social groups. With agricultural power shifting to the communes, the central fraction of coordinators was undercut. Similarly, the trend away from central to more local control of industrial firms also undercut the mechanisms by which the central fractions of coordinators amassed power. Likewise, the emphasis on politics in command, and on red as opposed to expert, meant that the transfer was less to local managers and technicians than to party cadre and officials. Finally, there seems to be at least

---

*Our understanding of the Hundred Flowers period is most cloudy. Maurice Meisner relates a complex analysis in his book, *Mao's China*, a volume which has an analysis of the entire revolution that is in many respects very similar to our own. He sees the movement as having been viewed and employed differently by different elements in the Party, but also argues that the response to growing liberalization regarding the expression of ideas was actually radical. We disagree, but in any case, the point is not critical to the rest of our argument.

some evidence, though it is very scanty, that party shake-ups during the period meant that the cadre and officials gaining in power relative to the coordinators were the left Maoists, while the bureaucrats were being criticized, purged from the party, or sent to do labor. There was also unquestionably a considerable egalitarian emphasis on the need for great sacrifice, hard work and modesty among the party's cadre—in stark contrast to the Soviet Stalinist experience where such contributions were entreated only from the non-party population.

How is the Great Leap Forward to be understood? On the one hand, one might reasonably argue that it was a bid for total power by the political elite, reducing the sway of the coordinator class in the economy as well as subjecting the workers and peasants to increased direct control by politically loyal cadre in order to extract increasing surpluses for use in crash industrialization. In this view the simultaneously apparent egalitarianism—the demand for material sacrifice by the cadre as well as the masses—would be explained away as a necessary compromise with the reality of stark and exceptionally poor circumstances rather than any sort of desire to move toward socialist equality.[23] The communes would be seen as simply the most effective labor intensive and disciplined approach to the extraction of agricultural surpluses from the peasantry. Divisions within the party would be seen to reflect differences over tactics and strategy necessary to develop the country on the one hand, and over the proper role of coordinators versus party reds on the other, but without any significant representation of worker or peasant interests or of serious desires for socialist outcomes. This somewhat cynical analysis can't, at least at this time, be completely ruled out. There simply isn't enough evidence. Yet, it does seem to us that another interpretation is more consistent with what evidence there is, not only regarding this period, but the whole process of the Chinese economic revolution.

In Maurice Meisner's view the Great Leap Forward was a conscious response of Maoists to the social/political deformations that resulted from the first five year plan. Industrialization was bringing bureaucratization, elites, growing differences between town and country and even spawning new class formations. There had to be a better way. The Great Leap was therefore to be social as well as economic. Industrialization would be accomplished at the same time as the preconditions for communism were laid rather than by a process that would impede the arrival of communism.[24] Given this view we can interpret the Great Leap Forward as a period of curtailing coordinator power in order to enhance (or at least preserve) the possibility of greater worker and peasant power through which actual socialist changes could eventually be made in various aspects of the human center and institutional boundary of the Chinese economy. If a particular revolution must tolerate or even promote certain coordinator aspects and institutional relations in order to achieve economic development, then the socialist route is to have periodic efforts to counter this development and prevent its encrustation into a new basis for a ruling class other than workers and peasants. Similarly, if a particular revolution must employ undemocratic political forms that have bureaucratic tendencies built into their very structure, again periodic episodes of struggle against these very institutions, despite their short-run importance, would be the only possible socialist course of action. Ideally, of course, such efforts would be clearly understood by the populace not as anti-capitalist, but as anti-bureaucratic and anti-coordinator and as means to ensure eventual participation and full democracy in both the polity and the economy. Furthermore, it would also seem most reasonable to employ and continually elaborate institutional forms which might provide an on-going center for the challenge to the party bureaucracy and planning technocracy. Now it seems that this "socialist ideal in difficult conditions" was not operative during the Great Leap Forward. Yet, it is still distinctly possible that decentralizing, promoting red versus expert, enforcing strict standards and material deprivation on cadre, advancing Maoist officials and cadre over right-wingers, and promoting the communes was simultaneously a periodic attack at both bureaucracy and technocracy, the later being the economic relations of the coordinators.* In any case, in Meisner's rendition the Great Leap Forward was blunted by party agreements reached over the

---

*Consider as a fragment of evidence the following formulation advanced by Mao in 1964 and reiterated by Lin Piao in 1969:

"[without an emphasis on class struggle] only a short time will pass, perhaps a few years or a decade, a few decades at most, before a counter revolutionary restoration inevitably occurs on a national scale, the Marxist-Leninist Party becomes a revisionist party, a fascist party, and the country changes color. Let our comrades reflect well on the danger that lies in this situation."

opposition of Mao in the Winter of 1958. Then, the following summer, bitter political struggles took place and steadily more restrictive rulings were applied to the communes. According to Meisner, all the meetings were presided over by Liu Shao-chi. Finally, Mao stepped down as head of state and the position was conferred on Liu in April of 1959. "Mao retained the more important post of chairman of the party, but he was no longer fully in command of the party apparatus. He later was to complain that after the Wuhan Plenum, he was treated 'like a dead ancestor'."[25] Then months later in a July plenum at Lushan Mao attempted to reinvigorate the Great Leap Forward movement. While criticizing himself for certain excesses of its initial enactment, Mao went on to assert that the communization movement could build the conditions of a communist transition and if the communes were to be further undermined vowed "to go to the countryside to lead the peasants to overthrow the government. If those of you in the Liberation Army won't follow me, then I will go and find a Red Army, and organize another Liberation Army. But I think the Liberation Army would follow me."[26] It was at this plenum as well that Mao purged the prior leader of the People's Liberation Army (PLA) placing Lin Piao in his place.

At this threat from Mao the Great Leap was revived but it was a "pale reflection" of what it had been before. Indeed, in the fall of 1959 and winter of 1960 the Maoist appeals for further radicalization "largely fell on deaf ears as floods and drought ravaged much of the countryside."[27] Mao apparently recognized the need to pull back from the program and indeed also pulled back from all government participation at least for a time. He thus "seemingly acquiesced in the reassertion of the power of the regular army and state organizations, personified in the growing dominance of Liu Shao-chi."[28]  In 1960, Mao was apparently no longer the central force within the Chinese Communist Party and government. Rather "Mao no longer commanded either the party or the state and no longer determined the policies they pursued. What remained of his victory at Lushan was tenuous control of the army through his protege, Lin Piao."[29] In Meisner's very palatable interpretation, Mao came to believe that the relative failure of his Great Leap policies was a function of their improper implementation by the party bureaucracy. That is, the party, threatened by decentralization, sabotaged the effort. This would obviously have been a powerful impetus toward the Cultural Revolution.

### The New Economic Policy: 1962-1964

The New Economic Policy (NEP) marked a clear turn to the "right," or in our terms an unmistakable trend toward a coordinator rather than socialist social formation.

All forms of regionalization were curbed in a return to greater centralization of decision-making. "Production was revived through a combination of the reimposition of centralized party control over the countryside, the virtual removal of communal controls over individual peasant producers, and urban assistance to the countryside. Hundreds of thousands of party cadre were sent to the villages, displacing (and criticizing) the Maoist inspired local cadres."[30] And in industry "direction over the economy...was returned to the economic ministries in Peking and the architects of the First Five Year Plan were restored to prominence."[31]

At the point of production the managerial fraction of the coordinator class increased its authority over the use of workers' and peasants' labor power. In Meisner's words: "Managerial authority in individual factories and enterprises...was reestablished. Managerial and technological experts...regained control over the operations of individual enterprises....And the traditional distinction between managers and workers reemerged with the new emphasis clearly on technical 'expertise' rather than political 'redness'."[32] Moreover, the increasing use of markets, prices, and profitability criteria granted the managerial fraction somewhat more autonomy from the central fraction of coordinators and political elite than they had hitherto enjoyed in China. In the countryside the communes were both diminished in size and brought under the sway of "full-time and salaried state functionaries."[33]

As might be expected there was also a drastic shift away from moral and collective incentives toward material and individual incentives for ordinary peasants and workers. Wage differentials increased, production norms stretched out, and piece rates were introduced. Moreover, there was considerable return to use of private plots in agriculture, to the extent that in some regions by the end of 1962 the private grain harvest was even greater than the collective harvest![34]

Perhaps the least significant change in policy from our point of view is the one that is most frequently emphasized in other analyses, namely the shift in sectoral priorities. Whereas the first five year plan had designated heavy industry as the priority sector, and the Great Leap Forward had pushed for all-out efforts in all sectors, the

NEP ranked agriculture as the first priority, light industry second, and heavy industry last. But while we attach no necessary social significance to shifts in sectoral emphasis in general, this change certainly appears to conform to the other changes discussed above, and the shift toward more agricultural and light industry output obviously facilitated the use of material incentives for the masses and provision of material "rewards" to the new elites.

In sum, both the fledgling coordinator class and the bureaucratic faction of the political elite made considerable headway under the leadership of Lui Shao-chi, Chou En-lai, and Teng Hsiao-ping. Accusations that these leaders of the NEP were acting under the influence of capitalists seeking some sort of restoration are ridiculous. But the idea that they were elaborating a course aimed toward a bureaucratic/coordinator social formation—that is, a non-capitalist but non-socialist outcome—is perfectly reasonable. The left response was the Great Proletarian Cultural Revolution.

### The Great Proletarian Cultural Revolution (GPCR)

Although all evidence is far from in, based on the accounts we have been able to assess it seems to us that the GPCR combined most elements of the Great Leap Forward with the critical addition of unprecedented mass participation not only in criticizing the bureaucracy and coordinators but also, to a lesser extent, in beginning to elaborate socialist alternatives. Whether the Maoist left political elite ever intended that the masses become involved to the great extent that they did, whether they were using the workers and peasants because they had a losing hand as long as the game was limited only to the political and coordinator elites, is important in assessing the revolutionary character of people such as Mao, Lin Piao, Chen Po-ta, and later the Gang of Four. But, no matter how manipulative and anti-democratic their strategy, procedures, or motives *might* have been there *was* mass involvement and there came to be a revolutionary socialist thrust at least among segments of the Red Guards, lower elements in the party, and sectors of workers and perhaps also peasants. Some estimate this supposedly ultra-left movement to have encompassed at times as many as 30 to 40 million people. This last fact, as well as the participation of hundreds of millions of people, distinguished that period from the Great Leap Forward and from any other epoch of construction in any other post-capitalist society as well.

The GPCR was characterized by a variety of features which we can briefly summarize here. First, at the movement's inception, there was a strong attack on the Mandarin system of education which was a linch-pin of the coordinator class mechanism for increasing its own power. The almost complete disruption of the prior system and institution of more just criteria for entry and participation in the school system were certainly socialist in orientation.[35] The process of students massively demonstrating, overturning norms, and criticizing faculty and administrators alike, while no doubt often extreme was also certainly an expression of radical dissent and reconstruction.

There were massive criticism sessions against those in power in schools, industry, and government—the latter two taking the form of anti-technocracy and anti-bureaucracy thrusts. Material incentives and individualism were attacked, and here no doubt there were many excesses. For in leveling wages often material hardships were placed not only at the highest levels but on a considerable majority of the population. Insofar as the GPCR was often imposed in the countryside and in certain industries by minorities of left rebels, no doubt it was often, despite the high level of participation, also rather arbitrary and undemocratic. One is reminded of the export of the revolution to the cities and the newly liberated parts of the countryside at the very outset of the Chinese revolutionary regime.

Not only was the Maoist faction within the party on the offensive against coordinators and party bureaucrats, but the whole party was called into question, *virtually immobilized,* and reduced in stature and power.* The institutional form that was to gain from this reduction of the party was, depending upon whom we are to believe, either the new "commune" or the Peoples' Liberation Army. In the cynical view, it was only certain popular extra-party leftists who supported the commune and were crushed by the Maoists who had spoken of the commune only as an opportunist tactic.[36] More positively toward the Maoists, and in our view, the Maoist faction did sincerely desire to experiment with new institutions even against the party itself, but they found these

---

*One formulation put forward by Mao in 1966, quoted by Lin and then widely throughout China, was that communists "should regard themselves simultaneously as a particle of revolutionary force and as a target of the revolution."

institutions unsatisfactory (or were outflanked inside the party) and then switched allegiance to the loyal and politically quite advanced PLA under the leftist Lin Piao.* There is no question that there was a considerable left that was repressed as the cultural revolution proceeded. After the Shanghai commune failed, there was a major reversal and the most radical red guards and workers' organizations were opposed from the top.[37] "More than a change of names was involved in the demise of the Shanghai Commune. It involved an abandonment of principles and the crushing of hopes. For the [new] 'revolutionary committees' in Shanghai as elsewhere, were not organs of popular democratic rule but essentially bureaucratic instrumentalities; initially dominated by the army, they eventually were to come under the control of, and merge with, a refashioned but still very Leninist Communist Party."[38] Was this a function of Mao not wishing to lose power? Were the left thrusts unexpected and undesired by his faction? And therefore was the Shanghai Commune a viable model for China as the most left elements claimed? Or *despite* the Maoists' desire for the commune, was it an institutional form that was just too far to the left for a) the human center in China at that time, and b) the remaining development tasks still facing China and necessarily requiring some viable alliance with the coordinator class? These are questions we are not able to answer with great assurance. We lean to an interpretation favorable to the Maoists, but very cautiously.

In any case, it is clear that whether the establishment of socialism via the commune was possible or not, the attempt to reach a victory short of this via the establishment of three-in-one committees for managing the economy and government—a consolidation of the Maoist elite in alliance with peasant and worker representatives and loyal leftist PLA cadre—failed miserably. In the

---

* Karol's volume gives ample evidence of the scope of the events and of the character of Mao's participation, if all the data can be believed. His (Mao's) public quotation early in the GPCR—"We are seeing the birth of the commune of China of the 1960s and its significance will exceed that of the Paris Commune itself"—is generally indicative, yet even more critical as it tentatively challenges both democratic centralism and the vanguard concept, is the following quote from a Central Committee meeting of August 1966: "We criticized the Kuomintang for its autocratic theory of a single monolithic party; to have no parties outside the [Communist] Party is in fact autocracy; to have no factions inside the Party is a mere optical illusion."

first place, the most left elements of the peasants and workers had just been repressed by the army cadre, thereby weakening the popular basis for this resolution. Second, the coordinators and bureaucrats harbored significant anger and desire for vengeance which would not be satisfied short of their retrenchment at the top of society and the purge of those who had supported the disruptive GPCR. Even the excommunication of Liu Shao-chi, "the number one capitalist roader," was denuded of broader meaning by making his deviance a function *not* of his role in the party and its impact on his ideology, but of a ludicrous formulation that he had been a traitor from the outset. Finally, if one remembers that in a country of 800 million perhaps upward of 100 million are either bureaucrats, coordinators, or members of the professional and managerial middle strata of intellectual workers who might easily come to align with the former elites, and that the left-most elements of workers, peasants and students were demoralized, it is possible to see how the retrenchment after the GPCR could occur.*

That the events should end with the peculiar death of Lin Piao and a propaganda story that he was a "capitalist roader" from the outset, an idea whose falsity is so transparent that the ease with which the bureaucracy was able to get the population to repeat it endlessly to visitors is quite frightening, is really testimony to the extent to which Chinese politics have always been authoritarian and top-down, and the Chinese populace subject to institutional

---

*The essay by Eduardo Masi in *Power and Opposition in Post-Revolutionary Society* is relevant to this argument. Consider the following assertions, for example (p. 75):

"The majority of people over forty years old in the urban middle class sincerely feel that the present situation represents a thaw. And they have not shied away from paying for what they regard as this liberation by handing down death sentences against young workers who 'rejected discipline,' 'sowed discord and indolence,' and demanded access to culture, thus threatening their own privileges...." "Recent directives condemn the tendency of the peasants to waste time in recreational and cultural activity...." "Professionalism and order have also been bolstered in the factories, at the cost of disbanding the revolutionary committees...in compensation, the workers, unlike the peasants, have obtained some wage increases."

relations in no way conducive to on-going critical and open debate and analysis.* One might reasonably argue that Mao's good intentions aside, his willingness to resort to extra-party institutions was too little too late. To fix the system only from within the system, to push it to the left only from within institutional forms that were intrinsically rightist, and to do this while often extolling the negative forms, was too contradictory to succeed.**

But what of the many upheavals and ideological formulations put forth during the period of struggle? What might have been the impact of these upon the consciousness features of the human center of Chinese society? First, Maoism became almost synonomous with the thesis that socialist development is characterized by active class struggle. The prevalence of this thesis was certainly to the good. But that the classes were misidentified as proletarians and capitalists, and that the non-class agents of history such as political elites, sexes and different ethnic minorities were not recognized as being critical forces in social change, has been and will continue to be horribly disruptive to potentials for progress toward socialism.

---

*If one reads carefully the essay, ''Whither China'' published by the Sheng-Wu-Lien organization and interprets in light of a broader class analysis, their view, as written, accords fairly well with our own. Consider for example these excerpts:

The January Revolutionary Storm was a great attempt by the revolutionary people under the leadership of Chairman Mao, to topple the old world and build a new world. The program of the first great proletarian political revolution was formulated at that great moment. Chairman Mao stated: "This is one class overthrowing another. This is a great revolution." This shows that the Cultural Revoluion is not a revolution of dismisisng officials or a movement of dragging out people, nor a purely cultural revolution, but is "a revolution in which one class overthrows another." With relation to the facts of the January Revolutionary Storm, the overthrown class is none other than the class of "bureaucratism" formed in China in the last 17 years....

Why did Chairman Mao, who strongly advocated the "commune," suddenly oppose the establishment of the "Shanghai People's Commune" in January? This is something which the revolutionary people find hard to understand.

Chairman Mao, who foresaw the "commune" as the political structure which must be realized by the first Cultural Revolution, suddenly proposed: "Revolutionary Committees are fine."

That Maoism and in particular the ideology of the GPCR has focused on the need to eliminate a number of inequalities that traditionally are not recognized as class differences and therefore not considered serious, including those between mental and manual labor and town and country, is all to the good. And similarly the challenge to the idea that the advance of the productive forces of a society is the key to the enactment of socialist economic relations is a powerful and important one. Emphasis on the quality and direction of development of economic relations between people is critical to the development of a socialist perspective and should be an

...Why cannot communes be established immediately? This is the first time the revolutionary people tried to overthrow their powerful enemy. How shallow thier knowledge of this revolution was! Not only did they fail consciously to understand the necessity to completely smash the old state machinery and to overhaul some of the social systems, they also did not even recognize the fact that their enemy formed a class. The revolutionary ranks were dominated by ideas of "revolution to dismiss officials" and "revolution to drag out people." The wisdom of the masses had not yet developed to the degree at which it was possible to reform society....

To truely overthrow the rule of the new aristocracy and completely smash the old state machinery, it will be necessary to go into the question of how to evaluate the past 17 years. This is also a major problem of fundamentally teaching the people why it is necessary to carry out the Cultural Revolution, and what its objective is.

To make the revolution really victorious, it will be necessary to settle the question: "Who are our enemies, who are our friends?" This "paramount question of the revolution" requires that we make a new analysis of Chinese society, where "a new situation has arisen as a result of great class changes," so as to revise the class standings, rally our friends, and topple our enemies.

(Sheng Wu-lien, "Whither China," in *China: The Revolution is Dead, Long Live the Revolution,* Black Rose, Montreal, 1979, p. 156, 157,165. Similarly, Gerard Chaliand has a critical assessment that minces few words:

> "The little that can be said about China without fear of error shows at least a few points which make short work of the pious image cherished by a goodly number of Mao's unconditional admirers. The personality cult of Mao Tse Tung; absurd, Stalinist-style accusations against political opponents after their fall (Lu Shao Chi, Lin Piao); a limitation of criticism of Russia to the post-Stalin era; extremely sharp and clearly defined hierarchies

ideological holdover for at least some of the peasants and workers who participated in the GPCR. That the old dogmas are now back in command in China does not negate that their sway over the populace may be weaker there than in any other coordinator country precisely due to the impact the GPCR had on people's thoughts. And in the same vein, all the rhetoric about the idea of the commune itself, about the "right to rebel," and about the need to oppose bureaucracy and even the party itself will no doubt provide the jumping off point for any future efforts at a truly revolutionary socialist transformation in China. Another factor on the negative side, however, which we discussed last section, is the considerable confusion introduced over the idea of right and left errors by the notion that the latter are only disguised versions of the former, and the parallel problem of secrecy and manipulation that was rampant even in the most democratic stages of the process.

Finally, there were at least temporary institutional gains which won't fade entirely from the memory of the Chinese population no matter how reactionary the new state may turn out to be. The existence of massive coalitions of movements in both the cities and countryside, often remarkably critical of the party and coordinator elites and eager for socialist policies, is unprecedented in post capitalist transformations that have had time to stabilize. Closing schools, establishing revolutionary committees, employing wall posters by the millions as well as opposition newspapers and pamphlets, the establishment of the three-in-one committees, and especially the abortive establishment of the Shanghai commune*
and perhaps (if some commentaries are to be believed) of certain others as well, were all major and important steps that can't help

within the leadership, suggesting that China's presumed grass-roots democracy has very narrow limits; and last but not least, a foreign policy and official diplomacy attentive not to the development of revolution but to the interests of the state."
(*Revolution in the Third World*, Viking, NY, 1977, pp. 162-3)
*Consider both in regard to the lasting impace of the commune idea and the assessment of the left Maoists' intentions the following excerpt from a Red Flag article by Cheng Chu Su, perhaps a pseudonym in the spring of 1966:

"We have been racking our brains for years to find a remedy to the danger of a split between the proletarian state and the masses, while the answer to this problem has existed since 1871

but find a place in the collective memory of the Chinese peasants and workers.

Nonetheless, there is no way to avoid the conclusion that the period ensuing at the beginning of the seventies and extending into the present has seen a steady entrenchment of the coordinator class and bureaucratic elite to the point where the likelihood of continuing struggles *within* the institutions of the Chinese state and economy are doubtful, save between elites. Any additional pressure for socialist outcomes would seem to us likely to come only in the form of new revolutionary non-party, non-state opposition to the now seemingly stable bureaucratic coordinator society.

### The Current Period

It seems to us that in 1969 and 1970 the attempt at a left consolidation after the GPCR failed. For reasons already mentioned the Maoist political elite was more or less isolated from widespread popular support and therefore relatively easy prey for the bureaucratic and coordinator elements. The Nixon visit and detente with the U.S. led by Chou and approved at least in appearance by Mao, signalled the rightist trend in foreign policy. The death of Lin and the removal from positions of leadership of upwards of a third of the Maoist cadre and loyal PLA forces signaled the turn-around in domestic relations. A rapid rehabilitation of "rightists" who had been the subject of severe criticism and a quick substitution of the refurbished party and other prior institutions for the three-in-one committees put the lid on the process. Lin's death and repudiation as a "capitalist roader" nailed it down.

The left's last stand appears to have occurred after Chou died but before Mao died, around the effort to link criticism of Teng Hsiao-ping to a criticism of Confucius and to the repression of rightists who demonstrated in support of Chou after his death. Apparently, the return of Teng Hsiao-ping, the second capitalist roader, was too much for Mao, even in his rightist mood. But resistance was finally quite futile. Whether the Gang of Four

and we need only adapt it to our conditions... In the commune the proletariat was the master... The leaders were elected by the workers and submitted to their control; they could by law be recalled and dismissed by the masses..."

actually tried some sort of coup or was simply rounded up by Teng after he gained the strength to do so, is quite peripheral to the main occurrences. For since 1976 there has been a trajectory toward rightist consolidation for bureaucratic elements, the extension of coordinator privileges and economic dominance, a reactionary foreign policy, and perhaps some liberalization for the intellectual and otherwise middle level sectors of the society. The retrogression to old schooling policies, to discipline in the work place, experts extolled over reds, and economics over politics, as documented by Charles Bettleheim in his essay "The Great Leap Backward," attest to the non-socialist orientation of the current situation.* Though some care is certainly in order, it would seem reasonable to assert that the coordinators and bureaucrats have the situation well in hand—all that remains is Liu Shao-chi's posthumous resurrection and perhaps even some level of attack on Mao himself.

Indeed, even as we put closing touches on this chapter reports are emerging from China regarding the initiation of a public trial of the Gang of Four and numerous other Cultural Revolution leaders, purges of perhaps millions of individuals who rose in stature during the Cultural Revolution, and even an initiation of criticism of Mao himself. This last trend may prove the only reliable—even if circumstantial—evidence for our complimentary interpretation of Maoist intentions. For if Mao and the Maoist faction were generally motivated not simply by a desire to maintain their own political dominance, but actually to move China as rapidly as possible toward socialism, then likely as not his writings and the memory of his life is going to have to be discredited, however cautiously. Should the "socialist thrust" of his lifework be substantial and evident enough, he will finally have to be denounced in one style or another.

But the flow of reports of lower level purges is itself quite indicative as to what is transpiring. In particular a report in the *Washington Post* of Sunday November 9, 1981, says that the Tachai Commune, once put forward as a model for all of China, is

---

*To provide flavor Bettleheim reports a Radio Peking broadcast in August of 1977 saying, "Rules and regulations ought never to be eliminated. Moreover with the development of production and technology, rules and regulations must become stricter, and people must follow them precisely. This is a law of nature. As production develops so must we establish rules and regulations that are stricter and more rational."

now denounced as a sham whose high yields were accomplished only by severe coercion. Many of the leaders who rose to prominence in the commune are being reduced in power and influence and finally purged from positions of authority. Topped with the spectre of a trial of the Gang of Four and other past radical leaders that appears to be as inhumane, manipulated, pre-determined and phoney as the best of Stalin's show trials (or of those of Judge Julius Hoffman in Chicago, for that matter) and in which the defendants may even appear in cages, the testimony and tapes be doctored, etc., it appears that the new government has certainly consolidated its hold and stabilized relations in its own favor. Whether there are stirrings beneath the surface and flaws in the armor of Teng's regime is impossible for outsiders to know. In particular, what is happening in Teng's prisons and punitive camps and especially in the Chinese countryside is, as always, closed to any meaningful outside view.

This study of Chinese economic history has hopefully clarified the importance of taking into account the existence of a third potential ruling class as well as the impact of institutional forms on economic relations. Even the most positive possible interpretation of Maoism leaves the important criticism that by employing the democratic centralist form and economic institutions furthering coordinator class power and by teaching that the struggle was between socialist and capitalist roaders, the left faction severely undercut the viability of its own efforts to support a revolutionary option. Obscuring all errors as intentionally reactionary and aimed to reassert capitalist relations, maintaining high level secrecy and therefore being forced to provide the populace with the most ridiculous propaganda stories, and failing to initiate centers outside the party and the coordinator relations of the economy until it was too late—these are failings which flowed from the underlying conceptions and institutional choices of the Chinese Communists, not solely from the exigencies of difficulties of social transformation in a complex setting.

### The Chinese Revolution and Kinship Relations

As with Soviet history, some describe the tremendous gains for women under Chinese socialism while others emphasize the continuation of patriarchy and the ways in which the Chinese revolution has been woefully incomplete for women.[39] We set ourselves in the midst of this debate arguing that there was a revolution in kinship relations in China, but that the new kin relations remained patriarchal. An analogy to a more familiar part of U.S. history might clarify this seemingly contradictory view.

Surely every analyst would agree that the Emancipation Proclamation, the Civil War, and Reconstruction eliminated slavery in the United States. Yet just as surely all but the most abject apologists for racism would admit Black gains were uneven. Residues from slavery persisted, and in any case the new community forms were far from the ultimate in justice, equality, or liberation. In our view there was a revolution in the community sphere but the new community relations still embodied oppressive distinctions among different groups of people. Slavery was abolished but the new social relations between Blacks and whites were still racist.[40]

## A Revolution in Kinship But Patriarchy Persists

In order to fathom the immense advance Chinese women have made and its limitations, one must have some idea of the barbaric conditions women endured before the revolution. "Bride-price and wife-selling were normal; so too were polygamy and concubinage. Girls were sold or kidnapped into prostitution."[41] A poem by the third century poet Fu Hsuan lost little relevance till well into the 20th century:

How sad it is to be a woman
Nothing on earth is held so cheap
No one is glad when a girl is born
By her the family sets no store.[42]

Footbinding, wherein girls' feet were tied to make adult women walk on stumps swaying in what Chinese men considered an attractive fashion, was but one of the more grotesque oppressions women endured. As Delia Davin quotes a Chinese woman's account:

My feet hurt so much that for two years I had to crawl on my hands and knees. Sometimes at night they hurt so much I could not sleep. I stuck my feet under my mother and she lay on them so they hurt less and I could sleep.

But by the time I was eleven my feet did not hurt and by the time I was thirteen they were finished.[43]

Women endured such barbarities in what were short and horribly constricted lives—when they lived at all. For beyond foot-binding, female infanticide was common as well. There can therefore be no denying the magnitude of gains that have been won. As Judith Stacy writes, "From female infanticide to crippled feet to child bride sale, wife beating, polygamy and more, Chinese women tasted no end of bitterness in their short, mostly poverty ridden lives." Yet, "today the situation is unrecognizably transformed..."[44]

With the revolution came a ratification of the dissolution of Confucian patriarchy that women had long struggled for. The new constitution declared: The People's Republic of China abolishes the feudal system which holds women in bondage... bigamy, concubinage, child-betrothal, interference with the marriage of widows and the execution of money or gifts for marriage shall be prohibited."[45] As with ending slavery in the U.S., the abolition of Confucian patriarchy was not immediate everywhere and resistance was great in some areas. Nor were the changes a "maximalist program" for women's liberation. But they did revolutionize if not fully liberate the situation of women. In time, "the husband-wife relationship replaced the father-son as the pivotal relationship in the family structure."[46] The Confucian patriarchal family as the center of both kin and economic life, and simultaneously as the locus of female bondage, was removed from history. As women entered the public workforce, gained some political and economic leverage, escaped barbarism of the past, and challenged many myths and cultural norms, there was certainly revolutionary advance. As Barbara Ehrenreich correctly pointed out: "There is a difference between a society in which sexism is expressed in the form of female infanticide and a society in which sexism takes the form of unequal representation on the Central Committee. And the difference is worth dying for."[47]

Yet the results to date have not been liberating in the way a feminist would finally require. The commune structure in the countryside, for example, offers many new opportunities for economic participation by women, but hasn't eliminated unequal divisions of familial labor, or altered women's status as sole nurturer. And as we found in the Soviet Union, "women uniformly perform the traditionally female tasks. All nursery and kindergarten teachers are women. Domestic production inside and outside the home is typically defined as women's work."[48] And "the largest concentration of women is employed in jobs often identified as 'female preserves' such as textile manufacture, food processing, and banking."[49] Finally, the continuation of unequal remuneration for men and women—not for the most part resulting from unequal pay for equal work but from unequal work—perpetuates female financial dependence.[50]

And while leadership roles in the political sphere are no longer totally barred to women, Batya Weinbaum reports that only 10% of the members of the Communist Party are women.[51] A more subtle source of differences in power between Chinese men and women is that the post-revolutionary kinship network has remained patrilocal. That is, when men and women marry it is invariably the woman who moves to the man's town.[52] Whether we understand this as a continuation of male-bonding and the "traffic in women" or not, there is no question that it is detrimental to women's advance. For women are invariably torn from their closest and most powerful personal ties and moved to where they have no reputation, no friends, and no contacts. Therefore young brides become psychologically and materially dependent upon their new husbands and their social ties. Judith Stacy remarks that the continued universality of this practice seems indicative not only of the maintenance of patriarchy, but of the relative absence of struggle against it by either men or women.[53] As the Chinese express no concern over exclusive female nurturing of children—"they believe women are better with children and seem to let it go at that"[54]—so they accept the movement of women to the man's locale. "There is evidence that Chinese women and men alike accept the asymmetrical arrangement unquestioningly. It is thought to be 'natural,' like sex differences, and that is simply that."[55]* But to move beyond the relatively simple task of demonstrating that qualitative changes for the better

*Another implication of patrilocal marriage is that to train women in a commune is often seen as a poor use of resources, as women will take the learning away when they marry. "We don't like to train young women for skilled jobs because when they marry they usually leave the village and take the skill with them. It is not worth it to us." (A production brigade manager quoted by Steven Butler in *The Washington Post*, Sunday, Oct. 19, 1980). Given the importance of patrilocal habits, Elizabeth Croll's report that in the model commune Dazhai (Tachai) "There has been some

have taken place while sexism and patriarchy persist, to the more difficult questions of how and why the changes occurred and whether or not China has progressed as far toward "woman's liberation" as the conditions of the Chinese human center allowed, we must delve into some of the history of these developments.

### Early Tendencies Toward Women's Liberation

By the turn of the century the Confucian kinship system in China was under serious pressure. Among the most notable factors undermining traditional patriarchal forms were the influx of Western norms and imperialist employment of women outside the home.[56] The longstanding tradition of exemplary individuals and small groups of women resisting extreme forms of oppression even by suicide has received less attention. In any case, even though attacks on the Confucian order were sporadic and uncoordinated, by the early 20th century cracks began to appear and Sheila Rowbotham even quotes one writer in 1920, Tai Chi-t'aio, who "thought a revolution for sexual equality between men and women would precede the workers' revolution for economic democracy."[57] Mao Tse-tung himself, sensitized by his own account to the indignities suffered by women at the hands of men in his own family experience, was moved to write at the time:

> If we launch a campaign for the reform of the marriage system, we must first destroy all superstitions regarding marriage, of which the most important is the destruction of the belief in predestined marriage. Once this belief has been abolished all support for the policy of parental arrangement will be undermined and the notion of the 'incompatibility between husband and wife' will immediately appear in society. Once a man and wife demonstrate incompatibility, the army of the family revolution will arise en masse and a great wave of freedom of marriage and freedom of love will break all over China.[58]

attempt to establish matrilocal marriage as a normal rather than an inferior form of marriage" is quite important. It not only demonstrates the correlation of radical advances in different spheres, but sheds further light on one of the contemporary projects of the new Chinese leadership—claiming this leftist model project was a fraud and purging its leaders, as described last section. Elizabeth Croll, *Feminism and Socialism in China*, Schocken Books, New York, 1980, p. 330.

In tune with this sentiment, the Communists passed a law in 1931 making sweeping changes in marriage practices in the areas they controlled. The principle was to be "free association in marriage."[59] But just three years later a new law was passed "which protected the Red Army soldiers from divorce by their wives."[60] For while the first law had aroused much support by young peasant women, it elicited resistance from men and older women as well. The latter groups proved more powerful, but the struggle was apparently a complex one: "Needing to attack the traditional family, if only to liberate women to mobilize their political and economic support, afraid to antagonize the men upon whom the liberated women were justifiably wont to vent their long pent up fury, the CCP leadership was racked with conflict and dissension on the issue."[61]

We can organize our analysis of trends in the alterations of kinship relations after 1949 in the same periods we used for examining the Chinese economy and polity. In the immediate aftermath of the triumph of the revolution "the family revolution was a political priority."[62] The marriage law of May 1, 1950 prohibited polygamy, concubinage, child betrothal, marriage by purchase and infanticide, abolished the category of illegitimate offspring, and also guaranteed women the rights of divorce, remarriage, property, and inheritance. In other words, the society-wide revolution included substitution of a legal framework of monogamous, conjugal, family relations with a variety of rights guaranteed to women, for the legal framework of Confucian patriarchy. Moreover, the legal changes were no mere paper reforms. There was also an immense popular mobilization to enforce the newly proclaimed rights for women. Judith Stacey reports that of the 21,433 divorce cases reported in the People's Daily, 76.6% were initiated by women.[63] But it was also the case that Chinese kinship relations remained patrilocal and patriarchal. That there were powerful forces at work opposing those mobilized to convert the legal gains into reality is indicated by the following quotation from a peasant woman during the period: "To get a divorce, there are three obstacles to overcome: the obstacle of the husband, the obstacle of the mother-in-law, and the obstacle of the cadres. The obstacle of the cadres is the hardest to overcome."[64]

In the next period, from 1953 to 1957, "Learn from the Soviets" was a motto as well suited to the kinship sphere as the economy. The worst reversal was with regard to divorce where the requirements were made much more stringent, and propaganda linked marriage with socialist advance and divorce to bourgeois reaction. Reports suggest that this policy on divorce has persevered to the present so that even women complaining of serious physical abuse have little likelihood of gaining a divorce hearing.[65] Moreover, the justification for this reactionary policy shift is almost as disturbing as the shift itself. The argument was that women were now liberated. Once the backlog of unjust, forced marriages inherited from pre-revolutionary days had been swept away, marriages were presumably the product of free choice between equals who should be held to their bargain. As a Chinese saying expresses it, the notion is that "if one makes one's own bed, one must lie in it."[66] It hardly merits pointing out the contradictory logic of excusing evidence of continuing sexism on grounds of the difficult historical legacy while justifying closing an important escape hatch for women on grounds that they were liberated when they chose to get married in post-1949 China.

Whether or not it was an intended by-product of the communization drive during the Great Leap Forward, it is a fact that this "economic" policy entailed an important increase in the potential for women's political participation and economic independence. The trend toward collectivization of "house-hold" tasks freed a portion of women's time that had previously been unavailable for political participation, although, to the extent that political practice remained sexist, there were continuing obstacles to prevent women from utilizing this new potential. Further, the fact that work points were calculated and wages paid individually rather than by family unit provided women for the first time with real income creating a measure of economic independence. But again, to the extent that wages and the responsiblity for children were not equal for men and women, and that the margin above subsistence was slim in general, Chinese women could still not translate this increased potential for economic independence into reality. Batya Weinbaum concludes that while there were gains for women as a result of these policies, predominantly in a first recognition of the potential and sense of contribution and worth of many women, the situation never approached one in which women were freed from the necessity of pooling their income with their husbands, or in which women's unequal dependence on men was seriously challenged.[67]

But as the New Economic Policy unfolded in the early sixties, and Liu Shao-chi, Chou En-lai, and Teng Hsiao-ping gained ascendancy, Chinese kinship activity was pushed in a reactionary direction again. Propaganda, party policy, and Chinese schools all returned to praising the traditional role of women, and emphasizing the importance of preserving marriages and the family. "As senior editor of *Women in China*, Tung Pein promoted the back-to-the-home revival by printing articles such as 'Women Live for the Purpose of Raising Children,' 'Women Should Do More Family Duties,' and 'For Women to Engage in Enterprises is Like Flying Kites Under the Bed.'"[68]

As with other periods of the Chinese Revolution, it is difficult to obtain a clear picture of the participation and situation of women during and after the Cultural Revolution and into the present. However, Elizabeth Croll's major study, *Feminism and Socialism in China*, does provide some information and insights. She describes how during the period of the Cultural Revolution there was an effort to redefine the meaning of "class consciousness" *to incorporate* a new attitude toward the equality and potential of women. In a sense this was a counter to earlier feminist approaches which attended to the situation of women in relative abstraction from class issues. It was argued that the earlier approach denied women any role in broader political and economic concerns by overly focusing on the household. Obviously there are two interpretations to the ideological change Croll records. On the one hand, it could have been an honest attempt to overcome the narrowness of an apriori "feminist" approach. On the other hand, it could have served to divert attention from concerns most directly bearing upon the lives of women so as to undermine any autonomous women's organizations and struggles. A statement such as the following appearing in 1964 would lend credence to the latter, critical interpretation:

> We must have a clear historical materialist viewpoint and make a clear class analysis of the ideological viewpoints of the women of different periods and different class positions, and not raise questions of conception of life and viewpoints of love, which have a strict class nature, as abstract, general questions of the 'female and the male.'[69]

Likewise, the general effort to move women from the home into the broader realms of social life doesn't seem to have ever been sensitive to the fact that this could have an anti-feminist as well as a pro-feminist component. That is, women often resisted the urgings that they diminish their focus on family matters and this was invariably attributed to their backward feudal consciousness. However, what if reticence to enter the public realm stemmed from an accurate recognition that one would simultaneously lose whatever minor dignity might have attended doing a good job at home, while gaining nothing more than a new kind of subservience outside the home? If the push for women to work was motivated more by the desire to raise production than concern for improving the status of women, reticence would not necessarily be due to backward consciousness at all.

Yet there are other indications which suggest that while these questions bear heavily on the overall character of women's experience in China, something else was also operative during the years of the Cultural Revolution. Croll reports that while before the Cultural Revolution, women "were carrying the hoe outdoors, handling the pot indoors, and taking a back seat in a meeting or in study,"[70] and that when women did attain positions of leadership it was invariably over other women and in matters confined to women's concern, there was a change during the new upheaval:

> As part of the cultural revolution to heighten class consciousness and involve as many as possible in political affairs, the government encouraged women to participate and lead in political and state affairs and recommended that all bodies and associations take steps to include women in their affairs.[71]

Croll also reports that "nearly all the films, operas and ballets produced during this period had a clear message for women. They reminded women that lots of them had led bitter lives when political power had been the monopoly of the warlords, the landlords, and factory employers."[71] Women were portrayed as courageous and politically astute leaders. These reports take on added significance when we remember that Madame Chiang Ching was directly responsible for cultural affairs during the period, a matter we will discuss further next section. Croll also relates instances of women and men making bargains over how to handle both household and non-household responsibilities and quotes a long report by Jan Myrdal concerning the great gains women had made by 1969 in a village he was visiting. The women related to Myrdal that the struggle had been difficult and had involved recognition not only of their right to participate in meetings but of the parallel necessity for men to concern themselves with housework and childcare if this right was to become meaningful.

Yet even in this period the motive force behind the advance was a class analysis and a desire for women to particpate so as to advance society. There was never any analysis pointing to kinship relations as themselves central to the determination of China's character. Quite the contrary, the idea was to communicate that women's oppression was rooted in mutable class relations not in what the Chinese called permanent biological relations. Of course, this was progressive and served to free women from beliefs that their lot was preordained as in Confucian ideology. But it nonetheless ignored that the mutability of sexual oppression could have its roots not only in the fact that economies alter, but in the fact that the social relations of kinship can alter. The absence of a focus on kinship relations meant that the issues of sexuality, nurturance, and violence against women never came to the fore. Regrettably, this meant that however substantial the gains of the period their foundation was not solid. To redefine class consciousness to include an awareness of the situation of women may at first appear to be a "totalist" innovation. But in a society with a level of sexual oppression and mystification as great as China, and in a movement saddled with underlying concepts that retain an economistic flavor even when they are used most flexibly, it was not. Consider the following quotation from a 1973 edition of *Peking Review*:

> We cannot discuss women's liberation, women's independence and women's freedom in isolation. I'm not for what is called women's rights in and of itself, as opposed to men's rights. We cannot make men the target of our struggle. Oppression of women is class oppression. When we talk about this we must remember that the liberation movement of women cannot be separated from the liberation of the proletariat. It is a component part of the proletarian revolution.[72]

Interestingly, according to Croll the anti-Confucian movement of the mid-seventies that constituted the "last gasp" of the anti-bureaucratic, anti-coordinator forces was also a very important movement for the rights and integrity of women.[73] The campaign argued that the view of women as inferior and of the inviolability of a division between home and factory was rooted in the false and feudal philosophy of Confucius.* Though this approach was not new, according to Croll during the campaign it was more thorough going and far reaching than ever before. "For the first time women have been widely encouraged to rediscover and study their own history with a view to understanding the role of the Confucian ideology, its origins, development and limitations in determining the expectations and self-images of women."[74] Remarkably, and with what justification we of course don't know, the parallel campaign against Lin Piao also emphasized that he slandered women, suggested the reimposition of feudal ethics and otherwise accepted and propounded that women were inferior.** Further, the "division of labor within the household and its repercussions for the position of women were discussed in the campaign. It was pointed out that just as women were to be fully integrated into the public sphere so men must undertake their share in the domestic sphere."[75]† Yet, as in the economy and polity, it seems that these far reaching formulations were insufficiently rooted in a long standing approach and in a clear institutional alternative. We know relatively little about kinship policy during the period since the anti-Confucian campaign characterized by consolidation of coordinator economic dominance and bureaucratic political rule. But some information is emerging.

In a long piece in the *Washington Post* of October 19th, 1980, Steven Butler reports recent experiences and interviews in China.

---

*Actually, it is rather unclear just who was behind this movement. It seems at its outset that it may have been Chiang Ching and others on the left—thus their last gasp—but, as it progressed it came rapidly under sway of rightists who used it to promulgate a mechanical materialism and to further denigrate Lin Piao.

**We repeat Croll's assertion with timidity.

†It should be remembered that often rhetorical flourish is aimed more at garnering temporary allegiance from oppressed people than at actually affecting their plight.

The accounts seem reliable and there is high likelihood that they give some indication of what is currently transpiring. It seems that the movement to have women participate in work and the great modernization campaign mesh nicely. For as the men leave the fields for the greener pastures of industry, the women enter farming behind them. "But increasingly, women have been left behind to labor in the fields. In the commune's richest production team, they do virtually all the field work."[76] But gaining a monopoly on menial farm work, whatever advance that may entail, does not lend itself to gaining a sense of equal power and influence. Butler reports asking a woman, "What do you do?" "Me? I don't do anything. I can't do anything. I have no skill at all." "Well, how many days did you work last year?" "About 300." "But what did you do?" "Nothing, I just farmed."[77] The implications of this answer for the position of peasants and of women in society are obvious. Butler goes on to report that even "though women perform most of the agricultural labor, which is the principal responsibility of the production teams, not one of the 96 production teams in the commune is headed by a woman."

Also reported in a *Washington Post* article, this time from the paper of Nov. 12, 1980 and written by Michael Weiskopf, is the recent release of a new Chinese sex manual directed at the broadest possible audience. In a country with such tight strictures regarding sexuality as China, a point we will return to momentarily, this represents a significant step. But does it serve to open a new area for serious critical analysis? With but a short article to go on it is difficult to be certain. While the manual includes explicit pictures of sex organs, there is literally no discussion of the actual practice of sexual intercourse. Furthermore, self-gratification or masturbation, literally translated as "hand lewdness," is castigated for detracting from work and potentially causing impotence and "severe nervous disorder." Proposed remedies to the inclination to masturbate include "washing the feet with warm water before bedtime, staying away from tight fitting trousers and heavy blankets and, of course, 'upholding responsibility for your country and the socialist system.'" Weiskopf quotes the report regarding sexual frequency as saying, "very, very frequent sex right after marriage: that is once every three to seven days," but then as passions cool, "once every two or three weeks." The guideline proposed to determine whether one is indulging too much or too little is the effect on one's ability to work the following day. (At no time does the manual suggest evaluating work according to its effect on one's sex or extra-work emotional life, of course.) Though it is difficult to know exactly what to make of all this, it seems reasonable to assert that beyond the simple fact of its release, this manual will do little to liberate sexuality or the condition of women.


## Conclusion

Before proceeding to a very tentative attempt to interpret and evaluate the history of Chinese kinship development, there is an underside to Chinese kinship history we must not ignore. Much as we wondered about the degree of regimentation in Chinese politics, we sense an unknown quality to the private aspects of Chinese kinship activity.

"In China, the work teams, production brigades, commune, neighborhood associations, state and party now provide more assurance of an individual's right to eat, work, study, survive, and prosper than the family ever did or could."[79] This could simply indicate a collectivist orientation, but it could also be a sign of incredible state power over all aspects of private life. Certain reports and writings on and from China portray a situation in which private relations are politicized and scrutinized to such an extent that private life is just about non-existent.[80] This would not be a mark of sociality, but of authoritarianism. It would mean that whatever the failings of family life might have been in the past, the improvements have had little to do with socialist kinship relations nor were they ever firmly "on the road" to achieving them. The idea that the "personal is political" must not be extrapolated into a view that all privacy is bourgeois, or that long standing relations involving intimacy, love and loyalty are without value. Stories of proletarian paragons asserting that private life is of no consequence next to party life, and of children turning in parents for crimes against the state are frightening if true.[81] If the stories are false and misleading, if the reluctance to dismiss them in the West is a result of deep-seated Western racism and cultural imperialism, that is one thing. But in no case should the actions in the stories be justified as simply the intricate ways in which another society solves problems differently from what we do in the decadent West. Similarly we wonder about the sexual chastity that appears to be the norm in

China. Consider this report from Tamara Deutscher based on impressions during a recent trip to the mainland:

> All contraceptives were, of course, available exclusively to married couples; sex before marriage was an unthinkable, unpardonable offense. If in consequence...an unmarried girl should get pregnant, she would become an outcast. She would be sent to some remote rural area to expiate her guilt. This topic, we felt, was so taboo that it could not even be broached at the family planning clinic. Somewhat later a woman guide, taken aside, was just a little more daring. She explained that no marriages below the ages of 23 for women and 25 for men were allowed. When it was remarked that sexual urges begin much earlier, she answered in a stern voice: 'Not in China.' On this reassuring note our conversation ended.[82]

That the party should govern the norms of premarital sex-life, set ages for marriage and withhold contraceptives from youth is, assuming it is an accurate picture, certainly quite frightening. The correlation of sexual abstinence and authoritarianism in general is often argued. Deutscher reports on a visit to a school for young children in a way that makes one wonder both about that relationship and, more simply, about how the schools, as extensions of kinship institutions, reflect familial norms. The description is also relevant to our hypothesis about trends in kinship likely paralleling trends in economy and polity in the recent period. For we know that the schools were scenes of many progressive alterations during the Cultural Revolution, though now something very different is transpiring:

> 'Two years ago,' explained the headmaster, 'we had an open door policy and accepted all children from the neighborhoods without explanations. But it was unfair to mix children of varying ability. Those doing well were helping the less gifted and thus they were wasting time needed for their own studies. Now we have very stiff competitive entrance examinations every three months, another examination at the end of the academic year, and a final one on leaving school.' ...there is a system of 'spiritual and material rewards.' Any student who does not behave properly or does not perform well is 'persuaded' by his

classmates to improve. In one class 14 boys and girls were watching an experiment in physics and listening to a teacher's explanations. They were all sitting with their hands behind their backs in complete silence. The little desks in front of them were identical: everywhere the pencil box was on the left, then a small inkstand, then something that looked like a sponge and further on a rubber eraser. In the adjoining classroom an English lesson was in progress. Here too desks were identically arranged, except that there was a textbook in front of each child. Answers to questions posed by the teacher were read out of the book aloud in unison by the whole class. Here again hands were crossed behind the backs.[83]

Is this picture frightening due to our cultural biases or a justified concern over State regimentation through the schools and presumably all of private life as well? Regrettably, on balance existing evidence is very disturbing. Likewise, if the perception of extreme sexual chastity is a false one due to the bias of Western eyes misreading a different approach to private matters, that is one thing. But if the perception is accurate, then a Chinese version of Victorian sexual morality is not immune from criticism simply because it exists within a "socialist state"! If human sexual potentials and well being are oppressed in China it would certainly be a very negative reflection on the kinship sphere. Finally, if reports are true that Chinese homophobia is so extreme that homosexuals are sometimes executed, no socialist should ignore the significance of the problem this indicates, much less condone the policy. And under no circumstances should an analysis of homophobia as rooted in patriarchal needs to preserve male/female role dichotomies—needs which might be expected to increase when extra-familial requirements tend to call these roles into question— be misinterpreted as a justification for such acts. Rather this analysis shows that the basis for extreme homophobia should it exist in China or elsewhere is quite likely to be an active pressure to maintain patriarchy rather than only a residual feudal or other peripheral mythology one might hope to see overcome in the immediate future. With these caveats, we are ready to offer a very tentative interpretation and evaluation of Chinese kinship policy.

First of all, it is obvious that how far and fast to push the transformation of kin relations was always judged by the Chinese political

leadership in the context of winning and consolidating the revolution as a whole. This was clearly the case concerning divorce policy
in the liberated zones during the early 30s and during the first eight
years after seizure of state power as well. And we do not wish to suggest that this is an inappropriate approach, assuming an appropriate
understanding of the meaning of "the revolution as a whole." Far
from it, we find this the only justifiable approach from a totalist
point of view. But agreeing that kinship issues should be determined in the context of overall societal transformation is not the
same as granting license to backslide on struggle over sexual divisions whenever that struggle is disruptive of political unity or economic aims, any more than one should forego struggle to attain
socialist goals in the economy or polity even though they may sometimes cause dissension among men and women. One must always
ask, political unity for what? What kind of revolutionary gains?
What kind of overall socialist transformation? Changes in whose
interests and fought for by what political constituency whose unity it
is crucial to preserve—and what kind of unity, gained at what cost?
A totalist approach recognizes the entwined character of change in
all four spheres of social life and sees the arrows of causality between
those spheres running in all directions. In assessing strategy
regarding kinship it is certainly true that one must not only ask
about effects on attaining ends within the kinship sphere. One must
also ask about effects on revolutionary aims in other spheres. For
example, how might failures to transform kinship relations *impede*
struggles for socialist rather than coordinator gains within the economy? Only when it is understood that anti-patriarchal revolution is
as much a part of and integral to the ultimate socialist program as
anti-feudal and anti-capitalist revolution, and that women are at
least half the revolutionary constituency, is it possible to proceed to
the practical questions of 1) the extent to which sex-based oppression is relatively active among the potential revolutionary constituency at any moment, 2) the extent of sexist limitations among sectors of the human center critical to a feasible strategy for socialism,
and how these might be overcome, and 3) the proper
program—both pace and scope—of kinship activity to pursue as
part of a totalist strategy of struggle. Naturally if demands at the
base of a society don't challenge patriarchy at its roots and if constituencies of the left are in fact sexist and threatened by anti-patriarchal formulations—both male and female constituencies—a

revolutionary movement cannot simply leap to a maximalist feminist stance. However, to forego efforts to move toward such a stance and also alter the basic makeup and orientation of the movement is inexcusable on two counts. For by such delay not only is the future well being of half the population being sacrificed to a continuation of patriarchy, but the possibility of fully liberating economic, political, and community relations is also being severely undermined. For as we have argued before, patriarchal kinship forms don't prepare citizens to be socialist workers, voters, artists, or friends. Even more, in a revolutionary situation where the road to socialist aims is difficult in all spheres, propelling change in kinship can act as a positive spur to progress elsewhere. These are the kinds of calculations of interrelationships between spheres that are not often made when the focus is instead immediately drawn solely to matters of how making demands about kinship might alienate this or that male constituency, and yet these calculations are critical to success.

Although we have far too little information to make a final judgment, it seems likely that in pre-revolutionary China the arousal of feminist concerns was generally limited to abolition of the most grotesque Confucian extremes rather than patriarchy per se. Furthermore, it appears highly likely that a "mass line" challenging patriarchy in all its forms would have been exceedingly difficult to maintain without sacrificing the allegiance of great numbers of men (and older women) critical to the highly activated anti-feudal and anti-imperialist struggles. If the kind of hostility toward women even among cadre described by William Hinton in the village of Long Bow was in any way typical, the condition of the pre-revolutionary Chinese human center was likely not appropriate for more than an anti-Confucian "mass line" on kinship.[84]

Yet there were women who asserted a feminist orientation and they were, it is essential to add, faced with great difficulties. "When they tried to participate as equal members of an integrated movement, they were required to overlook their specific oppression as women. Yet when they organized autonomously around women's issues, they were considered divisive of the cause of class solidarity."[85] Whatever the short run difficulties of developing a feminist analysis and program for the revolution, the failure to move resolutely in this direction couldn't help but create problems in the future. Indeed, to the extent that autonomous organizing and especially the extension of women's demands beyond anti-

Confucianism was prevented, one has to suspect the motivation of the pre-revolutionary period Chinese Communist Party. For it becomes doubtful whether their intentions to institute revolutionary alterations in the economy and polity ever extended fully to the kinship sphere—and more, given the character of the eventual revolution that was made in economics and politics, their reticence about kinship revolution might have had more than one basis: preservation of male supremacy *and also* preservation of social- ization practices well suited to an authoritarian future. Put in other terms, the question is, did the Party ever really envision an end to *all* forms of social inequality between men and women such that they would follow the path of such liberation wherever it would lead, or were they only concerned with eliminating barbaric excesses and appealing to women for their support on political and economic issues?

When we review the history of post-revolutionary policy we find supporting evidence for both interpretations of the Party's real intentions regarding the kinship sphere. But recognizing the fact that the Chinese Communist Party was far from monolithic, it seems most likely that there were factions within the party supporting each view. And since the periods of most active struggle against patriarchy appear to have coincided with periods when the Maoist faction was in ascendancy, and periods of backsliding on kinship issues tended to coincide with periods when the right faction of the Party dominated, it seems reasonable to conlude that the "two line struggle" within the Party—between a socialist and a coordinator/bureaucratic road—extended into the kinship sphere as well. Since the bureaucrats and coordinators within the Party were well served by the authoritarian psychological dynamics that patri- archal kinship forms generate, they would have had little reason to sponsor an upheaval in the kinship sphere that would have under- mined their positions in the political and economic spheres, as well as their positions as men, regardless of how resolutely they may have opposed the excesses of Confucian sexism. The Maoist faction, on the other hand, would have had more reason to support a deeper anti-patriarchal struggle because these dynamics would have strengthened them in their struggles against the right faction of the Party and the coordinators in the political and economic spheres respectively, by helping them to win allegiance of an immense constituency of women. This would certainly have made the Maoist faction more natural allies of any women (or men) truly committed to an anti-patriarchal brand of socialism even if important segments of the Maoist faction were not so committed themselves on kinship issues. That is, there could have been both an opportunist and a principled motivation for such alliances. In any event, the fact that the ups and downs of kinship development roughly coincided with similar shifts in economic policy and mirrored the changing fortunes of political faction fights suggests that these factions, whether consciously or not, had totalist programs which spanned Chinese society and recognized that stabilization in any one sphere required compatible stabilization in others.

If this is so it means that just as the position of workers and peasants and the potentials for their democratic participation were dependent on the good will of a particular political faction—the Maoists—in which they were ill-represented, on whom they could exert little direct pressure, and from whose deliberations they were excluded; so too was the situation of women dependent upon this same group of revolutionary men. If such a narrow, centralized approach was necessary due to conditions of economic poverty and illiteracy, it certainly should be made clear just how tenuous was the likelihood of its ultimate success.

Moreover, it would seem that in the kinship sphere, just as in the political and economic spheres, if the revolution was ever to be pushed toward socialist outcomes it would have been critical to encourage development of a militant, autonomous feminist movement as well as women's caucuses within the Party. That such movements would likely have been anti-authoritarian and anti-coordinator/pro-working class is all the more in their favor from our perspective. It is difficult to tell whether their absence was solely a function of patriarchal values or also of a recognition of their potential implications in spheres other than kinship. But in any case, with the advantage of hindsight, we might conclude that just as Mao's contribution to fighting party and coordinator power was impeded by many aspects of orthodox Marxist Leninist theory and thus too little too late, so too was his (or Chiang Ching's) attempt to unseat patriarchy in the Party and in China as a whole, if any such attempt was ever really consciously made. Limiting policy to abolishing Confucian excesses well beyond the time when that was all that could realistically be proposed, exclusive reliance on integrating women into the economy, lack of support for autonomous women's organizations that would really address the broad dynamics of kinship activity, and a theoretical framework that refused to recognize the importance of male/female categories in and of themselves, all contributed to the inability of the Maoist faction to struggle against patriarchy in China. All this can be said at the same time that we recognize that Confucian patriarchy was overthrown and the situation of Chinese women immeasurably improved.

## The Chinese Community Experience

This fourth section concerning the Chinese revolution must regrettably be quite limited. Not only is the "raw data" from which we must construct a history of Chinese community relations sparse and untrustworthy, but there are a number of reasonable ways to interpret it. We will confine ourselves to a discussion of religion in post-capitalist China as an important aspect of community relations we have not treated in our other historical analyses, and an analysis of the Maoist faction's cultural policy which we find to be quite non-progressive compared to their general political "line."

### Religion

In 1927, regarding the place of religion and its treatment by revolutionaries, Mao Tse-tung wrote, "it is the peasants who made the idols, and when the time comes they will cast the idols aside with their own hands."[86] Like other Marxist Leninists, Mao felt that religion would pass away with the development of socialism, and that this could occur through a process of free choice that didn't unnecessarily impose upon those with "backward" consciousness. In 1957, after solidification of the new government, Mao wrote:

> We cannot abolish religion by administrative decree or force people not to believe in it. We cannot compel people to give up idealism, any more than we can force them to believe in Marxism. The only way to settle questions of an ideological nature or controversial issues among the people is by the democratic method of discussion, of criticism, of persuasion and education, and not by the method of coercion or repression.[87]

So in 1957 the supposition was still that religion would become moribund and pass away without coercion from above. Yet scanty though the evidence may be, it suggests that whatever Mao's intentions may have been, the evolution of religious policy under the Maoists was less benign than these quotations suggest. In 1927 Mao urged that in criticizing religious traditions one should "draw the bow to the full without letting go the arrow, and be on the alert."[88] Yet one commentator suggests:

> Drawing the bow to the full without letting go the arrow does not begin to suggest the tremendous program of ideological education, propaganda devices, and subtle pressures used on religious leaders. There were lectures and study groups for everyone, regular visitation of those who were rightly suspect, reform by labor for those who never gave in or who openly criticized. Party officials preferred the first two categories involving discussion, criticism, and persuasion, as they put it, except when dealing with those who were 'stubborn' or 'obstinate.'[89]

Thus with respect to the relatively small Christian Church in China, the preferred approach seems to have been to struggle within the ranks of Christians for the redefinition of church beliefs and customs. For example, certain Protestant leaders met with Chou En-lai in 1950 and the result was a new Church Manifesto that presumably revolutionized the formerly reactionary content of religious belief.[90] Among other things, the new church called for "vigilance against imperialism," "support for the government's policy of agrarian reform," on-going self-criticism within the church, and "anti-imperialistic, anti-feudalistic, and anti-bureaucratic capitalistic education, together with such forms of service to the people as productive labor, teaching them to understand the New Era, cultural and recreational activities, literacy education, medical and public health work, and care of children."[91] Though this document can be cited as evidence that the Maoists were not interested in eliminating religion but only sought to insure that it evolve in tune with changes in the new society, it can also be interpreted as the first step in the process of completely subordinating the Church to the party line. Given the Maoist acceptance of Marxism Leninism's analysis of religion, there was obviously no call to discuss how people's legitimate needs for a place of worship or religious philosophy would be met in the new society, but only how the Church could be brought to fit within the strictures of party policy. The following description of St. Michael's Church in Peking during the early 1950s is indicative of the fact that religions were not totally unimpeded in the practice of their beliefs.

Red flags draped the main altar, communion rail, vestibule, and the path to the gate. The church columns were hung with streamers proclaiming 'Long live Mao Tse-tung,' 'Long live Communism,' and 'Christians Unite—Chase out the Imperialists.' Pictures of the Sacred Heart, the Virgin Mary, and various saints were replaced inside and out by pictures of Mao and other leading Communists.[92]

But replacing one orthodoxy with another is not the same as people revolutionizing the religious sphere of their lives from below, as the drop in worshippers at St. Michaels from over four hundred to under one hundred testifies.

The point is this: It is impossible for us to know exactly how the discussions and relations between the party and the various Christian churches proceeded. That the Christian church in China was an imperialist importation in the first place, that it had frequently been in the forefront of the ideological opposition to the revolutionary movement, that its leadership in all probability had little regard for the masses of China is all quite likely. None of this would have made the discussions about the future of the Christian Church in the new China easier. On the other hand, there was obviously a small minority of Chinese who were believers in Christianity and who chose to meet their spiritual needs through this institutional vehicle. Moreover, not all the priests could have been as distant from and callous to the needs of their parishioners as the top leadership. All we are pointing out is that the ideological stance of the party by not recognizing the legitimacy of religious needs made progressive relations more difficult than they need have been. The fact is that only a very few priests joined party-inspired religious movements and many were suppressed or arrested for their efforts in resisting these movements. That some were reactionary recalcitrants is beyond doubt. But that some were pushed toward an opposition stance by the fact that any cooperative relationship with the party was inevitably an admission that most issues sacred to the Church were illegitimate, and thus that religious leadership was illogical and due to be extirpated as painlessly as possible, also seems likely.

But a much larger yet even more obscure story concerning community relations in China revolves around the more traditional Eastern religions practiced by so many more Chinese. In 1949, Mao himself estimated that there were perhaps 100 million practicing Buddhists in China and 20-30 million followers of Islam. Yet many more were associated with the thought and practice of Confucianism. In 1940 Mao wrote:

> China also was a semi-feudal culture...whose exponents include all those who advocate the worship of Confucius, the study of the Confucian canon, the old ethical code and the old ideas in opposition to the new culture and new ideas.... This kind of reactionary culture serves the imperialists and the feudal class and must be swept away. Unless it is swept away, no new culture of any kind can be built up.[93]

Certainly, any socialist movement, no matter how much it emphasized the need for cultural pluralism and freedom of choice regarding religion, would face difficult issues in trying to evolve a policy toward a system of thought as oppressive in many respects as Confucianism. For within the Confucian philosophy five great relationships were stressed. The first emphasized that the oldest son must obey the father. The second admonished that the wife must obey the husband without hesitation. The third taught that elder brothers must be obeyed by younger brothers. The fourth established that age was to be determinant concerning the direction of authority between friends. And the fifth held that all subjects were to relate to the emperor as sons to their fathers. To judge whether there was anything within Confucianism which might have served religious or philosophical ends under socialism is beyond our knowledge. To evaluate whether Chinese conditions necessitated a harsh reaction against Confucianism, from the top down, is again beyond our knowledge of the relevant conditions. But as clear as it is that the Maoists turned shrines into schools, museums, and cultural centers; passed laws against public Confucian displays; worked strenuously and forcefully to prevent the continued use of agricultural lands for burial plots, and generally succeeded in eliminating the public influence and trappings of

Confucianism in China; it is not so clear that Confucianism's basic ideological hold has been uprooted nearly so comprehensively. And whether an anti-Confucian campaign that seriously assessed the legitimate needs Confucianism met, rather than only its role in justifying illegitimate hierarchies, would have been more powerful in not only uprooting Confucianism, but laying the ground work for development of new philosophies and moral codes is also uncertain but quite possible.

Taoism and Buddhism too seem to have been largely eliminated as visible movements and while certain reactionary ideas have thus been overcome, so too has there been a great loss of philosophical and religious wisdom. In any case, even the very brief survey we have made suggests that the Maoist approach to religion was a fairly straightforward application of orthodox Marxist ideas within what was in all likelihood a particularly difficult set of circumstances. While the effort to employ a non-confrontationist strategy may or may not have been as patient as we could hope for under the circumstances, there is little doubt that the goal was always the eventual demise of religious movements from China's past. It has been suggested that the motivation guiding this hostility toward non-Maoist philosophical and religious orientations was the view that Maoism itself was an encompassing orientation requiring the population's undivided commitment.

> The Chinese revolution isn't an occupation for amateurs. It isn't addressed to one part of the individual or to a certain section of the population. It takes possession of the whole being, of the masses in their entirety. It demands total and unreserved commitment. It is impossible to be revolutionary and religious at the same time. This would mean believing in two different religions.[94]

For according to orthodox Marxism Leninism, all pre-socialist religions are just one or another form of idealism only supporting reactionary class structures. As such, there is nothing positive to be learned from them or any reason to tolerate their existence any longer than necessary. In this view the religious question is reduced to the practical matter of how to eliminate religious institutions and beliefs most effectively and with least disruption. There is no need to build new religious institutions preserving the best of old religious forms, etc., because there are no legitimate spiritual needs to be met under socialism. And there is no need to study philosophical idealism because eventually everyone will embrace Marxism-Leninism Mao Tse-tung thought.

Perhaps most interestingly, it was the Maoist faction of the party that held to this analysis most firmly, and the period of greatest leftist influence, the Great Cultural Revolution, was also the period of most extreme repression of those who still held religious views.

> The Red Guards invaded the homes of religious believ-
> ers of all kinds, destroying sacred scriptures, art, and
> literature. The owners of such objects were often pub-
> licly harassed and persecuted. Churches, temples, and
> mosques were also broken into and stripped of many of
> their books, art works, and other religious objects, and
> were used as meeting halls.... To the Red Guards religion
> was an evil which had to be immediately eradicated,
> rather than a superstition which could be tolerated until
> it withered away.[95]

That religion was either "an evil to be eliminated" or "a superstition" that could be allowed to "wither away," but not a realm of human activity that might be revolutionized and play an important role in socialist cultural and philosophical advance was as axiomatic for Maoists as for all other orthodox Marxists, and for similar reasons. The community sphere was not seen as autonomous but only in term of its relations to economics. One didn't have to worry about intricate issues of spiritual needs, but about the relations of religious policies to class interests.

## Maoist Cultural Policy

The Maoist "line" on artistic practice (and indirectly on left culture of all types) was first elaborated in a clear and comprehensive form in Mao's "Talk at the Yenan Forum on Literature and Art," in May 1944, where he asserted: "The purpose of our meeting today is precisely to ensure that literature and art fit well into the whole revolutionary machine as a component part, that they operate as powerful weapons for uniting and educating the people and for attacking and destroying the enemy and that they help the people fight the enemy with one heart and one mind."[96] The rest of his talk detailed an approach to making art and literature effective propaganda for a revolutionary strategy for taking power. The first theme Mao stressed was the need for artists to learn from the peasants and workers so that their works might address the concerns of these classes and speak with a voice suited to their tastes. Next, Mao stressed that while art must be rooted in the daily affairs of the people, it must go beyond reflecting them to perfecting them at the same time. "Writers and artists concentrate such everyday phenomena, typify the contradictions and struggles within them, and produce works which awaken the masses, fire them with enthusiasm and impel them to unite and struggle to transform the environment." "Popularization" was another key theme, as was the practice we now call "consciousness raising."[97] The overall approach was, in Mao's words, "utilitarian," in the sense that art and literature, and presumably culture in general, were to be understood predominantly as tools of revolution. Mao argued that "in literary and art criticism there are two criteria, the political and the aesthetic." For him it was the political that was most important, and which therefore had to receive priority in guiding both the artist and the art critic. "Some works which are politically downright reactionary may have a certain artistic quality. The more reactionary their content and the higher their artistic quality, the more necessary it is to reject them." The point of the talks is clear. With regard to art and culture in general, "politics must be in command." What serves the needs and interests of the party and of the working and peasant classes is good; what opposes those needs and interests is bad. Mao asked what one would think of the doctor who didn't care what the impact of his or her work was on the lives of the citizenry, and argued that artists must also look at their work not abstractly, but always in context of its impact on the political landscape of class struggle. The artist is not to write spontaneously, but self-consciously to achieve political goals. Moreover, nowhere in the talks is any significant attention given to the worth of art or culture as other than a vehicle of revolutionary aspirations.

The artistic policies of the Cultural Revolution therefore have their roots in Mao's own pragmatic philosophy of cultural creation. When Chiang Ching suppressed "feudal forms," attacked "bourgeois artists" for their lack of revolutionary consciousness, reduced the number of allowable theatre and art works to a mere handful, and then virtually inundated all of China with these meager offerings, she was doing nothing inconsistent with the ideas Mao had laid down decades earlier. Moreover, this appeared to be a leftist policy of employing the energies of a special elite to eliminate reactionary ideas and forms as quickly and effectively as possible. That it also ran roughshod over a realm of human creative expression, lent energy to a similar suppression of cultural and aesthetic creativity in ethnic and religious forms, and thereby alienated large portions of the population, apparently went unnoticed by the Maoist leadership. So these Maoist cultural policies were in fact rightist (whatever their motive). For they not only suppressed diversity, they alienated many who might otherwise have supported other leftist policies of the Cultural Revolution. Ironically, the Cultural Revolution was a period of leftward thrusts in every area except culture.

The answer to why the Maoists had a rightest cultural policy alongside their generally leftist approaches to economic, political, and kinship issues lies in their failure to make any break with the traditional views of Marxism Leninism on culture. Whereas the Maoists forged creative revisions in other parts of the paradigm, they continued to deny the independent importance of community and culture, viewing them only instrumentally. The fate of the Maoist faction is in part a testimony to the fact that the Leninist goal of pursuing the homogenization of cultures precludes even the possibility for an intelligent approach to community matters no matter how well motivated a group of practitioners might be.

Though we will return to these issues from a positive angle in our chapter on socialist community as we envision it, to close this discussion it might be useful to note that though the left in China, the Maoists, had a right cultural policy, it does not follow—as some have in fact proposed—that the current leadership has a left cultural policy. It is true that in the period after the Cultural Revolution and the demise of the Gang of Four, the apparatchiks of the party and the coordinator class presided over a brief period of cultural liberalization in China. But as we pointed out in earlier discussions of class relations, the purpose of this has nothing to do with furthering political democracy, creative expression, or cultural diversity for workers and peasants. All that was desired was to remove certain restrictions from the shoulders of the Chinese political and economic elites themselves. And though there were some momentary gains for other citizens, more or less as a byproduct, the limits of this are easy to predict. Indeed, in an article dated March 22, 1981 from Peking, Michael Weisskopf reports in the *Washington Post* that the liberalization seems to have come to an end. His article suggests that a new crackdown has begun in response to growing criticisms of the government and its new policies. We can only hope that when a new revolutionary opposition arises in China, it will have a much richer and more pluralist approach to problems of art and culture than the Maoists were able to elaborate.

# 4
# THE CUBAN EXPERIENCE

> Let us go,
> Fiery prophet of the dawn,
> On silent spatial roads,
> To free the verdant isle you love.
>
> Che Guevara

Our overall assessment of post-revolutionary Cuba is that the outcome is still ambiguous: whereas certain characteristics are indicative of a stabilization of a coordinator social formation, there are also important dynamics still pressing in a socialist direction. In other words, unlike the Soviet Union where a non-socialist consolidation occurred relatively early in the post-revolutionary process, and unlike China where a more prolonged struggle between coordinator and socialist tendencies has only recently ended with a non-socialist stabilization of all spheres of social life, as Cuba enters the eighties there has still not been a clear-cut coordinator *or* socialist consolidation.

In our view this implies that Cuba remains an unstable society imbued with characteristics of two different social formations. Moreover, the history of the struggle between the socialist and coordinator "roads" in Cuba has been marked less by relatively clear cut periods in which all spheres of social life were moving together, first in one direction and then in the other, as was the case in China especially, but more often by conflicting trends between different spheres occurring at the same time as well as simultaneous conflicting trends within spheres themselves. All this makes for a complicated story that is difficult to relate and still waiting for an ending.

In this overview we offer only a few illustrations of the complexities and ambiguities we will find. The Cuban revolution was neither a revolution against capitalism for socialism, nor politically led by a communist party. Instead the revolution was directed at overthrowing a tyrant and imperialist domination, and the new communist party of Cuba was slowly built after the revolutionary triumph. Moreover, the twists and turns in the long and often torturous political process of constructing a traditional Leninist communist party (that did not hold its first party congress until sixteen years *after* the triumph of the revolution) frequently conflicted with contrary trends in the economic spheres and other trends in the political sphere itself. For instance, from 1965-1970 when the party building process of erecting a full hierarchical internal structure and establishing a vanguard relationship to the "masses" was literally put on hold, the mass political organizations were neglected and weakened as well. During the major period from 1970-1975 when a traditional communist party rapidly emerged as the dominant political force, there was also increasing emphasis on re-building the mass political organizations. And from 1975-1980 when the bureaucratic weight of a traditional communist party has been greatest, perhaps the most revolutionary development in post-revolutionary Cuba has also emerged in the political sphere—the organization of *Poder Popular*, people's power.

Economic developments have frequently displayed similarly contradictory trends. When the left economic program championed by Che Guevara in the mid sixties was launched by Castro during the latter half of the decade, the increased emphasis on moral incentives and building a "socialist man" was accompanied by a diminution of workers' participation in economic decision-making. While ordinary workers and peasants were increasing political power through the institutions of Popular Power in the mid seventies, a new coordinator class was being trained, rewarded, and given increasing control over the operation of the economy at the same time. And finally, after twenty years of rejecting the use of markets during which time there was no sign that the managerial fraction of the coordinator class held any significant power vis-a-vis the central fraction of the coordinator class and the political elite, the most recent evidence indicates that Cuba may well be beginning the eighties by embracing a classic policy of economic "liberalization" which would grant the managerial fraction of coordinators economic dominance.

We shall see similar contradictory trends within kinship and community relations as well as overall swings between socialist and non-socialist definitions in the kinship and community spheres that were frequently out of phase with policy swings in the political or economic spheres. For instance, the emphasis on creative socialist culture at the time of the 1967 OLAS conference was separated by only a few years from the heaviest repressive realist phase symbolized by the sordid Jaime Padilla affair which unfolded during the peak of left economic policy. And at the same time that anti-patriarchal aspècts of the new Family Code such as stipulation of equal male responsibility for household chores were being debated in all the mass organizations and confirmed as the law of the land, patriarchal relations were being given a legal re-enforcement in the economy by formally banning women from a list of male job preserves.

We close this overview with a reminder that however disappointing we might find some of the results of the Cuban revolution, and to whatever extent we might decide that Cuba's quest for socialism is still unfulfilled, the Cuban revolution, like that in Vietnam, Angola, Mozambique, and other third world countries, successfully extricated the society from direct imperial subjugation. In a sense it removed Cuba from the Latin nightmare Castro so eloquently described in his 1962 speech on "The Duty of the Revolutionary":

> The summary of this nightmare which torments America, from one end to the other is that on this continent... of semi-colonies about four persons per minute die of hunger, of curable illness or premature old age. 5,500 per day, two million per year, ten million each five years. These deaths could easily be avoided, but nevertheless they take place. Two thirds of the Latin American population lives briefly and lives under constant threat of death. A holocaust of lives, which in fifteen years has caused twice the number of deaths of World War I...it still rages. Meanwhile, from Latin America a continuous torrent of money flows to the United States: some $4,000 a minute, $5 million a day, $2 billion a year, $10 billion every five years. For each thousand dollars that leave us there remains one corpse. A thousand dollars per corpse:

that is the price of what is called imperialism! *A thousand dollars per death...four deaths every minute.*

And thus whatever failures Cuba might have experienced consolidating socialism, there was more than enough success to warrant Castro's injunction in the same speech:

> The duty of every revolutionary is to make the revolution. It is known that the revolution will triumph in America and throughout the world, but it is not for revolutionaries to sit in the doorways of their houses waiting for the corpse of imperialism to pass by. The role of Job doesn't suit a revolutionary. Each year that the liberation of America is speeded up will mean the lives of millions of children saved, millions of intelligences saved for culture, an infinite quantity of pain spared the people. Even if the Yankee imperialists prepare a bloody drama for America, they will not succeed in crushing the peoples' struggles, they will only arouse universal hatred against themselves. And such a drama will also mark the death of their greedy and carnivorous system.[1]

## The Cuban Political Experience

Like the Soviet Union and China, Cuba has a single, democratic centralist political party. But in spite of this important similarity, there are many aspects of Cuban political history that are quite different from that of China and the Soviet Union. Moreover, in the critical area of extra-party political institutions, Cuba appears to be blazing a new path much more conducive to socialist outcomes.

### Building the New Communist Party

In the anti-Batista movement there were two dominant organizations. Neither was Marxist or socialist. The Directorio Revolucionario was urban based and participated in organizing the urban underground and insurrection. The leader of the Directorate was Jose Antonio Echeverria, who formed the organization largely from Cuban university students in 1955. According to K.S. Karol, the organization was mostly "an alliance of fighters and not of politicians"[2] more concerned with Batista's overthrow than with what was to be done after Batista was gone. The relationship between the non-Marxist Directorate and the old Cuban Communist Party (Partido Socialista Popular, or PSP) was often hostile. The Directorate "fought against communist ideas at the university on the grounds that these allegedly turned the students from their prime objective, the struggle against Batista.[3] The second anti-Batista organization, the July 26th Movement headed by Fidel Castro, was also non-socialist and non-Marxist at the outset. "It was ultra-left with respect to strategy and tactics... [but] the program of 1953 contains no Marxist intentions whatever. It contains nationalistic, populist, and anti-imperialist elements [but] there is no trace of Leninist features."[4] Furthermore, and this was critical to later developments, "the movement had no institutional character whatsoever. It was a creature of its founder [Fidel Castro] and of his closest confidants.... " Despite having no "clear-cut class basis," and being defined by "the person of the leader and the mutual enemy," which served as the "decisive integrating factor" for what was otherwise but an "amorphous coalition,"[5] by engaging in rural guerrilla warfare the July 26th Movement built a strong base of support among the peasantry and rural proletariat and became the leading organization in the war to defeat Batista.

The last important revolutionary organization in Batista's Cuba was essentially a non-actor in the anti-Batista struggle. The PSP was an old-style Communist Party whose membership was very loyal to the Soviet Union's line. Its heroic days were the 20s and 30s, but since then it had been involved in much bureaucratic manuevering including (on and off) collaboration with Batista to avoid government attacks on unions where it held significant influence. As Karol reports, "the PSP saw fit to collaborate with Batista on the eve of, and during the Second World War, and it opposed Fidel's armed struggle until his triumph was a foregone conclusion."[6]

Though modern circumstances dictate that Castro discuss pre-revolutionary history in ways that remove doubt over the credentials of old PSP members, the actual merging of these three organizations into a new Cuban Communist Party was a very difficult task. Where the Bolsheviks outlawed and suppressed competing leftist parties rather quickly after their revolution, and the Chinese Communists prohibited development of other leftist parties within the territory they controlled, the Cubans chose amalgamation of the three major revolutionary organizations after their revolution was won, in the face of great mutual hostility, and when one organization held literally 100 percent of the political power. Why? The most plausible explanation comes from Castro himself.

In 1959 the revolutionary leaders of the July 26th Movement found themselves in a very difficult situation. Castro had virtually unchallenged and unlimited power, but no political apparatus to speak of. There was a small and politically inexperienced rebel army, experienced in guerrilla warfare, but not in administering a new society. The movement had no well-defined social base; middle class, worker, and peasant elements were rapidly diverging in their conceptions of what should be done.[7] Fidel's reaction was essentially to start over from scratch. He destroyed the old July 26th Movement by merging it into a new political organ. He described this sequence of events to Simone de Beauvoir in an interview in March, 1960:

> Why, we asked, doesn't the Revolution have cadres, no apparatus? Allowing for all differences, the replies coincided in the essential points; the Movement of July 26th, which had carried the Revolution, did have an apparatus but it was a petit bourgeois apparatus which could not keep up with the continuation of the revolution, with its radicalization and particularly with the progressing agrarian reform. That is why the Movement was dropped.[8]

With the old state apparatus destroyed and only the PSP politically structured, there was a threatening organizational vacuum. Perhaps new organs could have been built from the bottom-up, but in the pressing historical circumstances of the day it doesn't seem likely. In any case, Castro opted for the creation of a new political apparatus, a new party, but from the top-down. The first merger, the Integrated Revolutionary Organization (ORI), was announced on July 26th, 1961. It was effectively a simple summation of the memberships of the three prior organizations yielding a total membership of 15,000.[9] But as the PSP membership was organized and disciplined, its leadership was able to quickly seize preponderant organizational influence in the new amalgam. This predictable outcome became publicly apparent when the character of the leading element of the new organization was made public:

> On March 8th, 1962, the composition of the National Directorate of the ORI was announced in Havana. Previously this organization had functioned in a somewhat mysterious fashion, and no one outside could have told you precisely who were its leading officials. Now it was officially made known that its 25 members would be made up of thirteen delegates from the old July 26th Movement, ten from the old PSP, and two from the old Directorio.... It looked very much as if the Communist old guard would have the upper hand in the new organizations.[10]

Karol's prognosis seems even more reasonable in light of the PSP's still greater comparative advantage at regional and local levels. But this was not to come to pass. Very quickly internal feuding and factional hostilities were brought into the open as Castro publicly castigated the leadership of the ORI and sanctioned its rapid destruction. In its brief tenure the ORI had presided over what is sometimes called the period of mini-Stalinism in Cuban history, to be discussed in more detail later. Fidel's own characterization at the time is instructive.

> The party secretaries have erected an arbitrary dictatorship over the whole country. Everywhere it has come to despotic measures, to individual acts of violence. Honest revolutionaries have been delivered up to the terror... These gentlemen, who want to force their ideas on others, can scarcely be distinguished from Batista and his hangmen.
> (The organizational secretary of the party) Anibal Escalante has called a sect of privileged people into life. The provincial secretaries have behaved like Gauleiters. Nepotism and terrorism are spreading. We have founded the ORI but excluded the revolutionary masses. We don't have an apparatus but a yoke, a straightjacket...What does that mean, Integrated Revolutionary Organizations? The only ones who have organized themselves here were the people of the PSP... It's the same in every province: who became the party secretary of ORI? The former

provincial secretary of the PSP. It is the same thing in every local chapter: who became the local secretary of ORI? The former local secretary of the PSP!... If we look at the results we are forced to conclude: that is a pile of shit.[11]

But however great was Castro's hostility to the PSP bureaucracy and thus to the ORI which was dominated by that bureaucrcy, some form of political apparatus had to be created in the vacuum left when the ORI was disbanded. By spring 1963 the United Party of the Socialist Revolution (PURS) had been established in which the overbalance of PSP leadership was corrected. But it wasn't until 1965 that the Central Committee and Political Bureau of the contemporary Cuban Communist Party were formed.[12] Moreover, the five year delay in the party's formation was followed by another five years in which the party organization was allowed to stagnate. The first meeting of the Central Committee itself took place a full year and a half after its creation and then it was only to respond to a Venezuelan attack on Cuba before the Organization of American States. The new party organization was neither an important policy-making nor administrative organ during the remainder of the 1960s. Instead the political leadership of Cuba was dominated by July 26th veterans  who apparently functioned with little or no connection to their party base throughtout the rest of the 60s.

But whatever the reasons for the delay in constructing the Party during the latter half of the 60s, there was a drastic shift in party building policy at the start of the 70s. Not only was a large democratic centralist political apparatus quickly constructed in the early 70's, but much of the old PSP leadership was ressurrected. Although we will discuss the most important reason the party was hauled out of dry dock and steadily strengthened as an ever more powerful and influential actor on the political scene in the economic section to follow, it is worthwhile to note here that the number of members increased to 101,000 in 1971, 122,000 in 1972, 153,000 in 1973, 186,995 in 1974, and 202,807 in 1975.[13] This process—so long delayed during the first decade of the revolution—was finally culminated in late 1975 when the first Party Congress "elected 1) the new General Secretariat, expanded to nine members, with Fidel as First Secretary and Raul as Second Secretary...and including for the first time three 'old' Communists... 2) the new Political Bureau, expanded to thirteen members including three 'old' Communists, and 3) the new membership of the Central Committee expanded to 112 members including 26 'old' Communists."[14] The result was that the Cuban Communist Party, for all the unique aspects of its historical evolution, had become in many respects similar to the Soviet and Chinese parties by the late 1970s.

So what is the meaning of the history of party building in Cuba? The Cuban revolutionaries chose the different route of merging parties rather than outlawing all but the July 26th Movement after the revolution. Certainly this was a choice with much to recommend it. On the other hand, they did not opt for simply allowing the organizations to continue functioning separately in open competition with one another. This "optimal course," from the point of view of democratic debate, was likely excluded for fear that open signs of disunity would have been dangerous in face of the severe U.S. threat, counterproductive in face of a lack of any significant socialist consciousness in the population, and risky in light of the possible emergence of anti-Communist rhetoric (in political in-fighting) which might have fanned anti-socialist fears still strong in Cuba's citizenry. Furthermore, in orchestrating the merger, the Fidelistas did not get what they had hoped for in the ORI and likely concluded that a relatively long period would be required to build an apparatus whose ideology and policies they would be happy with.

A positive assessment would say that policy toward party development in the mid to late 60s was motivated by a desire to prevent the development of a large dictatorial, bureaucratic apparatus. One might interpret it as a holding action until the development of new popular leadership and mass political organs could be achieved. On the other hand, this policy led to the most politically centralist period of the Cuban revolution. Our evaluation is not too dissimilar to our evaluation of the Great Leap Forward in China: the elite rule in the late 60s in Cuba was beneficial insofar as it was a left political faction in control and the size of the bureaucratic apparatus was kept minimal. But the extreme centralism had negative consequences as well. For example, there was little increase in mass political participation much less any move toward creation of institutions of direct people's democracy. Was it impossible at this time, or simply beyond the conceptualization of the leadership? If the motivation was to hold off a rightist political consolidation until the political maturation of the masses was sufficient to preclude any form of bureaucratization, then why were there so few policies aimed at increasing mass participation during this period? On the other hand, the period of left-centralism in the 60s does not appear to have been a function of any drive toward dictatorship. For if that had been the case, institutions furthering the likelihood of popular participation and democracy at the base would have been blocked for good where, in fact, such institutions were promoted during the 70s, as we shall see shortly.

The picture that emerges is complex. The leadership appears to have been committed to popular democracy, yet doubly hampered in pursuing such a course. If the party had operated more democratically in the late 60s, it would likely have been old PSP members who would have benefitted, something the Fidelistas were quite adverse to allowing. Moreover, the situation with respect to the population as a whole was also constraining. The populace was immensely supportive of Castro himself, as a leader who was coming to socialism in a sense right along with the people. At the same time, the brevity of the Cuban struggle against Batista meant that neither revolutionary ideas nor experiences were widely shared among the populace. As a result, democracy within the political apparatus would have benefitted the PSP cadre, and democracy at the base may well have led to pressure for many rightist policies, or so the leadership might rationally have believed. But whatever the reasons, and however restricting the circumstances the failure to increase mass participation during the "holding pattern" in party building left the Cuban polity less well equipped to resist the impact of a rapidly growing party bureaucracy during the 70s than it might have been. As we will see, the increased emphasis on mass organizations and the advent of Poder Popular (People's Power) have served as strong counter-trends to party political domination in the 70s, but in retrospect one can only wish that these policies had been unleashed as early as 1965, and that building a massive traditional Communist Party had been shelved forever.


## Building Democracy at the Base?

The major Cuban mass organizations are the unions, the student organizations, the Committees for Defense of the Revolution (CDRs), the Small Peasant Association (ANAP), and the

Women's Federation (FMC). The last three organizations were all created, and even the unions and student organizations were drastically restructured, after the triumph of the revolution. But while all these mass organizations played a major role in carrying out the agrarian and urban reforms and defending the revolution from internal and external reaction in the first few years of the revolution, they were allowed to stagnate in the latter part of the 60s. We can only speculate about the reasons for neglecting the mass organizations during a period when, as we shall see, the Cubans were consciously pursuing an economic path opposed to the traditional "socialist model." One gets the impression that the leadership was committed to bringing about a revolutionary transformation of the human center by direct appeal to the Cuban masses. All previous institutions were unnecessary, if not suspect for their less than revolutionary characteristics. Mass mobilization based on direct appeals from the highest leadership to the revolutionary zeal of the masses, rather than institutionalization, was the order of the day. In any case, regardless of the reasons, even the fledgling mass organizations—offspring of the revolutionary triumph—suffered as a consequence.

In the early 70s all the mass organizations were, however, revitalized, at least to some extent. Whereas in the late 60s they had all degenerated to vehicles for arousing and mobilizing masses of people to carry out policies conceived from above, in the 70s, according to Arthur MacEwen's study, "The re-emphasis of the mass organizations has meant most importantly that they have begun to have a decision-making role. Specifically, for example, a new process has been developed of circulating draft laws for discussion and amendment among the local units of the relevant mass organizations."[15] In this section we will focus on the CDRs as the mass organization that fits most neatly within the political sphere. According to MacEwen, it was  "in the CDRs—the neighborhood clubs—that the increase in local authority seems most apparent. Today the CDRs take the responsibility for innumerable local tasks from organizing the innoculation campaigns to keeping the streets clean and in repair; from organizing night guard duty to recycling bottles and newspapers, from organizing neighborhood political discussion groups to making sure women have had recent pap smears."[16]

The idea of the CDRs certainly seems like a step toward popular political participation. The actual list of subjects for CDR attention makes one wonder about limitations on their activity that might serve to channel CDR energies toward relatively inconsequential matters. The most significant policy proposal to be actively debated in the CDRs was the new Family Code debated for over two years before being enacted on International Women's Day, March 8th, 1975. But we will discuss this in greater detail in the section on Cuban kinship. However, MacEwen's discussion of the limits on trade union debate over new incentive and wage policies in the early 70's is relevent to the question of limitations in the CDRs as well.

> There were, to be sure, limits on the extent of this discussion. Carmelo Mesa-Lago has pointed out that the context for the discussion preceding the Congress was determined by the issuance of nine theses by the central authorities of the labor unions. Furthermore, he offers the following statement by a leader of the labor unions (Lazaro Pena) as an indication of the limits of the pre-Congress debate. 'During the discussion (of the theses) every worker who wanted to criticize the administration about concrete aspects of its work was given a chance to do so... No political, moral, or any other pressures were applied to him... The criticism voiced in the assemblies (however) cannot be viewed as the expression of any anti-administration trend, because, if such were to develop, the CTC would be the first to oppose it... (The kind of criticism expressed was) in line with the role which the trade union can and should play.'[17]

### Poder Popular—People's Power

But beside revitalizing the mass organizations in the early 70s the Cubans also introduced a major, totally new political institution they call "poder popular," or people's power. It was tested in Matanzas Province in 1974 and extended to the rest of the country in 1976. According to Arthur MacEwen:

> The creation of a new system of political organization—known as Poder Popular—has been an

event of considerable importance. On one level, it would appear that Poder Popular is simply the introduction in Cuba of a form of electoral politics similar in structure to electoral systems in several other countries. Local assemblies are popularly elected; they elect district assemblies; and so on up to a national assembly. However, even if there were nothing unusual in the Cuban system, its introduction after many years without mechanisms of popular participation would indicate a significant shift in Cuban politics.[18]

But according to MacEwen the popular assemblies are involved in a far broader range of political decision-making than is usual to such institutions, including having a say in the operation of economic units in their regions and in national economic matters. "This means that the Cuban political process is much wider than in many nations, and as compared to political processes in capitalist nations, is not constrained by the independent activity of economic units."[19]

Carmelo Mesa-Lago reports that in the 1976 elections 10,725 delegates were elected to municipal assemblies for 2½ year terms, who in turn elected 1,084 deputies to provincial assemblies, who finally elected 481 deputies to the national assembly for five year terms.[20] He also reports on the character and mandate of Poder Popular (which he calls the OPP) in a way that corroborates MacEwan's description:

> There are OPP at three levels: municipal, provincial, and national. The first two are entrusted with the municipal and provincial management (through administrative departments) of services such as schools, day-care centers, hospitals, stores, hotels, restaurants, cinemas, night-clubs, transport, retail trade, housing, public utilities, and sports as well as some local industries... The municipal and provincial OPP also select the judges for the corresponding people's courts. The national OPP is the National Assembly... it elects the Council of State from among the Assembly members, appoints the People's Supreme court magistrates and the Attorney General, approves the *general outlines* of domestic and foreign policy, economic plans,... and can modify or revoke decree laws.[21]

There is no doubt that Poder Popular is a significant new democratic and participatory political institution. But the extent to which popular opinions are really expressed and acted upon through its structures is harder to determine. It is certainly the case that there is still a dominant central leadership that coincides with the Party Politbureau. The National Assembly is also predominantly white, with members who are "typically male, either an executive, a technician, or a military man, above forty years of age, educated, and a member of the party,"[22] despite Castro's complaints about similar election results in the Matanzas trial run. Apparently, without quotas, consciousness and social relations in the human center of Cuban society still militate for elite male representation. That quotas could have been discussed and hopefully agreed to as a means of insuring a more representative outcome, seems a reasonable complaint. But there are further restrictions on the operation of Poder Popular which must be recognized. According to Mesa-Lago:

> ... the powers and functions of the municipal and provincial OPP are significantly limited: (1) the party decides in practice who is eligible to sit in and chair the OPP Executive committees which are the decision-making and managerial bodies of poder popular; (2) the OPP manages the least important sectors of the economy (basically services) while the central state agencies administer the key industries, all agriculture, mining, and finance; (3) the size and distribution of resources allocated to the services administered by the OPP are also centrally decided; (4) the Council of State supervises the OPP, and the Council of Ministers (through the state central agencies) exerts direction and supervision over the OPP administrative departments, and, (5) the OPP decisions can be annulled, modified, or revoked by other organs of the state and the government.[23]

MacEwan also equivocates somewhat in his assessment of Poder Popular while praising the move toward greater democracy:

> Poder Popular, and Cuban politics generally, are not immune from criticism as vehicles of democracy. The rights of opposition are seriously limited in Cuba. The PCC dominates political affairs, and there is no pretense

that the electoral system allows leeway for altering that basic fact of Cuban life.[24]

But the positive side of the inauguration of Poder Popular should not be underestimated even while recognizing these restrictions on its operations. Candidates for office need not be Communist Party members.[25] This means that the institutional structure of Poder Popular exists parallel, rather than subordinate to the party apparatus. In discussing the Chinese experience we specifically criticized the left faction for never extending their opposition to political bureaucracy beyond disagreement within the party to the point of establishing extra-party organizational forms except in the case of the explicitly emergency and transitory "three in one committees" of the last stages of the Cultural Revolution. It would appear that the Cubans have taken that additional step toward creating permanent extra-party political institutions. This becomes especially striking when one notes that representatives at each level of Poder Popular, in addition to holding the political position of representative, also continue to hold their prior job—if this is possible—and in any case continue to be reimbursed at the same salary they had been receiving before.[26] This is a powerful obstacle to the growth of a privileged bureaucracy. As Castro expressed it, "We see this [Poder Popular] as a large school of government, because everyone will have to participate in the organization, direction and control of all these activities."[27] Furthermore, each week delegates must set aside consulting hours for their constituents, and once every three months they must meet with every CDR within their municipality to receive criticism and instructions from their constituents. Finally, and most important, at every level constituents can recall any official by a simple majority vote.[28] This skeletal structure represents a serious attempt at direct democracy wherein each level of decision making is composed of representative, recallable bodies accountable to the whole consitutency at that level. That the skeleton may not yet have flesh in the sense that there may still be institutional and psychological restrictions on the scope of its operation and the process by which people are chosen to positions, by no means diminishes its significance as an alternative to a Communist Party-dominated bureaucratic state apparatus.

But before drawing tentative conclusions on the state of the Cuban polity, there is another area of Cuban political life we must mention. There is still nothing resembling an independent, free press in Cuba, and there does appear to be a considerable police apparatus. At the same time, it is difficult to assess where one should lay the blame for these phenomena. For beyond any trend toward coercion within the political process of Cuba, there is also an external cause for repressive developments. For decades the U.S. has sent in disruptive forces led by CIA agents, has made numerous attempts on Castro's life and has generally represented a quite real, rather than imagined threat to the Cuban revolution. None of this would make the presence of a powerful repressive apparatus that was undermining the democratic aspects of Poder Popular by creating a climate of regimentation less regrettable. But it would bear upon where blame should be laid, and offer hope for a brighter future when such external pressures might be diminished or no longer exist.

## Concluding Evaluation

The situation within the political sphere does not appear to have stabilized. On the one hand there is the negative trend of the on-going bureaucratization of the party and its continued primacy with regard to all major policy matters and economic planning. In Cuba there is only one political line and it is the line of the party and its leadership. On the positive side, there is the elaboration of a vast network of mass organizations and, more significant, the on-going experiment in Poder Popular. The many layered structure of people's power is obviously conceived as an anti-bureaucratic, participatory device. But there is also evidence that it is conceived by some of the Cuban leadership as the socialist embryo that will eventually devour all less socialist institutions it competes with for hegemony. On the other hand, that there are severe limitations upon its activity is clear. And especially from outside Cuba, one cannot totally discount the possibility that there are some "window-dressing" and/or "escape valve" aspects associated with Poder Popular. But even were this true, the institutional arrangement does undeniably open the issue of extra-party decision-making, enlarge the populace's experience with decision-making and politics in general, and most important, it represents a framework in embryo for a full system of socialist democracy. For these reasons Poder Popular is exceptionally important. It may well turn out a major advance in both the theory and practice of socialist politics.

Presumably one could explain the "party trend" in Cuba in the same terms one explained similar trends in the Soviet Union and other "socialist" societies. But why did a participatory, extra-party political structure appear only in Cuba? We can only hypothesize that the left faction within the Party, the Fidelistas, never bought the entire Marxist Leninist paradigm. Moreover, they appear to have been more able to continue struggling for innovative policies in the political sphere than in other spheres of Cuban society, as we shall see in coming sections. A quotation from a Castro speech given at the outset of the decade, is certainly illustrative of the trend toward democratization:

> The formulas of revolutionary process can never be administrative formulas.... Sending a man down from the top to solve a problem involving fifteen or twenty thousand people is not the same thing as the problems of these fifteen or twenty thousand people—problems having to do with their community—being solved by virtue of the decisions of the people, of the community, who are close to the source of these problems... We must do away with all administrative methods and use mass methods everywhere.[29]

But to explain how the two opposing trends can continue to exist side by side in the political sphere is the real trick. If the Fidelistas are dominant in the government, and if the more conservative faction with roots in the old PSP has always held power only by grace of the Fidelistas, why aren't they now removed from power as the ORI was once abolished? Why don't the Fidelistas begin to replace the party with the democratic organs even at the national level of decision-making, leaving the party as simply a "consciousness raising" and ideological device, perhaps to be joined by other parties with somewhat different ideas? To say that this can't be done because the population is unprepared, begs the question only to raise another—why? Why, after two decades, can't democracy be pushed still further? Are there structures in Cuba that are acting as an impediment, structures that are diminishing the capacity of the populace for self-management at the same time as "Poder Popular" is enhancing that capacity? To answer this, and further our understanding of the strange duality of Cuban politics we must proceed to a discussion of Cuban economic history.

## The Cuban Economic Experience

Whereas we found a mixture of conflicting trends operating simultaneously in Cuban politics, Cuban economic development seems to be characterized by rather clear cut trends that dominated different periods. Moreover, whereas the ideology and economic programs of the mid and late sixties were characterized to a great extent by socialist trends, regrettably the trend in the seventies and early eighties has been increasingly toward consolidation of a coordinator mode of production and consumption.

### Leaving the World Capitalist System: 1959-1961

The Cuban revolution was fought under the banners of anti-tyranny, anti-imperialism, and social justice. To the extent economic issues were stressed the focus was land reform, ending the abuses of foreign business, and due process for labor organizations. The leadership of the revolution was neither Communist, nor socialist, nor Marxist. Furthermore, since communist and socialist parties existed in Cuba at the time but were not significant participants in the revolutionary events, the popular notion that the Cuban revolution was not a socialist transformation was quite reasonably founded. Even the extensive nationalizations were seen as acts in defiance of U.S. imperialism, not as first steps on a road to socialism. And since the revolution was relatively quick (as compared to the sustained struggles of China and Vietnam) the percentage of the population involved for prolonged periods was relatively low. In sum, there was popular support for the revolution—Batista was certainly hated—and mass consciousness favored economic justice including land reform, abolishing exorbitant rents, and responding resolutely to imperialism. But there was little socialist consciousness. On the contrary, McCarthyism in Cuba had left a rather generalized level of anti-communist and anti-socialist sentiment.[30]

In this context, on the third of March in 1959 the Fidelistas nationalized the Cuban Telephone Company, "a yankee monopoly which had been involved with the tyranny in dirty dealings against the peoples' interest."[31] On March 6th, rents were reduced by 50 percent. The urban poor and working people were elated, the bourgeoisie in shock. In May: a sweeping agrarian reform. In June: a nationalization decree was passed and Cuban Electric, Standard, Shell, and Texaco oil, and 21 sugar refineries nationalized in the months that followed. By the end of 1960 the state had expropriated over 11,000 companies accounting for over two thirds of Cuban industry.[32]

It is somewhat remarkable that motivated by anti-imperialism and social justice, nationalization proceeded much more rapidly in Cuba than it had in either Russia or China where the revolutions were led by socialists. But for the most part the United States was responsible for this phenomenon. Adopting a hostile view of the revolution, the U.S. cut sugar quotas, broke diplomatic relations, imposed an economic blockade, and generally compelled the Cuban leaders to retaliate with nationalizations. Since much Cuban industry was either U.S.-owned, or owned by Batista supporters who fled to the U.S. in fear, or abandoned by businessmen who felt they could not function after the U.S. cut off input supplies, the revolutionaries had little choice but to assume management of most of the economy.

At the same time the United States imposed an embargo which shut off not only commercial credits, sugar quotas, spare parts, and fuel deliveries, but also many foodstuffs and medicines, it opened its doors to those who wished to leave Cuba, especially the educated middle strata: doctors, lawyers, teachers, technocrats, architects, engineers, etc. Given the option of staying in a third world country suffering turmoil due to an unpredictable revolution and the quite predictable effects of the embargo, or of going to the world's wealthiest nation, many chose the latter course. The Cuban coordinator class and middle strata were rapidly depleted. The revolutionaries made no effort to force people to stay—feeling instead that reconstruction could be better accomplished without those who had little allegiance.[33]

But how did a non-socialist movement come to embark upon socialistic policies? Were there no other possible choices with regard to agricultural and industrial policy? Were there forces intrinsic to all small economies anxious to achieve economic independence and development pushing the leaders toward socialistic policies? Or was it a question of "socialism by accident" as conditions conspired to push the Cuban revolutionaries in directions they may otherwise not have chosen?

Given the prevailing consciousness, one might have expected the Fidelistas to adopt a "land to the tiller" policy in agriculture. Certainly the small and medium-scale capitalistic countryside this would have yielded would have been consistent with the norms of justice and anti-imperialism that were guiding their choices. And indeed this was the policy adopted in the poorer mountainous areas dominated by share-cropping, and in the tobacco land of the western provinces.[34] But the bulk of high quality land had been in sugar, and if you added the land devoted to cattle raising then all this had long been managed as large scale production units employing wage labor. There was no clearly defined tiller; the wage labor was usually seasonal, in fact. How could one sensibly allot small pieces to individuals in this situation?[35]

The Cuban revolutionaries were also aware that in addition to economies of scale there were reasons for not breaking up the large holdings associated with provision of social services. Dividing the land would not only have made road construction, irrigation, electrification, and sewage treatment more difficult to provide, but would have made providing modern housing, health, education, and cultural services to the rural sector impossible in a foreseeable time frame. Therefore, despite a political orientation that might have been willing to create a capitalistic countryside, the revolutionaries were propelled toward a cooperative approach instead. Most agricultural workers were not opposed to such a choice and had scant opportunity to stake a claim to a particular plot in any case. The result of this combination of factors was that by the end of 1961 55 percent of agricultural production originated in collectively managed units.

The situation in the industrial sector developed in a similar way. As Arthur MacEwan points out, "In the industrial and commercial sectors of the Cuban economy, the process of nationalization was not guided by a comprehensive program.... Nationalization commenced with the takeover of assets owned by persons closely involved in the old regime. Then... it incurred the hostility and non-cooperation of both Cuban and foreign business. In response to such general opposition... the government took over numerous enterprises.... By the end of 1961, measured in terms of value of production, 85 percent of Cuba's industry was in the state sector."[36] Again, to a great extent there was "socialism by accident."

But with the coordinators and middle strata on their way to Miami and the revolutionaries not having undergone decades of "schooling" in the administration of liberated zones, there were considerable problems administering the new economy. "All at once the people had to fill state posts, and take charge of the administration of all the basic production centers. The monopolies and the bourgeoisie and the most skilled managers and technicians had left Cuba. Ordinary men from the ranks of the people, very often with less than six years of schooling, had to assume the functions of direction of industrial and agricultural processes for which the ruling classes had been trained generation after generation, from father to son, in the country's few educational centers. We revolutionary leaders ourselves, who had been able to solve difficult problems related to the insurrectional struggle and the take-over of power, were, by contrast, quite ignorant of the most essential aspects of economic science and socialist construction."[37] Castro's assessment, however, is open to challenges. One commentator, Rene Dumont, argues that many errors committed by the leaders in this period due to their lack of experience might have been avoided if "experience" had been understood somewhat differently. That is, of course there were problems with inexperienced and unschooled individuals seeking to administer the new economy from the center, but in Dumont's view, had more reliance been put on autonomy and the initiative of workers in their own workplaces where they did have vast experience, many mistakes might have been avoided. The counter argument is that the workers were not, in fact, prone to such initiative. They were willing to support the leadership but evinced little disposition to take the initiative themselves. After all, the population at large had not pursued the land reforms, nor nationalizations, nor set up soviets, nor even engaged in any significant localized violence against the old regime.

Whatever the case, the period from 1959 to 1961 can be easily summarized. Land and industry were nationalized. Coordinators and many members of the middle strata left. Economic leadership and activity was exceptionally enthusiastic, yet haphazard and inefficient. While the top leadership felt the damage done had not been too great, they also felt it was time for a regularization, a tightening up, and a level of coordination previously absent. 1962 was to be the "Year of Planning."

## Mini-Stalinism: 1962-1963

As a result of the embargo, trade with the Eastern bloc and with the Soviet Union had expanded and Che had become a booster of not being choosy over what kind of socialism Cuba should subscribe to.* After a trip to Russia he came away impressed with a smoothly functioning developed economy. Surely this was a reasonable direction for the Cubans to turn.[38] The Russians, Czechs and the old PSP members in Cuba as well, certainly had considerable experience to offer. Why not make use of it? The experts began arriving in large numbers, and though great debates were being conducted over the proper balance between markets and central planning in the Soviet Union and Eastern Europe, there was no need for such confusion in Cuba.[39] Rather, in Cuba the situation was germinal. Regularization was in order. And in the eyes of both the foreign experts and the Cuban leadership it could only bring good results. As Karol put it, "Russian and Cuban optimism thus came together and reinforced each other. 'Veterans' of Eastern socialism and their young Caribbean disciples vied with one another in making happy forecasts. Cubans already saw themselves enjoying a Swedish standard of life, convinced as they were of Russian generosity and the efficiency of the planning 'clock'."[40]

The actual transition to planning was inaugurated at a National Convention on Production to which Fidel summoned some 3,500 economic experts. According to Karol, amidst great optimism for the future and free flowing criticism of the chaotic inefficiency of the past, there was ominously not the slightest reference to worker participation:

> Other details of varying importance showed that the
> Cuban masses had been won over to the Revolution and

---

*At no time are we going to seriously assess the importance of the boycott or Cuba's small size for the course of Cuban economic development. Whether the paths chosen would have been followed in any case, which we doubt, or would have been different had it not been for these factors, which we expect, is not so critical to an assessment of where the Cuban economy has been and where it is going, only to some aspects of why it is on its present course, which issue is not our chief concern.

were only too willing to play an active part in its
administration and development. In Cuba, it was
impossible to speak of lack of political awareness or of
apathy—the very stings that were poisoning the social
foundations of the Eastern European socialist countries.
To be sure, Cubans lacked the political education needed
to run their country efficiently, but was this a reason for
considering them so much clay in the hands of young
leaders who themselves were not the world's greatest
political or administrative experts? And yet, during the
three days of the National Convention on Production, no
one so much as raised the question of popular democracy
or workers' control of the factories.[41]

But no miracle came from the "planning clock." The system of
centralized planning and administration developed under Stalin's
long rule in the Soviet Union led to no great improvement in
economic output or efficiency in young revolutionary Cuba. Instead
rationing had to be initiated and "the Cuban leaders introduced
sweeping administrative reforms, abolishing certain ministries and
creating others, moving the managers of the *empresas consolidadas*
from pillar to post, and constantly enjoining the workers to keep
discipline."[42] Parallel to the emulation of the old Soviet economic
system, there was a growth in power of the leaders of the old Cuban
Communist Party. For who else was available with knowledge of this
approach? There was a new central planning apparatus with an
ideology and staff imported from the East, and old PSP members
taking over the economic levers to exert discipline over the workers.
The trade union movement was an immediate casualty as, in
keeping with the model, these institutions became agents for state
economic policy.*

While the guerrilla administrators of the first period had been
top-down and inefficient, they had at least kept up morale and the

---

*Karol reports,

"My informants may have had a grudge against them [the PSP
old timers], and I was ready to make allowances for their prejudice, but the countless cases of administrative incompetence they
quoted sounded genuine enough. To be sure, no one can say
with any certainty that the more rapid promotion of the Castroist
rank and file would have made for a better administration. Yet

peasants' and workers' enthusiasm for the future. Under the "old communists" however, there was still authoritarianism and inefficiency, but also a worsening economic situation, more emphasis on worker discipline, and a group of identifiable culprits with a poor reputation dating from their lack of participation in the revolution itself. Grumbling became commonplace. Before long, flagging morale and economic performance as well as a growth of political dissidence led many Cuban leaders to question the wisdom of the Soviet system. As we shall see, Che Guevara led the way this time as well.[43]

### The "Great Debate": 1964-1965

The great economic debate in Cuba resulted from dissillusionment with the traditional Soviet model and from the fact that the considerable questioning of this system occurring in the Soviet Bloc during this period appeared to be a challenge from the right and not the left.[44] The palliative of markets was not the kind of medicine the youngest revolution was interested in. Revolutionary fervor had not dissipated in Cuba, the ills of markets were a recent memory, and there was no longer a Cuban coordinator class to benefit from or administer a turn toward markets in any case. Many Cubans, and especially what we might call the left political faction of revolutionaries most concerned with developing socialist relationships, were thus forced to address problems of economic organization themselves. Where before Che had argued that the Soviets had things to teach as well as material assistance to provide, the new emphasis was on independence on all fronts. After all, the PSP with their Soviet advice had not made the revolution, the guerrillas had. Mightn't the guerrillas succeed also where the PSP had failed in creating a socialist economy?[45]

The two dominant personalities in the debate were Che himself and Carlos Rafael Rodriguez of the old PSP. The main concern was what kind of economy did Cuba want in order to achieve both

there is little doubt that when the old PSP took charge of Cuban industry, it became an obstacle to all original research on the role of the trade unions and on rank-and-file participation in the control and management of the economy.''

sufficient economic growth to overcome underdevelopment and to create the "new kind of people" necessary for the success of socialism. The principal focus of the debate was 1) the choice between moral and material incentives, 2) centralized planning without regard to each unit's profits versus "self financing " where firms would benefit or lose depending on their own "profit/loss" situation, and 3) economic diversification versus emphasis on sugar as the leading sector.[46]

Rodriguez argued that material incentives were necessary and valuable instruments, that careful attention should be paid to the profit/loss situation of individual units rather than simply transfering surpluses to the center and subsidizing deficits from the center, and that sugar exports had to be expanded as the means to obtain sufficient foreign exchange to purchase machinery for industrialization.[47]

Che took contrary positions against material incentives and commercial accounting as inappropriate to the task of creating socialism, and for industrial diversification that the Soviet bloc should underwrite out of socialist solidarity. His arguments were in certain respects akin to the theoretical approach we summarized in the first chapter of this volume, and argued in much greater detail in the companion volume, *Marxism and Socialist Theory*. Che argued the need for socialist enterprises to fit into a wider process of social service and development, and therefore against any notion that each firm should be pitted against others in competition for profits. And he argued that material incentives only led to competition and division among workers where what was required was the growth of consciousness and of solidarity that moral motivations might impel.* In essence he was dead set against the

---

*Che did not rule out material incentives but argued that they were a necessary evil to be steadily phased out. "One thing must be made very clear: We do not deny the objective need for material incentives, but we certainly are unwilling to use them as a fundamental driving force. We believe that, in economies, this kind of force quickly becomes an end in itself and then exercises its power over the relationships among men. It must not be forgotten that it comes from capitalism and is destined to die under socialism."

dynamics associated with commodity relations, not simply because of problems of economic imbalance, but more fundamentally because of their negative impact on workers' and consumers' consciousness. In a letter written from Africa in 1965 where he had gone in hopes of fomenting further revolutionary processes, Che writes of "Man and Socialism in Cuba":

> The new society in process of formation has to compete very hard with the past. This makes itself felt not only in the individual consciousness, weighed down by the residues of an education and an upbringing systematically oriented toward the isolation of the individual, but also by the very nature of this transition period, with the persistence of commodity relations. The commodity is the economic cell of capitalist society: as long as it exists its effects will make themselves felt in the organization of production and therefore in man's consciousness.[48]

> There is a danger of not seeing the forest because of the trees. Pursuing the chimera of achieving socialism with the aid of the blunted weapons left to us by capitalism (the commodity as the economic cell, profitability and individual material interest as levers, etc.), it is possible to come to a blind alley. And the arrival there comes about after covering a long distance where there are many crossroads and where it is difficult to realize just when the wrong turn was taken. Meanwhile, the adapted economic base has undermined the development of consciousness. To build communism, a new man must be created simultaneously with the material base.[49]

If we use hindsight to superimpose on Che's view a concern for the danger of development of coordinator relations, we can read him, with no twisting of his words, as arguing vehemently against relying on institutional forms conducive to such non-socialist outcomes, even in situations where optimal socialist institutions might themselves still be a ways off.

There is however, a blind spot, at least in our view, in the position Che took. If moral incentives are to work, and if the entwining of economic units into a social whole is to be socially meaningful, workers themselves must become increasingly responsible for economic decisions and not just for doing work itself and must gain possession of an understanding of all aspects of economic activity. If this is not accomplished it cannot be too long before the tedium of execution without self-management will blunt revolutionary zeal. When this occurs, moral incentives will begin to fail and in the absense of material incentives, only authoritarian coercion will be available to compel economic performance. When Che saw through the Soviet model as insufficient for creating socialism, regrettably he did not focus on the importance of workers' position along an axis of decision-making power.* Had he done so, perhaps there would have been another element in the great Cuban economic debate: that is, a call for institutions of direct workers' management over their own conditions of production and over the formulation of the economic plan itself. As K.S. Karol wrote in his excellent study of the first decade of the Cuban revolution, Che "seems to have misunderstood a crucial problem in the history of the workers' movement, namely the need and the right of workers to decide things for themselves, to determine their own fate under all circumstances."[50] Especially interesting from the perspective of other Third World revolutionaries, Karol also thought something better may well have been possible in Cuba. For in his view the Cuban trade union movement did have some heritage of militant struggle and was certainly loyal to the Castroist cause. Therefore even in the absence of workers' initiative to create councils of their own, perhaps these unions could have been forged into independent vehicles of workers' expression and power. This too would have meant a drastic reversal of policy, but then change was the whole point of initiating the debate in the first place. That Che bought the idea that workers should have no interests other than the furtherance of the economic plan and development, and that the

---

*Karol perceives the same failing in a slightly different manner:

"However, in this whole debate there was a major gap which genuine Marxists might have been expected to close. Neither Che nor his opponents had come to grips with the problem of political power in, and the political organization of, all those societies where centralized or reformist experiments in planning and economic management were taking place.... For Marx the entire transition period toward socialism and communism was characterized by the direct participation of all workers, free at last, in the running of communal affairs." (Karol, op. cit., p. 328)

revolution's leaders would necessarily know best "how to interpret the thoughts and needs of the working class" was a serious problem of his thinking. In any case, at least among the Fidelistas he won most points in the debate, and so ensued a period of "left leadership" in economic matters.

## 1966-1970: "Left" Economic Policies

This period sees enactment of Che's position on planning and incentives and of Rodriguez's on expanding the sugar sector, all administered by Castro and without Che, though with most old PSP members in positions of reduced power.

As a rough contrast one might liken the period to the Great Leap Forward in China. There was to be rapid economic advance to overcome underdevelopment. The left faction of the political elite dominated administration with little or no participation of other political factions, coordinator fractions, nor worker or mass organizations. There was much discussion of creating "socialist man," and again, like the Chinese parallel, there was great enthusiasm, but also immense confusion and disruption of the economy.

Part of the disruption was a result of departures from the national plan due to the perpetual intervention of Castro in favor of mini-plans which were generally very leftist local projects accorded the highest priority. No doubt another reason for confusion was the relative absence of coordinators and the enthusiastic but rather ad hoc approach to setting economic targets. For this was done more as a result of the hunches and desires of the top leadership than of any elaborate technical planning system. The expansion of focus upon sugar was marked by clearing new land for sugar cultivation, returning land used for other crops during the period of agricultural diversification of the early sixties to its former use, and the effort to reach a ten million ton harvest in 1970. One of the few institutional vehicles enhanced during the period was the army, for the immense economic effort, pushed by moral incentives and entreaties, was organized in a highly authoritarian fashion, often under the leadership of the army.[51] While material incentives were avoided, little was done to break with hierarchical patterns of decision-making. And as results demonstrated, half a socialist program can regrettably prove as bad in terms of concrete results, if not in

environment in which people would engage one another socialistically. During this period, the plan was used among other things to level wages as much as possible, to make as many necessary goods as possible free, and to finally sever the link between work and income and thereby eliminate insecurity. Since equity meant dignity and mutual respect more than plenty for all, it affected people's self-image more than anything else. As Castro put it:

> I am sure that if many simple people of the country were to be asked: 'What are you most grateful to the Revolution for? Your low rent? Your steady job? What are you most grateful to the Revolution for—the material benefits you have received or the moral benefits that you have received?' I'm sure that many, perhaps the great majority would say: 'What I am most grateful to the Revolution for and the reason I'm willing to die for the Revolution, is that since the Revolution I have felt like a human being. I've felt like a man of dignity. I've felt that I amount to something among my people, that I am somebody in my country. I've felt as I never felt in the past.'[52]

And if Castro too failed to perceive the importance of self-management and institutions through which common folk could manifest their desires and develop their capacities for self-management, he did not fail to understand Che's arguments about competition, money, and consciousness. And although his emphasis, if not his vision, has changed dramatically, if anything he was even more aggressive in implementing Che's theories during the late sixties than Che had been in arguing for them earlier.

> We will never create socialist consciousness, communist consciousness with a 'dollar sign' in the minds and hearts of our men and women. . . . But those who wish to solve problems by appealing to personal selfishness, by appealing to individualistic effort, forgetful of society, are acting in a reactionary manner, conspiring, although inspired by the best intentions in the world, against the possibilities of creating a truly Socialist spirit. . . ." "A financier, a pure economist, a metaphysician of revolutions would have said, 'Careful, rents shouldn't be lowered one cent. Think of it from a financial standpoint, from an economic standpoint, think of the pesos

involved!!!!' Such persons have 'dollar signs' in their heads and they want the people, also, to have 'dollar signs' in their hearts and heads!!!!'' "Such people would not have made even one revolutionary law. In the name of those principles they would have proposed to go on charging the farmers rent; in the name of the same principles they would have continued to charge the farmers interest on loans; they would have charged for medical and hospital care; they would have charged school fees; they would have charged for the boarding schools that are now completely free, all in the name of a metaphysical approach to life. They would never have had the people's enthusiasm, the masses' enthusiasm, which is the prime factor, the basic factor, for a people to advance, for a people to build, for a people to be able to develop. And that enthusiasm on the part of the people, that support for the Revolution is something that can be measured in terms incomparably superior to the adding and subtracting of the metaphysicians.[53]

It is not just a matter of Castro and Che's revolutionary spirit, nor their forthrightness and obvious love for the people. In our view the critical insight is that there is more to economics than a bottom line. It is the restoration of living people to the accounting ledger of the economist that is the major breakthrough in Che and Castro's formulations as well as their willingness to go against the grain to make this new claim. That they did not simultaneously address issues of power over decision-making, and new forms of planning is no reason to dismiss their efforts, but only reason to evaluate them critically when necessary. That the Fidelistas did cut against the orthodox grain, and that it was precisely the old PSP cadre who Castro had in mind when talking about metaphysicians, becomes obvious in the next quote. In light of the subsequent history of Cuban economic policy, the quote merits repetition in its entirety:

That is, the Revolution aspires—as one of the steps toward communism—to equalize incomes, from the bottom up, for all workers, regardless of the type of work they do. This means this principle will surely be given a name by 'learned,' 'experienced' economists—who will claim this goes against Marxist Leninist principles and against the laws of economics. The question is 'which' economics:

capitalist economics or socialist economics, the truly Marxist Leninist economics or a mercantilist economics. To these economists an assertion of this type sounds like sheer heresy, and they say that the revolution is headed for defeat. But it so happens that in this field there are two special branches. One is the branch of the 'pure' economist, be he capitalist or socialist. In short, just a plain economist. But there is another science, a deeper science which is truly revolutionary science. It is the science of revolutionary awareness; it is the science of faith in mankind; it is the science of confidence in human beings. If we agreed that man is an incorrigible individual, that man is incapable of learning; if we agreed that man is incapable of developing his conscience—then we would have to say that the 'brainy' economists were right, that the Revolution would be headed for defeat and that it would be fighting the laws of economics. . . . [54]

What we suggest is an alternative explanation for the defeat that did come, an explanation different from that of the "brainy" economists of both capitalist and socialist blocs, and an explanation different from the one that Castro appears by his actions and words to have accepted himself. Our explanation is premised on the belief that men and women—beyond feeling loyalty to a revolutionary leadership, beyond gaining dignity through equity, and beyond experiencing a kind of spiritual awakening through official recognition of their humanity—also need to begin to take control of their own life situations and exert their own creative powers rather than always depending on a benevolent leadership.

Osvaldo Dorticos, the President of the Republic, was apparently of the same mind as Che and Fidel, and according to K.S. Karol, was Che's successor as economic theoretician of the left faction of the revolutionary leadership.[55] He urged sowing the seeds of communism in the present and scoffed at the Soviet stopover in what he called socialism, and what we call a coordinator mode of production and consumption. Dorticos, like Che, was concerned with qualitative human issues as well as quantitative material issues and as he indicated in the interview he gave K.S. Karol which we quote below could even envision material sacrifices and errors as a reasonable price to pay in order to ensure a proper development of human habits and ideas.

We returned to the problem of material incentives. 'From each according to his abilities, to each according to his needs', is a basic principle of Communism. A truly communist society, Dorticos contended, will have put an end to all forms of exploitation, to commercial relationships of every kind. But as Fidel put it, a country like Cuba, which suffered from a heritage of misery heaped up over centuries, was much too poor to meet all its needs. It could not dispense with money, or level incomes, or eliminate private greed by decree. But it could and must realize that all these things are so many blots on the revolutionary escutcheon, shameful vestiges of the past. Men must be shown that life is more than a rat race to the top, must become suffused with fraternal ideas and must be given a larger vista of humanity. In the short run, this policy might well prove less economically efficient than one based on monetary rewards, and therefore more in line with old habits. But would it not be far better to make a costly long-term investment than run the risk of perpetuating the evil social values implicit in the old mentality?[56]

Nor did Dorticos suffer any illusion that all this could happen over-night. Like Che, he was simply concerned that the revolution be on a road that led to the desired outcome rather than some dead end.

Clearly it would be dangerous to impose norms of conduct that strained existing attitudes too far. The only result would be economic paralysis. What was needed was a fair balance between the desirable and the possible, always giving priority to the first. In Cuba many people clearly would be working for money and pursuing selfish aims for a long time to come. But the number of more fully integrated people seeking fulfillment in the great social liberation movement would keep growing steadily until, one day, they would be the overwhelming majority. In the long run, therefore, their work and devotion would be the determining factors in the economic transformation of Cuban society at large.[57]

Yet Dorticos, like Che before him, also talked of Cuba's industries being conceived as one immense factory with little awareness of either how differences in types of work are a cause of different human benefits and costs for the workers themselves, or of the importance of direct self-management instead of enlightened leadership from above. Instead, Dorticos recounted for Karol the ways in which Castro would represent ordinary Cubans, acting in a sense as the opposition within the bureaucracy he headed and insisting that all ministers do likewise as if this was democracy in action. Here, as in China it seems, socialism in the economy was dependent not upon the workers and peasants themselves and was promoted not by institutionalization of their direct power, but instead depending upon a beneficent leadership. And though the question Karol posed will always be relevant—"Who was there to keep an eye on the ministers themselves?"[58]—an even more fundamental question is how can socialist man and woman emerge in such circumstances. For though ordinary citizens were called upon to contribute in the name of socialism, they were not conceptualizing their own tasks, and they were not coming to know their economy better and better so as to increase their participation in planning. Instead they were subject to orders not of their making, no matter how benevolent, and therefore in a situation conducive to lessening initiative and increasing passivity.

In a recent volume on Cuba, forthcoming at the time of our writing, Arthur MacEwen assesses the "left period" of the late sixties in a way that diverges only at its endpoint from our own view. He first states, as we might ourselves, "The problem is one of creating the forms of organization—human abilities and behavioral patterns—that allow economic development without preventing or perverting the movement toward socialist social relations."[59] He goes on to argue that the Cuban working class did not seize power during the revolutionary process—"the underlying weakness can be interpreted as the inhibition on the exercise of power by the working class."[58] MacEwen then argues that to the extent that forms used in this and in the prior period inhibited the development of mass organizational capabilities, they were incorrect. What he does *not* do, however—and this is where we differ—is emphasize the importance of central planning itself as just such an inhibitory mechanism, nor the countervailing importance of direct economic self-management. This may well reflect the fact that MacEwan, like many other leftist economists, sees little to choose in the way of alternative economic forms. In this view, if one rejects markets there is nothing else but some form of central planning, and the issue is merely its character and that of the ancillary institutions that might be employed to offset central planning's (not often recognized) negative attributes. In Part Two of this volume we will argue for a different approach to socialist economic allocation—for a kind of decentralized planning that is qualitatively different from both markets and central planning and, in our opinion, more in tune with the ideals that Che, Fidel, and Dorticos put forward in the sixties. In our view this third alternative provides another pole for critical evaluation of this period in Cuban history. Where MacEwan emphasizes the need for greater popular participation in the *political* realm—something we certainly concurred with in the previous section—he is not able to suggest a parallel means for greater popular participation in the economy. Therefore his criticisms of the economic practice of the 60s all point to what was done badly rather than what might have been done instead. The following two quotations are indicative:

> In the Cuban revolution, the immediate struggle for power provided little foundation for the organization of socialist development. . . . Furthermore, the early reforms, while extremely popular, were decreed and carried out from above. INRA did not, for example, organize rural workers and peasants to carry out land reform themselves. . . . The experience of the Cuban working class did not provide a basis on which the Cuban revolution might build."
> The failure of the Cuban government to move more positively in the 1960's towards reorganizing economic structures reflected political weaknesses. The construction of economic structures to replace the market might have been accomplished by the development of more active participation of the Cuban people in *political* affairs. Yet in the 1960's, forms of mass *political* participation were being weakened rather than strengthened.[60] (Emphasis ours)

Short of having a positive alternative to the Cuban methods of economic organization, MacEwan's is likely the harshest criticism of Cuban practice that can be responsibly made. Ours, harsher still, asserts that the failure was not only political, but also economic, in that economic institutions could have more nearly approximated socialist norms. We believe that economic discussion at all levels, and especially participation of the workers in planning, might have propelled eventual self-managing forms far more effectively. However, the legitimacy of this criticism of course depends upon the feasibility of a non-central planning, non-market vision of socialist economic relations that we have still to present and argue for in part three of this book.

## The Turn to the Right and Increasing "Pragmatism": 1971-1974

The tone of Castro's speech on the 26th of July 1970 was forthright and self-critical. He not only laid the blame for the failure to achieve the 10 million ton sugar harvest on over-centralized, poor decisions at the highest levels rather than on any lack of enthusiasm and effort on part of the populace, but he seemed to promise greater worker participation, if not immediate industrial democracy, as the appropriate cure. Unfortunately, no such remedy was ever attempted. Instead, as the "left" political elite increasingly absented themselves from economic policy making, the vacuum was filled by the "right" political elite and a new coordinator class. Discredited "in practice," Che's ideas increasingly fell by the wayside as the modern Soviet economic system was slowly constructed by men who had opposed the "Cuban heresy" in the first place although, as we shall see, there was no lack of support for the new direction in economic policy by the likes of Dorticos and Castro himself. In spite of a few innovations that granted more worker participation, the dominant trend of the 70's was toward a more "rationalized" system of coordinator control over economic decision-making. The ground work for the rightward trend was laid from 1971-1974, and the new direction was consolidated under the New Economic Management System of the second half of the decade.

The interventionism of the "left" political elite was drastically curbed in the aftermath of the sugar failure of 1970, and the days of special "left" projects were officially buried at the first congress of the Cuban Communist Party in an official resolution stating that the national macroeconomic plan was reinstated as the main tool in the economy and that all lower level plans such as micro and sectoral plans would be subordinated to it. There was also an immediate decrease in mass mobilizations for agricultural projects. The deemphasis on the sugar sector at the expense of all other economic activity lessened the need for sugar mobilizations as did increased emphasis on mechanization of the harvest. The idea of a "green belt" around Havana, in which urban labor power was to be mobilized on a permanent basis to care for labor intensive agricultural products like coffee, citrus fruits, and vegetables, was also abandoned in the seventies as the quality of the largely voluntary work was deemed too low for such tasks, and the disruption of office and factory work deemed too costly.[61] Finally the most famous "special project," the effort to build communist institutions and create "communist men and women" in the Isle of Youth, was gradually de-emphasized in the seventies. Whereas in the late 60's the Island was literally administered separately from the rest of the country by groups of young volunteers and revolutionary fighters from the anti-Batista struggle living communally and running an economy without money, the Island is now referred to by its old name, the Isle of Pines, and has been re-integrated into the national economy and polity. Although it still retains vestiges of the profound social experiment that was conducted there in the 60's, it is now most noteworthy for the impressive secondary schools for young people from Angola, Ethiopia, Zimbabwe, Nicaragua and other African and Latin American countries attempting to overcome underdevelopment outside the imperialist orbit.

In the context of the historic debate of the 60's, the most telling change was the shift from emphasis on moral to material incentives. Based on a visit in the early seventies, Ron Radosh wrote:

> But now, a visitor finds that the Cubans are moving away from reliance on moral incentives.... The Cubans we encounter, such as the factory committee at the new steel plant, tell us about the new resolutions in the 'Theses of the 13th Congress of the Central Organization of Cuban Trade Unions.' These emphasize productivity, established norms of production, and the introduction of wage differentials linked 'to the fulfillment, underfulfillment, or overfulfillment of the norms.' In other words, the very mechanism of bourgeois competition between workers which Che rejected had been introduced as the mechanism for increasing productivity. At present, a worker who produces way above the norm and one who just meets the norm get the same salary. This, the plant

manager tells us, is unfair. When the new law is enacted, the bonus paid to the worker who surpasses the norm will be a material incentive.... To justify this new policy, the Cubans quote to us from Karl Marx's Critique of the Gotha Program. Cuba is now in the first stage of socialism, the basis of which is 'from each according to his ability; to each according to his work.'[62]

Of course it should not need pointing out that this famous quote can be interpreted just as easily to justify the Cuban system of the 60's as that of the 70's. If "work" is interpreted as "work time" the system being *replaced* by "the new law" was its literal embodiment, and the *new* system would be more in tune with "in order to get from each according to his ability; give to each according to his ability." If work is interpreted as "work effort" then the new system embodies this principle only to the extent that there are no differences of ability between workers and work conditions between facilities. But in any case, it is *not* our purpose to argue that a two-dimensional analysis of moral vs. material incentives is the most appropriate one, nor that the more "moral" the incentive system the more "correct" it is regardless of social context (or in our terms, the condition of the human center.) Rather we agree with Radosh who admitted that "the issue... is far more complex than I originally understood it to be."[63] "The simple question I ignored, I feel in retrospect, is what happens if the sense of duty does not universally exist?.... Without forward movement in the economy, dependency upon moral incentives might undermine a worker's identification with the Revolution and militate against the development of consciousness. In trying to stimulate productivity exclusively through use of moral incentives, the government came (in the 60's) to depend upon mechanisms of ideological control. 'A system of incentives that relies upon political directives from above' Silverman wrote (in his anthology *Man and Socialism in Cuba: the Great Debate*), 'becomes just another form of oppression.'"[64] Moreover, we agree with Arthur MacEwen's insistence that the distinction between individual and collective incentives can be every bit as important as the dichotomy moral/material. MacEwen has argued forcefully that individual moral incentives such as honors, medals and newspaper recognition for superior achievements in production can militate against the development of the kind of consciousness required to reach mature socialism just as individual material incentives can. MacEwen has also pointed out (correctly in our view) that collective material incentives do not generally display as perverse dynamics as those generated by individual material incentives.[65]

But we think it is a mistake to permit previous admissions of oversimplifications and recognition of important new concepts to cloud one's view of the overall trend of incentives in Cuba during the seventies. There is a moral-material dimension, a collective-individual dimension, and a participatory-authoritarian dimension as well in the development of socialist economic incentives. And on each of these axes, as well as for the entire space, there are practical constraints imposed by the condition of the human center inherited from both capitalist and previous socialist practice. But the socialist goal implies its own constraints—a development in the directions of moral, collective, and participatory motivations on people's parts. Movement need not be at a constant rate on all fronts, any more than the final goals must be achieved instantaneously. Trade-offs between movements along the different axes are always permissible if they are truly more rapid "turnpikes" to mature socialism. And backward steps to correct for overly optimistic "left" misestimations of the tension between the desirable and the possible should be taken. But in Cuba there has now been ten years of moving steadily backwards on the moral-material axis with no forward movement whatsoever on the participatory-authoritarian dimension. Furthermore, the gradual substitution of collective for individual material incentives begun in the early 70's has been reversed, as we shall see, in the second half of the decade. We can accept Fidel's statement as a truism during the transition to mature socialism: "Together with moral incentives we must also use material incentives without abusing either one, because the former would lead to idealism where some would live off the work of the rest, while the latter would lead to individual selfishness."[66] But we cannot accept it as it was offered: as a justification for the consistently negative trend in the Cuban incentive system of the seventies. Instead we must agree with Radosh: "The introduction of material incentives... seem to indicate a rightward shift that may very well lead to precisely the result Fidel hopes will be avoided."[67] And "the complexity of the debate over material versus moral incentives... does in no way negate concern for creating an institutional mechanism of socialist democracy. On this point, friends of the Cuban Revolution abroad should conceive their duty to be that of giving critical support, and not refraining from criticism when it is sorely needed."[68]

The shift in gears on the incentive question was probably one of the most difficult the leadership ever had to explain to the people and cadre. It is one of the few instances we know of where the Cubans felt it was necessary to re-write history. Rather than simply saying, "Che was wrong," the Cuban leadership allowed his once defeated, but now victorious opponent in "The Great Debate" to re-interpret Che's positions.

> Of course, Cuba's leadership has to find a way of dealing with Che's vigorous opposition to material incentives, which he argued would 'die out as we advance,' to be replaced by 'non-material incentives such as the sense of duty and the new revolutionary way of thinking.' How they are doing this is best indicated in a recent interview with Carlos Rafael Rodriguez, an old Communist who now sits on the Central Committee of the Party. This interview was given to us to read while in Cuba, and it is clear that Rodriguez's outlook indicates the direction of policy. 'Within the international left,' Rodriguez begins, 'a total distortion of his (Che's) views has arisen.... He has been projected as having a totally negative opinion of the utilization of material stimulus in the building of socialism.' Rodriguez claims that 'careful and systematic' reading of all that Che wrote shows that Guevara actually had 'a clearly dialectical position on that subject,' by which Rodriguez evidently means that Che really felt 'there had to be an adequate combination of material and moral incentives.' It comes as a shock that Cuba's top leadership sees fit to distort Che's own writings to gain credence for their shift in domestic policy. Rodriguez is careful not to try to quote from Che to prove his own interpretation. I cannot help but wonder whether Cubans are comparing this to their reading of Che's own words. Publicly, at least, one finds no evidence of any discussion of the fundamental issues Che had once raised.[69]

The beginning of the 70's also marked a shift from emphasis on "redness" to "expertness" in evaluating economic cadre. "Since late 1970 there has been a revival in Cuba of economic and accounting studies which had suffered a serious setback in 1966-70. Furthermore, two new careers have been introduced: 'systems analyst' and 'economic comptroller.'' The curricula of these careers include mathematical analysis, calculus, statistics, economic theory, planning, systems analysis, informational techniques, accounting, management, and production processes. Graduates are a mixture of accountant, economist and business administrator.''[70] And in 1973, ''President Dorticos warned managers of state enterprises that they had to acquire the necessary qualifications for their jobs or else would be fired regardless of their revolutionary credentials.''[71] And by the end of that same year the following stimuli were introduced: ''Promotion to a higher post must be based on the acquisition of the required skills; enrollment in higher education conveys a right to a paid leave of absence which increases from one to four hours per week according to the level of study reached; and completion of training is automatically rewarded with a salary increase.''[72]

The trend is clear enough: the pre-revolutionary professional-managerial strata and coordinator class had in large part fled Cuba by the early 60's. But whereas the greatly expanded educational effort of the 60's had objectively created the potential basis for a revival, the emphasis had officially been on increasing the level of education of the populace as a whole, and imbuing the rather small number of recipients of higher education with a deep-seated respect for less skilled labor as well as sense of duty to their brothers and sisters who had foregone the privilege of higher education. In the 70's however, old and would-be technicians, administrators, and planners were pushed through a curriculum reminiscent of their counterparts in capitalist economies in which the instrumentalist, manipulative bias of bourgeois cybernetics, accounting and management theories and techniques were woefully underemphasized. From an educated stratum with a consciousness of their relative privilege and special duties came the beginnings of a professional-managerial strata and coordinator class with a sense that their higher level of training ''naturally'' merited additional material privilege and decision-making power over the efforts of others.

But as much as a new managerial fraction of a future coordinator class was being trained in the early seventies, the levers of economic power were firmly retained in the hands of the ''right'' political elite and a technocratic group of central planners during this period. "The acceptance of the Soviet 'model' and the rise of the technocrats resulted in two clear changes: 'mini' plans were substituted by short and medium range central plans, and computation... for application to planning and management was rapidly developed."[73] Moreover, the Soviet Union and important members of the old communist party and Soviet school of 'socialism' were active participants in the transformation. "In December 1970, Carlos Rafael Rodriguez led a Cuban delegation to Moscow where meetings were held with a team of Soviet economists headed by Nikolai Baibakov, director of the Soviet Central Planning Board (GOSPLAN). As a result of such conversations, the Cuban-Soviet Commission of Economic, Scientific, and Technical Collaboration was established."[74] The first meeting of the Commission was held in Havana early in September 1971 where the Cuban delegation was led by Rodriguez and composed of top officials from the Central Planning Board (JUCEPLAN), and most of the important economic ministries. The second meeting in Moscow in April 1972 formalized collaboration in planning between JUCEPLAN and GOSPLAN, including Soviet supply of an electronic computer for planning to Cuba. Although it is very difficult for outsiders to know who within the Cuban leadership actually favor and administer different policy trends, it appears to us that Carlos Rafael Rodriguez was a central figure in the developments we have been describing in the early seventies. This is the picture painted by Carmelo Mesa-Lago:

> In 1970 when the new stage of the Revolution began, Rodriguez combined two key attributes: he headed Cuba's leading team of experts on central planning and computer techniques and—being a former member of the prerevolutionary PSP—had the confidence of the Soviets. The desperate internal need for economic rationalization and Soviet pressure for a technical approach in planning pushed Rodriguez back to the fore. In a rapid sequence of successes, he became the founder and chairman (on the Cuban side) of the Cuban-Soviet Commission of Economic, Scientific, and Technical Collaboration; the deputy prime minister of foreign policy; the chief negotiator of foreign trade agreements; the Cuban delegate to several socialist transnational committees on

planning, trade, and electronic computation; and the man with de facto control of domestic planning.[75]

But before describing how all these "rightist" trends were consolidated by ratification of the "New Economic Management System" at the First Congress of the Cuban Communist Party in December 1975, we should pause to mention two policies of the early seventies that did enhance worker participation in economic decision making.

Both the microbrigades and the revitalization of the unions had positive aspects. One of the most pressing social needs that was deferred during the 60's due to even more pressing social needs was housing. In the early 70's much of the increase in residential construction was done by microbrigades—construction crews composed of workers from factories whose regular assignments were being assumed by their fellow employees. The choice of who in a production unit would work in its microbrigade, the decisions about how to cover their jobs in the factory, and the particular mixture of merit and need that would govern the assignment of workers to housing as it was completed, were all decisions left up to the workers in production units that had microbrigades. Moreover, the management of the construction work was organized by the brigade members themselves, not by the regular production unit managerial hierarchy.[76] All this amounted to a significant increase in worker control over one part of the economic activity that affected their lives very directly. But it stood in stark contrast to the organization and management of the "regular" work process.

The first of the mass organizations to be revitalized were the trade unions who held their nation wide conference in autumn of 1973. We already discussed in the previous section both the advances compared to the 60's as well as the limitations on trade union initiative that marked this reorganization. But one further aspect of union revitalization deserves mention. In the early 70's Cuba was able to import limited amounts of consumer durables such as TV's, refrigerators, electrical appliances, etc. But there were not nearly enough for every family that wanted them. Rather than use exorbitant prices to ration these items, or ration them through the regular rationing procedure, many of these durables were assigned to production units to be distributed at readily affordable prices by special committees within the trade unions organized for this purpose. As in the case of the microbrigades, each union committee would formulate its own criteria of merit and need to govern the distribution of consumer durables.

In sum, both microbrigades and union distribution of consumer durables were progressive combinations of increased worker self-management and collective incentives. It is unfortunate that both these positive movements along the participatory and collective incentive axes were de-emphasized during the second half of the decade.

## The New Economic Management System and the Maturing of a New Coordinator Class: 1975-1980

The growth rate from 1970-74 averaged over 10 percent with the best years coming last. No wonder a writer like Mesa-Lago could conclude: "The economic results of this policy are positive in terms of industrial output, overall economic growth, and increased consumer satisfaction. Conversely, such policy may induce selfishness and some stratification. The goal of the 'New Man' in an egalitarian and mobilized society has been postponed, but for the man in the street this pragmatic decision probably does not look too bad after all."[77] That Fidel Castro and the Cuban revolutionaries came to a similar conclusion is more surprising, but in the First Party Congress in 1975 they did just that.

Fidel presented his explanation of the New Economic Management system at the First Party Congress in 1975 with a personal recantation for previous heresies:

> At this point, however, it is necessary to speak of our mistakes. Revolutions usually have their utopian periods, in which their protagonists, dedicated to the noble task of turning the dreams into reality and putting their ideals into practice, assume that the historical goals are much nearer, and that men's will, desires, and intentions, towering over the objective facts, can accomplish anything.... Now and again, the utopian attitude likewise goes hand-in-hand with a certain contempt for the experience of other processes. The germ of chauvinism and of the petty-bourgeois spirit infecting those of us who entered upon the ways of revolution by merely intellectual

means tends to develop, sometimes unconsciously, some attitudes that may be regarded as self-conceit and excessive self-esteem.... From the outset the Cuban Revolution failed to take advantage of the rich experience of other peoples who had undertaken the construction of socialism long before we had. Had we been humbler, had we not overestimated ourselves, we would have been able to understand that revolutionary theory was not sufficiently developed in our country and that we actually lacked solidly grounded Marxist economists and scientists to be able to make any really significant contribution to the theory and practice of socialist construction; we would have searched with a modesty befitting revolutionaries for everything that could be learned from these sources and applied in our country's specific conditions.... It is necessary to admit that in many instances our resources have not been used to the utmost. Our economic management has not been as efficient as it might have been.... The budget system of financing [that espoused by Che and employed in the second half of the sixties] turned out to be highly centralized and made very restricted use of economic levers, commercial relations, and material incentives.... Bank control was very weak; in general, the granting of credit was carried out automatically and there were no incentive funds financed out of the results of the economic activities of the cooperatives.... Putting an idealistic interpretation on Marxism and departing from the practical experience of the other socialist countries, we tried to establish our own methods. In consequence, the form of management established was a far cry from the economic accounting in general use in the socialist countries.... To some of us this seemed to be too capitalistic, because we failed to understand the need to preserve the forms of commercial relations between state enterprises.... The payments and receipts were in practice abolished from the second quarter of 1967.... In 1968, the connection between salaries and output was severed.... In 1967 interests on credits and the taxes collected from farmers were abolished.... When it might have seemed to us as though we were drawing nearer to communist forms of production and distribution, we were actually pulling away from the correct methods of first building socialism.[78]

Fidel then proceded to herald the introduction of the New Economic Management System:

The time has come to implement an adequate economic direction system.... The system worked out and being proposed to the Congress is based on the practical experiences of the socialist countries.... The proposed system takes into account the operation of economic laws that govern socialist construction, and that exist independently of our wills and desires. Among these laws is the law of value, the need to have receipt-and-payment relations among all the enterprises including those of the State, and that in these relations and in the various economic relations in general, money, prices, finances, budget, taxes, credits, interest and other commercial categories should function as indispensible instruments, to enable us to estimate the use we make of our productive resources and to determine, in the minutest detail, to the last centavo, how much we put into each one of our products; to decide which investment is the most advantageous; to learn which enterprises, which units, which collectives of workers perform best, which perform worst, and so be able to adopt the appropriate measures.... The enterprises producing over and above their inputs are the ones that operate with profit, with profitability. And as an incentive for their performance, the system envisages that a part of that contribution should remain in the hands of the collective of workers. The system also implies a certain autonomy in the use and handling of resources by each enterprise: to sell or rent out unused fixed assets, to decide to go into marginal production from waste, etc., without modifying their main production plan.[79]

Where is a concern for the development of socialist men and women? Where a concern for increasing socialist consciousness and motivation? Where is the rejection of social relations of production that foster individualism and greed? This is certainly not the kind of economics Che championed during the great debate of the mid-sixties, but rather a complete surrender to the manner of thinking and policy mechanisms of the "brainy economists" Fidel had warned against earlier.

In the first place, what Fidel's recantation conveniently deletes is that the Cuban economic heresy did not begin until *after* they had searched out "the rich experience of other peoples who had undertaken the construction of socialism long before." The Czech and Russians did come in, and the old PSP members did rush to mimic the "Soviet model" in the early years. Only after accepting just the advice Fidel claims they never sought and watching it fail on the anvil of their own revolutionary environment did the "unschooled" Cubans lose faith in the old ways and begin experimenting with new formulas of their own.

In the second place, it is true the young Cuban revolutionaries did not have all the answers in the sixties. And it is true, the Soviet "reform" model Fidel was declaring himself ready to mimic in 1975 was not exactly the same as the traditional central planning model Cuba embraced during the period of mini-Stalinism. But Che, Fidel, and Dorticos' criticism of the "Soviet road" and the thinking of the "brainy economists" in the sixties was right on the mark, and the failure of their own model in the second half of the sixties in no way invalidated this truth. It was a tremendous setback for Cuban socialism that by 1975 the party leadership was ready to bury the critical theoretical insights they had developed in the sixties.

An equally discouraging setback was the willingness of the Cuban leadership to parrot the methods of the Soviet/Eastern European "reform" model of "socialism" they had so resoundingly rejected before. In fact, as we have seen, this is not really a model of socialism at all, but a model for a coordinator mode of production and consumption in which a right political elite oversees (from a greater or lesser distance) the sharing of economic decision-making between the central and managerial fractions of a coordinator class and in which each of the coordinator fractions employs ever more sophisticated techniques to increase its power over others, and in which incentives are increasingly individual and materialistic. The central fraction of the coordinator class was clearly dominant in the first few years of the New Economic Management System as they continued to control virtually all investment decisions through the central plan and were better able to monitor production unit performance with the help of the national economic calculation system and the purchase and sale relations among enterprises which allowed for quick tests of financial success. However, in 1979 and 1980 the managerial fraction of the newly educated coordinator class has increased its power significantly. Once the new systems of prices, taxation, and banking, credit and interest were established and individual firm profits were not only calculable but existed at year end, it was a short step to the pilot project of financing out of firm profits in selected enterprises, and another small step to expanded self-financing in all enterprises.

Unfortunately, in our opinion, the results of these policies are only too predictable. Although many in the Cuban political leadership might desperately hope that these policies will increase worker effort by a system of more "efficient" material rewards and elicit greater initiative through greater decentralization of economic decision-making—as the international champions of the "reform" model have claimed since the early sixties—the actual results will be quite different.

In the first place, there is every reason to believe the new system of material incentives will reward privilege as much as effort. Which firms will have greater profits—and therefore larger incentive funds for their managers and employees—obviously depends on the prices used for evaluating all inputs and outputs. One set of prices could give all textile mills profits and all machine shops losses. Another set of prices could do just the reverse. How will relative prices be determined? To answer "on the basis of cost" is merely to beg the question since costs depend upon relative prices as well. To answer "supply and demand" is to forget that in a planned economy the public sector determines supply. Neither the Cubans nor the international champions of the "reform" model have an adequate justification for the prices they use and the material rewards they determine. Furthermore, even should a set of relative prices be found that discriminates neither against the textile mills nor machine shops, not all textile mills and not all machine shops are created equal. Workers in a brand new textile mill will generate higher profits per employee than will workers in a 50 year old mill, given equal skill, effort, and luck. So, in general, material reward based on individual production unit profits can be expected to benefit those "privileged" to work in the more modern industries and the more modern firms within their industry as much as it can be expected to reward greater effort.

In the second place, although the greater decentralization of economic decision-making—allowing individual units to invest their own profits and choose and market their own outputs after their planned quotas are met—might elicit more initiative from the managerial fraction of the coordinator class, there is no reason to expect it to increase worker initiative. In general, in the old system workers carried out a production plan determined by the central planners. In the reform system workers carry out a production plan determined in part by the central planners and in part by their immediate managers. But in the particular case of Cuba in this last two years, the situation as regards workers' power vis-a-vis the coordinator class as a whole has deteriorated. Whereas workers engaged in a limited form of reaction to proposed plans from the central planning ministry in the past, they are increasingly powerless vis-a-vis their local managers. "In the drive for profits, management is to get more responsibility, and freedom to dismiss unwanted workers. Unless workers got in trouble with police or wanted to emigrate, [in the past] they were almost completely cushioned against being fired. The Ministry of Labor had to authorize every move. Officials have now recognized that job security, combined with the fact that there is little to buy with extra earnings, has led to high absenteeism and sloppiness."[81] Moreover, the system of microbrigades that we praised as one factor that enhanced workers' participation in economic decision making in the early seventies has been cut back dramatically in the late seventies. Finally, the system of distribution of scarce consumer durables by union committees has atrophied due to a shift in import priorities toward consumer durables allowing for their distribution on an open market. For the first time in Cuba there are things worth buying with the increasing amounts of extra income received through educational or employment privileges.

Although our evaluation of recent trends in the Cuban economy is obviously quite negative, we hasten to add three caveats.

1) Unlike the Soviet Union, Cuba is still a small, underdeveloped, third world country that has not been pursuing a non-capitalist road for practically the entire twentieth century. So we must remember from where Cuba has emerged only relatively recently. A Cuban miner told Maurice Zeitlin the following:

The life under the capitalist system was a life condemned to death below the earth—and your children also; that's what they were good for. They were lucky if they made sixth grade; that was really special. Only the strongest could work. Those without good physiques could not.... Look, I don't mean this in any way personally, but listen American. There used to be a barrio here they called barrio americano, where only Americans lived, the administrators, technicians, and so forth; and on the door of their social club was a sign, 'Only for members.' Now that's a social club for all of us. We are all members now. Everyone.[82]

There is no denying the progress that has occurred. It must be recorded and the revolution for that reason defended. But this progress is not the issue at stake here.

2) Nor is the issue here whether or not the Cuban leadership has been "free" to do differently than they have done. The political, military, and economic hostility of the U.S., Cuba's dependence on the Soviet Union and socialist bloc for political, military, and economic sustenance, and the incredible international economic conditions to which all non-oil producing third world countries have been subject in the last half of the 1970s, all have greatly limited the possibilities for developing socialism in Cuba. But asking whether or not Cuba is developing a socialist society or some other kind of society is not the same as asking who or what is to blame to the extent the latter is the case.

3) Finally, as pessimistic as we are about recent trends in Cuba's economy, we are quite optimistic about certain political trends, as described last section. It is appropriate to note here that our overall theory suggests it would be remarkable if Cuba's political sphere could make great socialist progress while the economy was consolidating toward a coordinator mode, with little tension between the two trends. We believe there is in fact a great tension developing and moreover that the current development of the economy also has unintended implications for the possibility of new socialist trends in Cuba and in chapter five we will return to these issues in assesing likely future developments in the Cuban revolutionary experience.

## The Cuban Revolution Versus Latin Machismo

The Cuban revolution has brought major changes in women's economic conditions, and some changes in the relations between men and women as well. And while these changes certainly haven't spelled an end to patriarchy, it is not yet clear what will be the full dimensions of the transformation of Cuban kinship relations. While most evidence warrants a cautious appraisal, there are still prospects for an assault on patriarchy itself, not simply its most extreme manifestations. We have already seen that there is much confusion about the direction of the revolution in the Cuban polity and economy. As causal relations run in all directions between these spheres, it is not surprising that there should be similar ambivalences within the dynamics of Cuban kinship experiences.

### A Heavy Heritage

At the time of the revolution Cuban women endured hardships not solely due to their society's economic underdevelopment, but due to its archaic and repressive attitudes concerning the role and place of women in social life as well. "Nobody knows how many of our sisters were whores in Cuba during the last years of the Batista tyranny. In Havana (in 1957) there were some 270 overcrowded brothels, there were dozens of hotels and motels renting rooms by the hour, and there were over 700 bars congested with meseras—or hostesses—the first step towards prostitution."[83] According to Sheila Rowbotham there were only three options available to women in pre-revolutionary Cuba, "to be a slave to a man in the house, become a mother, or be an object of pleasure."[84] In interviews conducted years after the revolution one finds the residue of this heritage not only in the views of men, but also in women's attitudes toward one another. There was "low self-esteem and little support of women by women." Male children enjoyed preferential treatment. There was "a lack of empathy and trust between women, exploitation of women by women,"[85] and of course a pervasive and extreme level of sexism on the part of men. Moreover for most Cuban women the revolution had literally nothing to do with "liberation" in a feminist sense. Rather, what was most frequently sought was freedom "from outside work in order to take care of their own homes, and have time to spend with their own children."[86]

In this context, and given the underdevelopment of Cuba and the need to make use of all able-bodied workers no matter their sex, the main motivation for altering the situation of women was economic. They had to be taught, educated, and given confidence, all so they could participate in production to bring Cuba out of underdevelopment.[87] In the literacy campaign of 1961 women's illiteracy was brought down from 23 percent to 3.7 percent. "Girls who, prior to the revolution, could have aspired to little more than basic literacy skills were incorporated into the educational system at every level. By 1970, women composed 49 percent of Cuba's elementary school students, 55 percent of high school students, and 40 percent of students in higher education."[88] But the purpose of all this was not to confront anything so pervasive to the definition of Cuban society as patriarchy. Rather, the question was how half the population could do their share for development. Like in the Soviet Union and China, economic integration was immensely positive; but by itself there was no reason to believe it would lead any further in Cuba than elsewhere. Indeed, the same tell-tale aberrations gave evidence of the limitations of the process: "Many of the special education programs for women reflected both the government's good intentions and its stereotypical view of women and women's capabilities. For example, thousands of young girls were brought from the countryside to Havana on scholarships to study, en masse, 'feminine arts' such as cooking, sewing, and nursing. In other schools, established for the 'improvement' of wives of political prisoners, country women were encouraged to formalize their marriages and taught to curl their hair, shave their legs, wear high heeled shoes, nylon stockings, and matching accessories. Vocational training schools for women, such as those for former prostitutes, also often had personal grooming classes as part of the curricula."[89]

It is not only the fact that in the process of being inducted into the workforce women were urged to maintain their 'womanly ways' that undermined the program's impact on patriarchy. Perhaps more damning was that nothing was being done to overcome the sexual division of labor within the economy itself. Indeed, just the reverse seems to have been the case. Certainly women entering work tended to "be concentrated in those sectors in which they had generally worked before: in particular education, health, administration, and light industry [so that] much of the work women were doing could be seen as an extension of female functions in the home."[90] Of course there were exceptions, and these were often pointed out publicly, but most men and women could reasonably dismiss them as exceptions to the norm that would characterize Cuba's future. "In certain areas, such as daycare, what had been a necessity in the early days of the revolution was escalated to the level of theory. The fact that all those who worked daily in direct contact with children were women began to be given a 'scientific' justification: children needed female nurturing. It was 'only natural' that those who principally cared for children in daycare centers should be women."[91] There was a trend toward giving women "protected access to certain suitable work" and though this insured their ability to enter the workforce it was also a policy containing the risk of "permanently categorizing the least physically demanding and most unskilled jobs as 'women's work.'"[92] Indeed, in 1968 the sexual division of labor "received the force of law" with the passage of Resolutions 47 and 48 by the Ministry of Labor. For "these resolutions reserved some 500 job categories specifically for women and prohibited women from entering an equal number of professions."[93] This could not do otherwise than "strengthen notions of a 'natural' sexual division of labor,"[94] so it is reasonable to assume they were passed with the intention of combating what was considered an undesireable by-product of the rush to enlist women in the workforce— the potential dislocation of traditional attitudes about the role of women and men at the level of the principles of male supremacy itself.

But there was a grave problem with the scenario. The national commitment to women entering the workforce as a means of combating underdevelopment was unswerving. However, there was initially no national commitment to challenging the assumption that "children, laundry, and cooking were women's work."[95] It was expected that women in the home would be relieved of these functions eventually when the public sector could take on the work. And it was also a policy that working women should receive advantages to diminish the time required in certain tasks, for example special privileges at laundries and exemptions from waiting on lines at groceries. But by and large, for women entering the workforce, double duty as both industrial worker and as housewife/mother, was the order of the day.[96]

The burden was apparently too much for most to endure. In the first place it meant that in addition to doing "women's work" in their workplace, as we discussed above, new women workers would have little time for workplace meetings, development of their skills, etc. Instead they would need to rush home to clean up, care for kids, shop, and generally manage the household. As a result their chances for promotion in the workplace were exceptionally limited. And since it was often through excelling at work that one became a party member or grew in public stature sufficiently to warrant a position of political leadership, women were excluded here too. While keeping the country clean, fed, and populated, they did not have time or energy to compete politically and economically with men who were freed from those roles in the family. In 1974 women still made up under 13% of the party's membership and held only 15% of the leadership positions in all units of production, services,and administration.[97] Even as of 1976, "in the party, 2.9 percent of the municipal national leadership is female. There are no women members in the political bureau, nor in the secretariat, the two bodies which carry on the daily work of the party."[98] This means that the situation of women in Cuba has been dependent upon the will of governors who are overwhelmingly men.

But from the perspective of that male leadership, and in context of their desire to increase the "productive" contribution of women, the main visible difficulty of the program to enlist women into the workforce was that while entering the workplace in large numbers, they tended to leave almost as frequently. For example, "during the last three months of 1969, some 140,000 women were incorporated into the labor force. 110,000 of these women were still working at the end of 1969. However, this represented a net gain of only some 27,000 for that period, since at the same time some 80,000 other women had left work."[99] For the entire period from 1969 to 1974, "it has been estimated that more than 700,000 women had to be recruited into the labor force in order to achieve a net gain of just under 200,000 women workers."[100] In the case of Cuba, as with the Soviet Union and China, we are evaluating from a distance with only very schematic data and description. Perhaps the burden of the dual work role alone explains a high percentage of this flow of women into and then out of the workplace. More likely, it is the burden and implied permanence of this dual role, as well as the "redundant character" of work roles defined by a sexual division of labor, that were together critical. And in case any other pressures were necessary to induce women to leave jobs just as soon as it was economically possible, there is little doubt that husbands and male workmates pushed in that direction more often than not.

In the orthodox Marxist view the program to bring women into the workforce is inherently anti-patriarchal and, if brought to its logical conclusion will end by overthrowing patriarchy. In our view, this program has a contradictory implication for patriarchy. While it tends to erode the most extreme forms of patriarchy, and may under certain circumstances even challenge patriarchy itself, it will always be coopted to a form consistent with the maintenance of new forms of patriarchy and male supremacy so long as the basic roots of these oppressive features of kinship relations go unchallenged. At the point where the difficulties of the program of enlistment of female workers became clear, there were different options for the Cubans to follow. Certainly the Soviet economy has in the main succeeded in incorporating Soviet women. But as we have seen this was accomplished without undermining the basic idea of biological destiny, the asymmetry in the roles of men and women, and male supremacy. What was to be the outcome in Cuba? Could women be incorporated without undermining male supremacy and would this be the aim, or might there be a move toward a fuller revolution in the kinship sphere?

The most important evidence we have for evaluating this question is the Cuban "Family Code."[101] Although proposed from the top, it was discussed throughout the country in the Committees for Defense of the Revolution and unions as well as in the Cuban Federation of Women. The code has provisions for "equal rights and duties for both partners" in marriage including sharing responsibility for childcare and upbringing and for such household tasks as cooking and cleaning. The code guarantees both partners the right "to practice their profession or skill" and states that each partner has an obligation to make this possible for the other.[102] Thus, as Cuban political institutions took a markedly socialist turn with the institution of poder popular in the mid-70s, so did kinship institutions with the passage of the family code. For the enactment of the principle that men are as responsible for what had previously been deemed women's chores as law and revolutionary principle via a thoroughgoing participatory process is a step of major significance. Of course it did not mean an immediate transformation of all attitudes and practices. But the fact that in most public discussions "no men stood up to object to the parts that stipulate equal responsibility in the home,"[103] and that it is standard practice at weddings to read critical sections of the law, are testimony that the recent revolutionary trend in Cuban kinship institutions were manifested at least to some extent in concrete changes in kinship relations and attitudes.

But while the effort to establish new models for women has been substantial, there has been little equivalent "resocialization" of male role models. All the same, there has been some progress. For example, "there has been a dramatic change in men's relation to children. In the past a Cuban man would no sooner be caught on the street with a child in his arms than he would be caught hanging out the laundry. It is now commonplace to see men in public and at home playing with and fondling infants and toddlers."[104] Of course this is not a feminist revolution. After all, the same sights are quite common in the United States but it is nonetheless the case that it is women who have responsibility for children; men only help, at best. And indeed, in Cuba, though the trend is a desirable one, how far it will go is the real question. For at present it is still "female attention and love that is considered primary. The staff of the day care centers is female. To date there has been neither an attempt to change this, nor an analysis that argues the importance of men working with young children."[105] A poingant example of the prevalent attitude is the opinion of Marta Santander, a leader in Cuban child care:

> There are many fronts of work in this country and men are very much needed. There are many jobs a woman can do, but many others she can't. The man working with children would have to be a young man. But young men are working on other important things. Men are not going to work with children when women can do it. And in any case, since children need affection and special care, it's hard to find this in a young man.[106]

This almost total failure to address the resocialization of male roles serves as an appropriate reminder about what will ultimately determine the meaning of increased female participation in the workforce. The ultimate meaning of women entering the workforce will depend on the institutional and social changes which accompany it, both in the division of labor within the economy and in the family as well. To the extent that women entering the economy is seen by both men and women as a social necessity, a response to the need for more workers, and "women's work" is seen as not corresponding to men's and is accorded lower status, female participation in the economy will not be destructive of patriarchy. To the extent that gender based economic and familial roles are challenged both formally and in Cuban men and women's consciousness at the same time, on the other hand, female incorporation will be progressive.

Within the economy, for example, the establishment of female organizations, the "feminine front," in each production unit is a positive step. Yet it is compromised by the fact that it has no official power and is elected by all workers in the factory, not just the women. Similarly, the family code's injunction to share labor and responsibility in the household is immensely positive. At the same time, the absence of a vehicle that can propel the implementation of this injunction, one which can give women a collective power to enforce its implementation, is a major failing. The party's public commitment as expressed in a 1975 document on the situation of women presented at the first Congress of the Cuban Communist Party is positive: "a fundamental battle must be waged in the realm of consciousness, because it is there that the backward concepts which lock us in the past continue to subsist."[107] But the almost total absence of women from party leadership undercuts the statement's power.

There has yet to be any meaningful *public* discussion we know of concerning sexuality: either women's rights to control their own bodies, women's rights to equal sexual fulfillment, or the freedom of sexual preference. Obviously the incorporation of women into the workforce would more substantially undermine male supremacy if it were accompanied by a general reevaluation of male and female assumptions about behavior in general and especially sexuality. The fact that such a discussion has not occurred is evidence that the forces seeking a full kinship revolution are still far from ascendant. As Sheila Rowbotham commented on this issue in Cuba "both revolutionary homosexuality and active female heterosexuality imply the redefinition of masculinity—'revolutionary' masculinity included. At this point the most revolutionary of comrades become paternalist. Women told Elizabeth Sutherland: 'The idea that sex is for the woman's pleasure as well as the man's—that is the taboo of taboos....Less change has taken place in this area than in any other.' "[108]

The situation of homosexuals in Cuba is also indicative of the extent to which the battle to transform sexist forms of consciousness has just begun. There is no doubt that gays have been oppressed in revolutionary Cuba, although both the extent of the repression and the degree to which popular attitudes or official policy are to blame are difficult to determine. "In the first stages of post-Revolutionary Cuba" there were "mass jailings of gays as 'anti-social' elements."[109] On the other hand, this policy is "now admitted to have been a mistake by many Cuban officials...the practice was discontinued after a few years, and it is no longer a criminal offense to be gay."[110] In general, the policy toward homosexuals appears to to have improved over time. "Margaret Randall, an American poet and feminist living in Cuba since 1969 says that the Communist Party position on homosexuality has become noticeably more tolerant in recent years. One bit of evidence she offered was...a new textbook on sex education, a Spanish translation of a book written in the German Democratic Republic: *Man and Woman in Intimacy*. In the book homosexuality is not classified under the chapter on 'Sexual Deviations,' but appears as a short subsequent chapter. The introductory paragraph argues that there is no scientific basis for the widespread belief that homosexuality is unnatural, sinful, or a mental disease. It claims on the contrary that homosexual relations can be just as healthy, mature and responsible as heterosexual relations."[111] Moreover, reports indicate that homosexuality is no longer recognized as a category of mental sickness at Cuban mental hospitals, and homosexuals are much less discriminated against in the Union of Writers and Artists.

But there is little doubt that popular homophobia remains strong in Cuba, as the high percentage of homosexuals among recent refugees from Cuba testifies. Nor is there doubt that this homophobia is still reflected in, and encouraged by, some aspects of official policy. Gays are still not eligible for membership in the Cuban Communist Party, and the reason given is the traditional communist argument that they are potentially subject to blackmail by class enemies. That this is a totally invalid argument for people who are openly gay receives no response. Moreover, even the most sanguine of outside observers would be hard pressed to suggest that the government, even today, would tolerate formation of a counter-cultural "Gay Pride" movement in Cuba.

In sum, the status of kinship relations in revolutionary Cuba is mixed and the outcome ambiguous. The revamping of resolutions

47 and 48 in 1976 to limit women to taking 300 types of jobs instead of 500, coming as it did in context of women's demands that where they work should be a matter of choice, was certainly a negative step.[112] Likewise, the continuing heavy Latin machismo, largely uncountered, remains a paramount problem. "That oppression still exists is also beyond doubt, it is obvious in almost every aspect of a Cuban woman's life. The same woman who drives a tractor or studies at a sugar engineering school must daily confront the possessive imposition of a dozen commenting males every time she walks down the street. A National Heroine of Labor, who had cut more than a million pounds of sugarcane, will worry about the shape and condition of her fingernails. The anniversary of the attack on Moncada, the attack that launched the final phase of the Cuban revolutionary struggle, is still celebrated with something resembling a beauty contest to choose the female 'star' of the celebration and her court."[113] Yet the existence of the family code and the widespread discussions it has engendered, and of at least a verbal commitment throughout the society and especially in certain sectors of the party to deal with the code's injunctions in a principled way, does lend some hope for a continuation of the kinship revolution. Finally, although we know little of its impact or scale, there is in Cuba, at least among some, a more comprehensive awareness of the more radical dimensions of the struggle for the advance of women. Sheila Rowbotham quotes from a document that circulated at least around the University of Havana in 1967, and though the excerpt is long, it both demonstrates that a feminist spark burns in postrevolutionary Cuba and provides a good place to end this discussion.

> Economic independence is not enough. It is not a matter of a woman being able to pay her way but...of being able to transform her attitude toward life...the problem will not be solved simply by the incorporation of the woman in work. Extracting **her from** the role of housewife will not automatically change her attitude toward life. A woman working for the collectivity can continue to view problems through the prism of subordination and passivity. Change of occupation is only the basis for the transformation of woman...her whole attitude must change. It is a process of personal realization, which does not lie merely in dedicating herself to a creative task but in shifting the center of interest from the limits of one's emotional life

and events within the nuclear family, to a much broader area...which goes beyond individual interest, the interest centered in social activity. A woman realizes herself as a person when her viewpoint transcends egotistic interest. The true feminine struggle is the rejection of all those childhood teachings, all those family pressures during adolescence, and even the dominant social thinking which affects her as an adult...the ideas of femininity, of womanhood, as meaning the dedication of one's life to finding and keeping a companion generally, at the expense of becoming a man's satellite.[114]

## Cuban Cultural Policy and Community Relations

In each historical section on community relations we have selected only a few exemplary episodes or aspects and make no claim of comprehensive evaluation. As available information is greatest for the Soviet Union, in chapter two we deliberately focused on a little known aspect of national/racial policy both because that type of policy is the most difficult aspect of community relations to study over an extended period in any of the three countries and also because a worthy analysis of Soviet cultural policy is beyond our present capacities in any case. Regarding China, instead, we focused on government policies toward religions and cultural policies espoused by the Maoists, especially during the Cultural Revolution. In this section on Cuba we will focus on the well documented twists and turns in government cultural policies, and will also briefly summarize some meager evidence regarding race relations.

### Cuban Cultural Policies

Cuban cultural policy has closely followed shifts in economic policy, and particularly shifts in foreign relations with the Soviet Union. For example, coinciding with early revolutionary euphoria the Cubans emphasized cultural humanism from 1959 to 1961, but then during the period of mini-Stalinism from 1962 to1964 they turned toward socialist realism. The period of economic heresy from 1965 to 1968 was also a period of cultural heresy challenging many sacred cows of "existing socialist" theory and policy. Yet as economic problems mounted and relations with the Soviet Union were reemphasized from 1969 into the mid-seventies, there was a return to socialist realism culminating in the Jaime Padilla affair and mutual recriminations between Castro and the intellectual leftist community in the West. Finally, since the mid-seventies, like the mixture of policy in other spheres, cultural policy too has been ambiguous. Rather than well-defined swings between revolutionary humanism and heavy-handed socialist realism there has been a relatively stable and moderate cultural policy.

The shift from open, pluralist, cultural humanism in the first few years to closed, repressive socialist realism during the mini-Stalinist period is best illustrated by the experience of a magazine called *Lunes de Revolucion,* the cultural supplement to the daily paper, *Revolucion,* edited by Carlos Franqui. According to K.S. Karol, *Lunes* aired a variety of cultural perspectives on diverse topics not generally considered of mass interest even while it built a weekly readership of 250,000.[115]

> The weekly supplement discussed such topics as avant-garde art and the aspirations of the modern left. Trotsky's writings on art and revolution were deemed worthy of presentation to the Cuban public, and the space devoted to Andre Breton showed the group's attraction to surrealism. Yet they did not neglect the *Communist Manifesto* either, or the works of the great Bolshevik era, from John Reed and Mayakovsky to Isaac Babel. On January 18, 1960, on the sudden death of Albert Camus, they dedicated a whole issue to his writings; three weeks later, on the occasion of Anastas Mikoyan's visit, they published a special number on the Soviet Union, its films, theater, and literature. When Sartre came to Cuba a month later, they published his *Ideology and Revolution* together with a lengthy interview.... Moreover, [*Lunes*] published fundamental studies of the history of the Cuban revolution, and some of the most important works of Fidel Castro, Ernesto Che Guevara, and Camilo Cienfuegos.... And all the Cuban leaders acknowledged that [*Lunes*] met a specific need of a new generation, eager for knowledge and quite capable of making up its own mind. According to Ernesto Che

Guevara, *Lunes de Revolucion* was a striking contribution to Cuban culture. And Fidel Castro described *Lunes* as a worthy attempt to give expression to three similar things: revolution, the people, and culture.[116]

But as elements of the Communist old guard became increasingly powerful by mid-1961, they began questioning the wisdom of allowing an independent group to publish whatever works it chose, including those banned in other socialist countries.

On June 16, 1961, Carlos Franqui and his proteges were invited to a discussion at the National Library in Havana. They were told nothing about the purpose of the meeting and they expected a small, friendly gathering to discuss certain minor differences between them and their country's cultural leaders. Instead, they found themselves in a large hall, at a meeting attended by almost all the country's intellectuals, great and small. They had to face a board of inquiry chaired by Mrs. Garcia Buchacha and made up chiefly of PSP leaders; and they were addressed in a manner far more suited to a court of law than to an intellectual debate. They were accused of splitting the ranks of the Revolution, a serious crime at a time when unity had become a matter of life and death. They were accused of lacking a proper socialist perspective, of hankering after Western culture, and, more generally, of upholding dubious cultural trends. A terrible indictment, all told.[117]

The accusations aroused a varied response from the Cuban intellectual community. Some such as Roberto Fernandez Retamar (historian, poet, and later editor of *Casa de las Americas*), and Lisandro Otero (a veteran of the July 26th Movement, novelist, and later vice-president of the Cuba Council for Culture) spoke up for the editors of *Lunes* declaring that "loyalty to the revolution was perfectly compatible with the defense of avant-garde ideas and that they did not accept authoritarian definitions of socialist culture."[118] Some, such as Alejandro Carpentier, absented themselves from the debate, though still others, such as the poet "Jose Alvarez Baragano, were even ready to indulge in self-criticism for their contributions, and confessed that their supposed errors had been due to their bourgeois origin."[119]

In any case, as Karol reports, the issue was settled by Fidel's

declaration "that the Cuban revolution had not the least intention
of imposing a cultural ine on artists. There was no desire to limit
the freedom of research or expression of anyone on the side of the
Revolution. 'Within the Revolution, complete freedom; against
the Revolution, none.'"[120] But the publication of *Lunes* was
stopped nonetheless "not because the paper had been guilty of
crimes against the Revolution, but because Fidel decreed that it
was improper for so small a group to have so powerful a weekly.
He asked all writers and artists to combine their efforts in starting
a big cultural weekly, and to that effect a Union of Writers and
Artists was founded in August, 1961. It exists to this day, but has
never produced a journal—it does, however, put out a run-of-the-
mill magazine called *Union*, whose small circulation is a measure
of their lack of originality."[121] Although this likely seemed a good
compromise solution at the time, the turn toward mini-Stalinism
less than a year later confirmed that in fact the left intellectuals'
loss of their main vehicle in the cultural field was very important.

Still, the first period of socialist realism was short-lived.
During the mini-Stalin period the proportion of blue-jacketed
editions of the Moscow Foreign Publishing House increased while
the works of Trotsky, Kafka, Joyce, and others banned in the
Soviet Union disappeared. Blas Roca, then an editor of *Hoy*, not
published an attack on Fellini's "La Dolce Vita" as unworthy of
being shown in a socialist country even though he admitted he had
never even seen it. Yet immediately thereafter began a period of
cultural non-conformity (1965) when "everything related to the
Soviet cultural and ideological model was downgraded to the point
of open ridicule."[122] Indicative of the new creativity and coinciding
with the convening in Havana of the Latin American Solidarity
Organization (OLAS) in July of 1967, "the Paris *Salon de Mai* a
prestigious annual exhibition of ultra-avant-garde painting and
sculpture, was transported to Havana for the first time ever to the
Western Hemisphere, along with scores of prominent artists and
fellow-travelling writers. The display was the ultimate challenge
to socialist realism."[123] As Karol notes, "by inviting the *Salon*...the
Castroists were giving official blessing to the kind of art on which
other socialist countries had resolutely turned their backs." Even
worse, "the Cubans now declared that the only truly revolutionary
and progressive art was art that did not allow itself to be fettered
by petrified Marxism."[124]

But the full political significance of this dramatic shift in cultural policy was not apparent until the climax of the campaign of the week-long Cultural Congress in January 1968* at which Fidel exclaimed:

Where did the death of Che Guevara [three months earlier] have its most profound impact?...Precisely among the intellectual workers,...not [among] organizations of parties...who asked why Che Guevara died,...who are incapable of understanding and will never understand why he died, nor will they ever be capable of dying as he did, or of being revolutionaries as he was. [As Halperin notes, "there was no misconstruing the organizations or parties Castro had in mind or what his target was when he declared"] Marxism must act like a revolutionary force and not a pseudo-revolutionary church.... We hope, of course, that for stating these things we shall not be excommunicated or turned over to the Holy Inquisition.[125]

---

*The following description by Karol gives some idea of the magnitude of this extraordinary event: "Altogether more than five hundred intellectuals from seventy countries flocked to Havana. Bertrand Russell, Jean Paul Sartre, and Ernst Fisher, unable to attend for health reasons, sent warm messages of support. Such famous European writers as Michel Leiris, Jorge Semprun, Max-Paul Foucher, and Arnold Wesker; such renowned scientists as Pierre Vigier; such well-known painters as Matta, Lam, Pignon; such social scientists as Milliband, Hobsbawm, Guerin, Axelos—and this list is far from complete—mingled with prominant delegates from the Third World. Among these delegates, the Latin Americans and the Antillians, including Aime Cesaire, Julio Cortazar, and Benedetti, were the most widely represented. Nor was the conference remarkable for its composition alone; its agenda was no less extraordinary. Five working committees were to deal with five grand themes: culture and national independence; the integral education of man; the responsibility of intellectuals for the underdeveloped world; culture and mass media; art, science, and technology. A very full program indeed. The Cuban organizers made it clear right from the outset, that they were not interested in academic debates, but hoped for a concrete reply to the central question underlying the whole agenda, namely how the intellectual can best serve the Revolution. They did not shock anybody. On the contrary, the foreign guests had feared that, despite all their sympathy for the Castroists, they had been asked to

But "this small country, so exposed, so threatened," did not long feel "at liberty to prove to the whole world that socialism was not synonymous with intolerance and obscurantism."[126] Rather, when the left period in economic policy came to a close, when neither two, nor three, much less many Vietnams materialized, and when, seeking security, Cuba reoriented both its economic and foreign policies toward closer collaboration with the Soviet Union, cultivating support of the New Left and unaffiliated radical intelligentsia in Western Europe and Latin America declined in importance. It likely even appeared that the demise of cultural humanism was a small price to pay for Soviet support. In any case, the reversal in cultural policy both began with, and was best symbolized by the Jaime Padilla affair.

A few months after the Cultural Congress described above, Jaime Padilla won an annual international poetry prize for his collection of verses, "Fuera del Juego" ("Out of the Game"). Although

> he was the unanimous choice of a five-man jury of reputable literary figures of the left, from as many countries, an uproar by the directors of UNEAC greeted the award: Padilla's poetry was counter-revolutionary. However, in the face of sharp protests by the jury and others, a compromise was reached. *Fuera del Juego* was published, according to the rules of the contest; but in addition to the customary foreward by the jury the book also carried a blistering attack on the poet and his work—an attack that of course, he could not answer. Meanwhile, the army weekly *Verde Oliva* opened a slashing campaign against ideological and political heresy among the intellectuals.[127]

Perhaps the most insightful commentary on the affair was provided by Julio Cortazar, an Argentine novelist and long-time sympathizer of the Cuban Revolution who argued that—

> ...though Padilla believed in the revolution, as a critic and poet he needn't submerge himself blindly in it. Like

Havana simply to demonstrate their solidarity with Cuba, to be put on public display in the usual Soviet manner. All of them were most agreeably surprised to find that nothing of the kind was intended. (Karol, op. cit. p 398).

myself and so many others, Padilla is condemned to remain in part 'out of the game.' He has the courage to say so while so many others remain silent. His sadness, but also his hope in the future are expressed in these verses....They are not counterrevolutionary.[128]

But the wisdom of this insight into the useful role that intellectuals can and should play in developing socialist culture was lost in the face of the bankrupt Stalinist logic of Roberto Fernandez Retamar, the same Cuban figure who had formerly defended the editors of *Lunes* in 1961, but who now, as editor of *Casa de Las Americas* and Cuba's most prominent literary figure and intellectual, published a long essay justifying the Cuban government's actions in the Padilla affair and attacking those intellectuals who voiced objections. In defense of the government which arrested Padilla on March 30, 1971 and released him five weeks later *after* he had written a 4,000 word confession repudiating his work, admitting to cultural and moral torpitude, accusing French leftists K.S. Karol and Rene Dumont of being CIA agents, and opposing open letters signed by the likes of Jean-Paul Sartre, Simone de Beauvoir, Alberto Moravio, Julio Cortazar, Carlos Fuentes, Gabriel Garcia Marquez, Mario Vargas Llosa, and Susan Sontag, Retamar rationalized that "there is no reason to give any explanation to the sort of people who call themselves leftists but who, nonetheless, don't seem to give a damn about the masses and rush forth shamelessly to repeat word for word the same critiques of the socialist world proposed and promulgated by capitalism thereby merely demonstrating that they have not broken with capitalism as radically as they might perhaps think."[129] Halperin's evaluation of the logic of Retamar's (and the Cuban government's) position, is apt:

> He makes objections to left-wing repression akin to rejection of socialism itself, and the counterpart of support to imperialism and capitalism. Retamar demands support for Cuba entirely on the Cuban leadership's own terms. He asks for a suspension of all criticism. If the critics don't comply, Retamar has provided new grounds for Cuban dismissal of their complaints. They are irrelevant because they represent the voice of a colonized non-Latin cultural apparatus.[130]

But the political fallout of the Padilla affair was greater than the repression itself. For it marked a complete break between the Cuban government and the left intellectual community in the West, even though that community had always supported Cuba no matter how critical they had been of government policies in the Soviet Union or Eastern Europe. Moreover, the bitterness of the break provided backdrop for a wholehearted official Cuban endorsement of a cultural policy "fundamentally indistinguishable from the neo-Stalinist obscurantism that guides official cultural policy in Moscow or the cruder version that prevails in Peking."[132] Open letters published in *Le Monde* and *The New York Times* of May 22, 1971, by Western intellectuals stated:

> We hold that it is our duty to inform you of our shame and our anger.... The contents of this confession, with its absurd accusations and delirious assertions...recall the most sordid moments of the era of Stalinism, with its prefabricated verdicts and its witch-hunts.... The contempt for human dignity implied in the act of forcing a man into ludicrously accusing himself of the worst treasons and indignities does not alarm us because it concerns a writer but because any Cuban...can also become the victim of similar violence and humiliation.[132]

The final resolution of the First National Congress on Education and Culture held in Havana in April 1971 replied:

> In the field of ideological struggle there is no room for palliatives or half measures.... There is room only for ideological coexistence with the spiritual creation of the revolutionary peoples, with socialist culture, with the forms of expression of Marxist Leninist ideology....Thus all trends are condemnable and inadmissable that are based on apparent ideas of freedom as a disguise for the counterrevolutionary poison of works that conspire against the revolutionary ideology on which the construction of socialism and communism is based....

> We reject the claims of the Mafia of pseudoleftist bourgeois intellectuals to become the critical conscience of society. They are the bearers of a new colonization,... agents of the metropolitan imperialist culture who have

found a small group of mentally colonized people in our country who have echoed their ideas.... Many pseudo-revolutionary writers...who play at Marxism, but are against the socialist countries; those who claim to be in solidarity with the liberation struggles but support the Israeli aggression...perpetrated against the Arab peoples with the aid of U.S. imperialism; and those who in the final analysis turned leftism into merchandise will be unmasked.[133]

And Fidel's speech to the closing session left no doubt that the break was a personal as well as political one:

They are at war against us, brazen pseudoleftists, ...shameless Latin Americans,...fakers,...and intellectual rats....Now you know it, bourgeois intellectuals and bourgeois libelants, agents of the CIA and intelligence services of imperialism, you will not be allowed to come to Cuba!...Our door, will remain closed indefinitely.[134]

But despite this raging attack—an official declaration of policy that has never been rescinded—there is evidence that day-to-day Cuban cultural life in the seventies has been significantly more robust and healthy than in the Soviet Union or China, in the areas of support for authentic folk culture and cinema, in particular.[135] Whether this means government practice in the seventies has differed significantly from the official doctrines above, or that the perseverance of Cuban cultural workers has restricted government designs, is impossible for us to know. Given our overall analysis of the Cuban experience, however, it seems reasonable to hypothesize that fluctuations of Cuban cultural practice have reflected a contradiction between two tendencies with very different suppositions and roots. The pluralist and humanist tradition seemingly championed by Fidelistas and left cultural workers for its *cultural merit*, has contested a socialist realist trend promoted by the PSP's intellectuals and some "pragmatic" Fidelistas who presumably regard this as a low-cost means of appeasing Soviet ideologues of the loyalty of Cuban leaders to Soviet models. Thus, as with the other spheres of Cuban activity, there is much still to be resolved.

## Cuban Race Relations

For the half century before the triumph of the Revolution, the racial relations in Cuba bore many resemblances to race relations in much of the U.S. south. The segregation of night clubs and beaches were but two of the better known forms of special discrimination endured by Black Cubans in addition to the almost universal poverty they suffered whether they resided in city slums or formed part of the seasonal labor force harvesting the sugar crop. But the resolution with which the Revolutionary government opposed all forms of racial discrimination from its earliest days is undeniable. To our knowledge there has never been the slightest hint of official sanction for any racial bias directed toward Blacks, and, indeed, one of the chief prides of the Revolution is that whatever else might have been its failings, and however long the delay in overcoming other forms of injustice and oppression, the revolution ended sanctioned institutionalized racism almost immediately.

But it is precisely this very pride in having supposedly eliminated racism by simply curtailing racist laws and forms, an official view that denies racism is a continuing problem in revolutionary Cuba, that worries us. For we do not understand racism as a kind of social phenomenon that can be eliminated by fiat. If a new government came to power in South Carolina and ended all forms of legal discrimination, mounting a serious public campaign against racism as a deadly social disease, then even if that government was the sole employer so that ending public discrimination extended to more than the state sphere, we would still expect continuing racism due to its perseverance in the human center— that is, racist consciousness among South Carolina's whites and the debilitating human residue of racial oppression among South Carolina's Blacks. And likewise, to the degree that Cuba was similar to South Carolina in these regards before 1959, we would expect the same to be true there. In other words, we find it incomprehensible that racism has not been a continuing problem in constant need of being addressed in post-revolutionary Cuba.

This is not to say that the public posture of the revolutionary government doesn't effectively address the problem of racism in many respects. To treat racism as a social disease of the past that will not be tolerated, to make clear that racism is not an issue about which any compromises will be contemplated either in terms of trade-offs for social progress in other areas or in terms of concessions to the practical necessities of transition, are useful stances in conveying the deadly seriousness of the Revolution's commitment to overcoming racism. Moreover, the tremendous emphasis that has been placed on the leading role played by Black Cubans in every phase of the long revolutionary process that Fidel, as leader of the newest generation of Cuban revolutionaries, has emphasized tirelessly dates back to the slave rebellions, is extremely helpful in overcoming racist residues in Cuban consciousness. It is as if the U.S. government were leading the ideological movement to discover the true history of Black people in this country and develop the sense of pride this history merits.

But there is a significant difference between a "very clear articulation that racism is not to be given nurturing ground in Cuban society" and that "any existing remains of the old system will die of starvation without official space in which to operate"— which is how Bernice Reagan perceived the Cuban position during her visit in 1977[136]—and the more aggressive and in our terms socialist view that conscious efforts must be made to overcome racism including special transitional institutions such as quotas and caucuses. Although the following account of this difference is specifically addressed to the situation of women rather than Blacks, it reveals the logic behind the Cuban Communist Party position on race as well, and is so well expressed by Bernice Reagan that it is worth quoting in full:

> When we asked about women writers, we were told that their numbers were slowly increasing. Before the revolution, they said, there were few women writers and there had not been as much progress as they had hoped. UNEAC [The Cuban Writer's Union] had no women officers because it had to be run by the majority. When we asked why the revolution had not addressed the problem, they said it was difficult to make an artist— ....They talked about contests at all educational levels to stimulate writers. We asked: why not do that for women? That would be discrimination, they said. We talked about efforts in the U.S. to give special attention to lack of participation by minority groups and women, at times attacked as discrimination but generally seen by

our groups as one way to deal with a much-needed catching up. I asked how long it had taken to address illiteracy and was told it was taken care of in one year. I said: you saw illiteracy as a problem for your society, addressed it, and took care of it. You say not having women writers is a weakness. Then why have you not addressed it programmatically?[138]

To our knowledge racial quotas have never been used in post-capitalist Cuban society. Whether it be in selecting party delegates and leadership, assigning jobs of particular skill and/or authority levels in the economy, or admitting students to particular programs and levels of education, quotas have always been viewed as discriminatory. Nor are we aware of any instances in which minority caucuses have been sanctioned in post-capitalist Cuba. Our point is not that quotas are justified as reparations for past mistreatment of Blacks, nor that caucuses and quotas are required because post-capitalist leaders are consciously exercising racial bias, or that post-capitalist institutions contain racist role definitions. The argument for quotas and caucuses is instead that to the degree racism penetrated all aspects of the old society, positive programs and institutional forms, rather than mere neutrality, are required to overcome racism in the new society. Far from being an implicit admission that the new society is racist or a new form of reverse discrimination—which seems to be the only interpretations Cubans can imagine—*corrective* quotas and minority caucuses are a sign of the seriousness of the new society's commitment to overcoming racism precisely because they recognize the continuing injustice that Black subsidization of a lengthier than necessary transition process implies.

Yet in spite of their refusal to use quotas and caucuses we are happy to admit that the actual record of achievement of the Cuban revolution in improving the situation of Blacks in Cuba seems remarkably good. Even before the large scale Cuban military support to African liberation movements, the Cuban armed forces had Blacks represented more than proportionately in leadership positions. And although he is not one of the better known figures outside of Cuba, Juan Almeida, a Black leader in the attack on Moncada from which the July 26th Movement took its name, is the most powerful individual in Cuba after Fidel and Raul Castro. There is also no doubt that the early emphasis on improving the economic position of the least advantaged, providing literacy and lower education to everyone, and increasing the social status accorded those workers in the most physically strenuous production tasks such as cutting sugar cane all rebounded more than proportionately to the benefit of Black Cubans. And it is quite obvious that the public recognition of the Black contribution to much of what is heralded as the best in Cuban culture is such as to define Blacks as the leaders in Cuban cultural developments, rather than as uncultured unfortunates. None of this is to deny that Blacks are still underrepresented in the higher bodies of Popular Power, the Party, and economic management. But on the basis of the meager evidence at our disposal, it appears the Cuban Revolution has perhaps gone further toward overcoming racism than our appraisal of their official policies would have led us to predict. In any case, what remains to be discussed regarding Cuba, China, and the Soviet Union as well, is the likelihood for socialist programs in the coming decade, and that is a subject we will take up next chapter.

# 5
# PROSPECTS FOR SOCIALISM

> In our hands is placed a power
> greater than their hoarded gold.
> Greater than their mighty armies
> magnified a thousand fold;
> We can bring to birth a new world
> from the ashes of the old,
> For the Union makes us strong.
> Solidarity Forever

As we proofread the galleys for this volume, the international situation becomes evermore frightening. Confrontations between the two superpowers are building toward a new Cold War as each responds to the increasing disintegration within its respective bloc. If the handwriting on the wall was unclear when the Soviet Union "secured its southern flank" by invading Afghanistan and Carter fended off Kennedy's challenge in the democratic primaries by fanning the flames of American conservatism and patriotism, it is certainly indelible as the Soviets hover on the brink of invading Poland and the Reagan administration prepares for military adventures on any and all fronts. That Reagan could ask Walter Cronkite, "Can we abandon a country that has stood beside us in every war we've ever fought, a country that strategically is essential to the free world? It has production of minerals we all must have, and so forth," and within days five South African military intelligence officials secretly and illegally enter the U.S. for discussions with the National Security Council and the Pentagon's Defense Intelligence Agency is more than testimony to the oratorical and diplomatic "elegance" of the new administration.

Yet it is not pollyanaish to see signs of hope in the international arena. The revolt of the Polish working class, formation of the Polish trade union Solidarity, and the self-discipline and courage it has shown to date are events that even the most optimistic socialists would never have anticipated even a year ago.

In our opinion the events that have already transpired in Poland—regardless of what may occur in the future—are sufficient to challenge the currents of pessimism regarding the human feasibility of socialism that periodically run cold in all our veins. Moreover, one's depression over the Neanderthal Reagan policy toward the Third World should not blind one to the fact that it is in large part a consequent whose antecedent includes the overthrow of Somoza in Nicaragua by a militantly anti-imperialist, pro-socialist, and pluralist popular movement; the threat of similar movements to similarly precarious client regimes in El Salvador, Guatamala, and Honduras; and the consolidation of anti-capitalist governments in Mozambique, Angola, and Zimbabwe—not to speak of the "loss of Indochina." In sum, it would be an error to allow oneself to become so overwhelmed by the crescendo of the brutality of the superpowers' response to lose sight of the increasingly powerful challenges to imperialism, capitalism, hegemonism, and coordinatorism that are its target.

To comprehensively assess all these issues within a single book, much less a single chapter, is obviously impossible. Beyond the perennial intra-class economic struggle of the Soviet economy events are still too murky for definitive evaluation. Yet to avoid addressing the meaning of the events in Poland, the prospects for socialism in Nicaragua, Zimbabwe, El Salvador, etc., and the prospects for socialist developments in the Soviet Union, China, and Cuba would be as irresponsible as to pretend to provide definitive answers. We therefore offer this afterward not as a comprehensive analysis but as a rough preliminary assessment of certain contemporary events and prospects which are too uncertain to be definitively understood, but too important to be completely ignored.

## Socialist Prospects in the Soviet Union, China, and Cuba

The Soviet Union: In chapter two we argued that the Soviet Union had become a full-fledged coordinator society in the broad sense of the word, in which a political elite, the coordinator class, men, and the Russian minority were clearly dominant. We dwelled on these aspects of Soviet society in order to make clear that the present day Soviet social formation has nothing to do with socialism, and indeed, hasn't for quite some time. But while we have emphasized the extent of intra-elite struggles in post-capitalist Russia, we did not at all mean to imply that the Soviet Union is a kind of stable Reich one should expect to last for a thousand years. Quite the contrary, as the internal contradictions of a mature coordinator social formation unfold and as the Soviet rulers increasingly take on the role of an international imperialist power, destabilizing forces are likely to become more powerful. In this section we outline some of the possible ways in which the Soviet masses may increasingly enter the stage of Soviet history through the seams of intra-elite struggles and cracks of imperial disintegration.

While we argued that neither fraction of the Soviet coordinator class had any interest in establishing socialist economic relations, it is still possible that gains by one fraction or the other in their on-going struggle over economic power can have provocative effects that influence the possibility of movements emerging for socialist economic change. But to understand these possibilities we must recognize certain contemporary trends that are altering the context of the perennial Soviet intra-class conflict.

No regime rules by coercion alone. In the Soviet Union oppressive economic relations have persisted in part because they have been credited for the continual expansion of the Soviet economy. Yet lately Soviet economic growth has declined to the point of near stagnation. In a situation where production yields little surplus for further investment, it becomes difficult to motivate workers with rhetoric about present sacrifices for future comfort. In the past Soviet economic downswings have been reversed simply by expanding the workforce. But now the pool of peasants and women to be "welcomed" into industrial plants has been depleted, and this palliative is no longer sufficient for current economic doldrums. Another approach large countries often undertake is to seek a surplus through exploitation of the labor force and resources of other countries via imperial intervention. But even though the Soviet Union certainly has both the military capability and lack of scruples prerequisite to imperial behavior, in fact, in the post-war period its international machinations have brought into the Eastern camp countries which have acted as drains on the Soviet economy more often than as reservoirs of economic surpluses.

In any case, what remains as the most likely method for increasing output to continue the Soviet's efforts to industrialize, provide goods that will motivate and "buy off" the workforce, and prevent it from losing in economic competition with the West, is the extraction of more labor from workers *who are already employed* both by intensifying work and by diminishing waste. In broad strokes this is the picture: In the aftermath of the revolution the Bolshevik political elite held power over virtually all aspects of Soviet life. Though a broad coordinator class grew, largely as a by-product of the construction and elaboration of central planning, it was always this class's central fraction—itself nearly indistinguishable from a subset of the party elite—which held the upper hand in the economy. But now the context in which the struggle between this previously hegemonic central fraction and the local managerial fraction and its allies among conceptual workers has been waged has changed drastically. The local managerial/intellectual fraction has grown immensely. The workforce as a whole is better educated, the country has fully emerged from underdevelopment, and the peasantry no longer exists as a major social and economic class. As a result of these and other changes the internal logic of the Soviet economy now requires that means be found to extract greater labor from workers while losing less product through waste than in the past.* The obvious methods to these ends are to replace inefficient

---

*A recent study by Daniel Singer titled *The Road to Gdansk* and published by Monthly Review Press, New York, 1981, spends considerable time analyzing not only the recent events in Poland and their historical precedents, but also the contemporary situation in the Soviet Union and the prospects for struggle there. Singer's analysis is similar to ours in many respects but differs in two essential ways it is useful to note. First, Singer uses the term "apparatchik" to refer to what we call the political elite and then lumps what we call the central fraction of the coordinator class under this designation too. Thus, in Singer's analysis, the struggle between what we see as two fractions of the coordinator class is described as a struggle between an emerging united economic agent on the one hand, and the apparatchiks or political elite on the other, rather than that elite *and* the central fraction of the coordinators. Second, and adding to the impact of the disagreement over terminology, in this volume Singer doesn't take time to look deeply into the roots of the current non-socialist institutional relations in the Soviet Union and Poland, preferring to emphasize contemporary trends. But as a result, he spends

bureaucratic allocation with supposedly more efficient market allocations and strengthen workplace discipline and organization through investing more power in local managers and implementing new plant-level managerial policies. This incidently explains why Western managerial methods have become steadily more appreciated by Soviet elites. Together, we believe these changes in the context of the intra-class struggle are likely to rebound to the advantage of managerial and local coordinators. And though neither fraction of coordinators is seeking socialist ends, the change in the terms of the conflict can have implications accidently favorable to the emergence of movements which might seek socialist advances in the Soviet Union.

In the first place, greater power for plant managers will in all likelihood lead to employing layoffs as a tool of discipline.* These circumstances could tend to lead workers to see themselves not only in opposition to their local managers, but also as a class with its own interests and need for institutions of defense. That is, the change from central determination of economic decisions (reputedly in the service of workers by their representatives) to local decision-making by disliked managers, could demystify the economy by showing that it works not according to the will of the proletariat as translated through scientific planning procedures, but according to social decisions of a hostile, accessible and even-

little time criticizing democratic centralism and pays little attention to the *impact of planning mechanism themselves on class relations.* This may explain why his analysis is curiously lacking in criticisms of the *mechanisms* of central planning even though he looks primarily to class relations as the source of pressures for change.

*"Soviet managers too would like to hire and fire, to manipulate differentials in order to increase surplus value. But if the authorities were to move appreciably in this direction, if they were to grant the managers real powers of decision, they would by the same token destroy the fiction of the workers as co-owners of their factory. ...Faced directly with a boss who can decide on his own the level of employment and the size of wages, the workers would have to invent some forms of self-defense." And so, the odds are that the 1980s will witness a society in turmoil. The economic reforms from above, imposed on a reluctant leadership [by the need to reinvigorate the economy] will unleash forces from below, crystallize interests, reveal and intensify class conflicts. It may even see the revival of a labor movement in the alleged land of proletarian rule." (Singer, op. cit. p. 140)

tually vulnerable elite. Moreover the usefulness of local organs to defend and elaborate their interests would then become more evident to workers.

Second, local technocrats increase their power, the central political elite's dominance will diminish along with that of the central coordinator fraction. It is not that the party hierarchy will be superseded, but as it loses its economic hegemony, and as another force comes to exist side by side, so to speak, the party's freedom to exert unilateral force and coercive controls will diminish. And while the local coordinator fraction has no interest in socialist democracy for workers, they will certainly favor a political and cultural liberalization that diminishes restrictions they have had to endure themselves. But in such a climate of liberalization, naturally a potential exists for many different kinds of dissident movements against authoritarianism to grow. Certainly some will be reactionary, seeking to exchange a known dictatorship for a vision of Western political and economic freedoms that is but an illusion. Others will likely be more pragmatically opportunist, pressing for a liberalization extending to all intellectual elites, the whole coordinator class, and many middle elements in society whose allegiance can be coopted, but not to the populace as a whole. But there is every reason to believe, particularly in light of the Polish experience, that groups may also form to espouse democratic freedoms for all. In other words, the seams between the perenial intra-class economic struggle of the Soviet economy may be widened sufficiently to allow not only for working class organizations with the potential to elaborate socialist *economic* programs, but also for popular grass-roots organizations seeking socialist political and cultural freedoms as well.

Third, there seems to be growing evidence of an emerging feminist movement in the Soviet Union. As Soviet life becomes more cosmopolitan, as the populace becomes better educated, and as the spill-over effects of Western feminism continue, the likelihood that such a movement will grow increases. Moreover, there is an interesting possibility of interplay between an emerging feminism and the economic struggle we described above. The fact that women hold a disproportionately high percentage of middle level and local coordinator positions may have in the past strengthened the hand of the central coordinator fraction by enabling them to rely on patriarchal attitudes to help in their effort to deny power to local managers and intellectual workers. But now there is a precise reversal. If economic pressures compel the empowering of the managerial fraction at the local level and the broadening of prerogatives of all conceptual workers, then many advantages will necessarily accrue to women occupying these postitions—*if* women can maintain their present employment pattern—and this will certainly help strengthen any feminist trends just as feminist militance can rebound to the benefit of the local coordinator fraction in the short run, and to the prospects for a totalist socialist program in the longer run.

Finally, regarding community struggles, we have little reliable evidence to make an assessment. It seems reasonable, however, that as homogenization has never been totally successful, oppressed minorities within the Soviet Union will, as other movements begin to create room for dissent within the Soviet system, likewise express their own needs and greater autonomy. And certainly to the extent that Soviet imperial ventures such as the invasion of Afghanistan take place, the liklihood of nationalistic stirrings of kindred populations within Soviet borders is heightened.

Whether the possible trends projected above can yield a socialist movement, and eventually a socialist revolution that will overthrow the current coordinator social formation, or lead only to a modification of the present system with greater political and economic decentralization is, of course, unknowable. We have pointed to some reasons for being hopeful, but there are others that are sobering. There is even greater impetus for Soviet citizens to be cynical about the prospects of creating a better social system than there is for the U.S. citizen, since there "socialism" has supposedly been tried. Moreover, in the Soviet Union, far from being even a potential tool of criticism and providing a language suitable for expression of subversive desires, Marxism is the state religion and solely a means of rationalization.* Furthermore,

*In Singer's words, "Within the Soviet bloc Marxism is symbolized by the Soviet tank. Within the Soviet Union it is identified with the primitive, flexible, and hypocritical gospel designed to justify the privileges of the establishment. To resurrect the idea as the promise and instrument of human liberation is no mean task in itself." And we might add, it might well be a task which runs against the grain of what is practical or even possible, even though the mass appeal of socialist ideas and strategy "under any other name" might be very great.

there is no longer any remembered heritage of popular struggle. Most disturbing, there is a more ominous scenario and if the cold war heats up to the point of more hostile commercial and diplomatic relations, it is possible that we will see a retrenchment of Soviet society back toward still sharper repression and centralization familiar from the days of Stalin. After all, if the "Western Democracies" can bring the likes of Thatcher and Reagan to power, and flirt with the only slightly moderated neo-fascism of new-right "moral majorities" and born again McCarthyites, it is not unreasonable to think there will be neanderthal elements in the Soviet Union seeking to solve their problems by similar forays into reaction. But in any case, whatever intellectual vehicles the Soviet revolutionaries choose to express their will and aims, and whatever institutional forms they create, it is certain that the decade ahead will see much turmoil in the Soviet Union. Perhaps before too long the possibility will even exist for fruitful exchanges and mutual support between movements within the two "superpowers." Certainly, whatever we in the West can do to bring this day closer should be a priority.

China:   With regard to China, at least to our inquiring eyes, the future is more problematic. Because China has a coordinator social formation, many of the same basic ideas are applicable, but in a context that is fundamentally different. First, the peasantry still constitutes the overwhelming majority of the Chinese population. Second, China is still very much a poor and under-industrialized country, in which the working class is still quite small and relatively unlearned in the ways of industrial organization and struggle. Third, however, China seems to have moved somewhat further than the Soviet Union on the road to increasing the power of local coordinator elements and reducing the economic hegemony of the party elite. A further complicating factor, however, is the different experience of post-revolutionary struggle that has characterized Chinese as compared with Soviet history. The remembrance of the language of socialist struggle during the Cultural Revolution, and of methods of collective opposition, are still on the surface of Chinese consciousness, whereas at best they have long since dipped into the furthest recesses of the Soviet subconscious. Of course, it is also true that fear of a return to social chaos (which has been intentionally exaggerated by Chinese media) is a factor in China as is the reasonable desire for a period of stability. Yet on balance, it is certainly true that there is a much more significant residue of revolutionary struggle and socialist consciousness in the Chinese human center than in the Soviet. On the other hand, it is also important to note the negative aspects of the Maoist legacy which we noted in chapter three and which might best be summed up as 1) ideological confusion about the origins and nature of the "agents of history" in post-capitalist societies, and 2) a history of secretive, anti-democratic, commandism that is quite probably both remembered and resented by many who suffered its effects.

A second consequence of the recentness of the coordinator consolidation in China is that the internal contradictions of a stabilized and mature coordinator social formation have yet to emerge. It is interesting to note that the post-Maoist leadership of the party has toyed with granting increasing power to the local, managerial fraction of the coordinator class as well as tolerating greater political and cultural liberalization. But neither of these policies is well established and there are already contrary trends emerging. One needs only to consider reports of cessation of liberalizing trends coming from China to begin to suspect that Deng Tsao Peng and company are but fair weather friends of democratic innovations, even when these are limited to very narrow cultural, political, and economic elites.*

In any case, while it is hard to justify a note of optimism at precisely the moment when pressures for socialism stemming from the original Chinese revolution seem to have been silenced by entrenchment of non-socialist structures and programs, it would also be unwarranted to conclude that there has been an

---

*Consider, for example, the report of Edwin Reingold in *The Washington Star*, April 26, 1981, which describes the arrest of two dissidents, party complaints about "lax morals, undisciplined personal behavior, 'leftist tendencies' among intellectuals, writers and musicians, and a lack of patriotism." Apparently the two were arrested for calling the Party Vice-Chairman "a dictator" and they received sentences of 15 years. Reingold also quotes from *Peking Daily* an attack upon Pei, Hua, "a Peoples' Liberation Army script writer, for his film 'Bitter Love'." "*Peking Daily* raged that the film reflects a trend 'among a handful of people' toward 'anarchy, extreme individualism, bourgeois liberalism,' and warned that 'if this erroneous trend spreads unchecked, it will cause harm to the political state of stability and unity.'"

"end to history" in China. Instead, it seems to us that although China may exhibit the semblance of a stable institutional structure, the residue of political experience and idealism within the collective consciousness of the Chinese people *may* represent an insurmountable barrier to the complete stabilization of anything short of a socialist society.

Cuba: Cuba exists in a very difficult international setting characterized by diplomatic, economic, and threatened military hostility from the United States, coupled with material, military, and even ideological dependency on the Soviet Union. Moreover, as we described in chapter four, after a period of creative experimentation with economic policies in the sixties, the economy has come to assume a solidly coordinator cast, a full-blown hierarchical party structure has finally emerged on the political scene, traditional latin machismo continues to dominate family life, and whatever cultural turmoil there may be, there is certainly no consistent socialist policy in the cultural sphere. None of this enhances the prospects for socialism in Cuba.

Yet happily this is not the whole story. As we examined in detail earlier, within the political sphere, alongside the party apparatus, there is a fledgling infrastructure of popular organizations potentially suitable for pursuing participatory democratic political aims. Moreover, the mandate of Popular Power is open-ended concerning the extent to which it can grow to assume increasing power over political *and* economic affairs. Furthermore, within the kinship sphere, alongside persisting patriarchal forms and policies, there exist projects favoring a broad challenge to almost all forms of sexism. Finally, we have also seen that while Cuban community dynamics are certainly not socialist in the fullest sense of the term, they too have aspects which are considerably more creative and liberatory than those pursued by other post-capitalist societies. But all this is only what has lead us to the conclusion that the situation in Cuba is indeterminate. What else can we say about Cuba's future beyond the obvious conclusion that major social struggles are still to come?

Inside Cuba, the immediate cutting edge lies on the border between the political and economic spheres, in the struggle between the political organizations of Popular Power and the economic institutions of coordinator domination over control of daily life. If its socialist political institutions are not to stagnate

and eventually become hollow shells, they will have to become a
forum for popular expression of desires, discontent, programs,
and vision. As such, they will inevitably conflict with coordinator
efforts to dominate the economy. A workforce enjoying democratic participation in one sphere, the polity, will not take kindly
to enforced fealty in another, the economy. Either its taste for
initiatives will lag in tune with its economic subordination and
thus its participation in Poder Popular decline, or its reticence in
the face of managerial authority will pass due to its growing
political sophistication, and struggles will move from the interface between politics and economics into the economy itself. Will
the institutions of Popular Power then provide a model for spon-
taneous elaboration of new council forms within the economy?
Will progress within the kinship sphere spur anti-authoritarian
modes of thinking and acting that will fuel both political and
economic advances? Or will a technocratic economic apparatus
deaden popular morale so effectively that other spheres of Cuban
life will eventually consolidate in non-socialist ways? The many
factors that will influence this are complex and far beyond any
simple prognosticating. Among others, the role of the United
States and of the Soviet Union are critical, and each superpower
will be affected not only by the other, but by the evolution of the
whole international scene. Likewise, the development of socialist
movements or consolidation of reaction in other parts of Latin
America or Southern Africa will be significant. And finally, within
Cuba, there is the large question mark hanging over the final role
to be played by the Fidelistas themselves. We are in no position to
conjure a guess at the outcome of the impending struggles in
Cuba, but we can say that both as interested spectators and as
potential supporters and friendly critics, outsiders will do well to
play close attention to the fate of Popular Power in the coming
years. For it is on these popular political institutions that the
socialist prospect rides, and their advance or decline will be an
easily read signal communicating much about the prospects for
socialism in Cuba.

## Socialism in the Third World

This is not the place to chronicle the relative and even
absolute decline in the standards of living of the Third World. Nor
is it the place to describe the increasing obstacles that the interna-

tional context poses for countries trying to emerge from underdevelopment and overcome the debilitating international division of labor. Instead, we will start from what, for us, is a painfully obvious fact: the current world situation compels any Third World country that wishes to avoid economic stagnation and political and military subordination in the coming decades to successfully extricate itself from the capitalist world system. Moreover, this is an increasingly urgent imperative as the populace of Third World countries face possible mass starvation unless they can assert their wills against both imperial outsiders and reactionary neocolonial regimes imposed by their own brethren. The question we address is: As more nations seek roads to independence and as new popular movements arise seeking economic development and redistribution of wealth and power among the different classes and sectors within Third World countries, what are the prospects for a fully socialist transformation to take place?

A number of factors must be weighed in the balance. First, it is very important what kind of movement leads to struggles for liberation in these countries: what ideologies they generate and with what sorts of institutional vehicles they choose to manifest their strength and construct a new society after their victory. Second, the actual character of the struggle for change—its longevity, brutality, scope, and character—is critical. And finally, there is the matter of the world context into which the newly liberated country must fit and seek to survive. To be perfectly frank, taken abstractly all three of these factors militate strongly against the likelihood for a fully socialist victory. Yet that does not mean such a victory is impossible.

We have seen that the choice of Marxism Leninism as a guiding ideology, and especially of democratic centralism, vanguardism, and central planning as the cornerstones of revolutionary programs, all have a deadening effect upon socialist potentials. For whatever their usefullness in opposing reactionary regimes, organizing mass opposition, and inducing new and orderly relations conducive to economic development, these features also tend to impose authoritarian and coordinator oriented outcomes and to impede progress in the cultural and kinship spheres as well. Insofar as movements in Third World countries have no choice but to employ these forms—and this presumption is one that should be subjected to the most vigorous cross-examination every time it is used—they will do so to their own detriment *unless* they also develop strategies for developing socialist forms to replace these "combative forms." In any case, although, it is beginning to seem that some Third World movements may not adopt all these forms initially (remember that this was true of the Cubans in the past) *nor* necessarily turn to them upon achieving power (as appears to be true in Nicaragua and Zimbabwe so far), the lesson that emerges from our analysis of the post-capitalist experiences in the Soviet Union, China, and Cuba is straightforward: to the extent that Third World movements can 1) elaborate forms comparable to Cuba's Poder Popular in the political sphere, 2) simultaneously incorporate self-managing economic institutions and "qualitative calculations" in economic decision-making, while also 3) propelling feminist demands and programs as much as conditions permit and 4) engaging in cultural pluralism rather than a reflexive attack on religions and minorities, they will stand an infinitely better chance of embarking on a socialist development path.

Yet, we do not mean to imply that success is guaranteed by even these important efforts since two kinds of uncontrollable external circumstances can destroy even the best laid plans of Third World movements. Some countries are going to emerge from colonial subservience only by way of the most bloody and vicious warfare. This not only leads to immense post-war problems of hunger, disease, and dislocation, but also the human heritage of a military mindset and the inescapable memory of vengeful bloodletting. The American effort in Southeast Asia was disgusting not only for the outright military massacre and destruction which has left Vietnam, for example, a bombed out country with a nearly inoperative agriculture, a massive residue of unexploded mines and bombs still doing daily damage, and an immense health problem; but also for its conscious effort to divide people in Southeast Asia along every possible ethnic, religious and national axis so that post-war construction would be that much more difficult. It is hard enough for a poor country to embark upon development of a socialist infrastructure under the best of circumstances, but to do so in a poor country suffering post-war deprivations, internal "blood debts," and attacks from one's neighbors, may be asking the impossible.

And even should a movement carefully choose institutional

forms suited to socialist development and manage to avoid or overcome the ravages of anti-imperialism and/or civil war, there is a third serious impediment along the road to new social relations. The emergent society has little choice but to function within the worldwide division of labor. Yet this imposes the necessity of either joining the Eastern or the Western bloc to find trade partners and aid. On the one hand lies the problem of relying on the Soviet Union while trying to chart a social path that is anathema to Soviet leaders. On the other hand lies the problem of finding ways to entice Westerners to provide aid and/or investment without succumbing to pressures to compromise socialist goals.

Zimbabwe has decided for the moment to preserve far greater amounts of private property than the country's situation would require to embark on a program of socialist development, out of an understandable desire to retain ties with the West. Nicaragua has cut ties with Salvadorean comrades in desperate straits and virtually halted nationalizations in order to avoid being pushed out of the Western financial community and forced to depend solely on Soviet ties. And of course our earlier discussion of the effects of Cuba's dependency on the Soviet Union is relevant, as is the Cubans' own implicit testimony in the form of advice given to every Third World movement they have aided—from the Chileans to the Angolans, to the Nicaraguans—not to repeat the Cuban "mistake" of losing all ties to the West, if possible.

But as serious as the problems facing Third World countries seeking socialist development are, all is not gloomy. Neither Mozambique, Angola, Zimbabwe, Nicaragua, nor Salvador have so far had to endure the kind of massive U.S. intervention that was evidenced in Southeast Asia. Even Reagan has no choice but to recognize the international and domestic circumstances within which he makes decisions, and it is at least possible that even this militarist will have his hands tied to some extent, and his possibilities of direct military intervention abroad significantly limited. Of course in some cases less overt interventions can prove even more disastrous, as in Chile, but at least it is possible that in the coming decades there will be limits on Western interventionism so that Third World countries will endure lesser internal destruction on the road to their liberation. And while it isn't likely that

Western aid will be provided magnanimously to serious socialist leaderships, and there is much in the international economy that does not bode well for the prospects of Third World aid in general, some trends in the international context—Social Democratic governments and parties in Europe providing a political counterweight to more reactionary U.S. postures, and inter-capitalist economic rivalry between the U.S., Europe, and Japan providing more leverage for Third World countries in bilateral economic negotiations—do promise a little more flexibility in the years ahead. Finally, there is no reason to suppose that the movement of non-aligned nations cannot become a more powerful force on the world scene than it has been, thereby providing a somewhat sturdier life-line for small nations attempting to stay afloat in stormy international seas. In any case, the more multipolar the international setting, and the stronger the non-aligned bloc, the better the chances for anti-imperialist Third World movements to succeed in pursuing socialism as well as economic development. But the duty of socialists in the West is quite clear no matter what the polar movements prove to be: we must provide direct aid by opposing the imperialist policies of our own countries while providing whatever other assistance liberation movements might call for as conditions evolve.

## Socialist Revolution in Poland?!

The Polish events of 1980 and 1981 are not without precedent. The recent uprising is only the latest in a series that stretches back over the last two decades. Moreover, Polish nationalism has always turned a hostile face toward the Soviet Union, and the relative power of the Catholic Church in Poland has always acted as a partial brake on the monolithic designs of the Polish Communist Party. But despite their place in a broad process, these most recent events in Poland are unique and will come to mark a watershed in the history of the Soviet bloc.

For this time, in addition to demonstrating that the Polish working class has the strength to impose a veto when a party program is found seriously wanting, the movement has won significant positive social changes: the official recognition of Solidarity, the independent workers' national labor union, and the solidification of collaboration between Solidarity and the oppositional political institutions, for example KOR, of activists like

Jacek Kuron. Finally, the Polish workers have demonstrated to everyone with eyes to see, both East and West, the overwhelming power that accrues to a disciplined majoritarian movement in an industrialized country. Without outside interference, such a movement is virtually impossible to repress. It can only fail to attain its ends by its own limitations or as a result of international intervention.

In *The Road to Gdansk*, Daniel Singer outlines in considerable detail the history of the recent events and their precedents, and we won't reproduce that material here. No doubt, in the immediate future there will be many other studies emerging as well, some hopefully from within Poland and by members of Solidarity or KOR. What we would like to do, therefore, is simply make a few comments regarding the meaning of the Polish events and the possible directions we might expect them to take in the near future.

In the first place, the rising of the Polish working class shows the immense power that resides in collective organized political action. Whereas in past uprisings the Polish workers have taken their grievances to the streets and there been met by police intimidation and bullets, this time, "there was no shooting, no skirmishes, no street demonstrations. Calm, confident, determined, the workers stayed in their plants as if they were impregnable fortresses."[1] Having occupied the plants the workers had a hostage, so to speak, with which to coerce the authorities into restraint. Furthermore, the workers were well aware that "if the regime were to collapse, for instance, the Russians would not hesitate to invade."[2] Thus, while they could fight for significant changes, the Polish workers could not immediately take their struggle "to its logical conclusion, the seizure of power."[3] Rather, they had "the complicated task of winnning concessions from the authorities while simultaneously propping them up."[4] And while it is true that speculations about might-have-beens are usually rather useless, it is not at all beside the point to note that if not for the threat of Soviet tanks there is every reason to believe that the Polish workers would already have unseated the present Communist bureaucracy.

But then the questions arise: would this necessarily mean a turn to socialism in Poland? Isn't it possible that Solidarity would instead lead Poland down a Yugoslavian-like path ending in a different form of coordinator consolidation? Would Solidarity opt for true non-alignment or hitch onto the Western Alliance in one way or another? We cannot answer these hypothetical questions or even the practical ones of whether or not the Polish movement is seeking and winning everything it could given the actual international constraints within which it must operate. We can only catalogue some things we do know, list the areas where we know too little, indicate where what we know is inconclusive, and outline possible coming scenarios as we see them at this point.

In the first place, we know much too little about the situation of the kinship sphere in Poland and the role of women and potentials for feminist advance in the current situation. Less excusably, given the greater amount of information on the subject, we still know too little about the community sphere in Poland and in particular about the role of the Catholic Church, the nature of its political and philosophical attachments and the depth of its support among the population. We do know something that seems particularly instructive for Westerners about the relations between KOR and the broad popular movement. KOR is a revolutionary organization that seems to be democratically organized. It appears to have no pretentions to power over the movement at at large but instead acts as a catalyst to that movement both by exemplary behavior and by providing analyses and critical suggestions which the workers can treat as they like. In any case, indicative of KOR's style and role is the following bit of practical advice published in their weekly four page off-set paper called Robotnik (the worker): "One can distribute pamphlets from the highest landing of tall apartment buildings.... Don't forget to include a few issues of Robotnik.... Another useful way to protest is to paint slogans in aerosol—it's faster that way—in public places.... Action in defense of arrested workers is essential, especially by their co-workers. If other methods fail, one can resort to strikes.... The demands of each strike must contain, in addition to economic matters, specific demands for an end to political repression as well."[5] As another example, "The August 15th Robotnik carried a long editorial entitled 'What to Demand' which again showed the editor's meticulous attention to social and political ramifications of labor unrest. In addition to economic demands, the editorial urged the workers to press for the formation of free trade unions, freedom of speech and association, and an immediate change in the government's agricultural policy."[6] Insofar as the members of KOR are more or less what we in the West would call "professional revolutionaries" it is possible that they are demonstrating a way for individuals who group together to influence revolutionary events to have a large impact and yet neither thwart popular initiatives nor accrue to themselves undue power or influence. In short, the Polish events seem to demonstrate the possibility for communication and mutual aid between politically and economically demarcated institutions of struggle, and between organizations with a mass membership (Solidarity) and ones with a much narrower membership of political cadre (KOR), with no apparent subordination of the former to the latter; rather, as should be the case, it appears that in the Polish movement the power relations run in the opposite direction.

But beyond admiration for KOR's style of work and self-conception, in trying to assess the likelihood for further advance or cooptation, it is useful to turn to Kuron's own analysis of the situation. In an article titled "What next in Poland?" he writes: "Imagine for a moment that our railway system, whose timetables are all determined by some central authority, suddenly has to cope with an influx of trains whose schedules are to be worked out jointly by passengers and railway workers. Much the same problem will arise for a social system all of whose institutions are directed by a party-government that suddenly has to deal with independent trade unions. Surely, a social system, even of a totalitarian nature, is never as perfect as a timetable, and surely it cannot operate according to two mutually contradictory principles."[7] Obviously the two principles Kuron has in mind are those of the party planners on the one hand, and of the workers themselves in the factories, on the other. This, quite obviously, smacks of a revolutionary confrontation: on the one side we have a party bureaucracy and central planning, and on the other, in opposition, a call for self-management and power for workers to run their own lives in the workplace. Yet, in the very next paragraph Kuron deflates the images his analogy brings to mind: "Every fall, between September and October, the managers and employees of our enterprises are presented with a meticulous economic plan for the forthcoming year. This plan usually invites considerable criticism—some of it severe, some less so; as a result the central authorities come forward with a plan that altogether ignores the criticism. But now this scenario can no longer be repeated. Now that the people have created their own organizations, they are conscious of their strength. Now, at meetings of the workforces at various enterprises, the plans for the following year are being seriously questioned and rejected. Will the authorities then be able to work out a plan that will be effective as well as truly consonant with the demands of society?"[8]

What Kuron is describing is an advance, to be sure, but it is not a stable one, as we have seen in our analysis of central planning and as Kuron himself pointed out in his analogy to the railway system with two irreconcilable mechanisms for setting a timetable. For the time being, the planners will respond to the complaints of Solidarity due to Solidarity's ability to force this attention. Moreover, while enlarged, the workers' role, as Kuron projects it in the second quotation, is still far from a self-managing one. Kuron does not have workers doing the planning and thereby becoming ever more confident and informed concerning the possibilities and limitations of their economic situations. Instead they are exerting a veto power over the planning carried out by the central planners and higher echelons of the party. Yet to envision more would be quite dangerous under the circumstances, and much of the leadership of the Polish movement seems aware of the dangers of this type of cooptation. Disillusioned by a similar form of cooptation in the aftermath of the 1976 revolt, Solidarity has so far resisted the pressure from the party to participate as a "responsible partner" in the *existing planning organs*. So far it is the party pushing such a resolution and the most militant and class conscious Solidarity leaders who have opposed such participation. For given the state of the Polish economy, Solidarity's role would quickly degenerate to that of a gendarme for coordinator economic relations. A kind of stand-off confrontation within coordinator planning forms is not socialism and cannot be preserved indefinitely. In lieu of a growing popular awareness of the meaning and possible ways of implementing an economic system embodying collective economic and political self-management, regrettably either the old central planners will regain dominance or a new planning elite will emerge.

So, in broad terms, there are four possible outcomes we can see to the Polish "crisis." Solidarity could slowly lose influence

and membership through lack of a clear program leading to the
reassertion of party authority and coordinator class rule. This
might occur by way of participation of Solidarity at the highest
levels of planning, and thus its cooptation, or by its dissolution
through lethargy and apathy as its watchdog role becomes progressively less interesting and productive for its mass base. Even
in this depressing scenario, the history of the recent events will be
inscribed in the Polish consciousness and the next round of struggle will occur at a higher level than this, as this round occurred at a
higher level than last. Second, the movement can progress further
toward the creation of socialist institutions, yet carefully tread the
line beyond which it would provoke Soviet intervention. This
path would involve the gradual development of new political
forms perhaps like those of Popular Power in Cuba as a counter to
the party's dominance in the political sphere, but especially new
council forms within the factories as fledgling self-management
bodies which would increasingly consolidate their *own* network
through which to become involved in more aggregate levels of
economic planning. Presumably, in this scenario there would also
follow the emergence of a womens' movement and further development of cultural movements, but our ability to comment on this
in Poland is virtually nil. Third, the movement might progress
along the lines suggested above, yet not maintain discipline about
not crossing the line of actually invoking a revolution within
Poland. In this case, Poland could evolve toward socialism, or the
fourth possibility would be that the movement would be drowned
in its own blood compliments of the Soviet Red Army. While the
third scenario is obviously the most desirable, to our thinking it is
also the least likely; not so much because it is ruled out by Poland's
internal constellation of forces, but because we believe that even
in the face of tremendous international pressure and domestic risk
as well, the Russians *would* invade Poland. The Russian leadership could simply not afford to allow a serious socialist experiment on their border, for fear of its showcase effects.

Therefore, we are forced to hope for the second scenario. In
general terms the success of the second scenario hinges on playing
for time without allowing the movement to degenerate either
through cooptation by participation in the present system of
economic institutions or through a decreasingly unproductive
oppositional stance. In order to avoid both these forms of degen-

eration Solidarity and its allies must quickly hammer out an effective network of workers' councils capable of tackling planning tasks at the local, regional, and eventually national level. And if this is what the Polish movement decides to attempt, they will have to incorporate those sectors of intellectuals and conceptual workers who wish to join the movement and possess the skills necessary to translate local desires into national implications without diminishing the movement's comittment to full democracy and especially to workers' self-management.

But whatever its outcome, the Polish movement has already demonstrated that the coordinator economies of the East are not Orwellian societies along the lines of *1984*, but instead vulnerable to change once the momentum of their development swings. Hopefully the Polish experience augurs change not only for Poland and other countries of Eastern Europe, but also for the Soviet Union and all coordinator societies. Hopefully too, Western Marxists will all finally recognize the obvious truth made evident by the movement of Polish workers: that in the countries which go under the label of "existing socialism" not only is there patriarchy, cultural oppression, and a bureaucratic authoritarian state, but also a mode of production and consumption that is not socialist but instead organized to benefit a class other than workers.

# Part Three

# Socialism Tomorrow

Let me say, with the risk of appearing ridiculous, that the true revolutionary is guided by strong feelings of love. It is impossible to think of an authentic revolutionary without this quality. This is perhaps one of the greatest dramas of a leader, [to] combine an impassioned spirit with a cold mind and make painful decisions without flinching one muscle.... In these conditions one must have a large dose of humanity, a large dose of a sense of justice and truth, to avoid falling into dogmatic extremes, into cold scholasticism, into isolation from the masses. Every day we must struggle so that this love of living humanity is transformed into concrete facts, into acts that will serve as an example, as a mobilizing factor.... Above all, always be capable of feeling any injustice committed against anyone anywhere in the world. That is the most beautiful quality of a revolutionary.

Che Guevara

# 6
# SOCIALIST POLITICS

Every power is animated by the wish to be the only power,
because in the nature of its being it deems itself absolute
and consequently opposes any bar which reminds it of
the limits of its influence. Power is active consciousness
of authority. Like God it cannot endure any other God
beside it.

Rudolf Rocker

In the following chapters we will discuss our vision of what
socialism can and should be like once it is well established and
functioning smoothly and effectively. Obviously it is not a
comprehensive picture: we do not address all sides of daily life. Nor
is it a very detailed picture: we do not delve into intricacies, even in
the institutions and relationships that we do discuss. Furthermore,
the discussion isn't entirely balanced. Certain topics receive
inordinate attention for two reasons. First, there are certain
institutions that we find more critical, as we have emphasized
throughout this book. But second, even among those special equally
central and critical institutions, we are better able to envision future
possibilities for some than others. We will discuss politics,
economics, kinship, and finally community much as we did in prior
chapters that addressed specific historical experiences. In most
respects the vision we offer is quite different than the reality we
discovered in our studies of the Soviet Union, China, and Cuba. We
will also briefly discuss those differences and also some issues of
socialist transition as we proceed.

267

## Socialist Politics

Democratic centralism, vanguard leadership, and state bureaucracy have nothing to do with an established socialist democracy. They are institutional forms which intrinsically impede the development of popular participatory impulses and which instead promote popular passivity and governmental authoritarianism. We have already seen this in our discussions of certain historical experiences and our initial theoretical work gave us tools to understand it. In this section, however, we have a different task. We must come up with rough outlines and guiding norms of an alternative political approach. To start it might help to repeat again our understanding of exactly what we mean by politics, and to then set out very briefly our criticisms of the kind of electoral or parliamentary democracy found in many "Western capitalist societies."

## Politics and the Failing of Electoral Democracy

Political activity mediates differences among citizens. It determines guidelines and implements diverse programs to enforce them. This is necessary, but how it is to be accomplished, according to what guiding norms, and by what institutional forms, is a social choice.

Most societies have had authoritarian decision-making. Even capitalist societies with parliaments, free speech, free press, free assembly, and free elections suffer from three authoritarian failings.

First, though in rhetoric basic freedoms are preserved for all citizens, in practice they are often violated for women, third world people, working people, and other sectors of the population. Voters choose, to be sure, but only between preselected candidates and with only skewed information to guide our choices. Second, for the electoralist, freedom means "freedom from restraint." For the socialist however, freedom must mean "freedom to do." There is an immense difference. No one stops a worker in the United States from not working for a capitalist. But nonetheless this worker is not free to escape the indignities and exploitation of the workplace because there are no other locales for making a liveable income. With respect to the government, it is likewise not enough that people are free from incursions (however important this freedom undeniably is); in addition they must be able to express and enact their desires. Direct coercive barriers are not the only impediments to free activity. Others must also be overcome.

Finally, expressing one's desires through a representative involves action only in the choice of the representative, and then passivity till the next choice. Though it would be an important advance over sham elections, even a multi-party socialism that extends bourgeois democracy with basic bourgeois rights in tact and popular choice of candidates would still ignore people's need for self-management. It would reduce social participation to an occasional electoral choice and continue the subordination of the populace to the "expert politician." If this expert were a woman or a third world person, it would still not be all women or third world people. It would not be the people, but the leaders or bureaucrats who would enact desires. Electoral democracy is not participatory democracy.

Insofar as socialist politics must be concerned with reconciling diverse opinions into actual social programs and common expectations concerning social behavior, we can enumerate a few values which should be embodied.

In the first place political outcomes have got to be "fair." This means the interests of all parties and especially of those involved in the actual interchange have to be effectively translated into programs respecting the needs, inputs, and potentials of each. The outcome must reflect the desires of participants more or less in proportion to the extent each will be affected by the decisions made.

Second, the process of political activity has got to reproduce the conditions that guarantee "fairness." Since equity will generally result only by the participation of actors all of whom are well informed, and all of whom have the requisite skills and disposition to function politically, political activity must itself generalize these traits rather than monopolize them among some small subset of the population.

Last, and perhaps least well understood, political activity must embody "self-management." It is not simply that self-management produces fair outcomes and reproduces conditions necessary to fair outcomes—rather self-management as an end itself is necessary for the fullest development of human potentials. As beings of praxis who create ourselves through our activity and as social beings who can reach fulfillment only in interaction with others, we need collective self-management over our own development.

## Knowledge and Authority

Under socialism all people do not know all things. We will inevitably continue to have diverse interests and spend our time in different pursuits. As a result, on any given matter different people will have the most relevant and informed things to say. To the extent that authority—meaning the accretion of respect and influence—is an outgrowth of knowledge, there will be authority differentials under socialism. We will not take just anyone's advice about how to build a house nor about how to cure a disease nor about what kind of transportation system is most apt to serve social needs. But there is nothing fixed about such differences in experience, knowledge, or influence. And further these inevitable differences in knowledge and authority need not create a difference in decision-making power.

If people in a given society are demarcated by knowledge, experience, and personality in ways such that one sector has more facility in operating within the society's political forms, then that sector will indeed dominate political activity. Even if a society's political institutions could allow for fair outcomes given equal participation by all members of society, they will not likely yield such outcomes with unequal participation. This is why socialists have to recognize the need to reproduce the conditions of fairness. Under parliamentary forms, for example, certain sectors are propelled toward political inactivity while others are propelled to political involvement and leadership. In all but the most rebellious circumstances, the latter groups dominate and this is not democratic.

How a society deals with knowledge and authority is thus critical to whether or not its institutions will be fair and reproductive of "fairness." The continuous increase and dissemination of knowledge is good; its undue centralization is bad. Though the development of expertise increases knowlege and is often desirable, it can also concentrate knowlege in a negative way. It is therefore necessary that the general distribution of knowledge be sufficient for all citizens to intelligently evaluate "expert suggestions" and make up their own minds concerning the implications of proposed social programs. Only under these circumstances can the advantages of expertise be enjoyed without also suffering the disadvantages. While respect is due the opinions of people better trained in a particular realm of thought, it is only their opinions of the intricacies of programs and their implementation that deserve such respect. The knowledge sufficient for people to evaluate and to choose has got to be generalized. Similarly, the personality traits necessary for active involvement have to be generalized as well.

These abstract requirements are of immense importance and yet they are not met by any existing political systems. Instead existing systems have one or another form of hierarchy whereby some people make decisions governing the life situations of other people from above.

### Socialist Decision-Making Relations

A non-hierarchical solution to the problem of decision-making must be built upon power among the citizenry itself. In our view such a solution can be based on a nested network of many communes and other living units into a neighborhood assembly, of many neighborhood assemblies into a township general assembly, of many townships into a regional federation, and of many federations into the national state.

Built upon local living units, this network includes all citizens. The principle of self-management is the touchstone of its governing methods. Each unit is responsible for coordinating the wills and dispositions of its members into shared decisions concerning its own level of activities. The commune runs itself. But the regional assembly sets certain regional policies which impact upon each commune's situation. The agents affected by decisions partake of them. It is they who decide and vote.

The "bureaucracy" at the higher township, regional, and national levels, is only a working staff. It is responsible for investigating policy alternatives, spelling out implications, setting up debates concerning opposing viewpoints, ensuring wide dissemination and discussion of all relevant data, etc. But all major policy votes are at the base. Implementation of policies and further votes about alternative and relatively mechanical implementation schemes are carried out by the staff; but this is done publicaly, and is reviewed and subjected to popular veto. These individuals are simply government workers. They are doing this part of their total work for different levels of the legislative network. They may be recalled and replaced. They hold their jobs only for a predetermined period. They receive no special rights, privileges or status. They self-manage their own work but are simultaneously responsible to carry out the will of the involved populace. And they have no interest in doing otherwise: 1) There is no way to dole out favors to receive others later in return. 2) People rotate through staff positions like they rotate in and out of all other jobs. 3) It is impossible for staffers to accumulate either wealth or power; for neither really even exist in the traditional forms in a socialist society of the sort we are describing. 4) Staffers may serve themselves only by serving the community while defining their work relations in suitable developmental fashion—in this regard, "staffing" is the same as any other socialist work. 5) Overall power rests in the network of people's assemblies, as it rests in the council network in the economy.*

### Socialist Pluralism

One of the most fundamental changes in the approach to decision-making, in addition to emphasizing participatory self-management, is a redefinition of "pluralism." Under socialism, beyond a pluralism of approaches, we also seek a pluralism of outcomes. The orientation that there is "one right way," a view common to patriarchy, racism and authoritarianism alike, is superseded. Diversity and the possibility of more than one valid policy on any issue of concern are the values socialists respect. Choosing a particular path forward does not preclude trying out alternative paths as well. There is no necessity for conformity of approaches between regions and in different townships much less between nations and cultures. Governing should no longer be conceived as a process of seeking one truth, but of choosing some among many truths for simultaneous implementation. This allows a constructive approach to what is usually considered the problem of dissidence. In a socialist society, the premium on diversity and experimentation could actually make the role of critic a valued and respected one. Contrary to the traditional role of the state in

---

*These points are a powerful argument *if* the underlying argument about material interests and the definition and character of work in general are valid. For now the points will have to stand as only somewhat substantiated assertions. Next chapter, as we deal with socialist economic relations, work, consumption, and allocation, hopefully we will also provide a more solid foundation for these "five points."

capitalist and other stratified regimes—the repression of dissident views, periodicals, ideas—the socialist state would be responsible for ensuring that resources are available for groups with divergent ideas, living styles, and the like. But what form would these varying groups with different approaches take?

## Socialist Freedom

The cornerstone guaranteeing the development of democracy throughout every sphere of socialist society is the right of all groups of citizens to form political organizations addressing any issue or set of issues they are concerned with, and specifically the right to form on-going political parties. These political interest groups and parties would exert themselves in all the political forums created by the extension of civil liberties, but would carry the debates into all the various councils and federations of councils in the economy and communities as well. Since the socialist institutions defining economic, community, and kinship relations are no longer such as to *generate* class, sex, and race divisions, the political coalitions and parties would not be based on promoting the interests of particular groups and/or coalitions of groups against the interests of others. *
But socialist politics should not be viewed as a relatively dull affair compared to the antagonistic struggles of previous societies. There will be a host of issues that fan the flames of controversy. As we've argued, to the extent that diversity is both a perceived and implemented goal on a number of issues, socialism will be characterized by a plurality of outcomes rather than merely a plurality of proposals. But there will be many issues where only one way can be chosen, and the decision will matter greatly to people who do not agree. A number of activist political organizations are a necessary and desirable means of guaranteeing the fullest possible debate.

*For a time however, whose length we cannot now know, there would certainly be residue race, class, and sex inequalities, oppressive consciousness, etc. and one of the critical functions of the state in this period would be mediation of disputes based in these inequalities. Certainly parties would hold positions regarding such issues, but Blacks, Latinos, or women per se would not constitute themselves into what we mean by "parties." They would instead continue as autonomous movements with a presence in all parties—and in any case with more direct political power than parties will have, a point we will elaborate later·

Beyond recognizing the desirability of many different—and ideologically competing—political organizations and political parties, remains the interesting question of the extent people's views on the various issues of concern would tend to cluster in the absence of  continuing regeneration of class, sexual, and racial antagonisms. To the extent that the attitude of socialist citizens on any one group of issues tends to correlate with their attitudes on other issues, we would find that the environment of full civil liberties and encouragement of political organizations would result in ongoing political parties. That is, this freedom would result in political parties with a standing membership and a continuity of stands on major issues. To the extent that people no longer defined by class, sex, race, and authority roles tended to adopt views on major issues that did not cluster, we would find that political formations were more likely to take the form of fluid movement coalitions. That is, activists would work in relatively temporary coalitions organized around single issues, where the typical citizen would belong to many such groups. But as interesting as questioning the degree of ideological correlation in the absense of social divisions might be, it is unnecessary to know the result in order to know how to proceed. All manner of political organizations must not only be tolerated but actively encouraged, funded, and provided with all the tools that civil liberties define. If political parties result, fine. If the dominant formation is temporary coalitions, that is fine as well. * In any case the internal structures of all such political organizations would be participatory.

*Obviously, as throughout this discussion we are discussing not only a new kind of socialist society, but also one that is well-established and largely without scars from its past. In the earlier stages while freedom of belief and expression is enforced, the additional socialist norm of the collectivity actually supporting *all* political tendencies is not. Bourgeois, racist, sexist advocates would be morally isolated, denied material support for propagating their views, and generally recognized as deserving only the most formal toleration. But the issues of "transition," difficult and important as they are, are not our primary concern here. For surely one needs some idea of where one is headed before one can grapple with the details of getting there. This is critical if for no other reason than at least to prevent the use of otherwise effective strategic or transitional means which, as a byproduct, create norms and social relations antithetical to one's ultimate aims—for example, censorship or even dictatorship. In any case we will return to issues of socialist transition later.

## Socialist Elections

We have outlined a framework emphasizing direct democracy in local assemblies and federations of assemblies on a regional and national scale. In each case we have argued that while "experts" would likely be very influential in explaining and even in determining the parameters of certain discussions, everyone would have an equal right to participate in actual decision-making. The technology for mass votes at any geographical level obviously exists. Through T.V.-like technology not only could immense forums, public debates, question and answer sessions and the like be held, but issues could be framed and votes taken and tabulated almost instantaneously.

But we do not mean to imply that plebescites are the ultimate tool of socialist political decision-making. Votes are certainly a powerful agency for summing the individual wills of many people into one mutually respected decision. However, they also have many flaws. In the first place, votes must always be either "yes" or "no" or between this and that. They intrinsically involve a polarization of issues. Moreover, votes don't allow for a resolution of this polarization via the redefinition of possibilities. A debate which must be resolved via a choice between two sides and which is settled by a well informed vote will almost always guarantee victory to the side which appeals to a greater audience. But this is not necessarily the best result. In the first place, each individual's vote is counted equally, yet the outcome may affect people to different degrees. People should really have different numbers of votes to reflect their different levels of involvement in any decision and its effects. Furthermore, it is always possible, and often likely, that neither of two proposed alternatives are "best." Perhaps what should occur is a flexible interchange which leads to a redefinition of the issues and possibilities at stake. This kind of dialogue is often precluded by plebescite approaches. If you think of a neighborhood forum making decisions about their local living groups, it is easy to see that while some issues will be most suited to simple one person one vote resolution, others will be better left to a longer period of resolution through compromise, while others will require more subtle choices which pay more attention to the quality and character of people's opinions than to a simple counting of hands. How exactly these different ways of making decisions can be elaborated for larger issues affecting many more people, we don't know. But that some techniques will have to be evolved seems obvious. Still, the use of votes, especially with quick tabulations and following widespread discussion and education about the alternatives, will be an important means of making socialist decisions and one that is, whatever its limitations, much more democratic and participatory than parliamentary alternatives.


## Socialist Law and Law Enforcement

In societies that have oppressive core characteristics the main purpose of laws is to enforce the maintenance of those characteristics against the interests of the oppressed. Examples of laws with such purpose are those defending property in capitalist society or those outlawing certain kinds of popular organizations in "existing socialist" societies. Yet a secondary purpose of laws, even in oppressive societies, is simply to delimit certain agreed types of behavior which are to everyone's benefit. For example, laws about how one can drive or cross streets, certain kinds of zoning restrictions, and the like. There is a very real and difficult question as to whether these latter reasonable laws—including those against assault, rape, and theft of personal property—really require enforcement. Are they broken only due to alienation, confusion, and maladaptations that will disappear under socialism? If this proves true, then under socialism there would be little need for law or law enforcement in the usual sense. For certainly there won't be laws which defend oppressive social institutions or individuals from the oppressed as such divisions won't exist. And if the only reasons people harm one another or disobey simple and socially useful norms is because they suffer oppressive indignities, or *need* to steal or otherwise act anti-socially to survive, then such norms will hardly ever be broken under socialism. If so, these norms would be common knowledge and changed only by socialist decision-making. Their enforcement would be almost automatic, and presumably if there were violations they could be addressed on a community level by one's peers. The exact form of institutions which would serve this end would be worked out as situations evolved but they would be some type of adaptation of relatively informal community courts.

On the other hand, it is possible that even the most effective imaginable enactment of socialist institutions will not eliminate crime in the usual sense of the word. There might remain, for example, acts of criminal violence concerning sex, jealousy, passion, and perhaps even theft. Likewise, there could be cases of fraud, and so on. If this proves true there will need to be enduring institutions for law enforcement including police. And police would not only direct traffic and act as social servants in cases of loss or in times of stress or accident, but they would also seek to arrest law breakers and "bring them to justice." These police officers would be workers, more or less like any others; and *as workers* their "methods of work" will be addressed next chapter. Here we must simply say something about what 'socialist justice" would be.

The typical meaning of "justice" in contemporary practice is retribution and little more. This is a function not of the character of the second type of laws—those serving the maintenance of *useful order* and protecting people's real interests—but of the first type of laws, those serving the maintenance of unjust and oppressive social institutions. For the mark of these "first type laws" is that by the standards of the oppressed, and this includes most of the people who will break these laws, they are irrational. They do not correspond with social realities, as felt by the lawbreaker. The lawbreaker cannot easily be educated to understand their logic. Moreover, education is not really a priority. Rather, what is essential is to convince others that lawbreaking is not a good idea no matter how enticing it may be. If bank robbers were simply educated about life and society, rehabilitated, and quickly released all the while treated with respect and solicitude, the line at the First National teller's window would be long with hooded clients. As a *deterrent*, therefore, everyone must be well educated about the consequences of doing what would otherwise be quite sensible. And this dialectic of punishment and retribution then penetrates the whole legal apparatus till it is absolutely paramount.

Socialist law would be quite different. Retribution and punishment are not the issue. First comes the well-being of society as a whole. If an individual engages in crime, he or she can't be allowed to endanger others. Next comes the well being of the violator. Can this individual be made to accept and understand the rights of others so as to be able to again participate equally in society? And if not, in what ways can he or she be allowed the greatest possible personal freedom and development, the greatest opportunity to develop and contribute to society short of being free to enter every-day' exchange? Perhaps, if such violators of social norms exist under socialism, they will be sequestered with one another in colonies which are effectively no different from any other save for being isolated. Or perhaps there will be "penal institutions" within regular townships. But what won't exist is a system of forced and violent repression of people's capacities for expression, joy, love, and social production. For this would have no purpose. It would not deter socialist crime because socialist crime will never be motivated by a simple calculation of *material* cost and benefit. And it would not aid society because society would both lose the potential contributions of the "prisoners" and society would also have to become party to their incarceration in "prisons" that were inhumane. One might say, no society is any more just and merciful, any more wise or loving, than its most degrading and despicable prison. For this is a socialist sentiment and one that will govern the evolution of socialist law enforcement should there prove to be need for such law enforcement at all.

### The Benefits and Feasibility of Socialist Politics

The benefits to society of the new socialist form of decision-making are multiple. Self-management needs are finally fulfillable. Elites no longer manipulate social outcomes and consciousness, and the character and results of human cooperation are thereby enriched. The reality and the fear of big brother are gone though more than anything else it is "the fear of freedom" which is finally erased. Individuals are no longer beholden to powers greater than themselves. We are no longer beneath political authorities; docile, and worried at how we will be appraised. We are eager to step out, to initiate, to exercise our talents and wills. There is no one waiting to suppress, legislate, enforce, or deprive us.

The whole meaning of leadership is altered. There is as much attention paid to development and process as outcome. The admirable attribute is not the knowing but the teaching. A leader in accomplishing a particular task is someone who has developed skills or ideas necessary to that task which others have had neither time nor experience to master. However, leadership consists not only in helping to get the project done, but also in spreading the relevant insights and skills. The good leader is the one who displaces her or himself as leader by extending the conditions of "leadership" to others. The monopolization of information for power and status is gone and so are all the "paternal" attitudes generally associated with being in a position of "expertise." Differences in knowledge about particular issues are understood as natural outcomes of variety of experience and learning and in no case are they a basis for privilege. Instead, as social products, they bequeath the social responsibility to contribute and teach.

And in what do we see the possibility for such an advance in decision-making forms and consciousness, even over an extended period of new relations? In the hierarchical governing mode—of whatever particular form—coordination is achieved by the subordination of the mass of wills to one, or at most a few, with these representing the pinnacle of authority. The only conceivable argument for this mode in light of its failings we have pointed out, is that a truly democratic alternative is impossible. Supposedly letting all have equal power, since people have different levels of expertise and everyone has divergent aims, precludes efficiency and coordination. Therefore unified leadership is necessary, the only question is who will undertake it. But this conclusion rests on the vulnerable assumption that unbridgeable differences between people are permanent, and that the only road to their efficient resolution (determining *the* superior option) is autocratic.

But what if seemingly unbridgeable differences are actually byproducts of contingent social relationships that can be eliminated or at least made non-antagonistic under socialism? And what if in most cases there is more than one right solution to a given problem? These are our contentions and the basis of our belief in a participatory state. It is not that there will be no differences or struggle. As we've seen there will more than likely be a plethora of parties struggling over major social issues thereby generating wide debate. One kind of issue there might often be disagreement over, for example, will be the trade-off between immediate fulfillment and "investment" for developments aimed at greater potential for later fulfillment. We anticipate no diminution of people's struggles to uphold their beliefs under socialism but quite the contrary. What won't exist on the other hand is a division of society into antagonistic sectors represented by interest group based parties. It is not the existence of politics per se we deny—for politics is an inevitable part of the process of socialist decision-making. What we seek to eliminate is only the politics of domination. Governing must be but another part of socialist daily life, and like all others it comes under the auspices of the people themselves and is characterized by self-management, solidarity, and diverse solutions to political problems.

## The Transition to Socialism

In the first place the transition is not an epochal period. The transition is not itself a kind of society. When we speak of the transition to socialism we simply refer to the period of creating the basic institutions characteristic of socialist society in all its spheres. This process begins in the earliest stages of the revolutionary movement and continues through the "moment of victory" till the eventual regularization of socialist social relations, though obviously it receives most attention right after victory. The most important point about this "bridging process" is that the bridge must touch the ground at both ends. The transition must take off from the practical realities of capitalism as it is initially encountered by the revolutionary movement, and it must land in firmly established socialist institutions. The transition, therefore, cannot be based on institutions which cannot be constructed out of conditions as we find them, for then the transition would never begin. But neither can it be based on institutions which lead somewhere other than to socialism which is in our opinion the point most frequently ignored in socialist writings. So the overall task of transition is to create socialist institutional and ideological relations beginning from where we are. If these relations must be more severely adapted to compromising realities in the earliest periods when the capitalist heritage is more constraining, and less so as the movement for socialism advances, so be it.

But if social relations and ideology diverge ever further from socialist norms as the movement gains power and eventually hegemony, then this "transition" is no longer to socialism but a path leading elsewhere. So the fact that the economic, political, kinship and community insitutions outlined in this book are fully socialist, "ideal" one might almost say, is neither an accident, nor a sign of muddled utopianism. If there is no in-between society, only an in-between program, then the institutions for the future must be established as closely as possible in the present. The only other possibility is the consolidation of a new form of stratified society, and if history has anything to teach us, this is the most pressing danger for "successful socialists," not dissolution due to reaching too far. To avoid the elaboration of a coordinator dominated class stratified economy, rhetoric about the interests of workers will not be enough. Institutions of real economic democracy and self-management will be required, institutions which yield socialist and not coordinator consciousness. To avoid authoritarianism, it will not suffice to modify the word centralism by the word democratic. Nor will an elitest conception of leadership be sufficient. Rather we will need new decentralized and participatory political institutions. To avoid the recreation of patriarchy in new forms will take more than an assumption that the relations between genders—the "woman question"—will be solved by changes in the economy. Rather, we will need to carefully assess our interpersonal habits, our understanding of "family," "sexuality," and "socialization" and construct new institutions true to the potentials of all people. Finally, to avoid a culturally homogeneous, barren society or one with diverse inward-looking hostile cultures, we will need a new attitude and set of relations—socialist intercommunalism—whose character will determine not only many of our attitudes about community formation and interrelations, but also art, competition, and the meaning of diversity in a framework of solidarity. Whether the transition to socialism from a coordinator society is any shorter or less arduous than the transition from capitalism is not something we should wish to have to find out. Therefore one of the purposes of this book is to provide enough of a vision of socialism in all institutional spheres to allow us to begin to address the question of transition in a new, and ironically more pragmatic way. But for the most part that task must be undertaken elsewhere, and likely largely in practice.

Fidel Castro recounted in a 1966 speech the response he encountered when he put forward this same view in another form and as the Cuban experience was certainly important for the development of our own thought, whatever its final resolution may be, this recounting is instructive and provides an excellent note upon which to move toward some more concrete issues of political transition.

> On one occasion, when the Central Committee was organized, we said that we did not believe that communism could be built entirely independent of the construction of socialism. That communism and socialism should be constructed, in a certain sense, parallel with one another. To invent a process and to say, "up to this point we are building socialism, and at this point we are building communism" can be an error, a great error. Because obviously, among other things, in our eagerness

to reach our goals, we must not renounce or endanger the development and the formation of the communist man.
When I expressed this idea—not the pronouncement of a teacher, nor an apostle, nor a professor, nor an authority on revolutionary theory, nor much less a kind of petty ideological Pope—some were surprised, and more than a few readers of manuals were astonished. More than a few people—they weren't counted, but I estimate their number based upon the number of those who have been intrigued by this statement, people accustomed to having the ideas in their minds as well ordered as the clothes in their closets—even became disturbed at these statements, and I do not doubt that some asked themselves if perhaps we weren't somewhat sacrilegious.
And, of course, I believe that in this category the worst of sacrileges—and when I speak of sacrilege, the catechism I was taught as a child comes out, at least in words. . . . The worst of sacrileges (and it would seem that Marx also studied catechism, since he often employs this type of terminology, which of course, is not copied but is something that I have observed in my reading of Marx)—the worst of sacrileges is stagnation in thinking. "Thinking that stagnates is thinking that 'rots'."
And we must not permit our thinking to stagnate, much less to rot. When we made these statements, we were simply asking certain questions, about which we must all meditate and which we must all study a great deal.

### Political Transition

In the countries we've studied the main problems of political transition had to do with repressing enemies of socialist change and constructing democratic forms in the presence of a vanguard party geared to monolithic and hierarchical rule. The problems proved intractible in the Soviet Union and China and the score is not yet in on Cuba. In the discussion of the problem of transition, if the socialist movement must employ a Leninist party the key lesson we have learned is the necessity to begin elaborating political forms *outside* the party and democratically rooted in the local community as early as possible and to ideologically admit that *those institutions* represent the shape of things to come while the party is merely a temporary governing vehicle to be jettisoned as early as possible. Our analysis of how the Leninist party's structure and ideology make this task exceptionally difficult suggest an obvious parallel lesson for industrialized countries. If Leninist approaches aren't necessary, don't use them.

We can take this logic further, however. The Leninist approach allowed a political elite to stand in for a small coordinator class in a revolution that was not even socialist. Where the working class is quite strong and where the coordinator class and middle strata are also powerful, there is no economic thrust in favor of centralized, elite political institutions. Quite the contrary, in a society used to bourgeois democracy, Leninism flies in the face of the aspirations of *both* opposition classes and of other groups likely to be revolutionary agents as well. Women, for example, have nothing to gain from the elaboration of a vanguard hierarchical party that will inevitably be male, nor do minorities have any reason to support such a party as it will only allow them peripheral entry and participation.

We assume that a socialist transition period in a country like the United States will begin with a very rich council structure elaborated in workplaces but also in communities, with autonomous yet totalistically linked movements in all four spheres of social life, and with one or more political parties elaborating socialist philosophies and programs, but solely from a position of participation and in a mode we might call advisory. Decision-making power and implementation capacity will both rest solely in the movement and council structures in which the parties would only be participants.

Then the most substantial kinds of political transition problems we see are how to overcome past habits regarding political behavior in general, how to elaborate new political institutions, and how to ensure that old hierarchies are not reproduced in these new forms. The past habits that must be addressed can be labeled "political passivity" and "political aggression." The former refers to the practice of bending before the will of others, being uncritical, or at the extreme simply abdicating participation entirely. It is a product of one's previous roles in hierarchies as an "order-taker," and is therefore pervasive. Political aggressiveness has similar roots, though now due to order-giving, and is therefore similarly pervasive. It is characterized by arrogance, the presumption that one's will is to be enacted without question, a reluctance to explain oneself, and an aversion to being questioned or criticized. Obviously such attitudes prevent true democratic participation. For a real democratic polity can exist only where people have mutual respect, want to criticize and be evaluative, and want to be criticized and have their ideas evaluated. If the aim is only to win or to follow gracefully, then there will be no on-going criticism yielding socially optimal results. Moreover, there will never be recognition of the need for a plurality of options *and* outcomes. The idea here should be clear: there is a basic contradiction between the maintenance of center intellectual and behavioral patterns associated with authoritarianism, and the construction of democratic participatory political institutions in the boundary. While the very construction of those institutions will be a pressure for change in the center, and while the successful effort to win power from prior political elites will have been a similarly positive pressure, still, without additional special attention there is the possibility that old attitudes will compromise new institutional efforts. Thus the main transitional problem in the political sphere is to develop extra means for countering this residual force, means which are, however, not contrary to other socialist desires. That these means will likely involve certain kinds of exercise in taking and in giving criticism, certain kinds of safeguard against abrupt acceptance of proposals before proper evaluation, and certain special modes of debate and of allocation of tasks to enhance participation and learning, seems certain.

The second two political problems, constructing new institutional forms and avoiding reproduction of old hierarchies are obviously intimately related to the problem of attitudes already discussed. The absence of a mature socialist political orientation among the populace cannot be allowed to thwart construction of socialist political institutions even though such institutions will not immediately be the most comfortable or familiar way to operate. That is, people will still have many expectations and traits due to their life histories under capitalism. The creation of socialist political forms will involve unusual behaviors and will seem to elicit undo amounts of effort, disruption of accustomed ways, and so on. In order to achieve socialism it must be understood that these costs reflect progress, not some error in calculation. They are not a product of trying to accomplish too much too fast, but of the necessary tensions which accompany changing one's most basic patterns of daily life. It is going to be all too easy to fall back into old habits as a means to avoid these tensions. The old hierarchies could easily reemerge as shortcuts to getting decisions made or as ways to avoid the unaccustomed and therefore uncomfortable practice of taking ideas and proposals seriously rather than simply implementing them unquestioningly. The point is that the transition period can't be guided simply by the immediate desires of each individual participant, unless these desires are premissed on a self-conscious recognition of the necessary price—temporary though it may be—of making major changes. The way to prevent the reemergence of old hierarchies is not to repress, outlaw, or otherwise destroy those who were previously most aggressive. It is necessary instead to redefine roles, and to create ample room for the expression of all people's political tastes and capacities. And this must be done against the understandable desire to quickly settle into a comfortable pattern.

# 7
# SOCIALIST ECONOMICS

> Before [the workers] now the problem arises of how to
> unite freedom and organization; how to combine mastery
> of the workers over the work with the binding up of all this
> work in a well-planned social entirety. How to organize
> production, in every shop as well as over the whole of
> world economy, in such a way that they themselves as
> parts of a collaborating community regulate their work.
>
> Anton Pannekoek

Having discussed the strengths and weaknesses of central planning and markets, and the compromised history of "socialist
practice," we must now offer an alternative. We will start with a
brief restatement of the guiding criteria we wish socialist economics
to measure up to. Then we will discuss the institutions governing
economic activity within individual economic units, or what we call
intra-unit forms. Having done this, we will be in a position to
discuss the institutions for coordinating the units, or what we call
the inter unit form of decentralized socialist planning.

But we would like to apologize at the outset for the fact that
this discussion is neither particularly emotive nor straightforward. In
another work we have presented a more general vision of socialist
economic possibilities. It seems pointless to repeat. Moreover, given
the prevalent skepticism even among socialists concerning the existence of an alternative to hierarchial authoritarian structures and
central planning and market allocative institutions, what is in order
is not a general description, but one including detailed and
sometimes technical discussion. How would socialist economic relations actually function? Taking this question seriously actually
makes our presentation somewhat drier than we would like. Our
apology, then, is not for undertaking this task, but for our inability
to do it in a way that properly communicates the "flavor"—the
emotional and ethical character—of the system we are describing
while also attending to its "nuts and bolts."

As a last introductory comment, it is important to note that the ideas in this section are not mere dreams but part of an enduring heritage of socialist thought and practice. This heritage emphasizes economic democracy, councils, and a participatory alternative to central planning and markets. It includes council communists of the last and this century, the Guild Socialists in England, the anarchists in Republican Barcelona, the workers' opposition and left communists in Soviet Russia, the Italian revolutionaries of the 1920s, the Hungarians' rising in 1956, and many contemporary socialist theorists and activists. There has long been a conviction that a third and better alternative exists. We simply count ourselves, along with many others who came to political awareness in the New Left in the 1960's, as recent converts to this fiercely stubborn heritage. Our hope is to give it more concrete substance and clarity than it has possessed in the past.

### General Aims

In thinking about both intra- and inter-unit economic forms we want to emphasize the need to attain conditions of self-management, variety and human solidarity as well as material sustenance and security. For the former are as important to providing a healthy developmental environment for people who are social beings of praxis as the latter are necessary for immediate need fulfillment.

We therefore want economic institutions that require initiative rather than passivity, sharing rather than competition, friendship rather than aloofness, and love rather than callousness. Socialist economic institutions must promote initiative and participation in decision-making, must guarantee equity of consideration *and* outcome, and must provide full information necessary for people to consciously apply the decision-making criterion of well-being for all. Finally, socialist economic relations must allow us the freedom to experiment and alter our choices so we can continually deepen our understanding of our own needs and capacities and thereby continually advance ourselves. These, in our view, are conditions which are consistent with the full elaboration of self-management, variety, and solidarity and therefore with the development of a network of truly socialist economic institutions controlled by women and men of socialist consciousness.

## Democratic Councils of Workers and Consumers

We see the fundamental units of the new socialist economy as individual work places varying in size from a few workers to as many as several thousand, according to the nature of the work process; and individual neighborhoods of up to perhaps a thousand people who would constitute a collective consumption unit. Each of these units would be organized as a democratic council that would be entirely responsible for 1) the day-to-day management of the unit's activities, 2) initiating the unit's proposals concerning its inputs and outputs in society's economic plan, 3) revising these proposals during the back-and-forth planning procedures we will describe below, and 4) directing the council's participation in a variety of federations of councils in which it may have membership.

The council form has obvious advantages for local intra-unit organization. Councils are conducive to direct communication, long-term personal relationships, and direct conflict mediation. Even in a hostile capitalist environment, small groups enjoying intimacy and long-standing familiarity are often able to generate considerable solidarity; the results should be that much better in a socialist environment where the councils are aided from without and able to establish various internal practices, rules, principles, or intra-unit institutions to foster initiative and solidarity. In the words of Anton Pannekoek:

> Thus council organization weaves a variegated net of collaborating bodies throughout society, regulating its life and progress according to their own free initiative. And all that in the councils is discussed and decided draws its actual power from the understanding, the will, the action of working humanity itself.[1]

All decisions within the workers' and consumers' councils would be subject to direct majority rule, with special attention to the intensity of dissenters' feelings. So why is there any need for additional intra-unit rules and policies? The idea is to provide an institutional context to safeguard against an alienated, unconscious reemergence of old, self-defeating habits. While this may not be necessary in fully mature socialism, it certainly would be necessary in the formative years. In the early stages of socialism we will not yet be the people we want to be, so it would be sensible to democratically adopt a set of guiding principles for subsequent debates, where otherwise, some of our holdover undesirable traits might run unchecked. In other words, analyzing in calm moments the conditions we wish to generally fulfill, we can develop principles that can guide debates and decision-making in more difficult conditions when if we weren't prepared, detrimental habits might obstruct our true aims.


## Consumers' Councils

The most general decision-making criterion of the consumers' councils would be to maximize the fulfillment and development of each member of the council, granting equal consideration to all members and to the well-being of the members of all other councils. This is the kind of motivation Che and Fidel were urging in the Left period in Cuba. What makes this criterion likely, rather than a utopian dream, is that all internal decisions are ultimately subject to majority vote, and the final proposal of each council must be accepted by all other councils and federations of councils. Because each council member has one vote it would be difficult for any individual or group within the council to successfully insist that their well-being is more important than others. And since all the other councils have a kind of veto power over any proposals they consider unfair (as we shall see when we consider the social planning procedure), it becomes critical for each council to convince the rest that it is not demanding a higher priority for the well-being of its own members than for members of other consumption councils. In time, as socialist values pervade consciousness and desires, such a collective approach will come more naturally. In the shorter term, however, the fact that a collective attitude is the most sensible approach for individuals and councils to adopt given the proposed institutional arrangement should be seen as a useful "pressure" toward equity rather than as either a crutch or coercion.

In the process of attempting to maximize the well-being of each council member consistent with equal consideration for all other members and all other consumers' councils,* each neighbor-

*In order to take into account all other producer councils, which in our view is also necessary, the consumers would have to have access to information allowing an assessment of the implications of their consumption requests for all producers and also the means to bring their decisions based on this information to bear on social outcomes. But since this is primarily a problem of inter-unit relations we will leave its treatment to a later section.

hood council would have to decide 1) how much and what form of "individual" consumption items to request, 2) how to distribute "individual" consumption items among its members, 3) how much and what to request for "collective" consumption within the neighborhood itself, and 4) how much and what "collective" consumption to propose or vote for in the various federations of neighborhood councils of which the neighborhood is a member. We would expect that a set of principles such as those below might be agreed to within a consumers' council to guide the process of arriving at these decisions.

Beyond guaranteeing the fulfillment of all members' basic survival needs, councils might adopt principles of general equality of individual consumption, priority of collective consumption activities over private ones, and priority of developmental requests. Guaranteeing survival needs and material equity would be recognized as pre-conditions for developing solidarity in addition to being in each individual's interest given equal voting power. Granting priority to collective and developmental requests would be measures to correct certain extreme individualist/consumerist habits inherited from the capitalist past and predictably over-represented in the human center. The latter aim is consistent with the thrust of certain efforts of the Cuban and Chinese socialist factions, though here the relations would be institutionalized "from the bottom up."

So community lounges, neighborhood recreation centers and playgrounds would be given priority over individual family "rec" rooms and backyard playground equipment in the council's own requests, and preference might be given to schools, parks, and cultural centers to be consumed in conjunction with large federations of councils, as compared to consumption activities confined largely to the neighborhood alone. Furthermore, preference would be given individual requests aimed at developing talents and creative capacities over requests aimed at satisfying lingering needs for social prestige and recognition via status-laden conspicuous consumption.

An important feature of the neighborhood consumption councils is that decisions about "private" goods whose consumption primarily affects only a few people within the neighborhood council will be handled in the same contexts as decisions about "public" goods which affect everyone, thereby diminishing the incentives to "conceal one's preferences" and become a "free rider." A legitimate concern of every consumption council will be the proportions of relatively private and relatively public goods it wishes to request, but in context of a rough commitment to equal amounts of private goods for all members (though of course not the same goods for all members) there is no reason for people not to honestly express their views, since in this context to do otherwise would be self-defeating.

That many goods have effects extending beyond a single neighborhood is accounted for by federations of consumers' councils who also submit proposals for public goods of larger dimension. Although the role of these federations will be discussed more extensively in relation to the planning process, it is worth noting here that it is the provision for a pyramiding network of federations of consumption councils and their status as "proposers" on equal footing with individual units in the planning process, that distinguishes decentralized socialist planning from both market and centrally planned socialism in its ability to handle the subtle gradations of public versus private effects that different consumption choices have. Whereas market socialism treats all goods as if they were totally private, and centrally planned socialism treats everything as if it were a pure public good, decentralized socialist planning (DSP) provides for a wide gradation of size in federations of consumption councils through which people can express their needs for different kinds of private/public consumption activities, as well as a "basic" consumption unit defined on a neighborhood rather than an individual basis.

Finally, though principles guaranteeing basic subsistence, favoring general material equality, and granting priority to collective and developmental consumption requests might be agreed to, no council would have any interest in imposing standards of uniformity over individual consumption. Quite the contrary, councils would seek to encourage the greatest possible variety and initiative in this regard. For it is generally in the interest of every individual to be able to learn from others' experiments with the widest possible array of individual consumption activities. Yet in case this should not prove an adequate incentive to protect differences in individual taste, two provisions for safeguarding individual freedom and promoting variety might be incorporated. First, an individual would be free to leave his/her consumption unit and apply to join any other unit, or collaborate with others to create a new unit. DSP would contain no "passes," restrictions against "voting with one's feet," or restrictions against creating new forms of voluntary association. Second, the principle of general equality of individual consumption would protect social innovators who wish to remain within their original units even though their neighbors have in some sense disapproved of their "lifestyle." Although the members of a consumption council can insist on a discussion concerning any individual's proposal, and would in fact feel compelled to do so in cases where they felt the principle emphasizing developmental requests, for example, was involved, the individual could call the principle of material equality to his/her defense whenever an agreement was not reached. If an individual whose unorthodox proposal was challenged could show that his/her request was not a demand for a greater individual consumption bundle than the average for the unit, the council would be hard pressed to justify denying the request should the individual remain unpersuaded of the error of his/her ways. How different kinds of consumption items can be quantitatively compared we shall see when we discuss the planning process.

### Workers' Councils

As in the case of consumers' councils, the most general decision-making criterion for workers' councils would be to maximize the fulfillment and development of each member of the council consistent with equal consideration for the well-being of all other members and all other work and consumption councils because again, all internal decisions of work councils are subject to majority rule and each council's final proposal must be accepted by all other work and consumption councils. As guides to carrying out this goal we would expect each work council to adopt principles of equal work effort, equal degree of personal development or stultification, and equal boon or danger to life and health. But obviously these principles will often prove difficult to apply at least until socialism is well established.

Certainly, until massive restructuring of work is completed, and probably even after, all jobs will not be equally safe, pleasant, or personally rewarding. Furthermore, under the division of labor inherited from capitalism the components of conceptualization, coordination, and execution integral to human laboring activity will have been violently fragmented creating a situation in which those performing certain jobs will have considerable power over those performing others for a time period that cannot be willed away. One of the few antidotes available for achieving the goal of equitable work assignments is job rotation, but this is a limited remedy until job restructuring redefines work roles and technologies and until both formal and informal training spreads certain skills. In the meantime, limited rotation relies on the generous attitude of those individuals stuck in more demeaning, boring or dangerous work, and this attitude can only be nourished by trust in a common commitment to the transformation process.

For example, until the hazardous job of working in the coke ovens in steel mills can be eliminated, individual steel mill councils would try to arrange rotation so that no one ended up doing this work continuously while others worked in relative safety as crane operators, mechanics, warehouse stockers, or administrators. In hospitals doctors and nurses would "rotate" through jobs like changing bed pans and work in the laundry room immediately. In every work process involving large numbers of people the department "chiefs" and work team "captains" responsible for planning and coordinating would, to the extent they were needed, be democratically elected by the relevant unit itself, but enforced rotation of this duty would still be critical for preventing the consolidation of an elite coordinator class, for spreading knowledge, and for generating high morale and mutual respect. Yet there are practical limits to job rotation. Prior differentials in training, knowledge, and disposition cannot be instantly willed away. A worker in the coke ovens cannot operate a crane or help in factory redesign until he/she acquires the knowledge and confidence to do so. A doctor cleaning bed pans cannot simultaneously be tending the ill with surgical or diagnostic treatment. As long as there are too few doctors, this is a real cost to be recognized. And though new occupiers of conceptual, coordinating roles will certainly benefit by learning from doing, performance cannot be permitted to suffer excessively from beginners' mistakes.

The important thing is to recognize the nature of the issues every work council will face, and to be clear about the aims of the process of restructuring. Moreover, it is critical to avoid biasing decision-making to reflect the desires of the more highly educated and trained participants.

Judgments will have to be made between some not-so-subtle trade-offs: How far can rotation be pushed right away without unduly affecting the quantity and quality of the work place's outputs on which other members of society rely? How far can rotation be pushed without unacceptable increases in the danger to council members? And in the long run, how much time and energy should be devoted to training individuals in diverse functions so as to diminish the costs of job rotation? After all, time and resources used to generate new human skills and capabilities cannot be used to increase other outputs or devoted to leisure activities. The point is not to prescribe what balance individual workers' councils should attempt to achieve in these trade-offs. Since there is no "correct solution" for all members of society, we would expect—and welcome—a variety of outcomes on all these practical matters in different work councils. Rather, the point is that in every case the criterion for making the choice would be to maximize the fulfillment and developmen of each member of the work council consistent with equal consideration for all; and the method of deciding the practical trade-offs would be democratic choice.

Furthermore, the point is to recognize and make clear that to the extent that practical choices do not immediately lead to work schedules that completely eliminate inequalities in the overall desirability of human effects of different individual's work activities, society's progress will hinge on being "subsidized" by the generous attitude of those temporarily disadvantaged. It is not the highly trained and skilled individuals who subsidize the socialist transition by "donating" their skills at a lower rate of compensation than they could achieve by fleeing to a capitalist society, but quite the opposite. To the extent that their jobs are relatively safer and more rewarding *it is the advantaged few who are being subsidized by those who do not insist on an immediate equity of work outcomes in the socialist process, and who therefore continue to pay a price for the positions they were forced to hold under capitalism.* *

*Rudolf Bahro's discussion of the costs of too little rotation bear on our argument. "On the assumption that its personnel consists of an essentially similar level of education, there would simply no longer be any possibility of tying anyone permanently to activities that make little demands on people and are inherently unpleasant. If we hear today that 'no one who has completed his degree could be allowed for a long time to come to work in a field decisively below the level of his qualifications,' we do not

Finally, the long run aims of restructuring and rotation must be kept clearly in mind as a guide in practical short term (and more constrained) decision-making: to achieve equity, to provide variety of work roles, to promote solidarity and personal empowerment through mutual respect, to promote productive creativity through collective understanding of the whole work process, and to prevent class divisions along a coordination/execution axis. Having dwelt on this last point at such length in earlier discussions of markets and central planning, it behooves us to explain how our system will handle this issue.

The aim is the elimination within workplaces of the class distinction between coordinators and workers—of the fixed division of labor most responsible for creating disparities in social awareness confidence, and skills associated with planning, and therefore with making one's desires felt in the clearest possible fashion. In Marx's words what we seek to eliminate are the conditions that "mutilate the laborer into a fragment of a person, degrade the laborer to the level of an appendage of a machine, destroy every remnant of charm in work and turn it into a hated toil."[2]

In a given socialist work place, for any number of reasons there may be a division of roles—some involving more conceptual work, some more execution. For a long time residual capitalist technologies may impose such divisions even where workers would prefer more integrated role definitions. But also, council members could actually prefer such a division, for example, for many tasks where conception precedes execution and it is desireable that only a few workers do the conceiving at any given time. For example, five workers might plan a process while fifty carry it out, and this might be the most socialist procedure possible. We can't know in advance the extent to which workers will eventually retool their settings to merge all conceptual and executionary activity into unified roles or the extent to which they may consciously keep them separate. It is the lesser aim of *no fixed division in the involvements of people in different types of work* that we are aguing for. This is the aim which must be the guiding principle.

generally consider the consequences of this, i.e. that there have to be other people whom these college-trained specialists with their monopoly of development-promoting activity condemn to spend their whole lives in precisely those mind-numbing activities that they indignantly reject for themselves." (Bahro, op. cit. p. 279).

We are not suggesting that everybody must at some point do every imaginable job. That is ridiculous. Nor are we arguing that one must always be simultaneously equally engaged in both conceptual and executionary work. Rather, the point is that work norms must allow people equal access to skills, social consciousness, and collective self-managing power. To accomplish this, job redefinition, job rotation, and especially the generalization of "higher education" will be essential. "All people must obtain the real possibility of access to all essential realms of activity, and moreover right up to the highest functional level."[3] Though everyone doesn't do everything, everyone does have the sort of general knowledge and ability to think and conceive and the general intellectual capacities necessary to embark on a study program to master most any particular activity. More, the opportunity to do so must be provided so everyone does come to do comparable amounts of skill-inducing and conceptual work, of creative fulfilling executionary work, and of more rote and less desirable jobs as well. *
The process by which one moves from a highly stratified workplace—like today's factory, office, or hospital—to one which embodies this sort of equity of activity and empowerment will certainly vary from unit to unit both in length of time required and in actual steps taken, but the final aim is a principled classlessness that is part of achieving socialist economic relationships.

Providing we can elaborate an inter-unit form that would foster the council dynamics we have discussed, it should be clear that workers' councils would have every reason and the necessary means to pay full attention to the worker as "product" of the production process. Temporary inequalities of outcome would only be tolerated as means for hastening the transformation of skills, knowledge, and technology leading to their elimination. But what about the argument that this will be a frustrated aim because desirable levels

---

*About conception and execution, therefore, "the border between the two realms naturally runs *within* the factory, between creative activities, those oriented toward development and change in the reproduction process, and on the other hand that routine work in production and administration that is to a large extent useless as far as personal development goes. A better way of putting it might be that the boundary *could and should* run within the factory, and that it *must* run there in the future, and moreover right through the time schedules of all individuals involved, who must do their share on both sides." (Bahro, op. cit. p. 295).

of high productivity require advanced technology which will in turn impose job fragmentation and hierarchy? Our answer is, it's wrong. For the impression based on the experiences of capitalist and coordinator economies that advanced technology necessitates hierarchy and alienation stems not from technology itself, but from the fact that in those societies technology is developed according to the requisites of increasing managerial authority, disciplining workers, and preventing worker solidarity and initiative as interpreted by either owners or coordinators. It's little wonder that these criteria have produced the debilitating and fragmenting assembly line, information processing, office, and energy industries with their extreme divisions of labor. For these divisions serve both capitalist owners' desires for profit and coordinators' needs for power and dominance over the labor process. In contrast, rather than aiming at profit and/or control over workers, socialist technology would be chosen by worker's councils to minimize drudgery and to enhance solidarity and personal development. Technology would be designed to elicit artistry, foster self-management and initiative, and generate hospitable and healthy work settings. Computerization of the most dreary clerical tasks would be in workers' interests rather than threatening their job and financial security. And elimination of repetitive assembly line work would be high on any worker's list of requirements for new technology.

Finally, as job structures and human skills are increasingly transformed work itself will take on a new meaning. Instead of being a dreaded means to attain the end of leisure-time consumption, work will become an *end in itself*, or as Karl Marx put it, "life's prime want." The councils will eventually transform the workplace into an arena where people can effectively engage their creative powers. Jobs will be rotated not only to equalize the negative effects of work, but also to allow people to experience many kinds of enjoyable work in their lifetime; to provide a more balanced and complete development of human capabilities; and to ensure that new ideas are constantly brought to every job. The tasks of conception, coordination, and execution will no longer be the basis for a permanent division of labor but will be part of the yearly activity of every worker providing the only means for each person's complete fulfillment through laboring activities. In the factories workers will not only produce socially valuable goods, but also ever more fulfilled and capable human beings.

## Decentralized Socialist Planning

It is obvious, given our earlier discussion of the implications of market and central planning inter-unit forms, that the councils we have described would not long function as we have envisioned were they integrated by either of these economic forms. If connected by markets, consumption units would be pushed toward materialism and production units would be compelled by competition to act only in terms of narrow self-interest. As has occurred in Yugoslavia, profit-seeking, the voluntary sacrifice of self-management and collectivity to managerial authority and routinization, and an increasingly competitive materialism would follow. On the other hand, if integrated by a central plan, consumption units would largely lose their influence on production decisions. Likewise, worker's councils would be excluded from power over most economic decisions and therefore a continual diminution of self-management and increase of worker passivity would ensue, paving the way for imposition of a hierarchical managerial structure within workplaces, and for subordination of each workplace to a central chain of command. We need say no more here about a process we analyzed in some detail in our discussion of historical experiences earlier. But there is one further point to be made about the use of central planning and markets in combination. Though experience and our argument make clear that a combination of the two are little better than either alone, someone might still claim that either could be used effectively in concert with some other social technique used for allocating labor power and making major investment decisions. Thus we'd have markets or central planning for many non-essential realms and some alternative social procedure to apply in the essential realm. Markets (or central planning), someone might argue, are efficient and useful when confined to controlled areas even if lethal when used exclusively—much like many medicinal drugs. But this belief, however appealing, is wrong. For markets (and central planning) are not only lethal when used in excess, they are also addictive. Because both commercial and command relations have a tendency to inculcate non-socialist values and interests, they have a dangerous tendency to spread. So as comforting as it might be to think we could handle the "non-fundamental" aspects of the economy that are "mere implications" of the "basic" social decisions concerning major development directions and labor allocations with markets (or central planning), it would also be self-deceptive. Apparently, if we are to view markets (or central planning) in terms of a drug analogy, regrettably the only accurate one is to a lethal narcotic—small doses might ease problems momentarily, but the habit spreads until addiction makes the drug's use pervasive. The prognosis for the partial use of markets or command relationships is similar.

Our inter-unit problem is therefore to conceive of an institutional mechanism which will allow each council to settle upon a course of action of its own while also ensuring that the totality of their activities mesh into a viable economic plan. Inputs for one council must be made available by nature or by some other council. Outputs from each council must find their way to some other council where they can be put to a productive use. But this coordination must take place in a manner consistent with the development of self-management, variety, and solidarity as socialist aims we have already described.

We will propose, in the pages to follow, a social iterative procedure in which activities are proposed by those who will carry them out according to an estimate of their effect on the well being of all members of the economy as well as the well being of the proposing unit, and in which revisions of proposals are agreed to through direct participatory, collective self-management. *

### Initial Proposals

Each work place and neighborhood council proposes a list of all inputs and outputs—material, social, and human—for its proposed upcoming activity. Criteria used in arriving at these proposals are the worth to others of the proposed outputs, the difficulties for others implied by required inputs, and the effects upon the council's own members including effects on capacities, personalities, social relations, and need fulfillments.

In making an initial proposal each council would have to estimate the kinds of efforts required of others to supply a given list of proposed inputs, and the uses to which others would put a given list of proposed outputs. Indeed, estimating the effects of one's own unit's proposal on other units plays a pivotal role in getting one's proposal accepted in the iterative process of proposal, revision, and

---

* "Iteration" is a useful word from the field of computer programming and mathematical analysis meaning a series of steps that are taken repeatedly to yield a final solution.

new proposal. Since other units would not accept a proposal until they were convinced that it did not imply a greater concern for the well being of the proposers than for others in the economy, each unit is compelled by the nature of the planning procedure to offer a convincing explanation of why their proposal does not place greater burdens on others than they are willing to accept themselves, or deny others benefits that they seek for themselves.

In estimating the effects on others of its initial proposal each council would have to rely on information accumulated concerning other units from previous planning operations. It is helpful to think of the kind of information needed as being in two different categories, one qualitative and inevitably "subjective" in the strongest sense, and the other quantitative and "objective" to a greater extent. The quantifiable information is: 1) how much of different kinds of material products must be produced by other units in the economy if we are to receive the material inputs requested in our proposal, 2) how much of different non-reproducible resources must be used up to supply us those inputs, 3) how much labor of different kinds must workers in other units perform to supply these inputs, and 4) in what further production and consumption activities would the material outputs offered in our initial proposal appear as inputs. Ironically, even though the lengthy, complicated chain of implications that must be analyzed in order to arrive at estimates for this kind of quantifiable information is formidable in any modern economy—and not the kind of problem most people would choose to "solve in their heads" (or read about?)—it is by far the easier of the two categories of estimates to gather.

The qualitative information concerns translating these "material" consequences of our initial proposal into the "human consequences" they imply. Just as there are material and human inputs and outputs contained in our proposed activity, there are material and human consequences of our proposal for other units in the economy. But whereas we can rely on our knowledge of our own production or consumption process to evaluate the human effects of different choices of inputs and outputs for our own activity, we have no such "personal" knowledge of the human consequences of other units' activities. For example, personal experience won't give a "steel consumer" the insight of workers *in* a steel mill who can easily estimate and understand the effects of a change from open hearth to oxygen furnaces on both the amount of pig iron and coal needed to produce a ton of steel as well as on the danger and burdensomeness of work in their plant. Yet no information is more crucial in carrying out participatory, collective self-management. How can previous planning operations help each unit obtain both this quantitative and qualitative information?

Last year's plan tells us not only how much material output was produced by each industry, but how much of every kind of material input, both produced and non-reproducible, and also how much of every kind of labor was used directly in the production processes in each industry. By mounting last year's plan on a computer, and providing each workers' and consumers' council with an access terminal, each unit in the economy could calculate for itself all the indirect material effects of any initial proposal it was contemplating if everybody else's production and consumption were carried out this year as it was last. This would be done by determining how much of each resource, type of labor, and intermediate good would be both directly and indirectly necessary to create one unit of any given output, and in what proportions each final good was consumed by each unit, and then using this information to compute the implications of the proposal.* In other words, the lengthy complicated chain of material consequences listed above that is impossible to calculate in one's head, can be quickly calculated by each council, for itself, using access to a computer containing the information from last year's plan.

But knowing *how much* of every kind of labor and resource was needed to make what you are asking for is different from knowing the social value of all those inputs. So how can a unit evaluate even the *material consequences* of requests for material inputs? In

---

*By dividing the total amount of each material input used in any sector of the economy by the total output of that sector one can calculate $a_{ij}$, the amount of input i "directly" needed to produce one unit of output j according to last year's plan. By dividing the total amount of each kind of labor used in a sector by the total output of that sector one can calculate $l_{wj}$, the amount of labor of type W "directly" needed to produce one unit of output j last year. By dividing the total amount of each non-reproducible resource used in a sector by the total output of that sector one can calculate $b_{kj}$, the amount of resource k "directly" needed to produce one unit of output j last year. Calling the input/output matrix of direct material coefficients, $a_{ij}$, A, any council could calculate the sum total "direct" and "indirect" "material consequences" of any list of material inputs it might request for delivery by premultiplying that vector of inputs by the inverse of the matrix found by subtracting A from the identity matrix I, $(I-A)^{-1}$. Calling the matrix of direct resource coefficients, $b_{kj}$, B,

general, different proposals will require the use of different resources and kinds of laboring capacities in different proportions rather than in uniformly greater or lesser quantitites. Consuming a radio instead of ten pounds of meat requires *different* kinds of labor and raw materials, not just more or less of the same. If we assume the plan agreed to last year was optimal, then it contains even more information than we have used so far. There is a theorem of mathematical programming theory (the fundamental duality theorem) which tells that finding out how much of every product to produce via each conceivable way of making that product in order to maximize the human well being resulting from using the economy's limited resources and laboring capacities, is the same as finding out the value that a unit of each limited resource and laboring capacity has in producing society's optimal production plan. By requesting from the central computer the solution to this "dual problem" of resource and labor capacity "valuation" that accompanies the solution to the "primal" problem that was previously calculated by participatory planners and enacted as last year's optimal plan, each council can obtain means of *evaluating the material consequences* of different proposals, in addition to the means of *calculating* these consequences in their physical details. Multiplying the quantity of each kind of resource and labor capacity that a specific input proposal would require (both directly and indirectly) by what economists call its "shadow price" and summing them would provide an estimate of the overall "material" or "quantifiable" costs that any council's proposal would impose on the rest of the economy. These shadow prices from last year's plan as well as the mathematical process of using them to evaluate the relative

the council could calculate the total amount of each resource that would be used up producing any list of inputs requested by pre-multiplying the vector of inputs by $B (I-A)^{-1}$. Calling the matrix of direct labor coefficients, $l_{wj}$, $L$, the council could calculate the total amount of labor of every kind required to produce any list of inputs by pre-multiplying the vector of inputs by $L(I-A)^{-1}$. Finally, the further use that others in the economy would make of any council's proposed list of material outputs could be calculated by dividing the total amount of each material used as an input in each sector, and by all consumer's councils, by the total amount of that material produced in the economy as a whole. Obviously, these calculations assume that inputs requested and outputs offered this year would be produced and used by others in the same way as they were last year, a reasonable first approximation.

burdensomeness of different proposals in *material terms* as was just described could all be done quite easily by the computor at individual council's request.* In this way each council could evaluate and compare the overall "material" burden that different proposals would place on the rest of the economy.**

The fact that this year's plan will end up being somewhat different from last year's and that last year's was not perfectly optimal, implies that "material consequences" will be somewhat misestimated. But this is not such a serious problem as it might at first appear. In the first place these material consequences calculated by each council for a variety of possible proposals *are purely for information purposes*. We are not relying on these calculations to produce equality between demand and supply or to render a "feasible plan." If we were relying on these calculations for that purpose, inaccuracies would be significant. But DSP relies on a sequence of flexible social proposals to produce workable outcomes. Second, the imperfections in the estimates of the "material consequences" are minor compared to the inevitable inaccuracies in translating "material consequences" into "human consequences." In sum, the slight misestimation of material consequences   is inevitable in any economic system and no more debilitating to DSP than any other.

---

*The procedure is to call the vector of shadow prices for resources $p_r$, and the vector of shadow prices of different laboring capacities $p_l$. The overall material cost of any proposal would then be calculated by pre-multiplying the vector of inputs requested by $p_r B(I-A)^{-1}$ and by $p_l L(I-A)^{-1}$ and $p_l$.


**It might be noted that *if* there were only one kind of non-reproducible input to production, labor, and *if* labor were a homogenous input, i.e. there were no different concrete laboring capacities of any significance, and *if* the human effects of work were uniformly negative in all kinds of work, and *if* nobody cared when they performed their work activities or consumption activities, *then*—and only then—could the entire material and human "costs" of any proposed set of material inputs be discovered by calculating the number of hours of labor required to produce them. We deny the validity and therefore usefulness of all the above assumptions. In this section we have allowed for both heterogenous labor and non-labor primary inputs, and in the following section we will go to considerable lengths to estimate the human consequences in light of the falsehood of the assumption of uniform human effects of work and indifference to scheduling.

## "The Human Consequences"

Although translating the chain of "material consequences" into a chain of "human consequences" and evaluating those human consequences is far and away the more difficult—and important—of the two tasks involved in estimating the consequences for others of our unit's choices, the particular method of planning used in DSP is uniquely capable of providing some crucial help.

At each stage in the planning process every council proposes an economic activity described as completely as possible in terms of all its inputs and outputs, which means human as well as material. In addition to explaining the consequences that the proposal has for others, the most important information contained in the proposal is the expected human effects for members of the council itself. These effects are contained in the description of human inputs required and human outputs expected to result from the activity: the changes in individuals' personality traits, talents and skills, levels of understanding, attitudes and values, the changes in social relations within the group, and the degree to which different needs would be fulfilled or thwarted. Indeed, it is an evaluation of these consequences for human fulfillment and development for participants in the activity, combined with an evaluation of the "fairness" of the consequences for others, that will determine whether or not other councils participating in the planning process will accept the proposal. So it is in the interests of each workers' and consumers' council to provide as full an understanding of the direct human effects of its own proposed activities as possible. And as part of every proposal we would expect to find a qualitative decription of the different kinds of needs fulfilled and traits and capacities generated by specific consumption proposals, and the degree of dulling and degradation, or fulfillment and enrichment, that would accompany different work proposals. But all this means that in the process of generating last year's plan a tremendous amount of "qualitative" information concerning the human effects of different work and consumption proposals in different units is generated. Indeed, this is one of the major results that decentralized socialist planning is designed to elicit. And there is no reason this information cannot be stored in the central computer along with the material proposals from each unit.

The information would be stored in the following forms: First would be the description of the human consequences expected from the final proposal accepted from each council in the economy—both workers' and consumers'—as its part in last year's plan. This information would be partly in symbolic notation, including the numbers of people expected to have specific kinds of individual and/or group characteristics effected in a particular way, and partly in verbal descriptive form. For instance, if a training program were expected to increase the possibility of job rotation so that personal initiative and skills were enhanced and residual hierarchical relations diminished for seventy five members of the production unit, this would be noted in the accepted proposal. Second, there would be a similar record of the projected human inputs and outputs that accompanied each proposal previous to that finally accepted. In general, we would expect that the local beneficial human consequences of both production or consumption units earlier but socially unfeasible proposals would be greater than for its final proposal. Third, the federation of councils comprising each industry and consumers' region would prepare a summary report of the human consequences that were expected to accompany that industry's participation in last year's plan, along with an update indicating any deviations from expectations that occurred as the industry carried out its activities. Finally, each industry and consumers' regional federation would prepare for storage a report estimating the difference in human outcomes between the federation's most preferred proposal and the actual proposal enacted. This report would be based on the individual councils' descriptions of human effects in proposals submitted prior to acceptance. The "most preferred" alternative would not be of the nature of a "What we'd like to be doing 40 years from now," but what alternative set of activities appeared relevant enough to federation members to be incorporated in their earlier proposals during last year's plan formation, but proved impractical enough in light of others' situations and capabilities to be unacceptable in last year's outcome.

By getting print-outs describing the human outcomes of various activities required of others by its current proposals, each council could use the descriptive information to start to translate the material consequences of its proposals into human consequences. Gradually each council would be able to construct a more and more complete understanding of how it was situated in the social economic process of which it was a part. By requesting the summary report of actual human effects from each federation from which a council requested material inputs or to which it proposed to deliver material outputs either directly or indirectly—the council could obtain information about human consequences in an "averaged" form. So a neighborhood, for instance, requesting a new recreation center could obtain a print-out describing the average work conditions and human consequences in the construction industry, cement industry, lumber and steel industry and every other industry that either directly or indirectly would contribute to building the center. Moreover to the extent that a council's supply and delivery schedule was similar to last year's, it could access the particular reports of the individual councils within different industries and federations that it had had dealings with before, thereby generating a specific picture of the chain of human consequences that might reasonably be expected to result from its proposed activity. Finally, by consulting both federation and individual councils' "most preferred" proposals from the previous year, a council could attempt to roughly evaluate the extent to which any changes in its proposal this year might aid or hinder other federations and councils from achieving more desired activities. The neighborhood could then alter its recreation proposal. Or, as a production example, if a work council was considering a proposal that would increase its output of a new machine, it could evaluate the human benefits for others by analyzing the changes in work quality that would likely occur in other work places that requested such machinery last year but found it was still unavailable. Work places producing "consumer" goods would also discover in this way what kinds of new product or product improvements were desired by consumption councils, but previously infeasible. Likewise, if a council proposed to diminish its request for an input like coal, for example, it could evaluate the benefits for others by consulting the description of alternative human consequences under a reduced work load or more "job-enriching" organization of production in the coal industry.

In any case, all of the information discussed above would be generated by the method of planning used in decentralized socialist planning and accessible to individual councils wishing to assess the human consequences for others of different proposals they might make. Moreover, there is a strong incentive to *use* this information since it is in each council's interest to convince the members of other councils that its proposal has taken their fulfillment and development as seriously as that of its own members.

## "Iterations"

There is no reasons to suppose (even after each council's attempts to estimate the material and human consequences for others) that the initial proposals will "mesh" into a mutually consistent, enactable, and therefore feasible plan. In other words, when all the initial proposals are added up, supply will not equal demand for all of the hundreds of thousands of material products exchanged between units. As a matter of fact, as much time as might be saved if initial proposals were mutually feasible, much valuable information for next year's planning process would be lost if this occurred. By allowing each unit in the economy to initiate their own proposal we expect them to open a gap between what is desirable and what is immediately possible, and the discovery that demand is greater than supply for most items, or that the sum total of initial proposals are not feasible, is nothing more than confirmation of the fact that people have a clear vision of a better set of economic activities that still cannot be. The sequence of iterations in the planning process (back and forth communications and revisions of proposals) is viewed as a way to allow the individual units and federations to begin by expressing their optimal desires, but then whittle those desires down to a feasible set of economic activities themselves. So in their initial proposals consumer councils might well have asked for more than workers offered to produce, and some intermediate industry federations might not have offered to produce enough to allow for the proposed activities of workplaces producing finished goods to occur. But after summing the results of all units' first proposals, each council would have more information to go on:

1) For each material good or service there would be information about whether it was left in excess demand or supply by the sum total of all first proposals. 2) A comparison of the proposals of different neighborhood councils would reveal differences in the quantity of all the different kinds of "final goods" requested per member. 3) Comparison of workplace proposals would reveal differences in average work-time proposed per member, differences in the quantity of output proposed per member, and differences in

the amount of each input per unit of output requested. 4) The description of human inputs and outputs of different work and consumption processes in the initial proposal would reveal any changes from last year as well as differences in human outputs proposed by different workers' and consumers' councils. 5) Moreover, for each unit that included an attempt to justify its proposal by estimating the material and human consequences of its proposal, there would be a list of calculated material consequences, an evaluation of the material consequences using quantitative values determined from last year's plan and an attempt to translate these consequences into human terms. For any unit that did not care to prepare such an estimation, any other unit—or the unit's federation—could make the calculation for it. But before proceeding to discuss how all this new information would be used in a series of proposal revisions converging to a feasible plan, we need to discuss more fully the formation of federations of councils and the role of research and development departments.

## Federations of Councils

Up until now we have discussed the operation of decentralized socialist planning mainly in terms of the proposals and revision of proposals of individual workers' and consumers' councils. But we've referred to the fact that federations of councils would have to be formed. Each neighborhood consumers' council would belong to a Ward Federation of Consumers' Councils, which in turn would belong to a Regional Federation of Consumers' Councils, which in turn would belong to a State Federation, and finally a National Federation of Consumers' Councils. Each workers' council would belong to two branches of federations, one based on industrial filiation along product lines, the other based on geographical locale. Thus a workers' council would belong to a Regional Federation of all workers' councils in the area as well as a Regional Industrial Federation composed only of workers' councils producing similar material outputs. Both Regional Federations of all workers' councils and Regional Federations within industrial branches would belong in turn to their respective State and National Federations. The general purposes of these federations are 1) to facilitate the process of revising proposals so that many iterations can be worked out within an appropriate federation and need not occupy the time of all units in the economy, 2) to allow for the subtle gradations of public vs. private aspects of different consumption activities as well as the different degrees of mutual interaction involved in different production activities, and 3) to allow for the external effect and democratic direction of research and development operations at a variety of "levels" in the economy. We will discuss the first two functions here and the last in the next section.

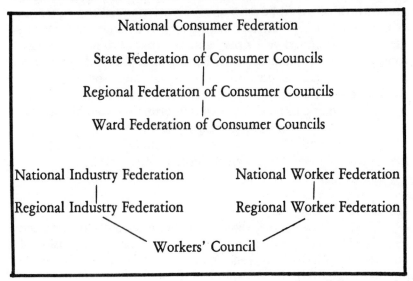

Every consumption council will not only request the goods to be consumed by its members, it will also vote its desires concerning consumption goods that will be requested and consumed by larger federations. The federations are the units which will make the proposals concerning "public goods" of varying extensions, but these proposals will be the democratic outcome of the summation of votes coming from all the member councils. So when every consumption council formulates "its" proposal, what this actually consists of is its votes concerning public goods that will make up the proposals of the National, State, Regional, and Ward Federations of consumption councils of which it is a member, plus its own requests. The actual proposing in the iterative planning process for goods that are more "public" than a neighborhood reflects would be done by the appropriate federations of consumption councils, based on the summary of votes from member councils,* so that the planning process would incorporate proposals from all individual consumer councils and all federations of consumer councils as well.

The federations of consumption councils could also facilitate proposal revision for member councils. Each Ward Federation would review the individual requests of each of its constituent neighborhoods for "fairness." Since each council in a Ward Federation receives the same "package" of public goods, there would be no reason for councils within a ward to tolerate any significant deviation above the average social burden implied by individual neighborhood requests. Of course high deviations of calculable material consequences do not automatically merit rejection. Just as in the case of neighborhood councils' discussion of individual's personal proposals that we can now see can be evaluated using last year's quantitative evaluations (shadow prices), the quantifiable calculation is more an indication of which proposals merited further discussion and investigation than which should be disapproved out of hand. As for individuals, just because a whole neighborhood's proposal is characterized by a high per member quantifiable social cost, it might still prove justifiable upon subsequent "human" translation. But in any case, most of this kind of neighborhood consumer council proposal revision could be handled within Ward Federations rather than necessitating a whole series of economy wide iterations. Similarly, each Regional Consumers' Federation could review the proposals of all its members

---

*There are two possible ways proposals of consumption councils could be formulated during each iteration: Each consumption council could formulate its own proposal and all its "votes" for its various federations simultaneously. Or, each council could vote its federation proposals, starting with the highest level federation first and working down, only formulating its next federation vote (and finally its own neighborhood proposal) after current federation proposal "votes" were tabulated and the results communicated to each member council. The first method allows for more rapid formulation of proposals. The second allows each council to know the actual proposal of each federation of which it is a member, before it proceeds to formulate the rest of its votes and or proposals. In the first case, a council might well base its individual proposal on a mistaken impression of what federation proposals it accompanied. As an example, suppose a council votes for low federation proposals and a high

Wards,* each State Federation could review the proposals of its regions, etc.

The two different systems of federations of workers' councils would operate so as to take account of the two different kinds of external effects most common in production processes. The kind of external effect usually analyzed under the heading of economies or diseconomies of scale (now broadened to take account of human as well as material inputs and outputs) would be handled within the Industrial Federations. For example, if raising the output of steel could be done more effectively by creating fewer large production units than more smaller units, this would be determined and evaluated first within the steel federation itself. The other kind of externalties between production processes in which the production possibilities of some unit are dependent upon the choice of production activities of another unit within the same locale, would be accounted for within the geographical Federations of Workers' Councils. In this way the effect of the pollution of an upstream plant on a downstream plant's access to clean water would be taken into account.

But the federations of worker's councils would also play a critical role in worker proposal revisions. What the economy-wide plan ultimately requires is national inter-industry feasibility and geographical supply consistency. The two kinds of worker federations can facilitate these goals immensely. If the last iteration left an economy-wide excess demand for coal, for example, this could be analyzed first at the level of the National Federation of Coal miners where the question would be: was an increase in coal output justified, and if so should it be achieved through increased material

neighborhood proposal—arguing in its "evaluation of consequences to others" that the overall package its members would receive is fair and reasonable. But then suppose it is out voted in all its federation proposals so the federations actually make larger requests than the council had voted for—yielding an overall package that is unintentionally "greedy." The question is simply whether to allow for correction within the process of proposal formation (option 2), or to leave correction for subsequent proposals and iterations (option 1).

*Here the ward federations would append the neighborhood requests to their own for evaluation purposes.

inputs, an increase in labor force, or a more intensive effort using the inputs already requested? We will see that a number of factors would enter into the answer. But once the answer to this question was settled at the level of the national industry, the changes in the industry's proposal of inputs and outputs could be communicated to other affected industry federations, and the distribution of new production burdens and any new inputs among individual coal mining units could be settled within the coal industry itself.

Geographical Federations of workers' councils, in combination with the relevant consumers' federation, could resolve the bulk of the intricate supply scheduling that must follow agreement on any national production plan by discovering which supplies could be taken care of from production and stocks within a geographical region itself. Only supplies that could not be met internally would have to be forwarded to a national level for coordination in the process of drawing up agreements and delivery dates.

Finally, the revision of work proposals concerning average hours of work proposed, and the specific kinds and quantities of new equipment requested, etc., could be worked out within industrial federations for the most part. If a council of coal miners wished to propose that all coal miners work a shorter week than previously, they would take the proposal to their federation. If the proposal was accepted by the federation, it could become part of the federation's proposal in the economy wide planning process to be accepted or rejected by other workers' federations. On the other hand, if a particular coal miners' council wished to propose a shorter work day or week for its own members than for other miners, this, along with the reasons for it, could be discussed entirely within the coal miners' federation.

## Research and Development Departments

A Research and Development department would be attached to each council and federation of councils. The purpose of all the R & D departments would be to carry out investigations that help its directing unit to a) develop new kinds of economic activities via development of new social relations, technology, etc. and b) assess the likely consequences of such new activities, both for the immediate unit involved and for the rest of the economy as well. The reason R & D departments would be necessary is that neither council members nor representatives to federations of councils would always have the time necessary to pursue and develop every new idea that deserved consideration. The staff and resources of the R & D departments would be available for councils and federations to "assign" the task of more time-consuming long-range, development and evaluation, though these special institutions would also be self-managed in context of the broad norms of participatory socialist economics.

R & D departments in individual councils would focus on changes in the immediate work process and consumption activities as they affected the human development of their council members. R & D in industry-wide federations would focus on large-scale changes in production techniques such as changing from open hearth to oxygen technology in steel production or assembly lines to work teams in auto manufacturing, or from central hospital treatment to local clinics and out-patient treatment in health care. R & D in regional consumer federations would focus on such issues as changes in the regional transportation system using a fleet of mini-buses instead of taxis. R & D in the national consumers' federation would investigate substituting local subway systems and long-distance high-speed trains for the "private" ecologically inefficient car and highway network. Perhaps the most important role of the R & D divisions would be to make specific the commitments to complicated investment patterns over lengthy periods that new activities imply so that these new activities can be meaningfully voted on by all who would be affected, and so that necessary commitments could be recognized and included in future plan allotments.

These R & D institutions are important precisely because they reflect a socially useful division of labor, but since they involve a high level of conceptual work and also have a large impact on the direction of economic development, it would be essential that their workforce not monopolize their positions. This would be most simply insured by requiring that R & D members come from the attached council or federation, holding their position in the unit for predetermined periods, perhaps retaining some of their prior council work even while at the R & D unit, etc. All criteria concerning the role structures within councils would apply to the R & D units as well, and the general criteria guiding their elaboration would be those of preventing harmful on-going divisions of labor, etc., throughout the economy.

## Converging to a Feasible Plan

The long run proposals agreed to as part of previous plans would entail commitments that must be honored in this year's plan unless the projects were being dropped. So the first step in each planning period would be a review of these "inherited" projects to decide a) if they will be continued, and b) if there are any reasons to change the list of activities that R & D councils projected as necessary for their realization. If the project was a major national program, such as a planned decentralization of cities or transformation of the national transportation system, it would be reviewed by a variety of national industrial federations as well as the national consumer's council. If it was a regional or local project it would be reviewed at a lower level. At the end of these reviews there would be an updated list of inherited commitments that would form an unchanging part of each iteration. With a graphic appreciation of the kind of investment commitment already programmed, every council and federation of councils would submit its initial proposal. The results would yield an excess demand for most items.

The "whittling down" would proceed at all different levels within the structure of federations of councils. But in order to see how this "whittling down" would proceed—just what would be "whittled"—it is best to break down the different reasons causing excess demand in order to see the different kinds of adjustments that would be made to eliminate them. Each consumption council and federation request is a list of net inputs requested which implies a calculable larger list of gross productions needed.\* Each request for investment goods by a production unit or federation is also a list of net inputs requested which implies a calculable larger list of gross productions needed.\*\* All of these lists of gross productions implied by various net consumption and investment requests can also be translated into lists of demands on limited raw materials and different categories of labor.† A set of proposals is infeasible if the

---

\*The vector of gross production requirements is $X=(I-A)^{-1}y$, where y is the vector of consumption requests and the A matrix is composed of the average production coefficients of produced goods for the industries according to their *new* proposals.

\*\*The vector of gross requirements is $X_i=(I-A)^{-1}i$ where i is the vector of investment good requests.

†The vector of natural resource requirements for the net consumption request would be $r_i=B(I-A)^{-1}y$ and for the net investment request i, would be $n=B(I-A)^{-1}i$. The vector of labor requirements for net consumption

ultimate demands implied by consumption and investment requests are greater than the total amounts of specific resources or types of labor available.\* There are four different ways in which these imbalances can be eliminated. One kind of adjustment can be made by consumption councils and their federations, and three can be made by workers' councils and their federations.

Consumption councils and their federations can reduce some components of their requests. The question becomes which councils and federations should be asked to make these adjustments, and which specific kinds of requested inputs should be sacrificed. Although the reductions would at first be voluntarily proposed by the various units in light of their *own* evaluations and the new information they receive about the results of the first iteration, attention would certainly be focused on the councils and federations whose requests implied a higher than average burden on the economy.\*\* In the first few iterations reductions would probably remain voluntary, but toward the end of the "social iterative" planning procedure, reductions might have to be imposed on member councils by a majority vote within their respective federations.

Beyond voluntary reductions and reductions from those consumption units with greater than average requests (and no supportable reasons for them), there would be a trend toward shifts away from consumption items whose production emphasized (both directly and indirectly) relatively great amounts of the resources and labor capacities in greatest excess demand, and toward items requiring (both directly and indirectly) those resources and types of labor in greatest excess supply.†

request y would be $l_i = L(I-A)^{-1}i$. The B and L matrices in all cases would be composed of the average production coefficients of non-producible inputs for all the industries according to their *new* proposals.

\*That is when the vector r contains components greater than in the vector r of available resources and labor capacities.

\*\*Here calculations would have to be based on last year's shadow prices with all the inevitable but not terribly damaging inaccuracies discussed earlier. And, as before, each federation must include all its member units' requests as well as its own.

†This "shifting process" could be facilitated by allowing units to substitute zero for the shadow price from last year's plan for all non-producible inputs in excess supply during the previous iteration. A "practical" formula for raising the calculating price above last year's shadow price according to the percentage of excess demand remaining after

Production units and federations could also be asked to reduce some components of their *net* inputs requested for investment purposes. Many of the issues are the same as those discussed for consumption above but the question of which units to focus special attention on for reductions in investment is slightly more complicated. Whereas there was no reason to assume that any particular consumption council or federation should place a greater burden on the rest of the economy than any other, some production councils and federations probably should be "investing" at a more rapid pace than others. What is called for is a scrutiny of investment requests in light of the structure of investment priorities agreed to in the earlier planning periods, and an analysis of new investment priorities in light of the relative discrepancies between the "most preferred" and enacted proposals in previous years. Industries designated as low investment priority should not have requests greater than units at the head of the line. And units within industries designated lower priority should not have greater requests than high priority production units.

But beyond changes in their investment requests, production units can make adjustments in the way they will carry out their activities. For example, by changing their techniques, duration of work, or social organization of work, they could alter the size of their production coefficients—how much of each input they need to produce any particular output—and thus individual production councils and federations could diminish excess demands for certain scarce inputs.* The federation would check to see which individual units proposed production techniques which made the best use of scarce inputs and then determine 1) whether the techniques proposed by these units could be adapted for use by others, and 2) to the extent they could not be, whether some production could be shifted to these more efficient units. Of course actual changes would be agreed to via the usual participatory procedures and therefore in

each iteration could also be voted on by all national federations prior to each iteration, or it could be chosen by a planning agency. Any positive function of percentage of excess demand existing to be added to last year's shadow price would hasten the shifting process, but of course some functions would be more practical in a given circumstance than others.

*In technical terms, the second way in which production units can modify proposals to help yield a feasible plan is to change the coefficients in the A and B matrices that translate net productions into specific resource and labor requirements.

accord with an analysis of the human attributes involved in all possible adjustments.

The third kind of possible adjustment for production units has to do with the amount of labor time and effort proposed. For scarce raw materials there is a physical limit to their supply. But the "available supply" of different kinds of laboring capacities is a fuzzier concept, determined in part by vacation schedules, overtime schedules, retirement schedules, and job training and schooling "schedules." In the final stages of arriving at a feasible plan, it might be desirable to modify some of these variables for laboring capacities that have remained in excess demand through numerous iterations. The adjusment this year, were it to be an inconvenience for particular kinds or workers, could be "paid back" at a future time when the demand fell more heavily elsewhere, or when investment and workforce changes eliminated the imbalance.

To this point, we have identified four different kinds of adjustments that can move the socialist planning process toward resolution, and we have also distinguished between "reduction-type" adjustments, and "shifting-type" adjustments. This operation would obviously entail a number of social iterations, the first few composed almost entirely of "voluntary adjustments," and the final rounds perhaps containing some "forced" adjustments. But in all cases where changes weren't voluntarily proposed by the parties concerned, they could only be coerced by a majority vote of the appropriate federation of which the coerced unit is a member and could be challenged by that unit by a variety of "extraordinary" means to be discussed in another section. In any case, we are not suggesting that decentralized socialist planning arrives at economic policy easily—especially in its formative years—but merely that it is capable of doing so.

## What Happens When People Disagree? Conflict Resolution

We expect that there will no longer be classes or class conflict in a mature socialist economy. We also expect that the kind of socialist kinship and community relations we will argue for in the following two chapters will no longer yield the kind of negative dynamics that generate racial and sexual hierarchies which intrude in the economy as well. But in a young socialism people will carry over many attitudes, habits, misconceptions, and unequal skills from their prior experience under capitalist class relations, racist community relations, and patriarchal kinship relations. Further, it will take time before economic imbalances and all institutional inequities are reversed. In short, neither the institutional boundary nor especially the human center will succumb instantly to revolutionary change.

We have already spelled out, in reasonable detail, how decentralized socialist planning will operate to eliminate class divisions by eliminating direct exploitation, the more subtle phenomenon of redistribution, and persistent divisions of labor which create differences in economic power. But we have not discussed all the mechanisms that can be incorporated into socialist planning to resolve conflicts from lingering class residues. Nor have we discussed mechanisms that can be used to eliminate racist and sexist outcomes that might otherwise continue to occur in a young socialist economy. Finally, conflicts will inevitably arise from simple differences of opinion about how things should best be done, and we have said little about them.

It helps to distinguish between two fundamentally different kinds of disagreement in a young socialist economy. Those arising from holdover, negative attributes, and those reflecting "honest disagreements" among equals. We have given a number of concrete examples of both types of disagreement elsewhere, and will only summarize the main approaches for solving each here.

In the case of an honest disagreement over what is just, wise, or desirable every effort would be made to settle the matter through frank discussion and compromise. Frequently, two different policies could both be tried, or a minority can be permitted to try out its own approach experimentally. In cases where a single program will have to be enacted, a substantial rotation of dissenters out of the role they feel is wrong and members of the majority into the disputed activity could be arranged. Only when all else fails must a resolution be forced by a majority vote of the appropriate council, federation, or society.

But when some individual or group proves intransigent due to holdover attitudes of class privilege, there will be relatively swift provisions for societal pressures to prevail. Individuals will be quickly stopped by a majority vote of their consumption or workplace councils should they persist in proposing unfair levels of consumption or consistently advantageous work assignments for themselves. Similarly, the individual workplace cannot long hold out against the industry federation, and consumption councils must finally succumb to consumption federations where the former deems an unequal proposal unjustifiable. And although a separate channel of appeals could be established whereby individuals or councils could go over the head of majorities opposing them to the next higher level of federation to safeguard against unjust or ill-informed pressures by local majority, we would suggest that a guaranteed appeal all the way up to the political electorate be utilized most often only for conflicts where the impinged parties felt that racism or sexism was a factor in the denial of their proposals.

For just as retraining, rotation, and other institutional techniques discussed above are necessary to overcome differences in consciousness, attitude, and skills between former members of different classes, so too are institutions functioning within the economy which safeguard against racist and sexist outcomes also needed. The most likely forms these institutions will take in any particular young socialist economy will likely depend most on the actual form of the revolutionary process overthrowing the old regime. But it appears to us from what we have already seen in the United States, that, at least here, the process will involve the continued development of autonomous third world and women's movements. We believe that federated councils of women's and minority caucuses will provide the best safeguard against racist and sexist economic outcomes in the early stages of socialism.

There would be autonomous third world and women's caucuses in every workplace and neighborhood council, and these would be federated in turn into regional and national third world and women's organizations. When a caucus felt that disagreements were the result of racism or sexism it would have the power to petition higher bodies. For example, if investment decisions in a particular factory appeared to perpetuate the oppression of Black workers, the third world caucus could appeal the decision (even though it had been arrived at by a majority vote within the workers' council) to the industry federation. If the industry federation refused the appeal, but the industry third world caucus still believed that racism was involved, the appeal could be taken to the national industry federation. Finally, if the national industry federation upheld the original decision, but the national caucus of third world workers in the industry still felt it was a racist decision, the appeal would go to the political arena and the national third world movement. Though in the end the resolution would have to be by binding majority vote of all races and sexes, presumably, in context of parallel revolutions occurring in community and kinship relations, such a process would lead to a just outcome as well as to sufficient struggle over racial and sexual concerns in the economy. The principle at work is quite simple. Throughout economic decision-making the aim is that people should decide in light of social need and potentials and in proportion to their involvement in activities whether as producers, consumers, or bearers of external costs like pollution. When economic decisions bear more heavily upon women or minority workers or consumers because they embody sexual or racial implications, following the same principle, it is these people who must take the lead in decision-making, though the final outcome is determined by the whole planning process.

Even though this brief section has been primarily concerned with special mechanisms for conflict resolution in early socialism to overcome the inherited residues of classism, sexism, and racism, it is important to conclude by stating that the premise of the system is that socialist institutions reward collectivity, empathy, and initiative and discourage selfishness, greed, and authoritarianism so that these latter traits will become weaker influences on economic decision-making as time goes on.

## Ecology, Growth, and the Pace of Development

One of the failings of modern economic systems, both East and West, is that they literally destroy the environment we must live in. This destruction takes two forms. On the one hand, production is undisciplined by any concern for the creation of dangerous by-products. Thus pollutants are dumped till Love Canal becomes a veritable cesspool of chemical disease and the air of Vladavostok a daily threat to human life. On the other hand, production also pays no attention to the delicate balances that characterize all ecological systems. We use up needed resources and strip mine or pave over vast areas, reducing them to homogeneous tracts of dead dirt or asphalt where once there were intricate life systems. We even destroy Brazilian rain forests which provide the oxygen the whole human species needs for survival.

Under capitalism these phenomena persist because of the profit motivation propelling production and because of the mentality of decision-makers. For our leaders see the world as clay to be molded rather than as an arena in which we must live and with which we must converse. This attitude is in part an outgrowth of economic dictates, but it is also a product of the white, male, and authoritarian attitudes that guide ultimate decisions about how we relate to nature.

Within the so-called socialist societies that are really organized in service of the coordinator class, political elites, minorities, and men, the reason for ecological decay is similar. Again, the criteria guiding production are skewed away from concern for the well-being of the whole community. Growth and accumulation are a powerful factor in all decision-making partly due to competition with the West, partly from economic pressures to provide people incentives to participate in otherwise alienated work, and partly because the underlying orthodox Marxist ideology is fixated upon "unleashing society's forces of production from all restraints." What would be the situation in the kind of socialist society we have been describing?

Obviously ecological choices, like all others, would be subject to criteria determined by producers and consumers. When people have control over their workplaces and live in the vicinity of those workplaces, and have nothing to gain from mindless productivity increases, they are obviously going to take seriously the quality of their air. This doesn't require further discussion beyond what we have already said about the character of socialist decision-making. It is self-evident. Additionally, our tiered system of councils is specifically designed to be sensitive to the interconnectedness of all economic choices eliminating incentives for people to ignore the "external effects" of their actions.

But the interesting points for discussion seem to us to revolve around another issue. Will there be growth or not under socialism? There are two powerful arguments concerning the question of growth, only one of which gets much airtime. The more aired is that growth will have to level off and perhaps stop because of constraints imposed by limited resources. There is only so much oil, aluminum, etc. As these resources become ever less plentiful what is left will become more and more difficult to get hold of and therefore we must conserve. The laws of thermodynamics—entropy—guarantee this, or so the argument goes. Actually, this argument may or may not be valid depending upon a number of factors; not least of which is how we define growth. For example, is the transition from gargantuan computers with tubes to lunch box sized computers that are more powerful and have micro-chips growth? If it is, it is also at least in a sense, conservation. Another factor of importance is the assumption that today's dwindling resources will continue to be critical tomorrow and will therefore act as inevitable breaks upon production. What if replacements for these resources are developed? We don't have answers to these questions. But it does seem obvious to us that the kind of economic institutions we have described allow for flexible handling of all these eventualities.

The second point about the question of growth is more subtle. Are there reasons why we might want to put *social* limits on growth and even on change, even if there are no natural limits? Mightn't we decide that the reconstruction of a society's infrastructure every ten years or so is too disruptive of social continuity to be allowed, even if each separate innovation and new creation that would constitute such a reconstruction were *itself* demonstrably superior to its predecessor? It is not impossible that there are certain human rhythms that should limit the rate of implementation of scientific innovations and of material construction, even if there are no technical constraints. Certainly to date science has far outstriped the development of social forms, ethics, aesthetics, and morality. It may be that alterations of these latter human attributes cannot be speeded up beyond a certain point and that we would not want to over accelerate such changes anyway. And if that is so, it may be that we will want to put *social* brakes on economic change, scientific innovation, and material reconstruction as well. Again, we don't have very well defined answers to these questions, but we do think that participatory socialism will allow us to decide what pace of development, change, and innovation we want in our society and allow us to enact those decisions carefully. Few socialists or social critics have paid much attention to the rapid developments that are taking place in computer sciences, communication, biology, and miniturization and their possible important implications for the organization of society. Yet these developments are obviously of potentially great importance. The changes they auger rival those of the last great industrial spurt, the industrial revolution itself. We are not in position to evaluate all these phenomena in a technical way, but a socialist economic vision that will eventually capture the imagination of millions is going to have to incorporate a recognition of the power of many of these innovations and also take a stand regarding which we may want to slow down because they are simply too different, too unpredictable, or otherwise too disruptive of how *we want* our societies to function. It is not true that everything the human mind dreams up has to be put to use. If we want to do craft work in certain areas of production, we needn't forego that desire simply because it has become possible to produce in those areas by automation instead. Under the socialism we envision not only will decisions take into account the preservation of ecological variety and balance, they will also recognize that technology is a human, social product, one which can be used or not used as social desires decree. To reply to the question why did you climb Mt. Everest with the phrase, "because it is there," may be a profound and complex expression of something very human. But for someone to reply years from now to the question why did you drop the atomic bomb, why did you develop a strain of bacteria that destroyed ten million lives, why did you automate away all variety, why did you blot out the sun, with the answer "because our technical know-how made it possible" would be an expression only of the most vapid and self-defeating ignorance of our real potentials as human beings. The struggle for ecological freedom and balance is an intrinsic part of socialism and cannot succeed without a socialist transformation, not only of the economy, but of all spheres of daily life.

### The Viability of Mature Socialist Economic Relations and the Problems of Socialist Transition

We have argued elsewhere why we feel that this participatory socialist economic system is humanly viable—people can act in the ways required—and we do not wish to repeat ourselves here. The essence of the argument is derived from our understanding of human motivation and development. Whereas capitalist and coordinator economic arrangements promote various kinds of individualistic and materialistic behavior of the crassest sort, decentralized socialist planning fosters solidarity, variety, and self-management. Therefore, unless one believes that people are intrinsically and irreparably anti-social and greedy, we can find no reason to believe that the institutional framework we have described would not be quite compatible with human capacities and therefore quite workable. But concern over the "viability of socialist economic relations" needn't rest only on concern about human potentials but may emerge instead from legitimate fears about the difficulty of "getting from here to there." And even assuming that the socialist period begins on a foundation of council and movement structures which have successfully won power throughout society, within the economy one can nonetheless enumerate many likely problems of transition to socialist relations.

First, there is the obvious issue of economic construction and this has two aspects. The new economic institutions must be fully elaborated for allocation and for proper communication within workplaces and consumer units as well. Likewise, however, there are immense rebuilding tasks at many levels. Within units, old technologies that embody the logic of capitalist relations must be progressively replaced. Thus the old assembly line, unnecessarily dangerous tools, and too sharp divisions of labor have to be transcended. At a broader level, it will be necessary to alter the whole character of certain industries. Some will be too dangerous, ecologically unbalanced, or needless—for example, certain kinds of mining, certain nuclear or chemical operations, and traditional advertising. And at the largest scale there will be major problems of reconstruction of over-crowded cities, retooling of industries like Ford, and construction of new public transportation, etc. We'd rather not focus on these matters here, not because they won't be immensely important, but because we think they are largely to be dealt with in the same fashion as all economic decisions, by a participatory process of prioritizing and deciding. Naturally, the fact that these unusually large and intricate decisions are among the first that need to be addressed, at the vary earliest stages of application of the new economic decision-making machinery, further complicates all sides of economic transition, but that simply can't be avoided.

Here, however, we would like to draw attention to three other more subtle matters. First, there is the problem of avoiding a coordinator drift in economic decision-making. Second, and related, there is the question of income distribution. And finally, there is the general problem of old habits, and expecially of consumerism and individualism.

During the transition of the economy, there is obviously going to be a crying need for technical innovation and expertise of many kinds. Though the socialist movement may have begun the process of elaborating skills as widely as possible, engineers, scientists, and intellectuals in general will still have immense advantages both in specialized kinds of knowledge and in psychological dispositions to spend lots of time thinking, planning, debating, etc. It will be very difficult to simultaneously have these people play a large role in transition but not become a new ruling economic class. How does one simultaneously allow the engineer to put his or her abilities to work, restrain the engineer from becoming overly powerful, and most important propel all the workers around the engineer to ever increasing levels of skill and confidence? These aims have never been consciously charted in this way before, much less fully accomplished. And the difficulties are not entirely on one side of the divide.

True, the engineers, doctors, city planners, and other professionals will present a large problem. They will be ready to design the new economy, to be sure, but they will want to be appreciated in a particular way for their contribution—and they will want to set the contours of the design themselves. The ideas that they should participate only as equals and that their expertise entitles them to no greater say in what is actually to be done—indeed, that it requires that they defer in many situations so that others with less expertise will be able to dominate discussion—will be largely foreign. Even if accepted in principle, these socialist themes will contradict the coordinators' prior experiences and deep-seated attitudes and seemingly even their current centrality in the economic reconstruction. There will have to be very specific mechanisms, even beyond the normal fledgling socialist economic forms, to address these peoples' old attitudes and to deal with their likely tendencies to be paternalistic and elitist toward others.

But on the other side of the coin, working people are not going to be universally eager for change either. There will certainly be a residual fear of participation, of taking on too much and getting in over one's head. Workers will often be hesitant to challenge the plans set forth by intellectuals, yet unless they do challenge those plans and rapidly develop their own, a coordinator drift in class relations is likely. Like in the political sphere, economic change is going to be quite threatening and disruptive of accustomed patterns. When one has long cultivated a certain attitude to work—"I want to simply get through the day with the least expenditure of energy and with as little attention paid as possible"—it is difficult to abruptly change to an entirely different stance: "I must participate at every level, be critical and alert, challenge authority, become a decision-maker responsible for this workplace." For example, many workers are likely to find rotation needlessly disruptive or inefficient. Even while thinking of the workplace socially rather than economistically, regarding say health and safety, many workers will be hesitant to assess job definitions and responsibilities, and racial, sexual, and class divisions of labor by the same social standards. For such assessments will imply need for many changes, some of which will be threatening to old identities and familiar ways. There will likely be a noticeable difference between the vigor with which socialist values will be thrown in the face of adherents to capitalism, and the energy that will remain for actual socialist reconstruction after capitalists are defeated. We're not suggesting socialism will have to be forced on workers (as capitalist and coordinator relations must be) but simply that like anything else profoundly new and different, its creation will require a real act of self-conscious will. It will be problematic, not automatic. The movement for socialism will have to instill not only a great desire for participation and equity and a considerable amount of skill and confidence in workers, and not only a sensitivity to the class issues of coordinator leadership, but also a recognition that while the transition period won't last inordinately long, it will involve a certain on-going tension and struggle, both with others and with one's own past habits.

The problem of achieving equity in the transition is also going to be difficult. The distribution of wealth in a country like the U.S. is sharply skewed. Expropriating the capitalists and making available immense amounts of real estate for daycare, parks, public cultural institutions and the like will make a large difference. But some people will still be living in suburban houses, while others live in ghetto apartments, and still others may have no home at all. There will be those with great personal property—clothes, T.V., car, stereo, and so on—and those who own almost nothing. And there will be those who hold jobs that involve high wages, those in low paying positions, and those with no job at all. How will income be redistributed and equity attained?

In general, this problem will be dealt with via the socialist decision-making mechanisms we have already described which contain powerful democratic forces preventing continuation of significant differences of income. But this still leaves two problems during the transition period that will require special attention: To what extent should socialist distribution grant larger material requests to those with lower initial wealth in order to achieve overall equity more rapidly than would be possible otherwise? And to what extent should socialist distribution "phase-in" equal income flows gradually out of respect for limits to everyone's capacity to absorb large changes in life circumstances cataclysmically? By formulating the issues in this way we do not mean to imply that practical political questions of consolidating and extending the political power of the socialist movement will not legitimately enter in to these decisions. But these do appear to us to be the two aspects of the question of income redistribution during the transition period that impact directly on social well-being. Moreover, it is critical to recognize the legitimacy of the former question without confusing it with punitive action against the formerly privileged but now "vanquished." And it is important not to confuse the latter with any concept of justifiable rewards to those supposedly contributing more to society than others. For both the concept of "the vanquished" and the concept of "justifiable material rewards" to those of greater talent or expertise are foreign—indeed poisonous—to socialist development.

However, beyond observing that an overly precipitous approach to redistribution would be disastrous, while prolonging a situation of gross inequality would be equally dangerous and more unjust, we can do no more than try to sort out the legitimate concerns and distinguish them from criteria deserving no place in a socialist transition. Whether the extra strain of mediating between extremes that would be absent in a well-established socialist society would be too much for fledgling council institutions to handle with only those mechanisms we have outlined, we cannot know. If so, the task of elaborating additional, temporary distribution institutions for the transition period ranks high on the agenda of work still to be done.

Finally, there is the issue of consumerism, individualism, and general economic habits left over from the past. For we have described a council structure whose successful operation not only requires a substantial increase in each person's confidence, skills, and knowledge, but also a willingness among all actors to behave collectively and to take into account one another's well-being. This will be a largely foreign notion for people used to market relations. For in the market, one takes into account one's own comfort, and that is all. There is no attention given to the situation of a worker who produced what you are about to consume, nor for those who might get less if you take more, nor for the possibility of sharing consumption or for the kinds of impact your different consumption choices may have on other people. The vision of socialist workplace or consumption councils carefully assessing societal, collective, and individual needs to arrive at a rich plan of action is very far indeed from the privatized decision-making we are used to under capitalism. Yes, there will be many safeguards which will insure and even enhance the individual's right of self-expression and opportunities for experimentation under socialism. But nonetheless, each socialist citizen will be socially compelled to a greater extent than today to parade the logic of their behavior in public and to take account of their neighbors' and workmates' self-expression as well. Again, the process of building a socialist movement and struggling for power will have begun to sensitize people to the need for this sort of outlook and familiarize them with how to carry it out. But there is something different about functioning under the duress of social struggle and normal commonplace decision-making. We all know, though sometimes social commentators forget, that people *are* capable of sacrificing for the social good. Wartime rationing is universally acceptable, and even less catastrophic circumstances like hurricanes and floods lead people to take seriously one another's claims on scarce goods. But will it be easy to foster such social attitudes as the norm rather than the exception? Won't there be a long period when such behavior will be unfamiliar and only practiced poorly so that the kind of planning we have described will take longer than it otherwise might and involve many confrontations? And if this is the case, won't there be formidable pressures to cut corners and delegate authority to experts and/or leaders? We think so, and so we also think that substantial collective discipline is going to be necessary to master the skills and habits associated with socialist consumption and production. Overcoming selfish and ultimately counterproductive individualism is going to prove very difficult, and while the new institutions we have outlined will provide a favorable setting, they won't provide any guarantees. It is likely that special transitional methods will be called for, but these will have to be worked out on the basis of experience.

The point is simple. Creation of a socialist economy is going to be a complex, demanding project. But the fact that the label "socialist" has heretofor been defamed due to its appropriation by coordinator societies is no reason to deny the desirability of true socialism. Nor is the difficulty of envisioning and creating a participatory socialist economy reason to deny the need. Rather, the oppressiveness of the class divisions of capitalist economic arrangements leave no option but to revolutionize our economy, and the oppressiveness of coordinator class divisions should convince us that during transition there is no point in compromising socialist economic aims for efficiency or an early stabilization. Regrettably, there will be no avoiding the potential pitfalls of trying to create a decentralized participatory economy despite the obvious fact that the originality of such a project will make it all the more problematic. For the bankruptcy of "existing alternatives" is undeniable.

# 8
# SOCIALIST KINSHIP

Mama, Mama, do you understand
Why I've not bound myself to a man?
Is something buried in your old widow's mind
That blesses my choice of our own kind?
Oh Mama, Mama.

Meg Christian

As Batya Weinbaum asserts, unlike the Bolsheviks our question must "become not 'how do women fit into the revolution,' but 'what kind of revolution do women need?'"[1] What must be the new living relationships between men, women, and children in the family? How must socialization be accomplished and how must its purpose change in socialism? If kinship networks are responsible for the production of sexual norms and preferences among adults, how must these norms and preferences alter, how must the institutions themselves be altered, how will the process of maturation be different from what it is in our society today? These are some of the questions we need to answer, however hesitantly and cautiously. What was true of citizens of the young socialist republic of Russia remains true today. Not only is there great interest in these matters, but there is intuitive understanding that changes in these areas are essential if life in any sphere is to significantly improve. If a blueprint is premature, silence is ridiculous. Orthodox Marxist theory emphasizing the preeminence of the economic sphere in determinations of the situation within the household and generally between men and women is certainly insufficient to the task at hand. Incapable of guiding a thorough analysis of sexual relations under capitalism, incapable of discerning the maintenance of patriarchy (even if in altered form) in the Soviet Union, China, and Cuba, this theory is also insufficient in guiding us in the elaboration of kinship institutions as we want to create them in a truly socialist and feminist revolution. This is a main result of the analysis to this point in this

331

book. We have begun assembling a theory to use in place of the orthodoxy, a totalist approach in our view more consistent with original Marxist intentions and certainly with the lessons of modern feminism, and we will now apply this theory to the problem of creating a "kinship vision" suitable for socialism in the United States.

## The Rejection of Old Norms

New kinship relations will be elaborated by women, men, and children of different communities according to their own preferences and through their own experimentation. There will be no single correct approach, but to be socialist, new kinship relations will have to embody the socialist values of self-management, solidarity, and diversity of development we have already emphasized in earlier chapters. What would this mean for kinship activity?

In the first place there will be a thorough rejection of the patriarchal kinship norms of modern Western societies. But traditional "communist" alternatives will not be the substitute. For example, socialists will not seek to solve the tensions of male/female relations by simply removing the problems of nurturance and child-rearing from the household to be turned over to "experts" in State nurseries and live-in schools. This solution eliminates the diversity of relations between adults and children at best, and reproduces patriarchy in a public socialization process at worst. Nor will simple-minded promiscuity be the solution. For although kinship forms will no longer be limited to the nuclear family and monogamy will not be forced on people, the richness of love and friendship are not fully developed in a single night but require longevity, continuity, and intensity. This is not to say there will not be an expansion of sexual desire and even an increase in short-term sexual encounters. Moreover, where recent trends in this direction have been characterized by new forms of degradation for women—as in the hippie formula: free love = free women—in the future these aspects will presumably be absent. But *among* all the multitudes of living modes that will blossom—nuclear families, extended families, singles, transients, and all manner of loose collections of friends and comrades—we expect that one new one, the socialist commune, though in no way enforced, will become increasingly common. This perception of the future is suggested by both practical and theoretical considerations.

From a practical point of view, there has been a dissolution of modern families in the U.S. and through much of Europe, and a parallel increase of interest in collective living arrangements of all kinds and in the reduced house work and more diverse friendships these can accommodate.[2] Even more important, in Black and white working class communities there is reasonable evidence that the extended family, including not only blood and marriage relations but also close friends, already exists as a prevalent form. These are not socialist communes because a) the sharing is motivated primarily for reasons of survival in an extremely hostile environment, and b) the situation of children and women is no less coerced than in nuclear families in the rest of society. But still, in the social solidarity and pooling of resources of these families, we can already see the seeds of socialist formations.[3] But to argue in support of the commune as a new kinship form we must briefly discuss the meaning of socialist socialization and sexuality.

### Socialist Socialization and Sexuality

Socialization is the process by which children become adults, habituated to fit the social roles which await them so they might contribute and receive from society in an orderly fashion. At the most abstract level socialist socialization is no different save for the different contours of the society the child is prepared to participate in. But how can a process which molds children to conform be part of a socialism synonymous with freedom, self-development, and diversity? Isn't socialization manipulative by definition and the exact opposite of freedom? Of all the countless directions a child can develop in, one necessarily emerges. But doesn't the fact that this one fits with what society requires betoken that the process of socialization is apriori determined and that it is therefore "unfree"? This seemingly compelling argument is wrong, and understanding the error is helpful in developing criteria for socialist kinship forms.

If socialization prepares a child to be an adult in a way that denies human potentials, then of course it is an intrinsically narrowing and coercive process. But if a society were structured in such a way that fitting its contours meant precisely developing in accord with one's potentials, then the fact that we could say in advance many things about how these potentials would most often manifest themselves wouldn't make their development less free. That we can predict that a U.S. citizen will most likely grow up heterosexual is due to our knowledge of the constraints that narrow his or her sexuality today. That we will be able to predict that future citizens will grow up in possession of their full sexual proclivities is evidence of the freedom of socialist socialization, not its narrowness. The point is that socialist socialization should free the individual to develop all of his or her potentials, while socialist society should be structured to accommodate, reward, and benefit from the resulting diverse adult dispositions. Furthermore, the fact that norms associated with any given period's understanding of "full development" could certainly conflict with yet to be evolved future understandings, adds another dimension to socialist socialization. What is required is therefore not no socialization, but socialization to freedom and a sensitivity to the requirement that like people, institutions and norms too must freely evolve in tune with the lessons of new experiences.

With respect to sexuality and sexual divisions, socialist socialization must not "produce" repressed men and women, nor a sexual differentiation in social roles and norms. Under socialism there can be no non-biologically imposed sexual division of labor—men doing one kind of work and women another—nor any demarcation of individuals according to sexual preferences or age beyond what is biologically justified. This means we need kinship forms which equilibrate the contributions of men and women and which respect the potentials of the young and old. If socialist sexuality is to be physically rich and emotionally fulfilling, yet not create unequal social skills and dispositions between the sexes, obviously life in the primary kinship unit and socialization in general must be redefined significantly.

So, theoretically we are looking for a kinship form which is democratically structured to allow and develop skills at self-management, egalitarian to promote solidarity, and flexible for diversity. New forms must overcome the possessive narrowness of monogamy while allowing preservation of the "depth" that comes from lasting relationships. They must destroy the division of roles between men and women such that both sexes are free to nurture and initiate. They must give children room for self-management and learning, while also providing the extra support and structure children need. They must return to the long-living the place of esteem they deserve and the opportunity to pass along their accumulated wisdom even while they learn from the experiments of the young. Living must not be by rote but by design. Continual development of new kinship arrangements must promote and accommodate such aims.

But the nuclear family generally attains the antithesis of these ends. While within a constrained setting it meets many survival and emotional needs and provides at least a partial solution to some problems of kinship, it is also at present the focal productive unit for the creation of genderized adults suited to market exchange, class stratification, instrumentalism, subordination to authority, anti-collective individualism, and racism. Even the extended families of some working class communities while better in some ways, still embody authoritarian parent/child and patriarchal man/woman norms.

So we see a need for socialist communes as a real alternative with roots in current practices and with the potential for elaboration into a key link in a network of socialist kinship relations. Of course there would be many kinds of communes as it is a complex form which can be varied in countless ways, but nonetheless we can outline some basic features.

The commune we envision is a voluntary, freely chosen home. Potential members are accepted (or rejected) by those who have come before. Commune work is shared equally. There are no special privileges, nor any non-biological age or sex-defined division of labor. There is collective democracy as in the economy and society as a whole. Everyone shares responsibilities. All adult members participate in the responsibilities and delights associated with raising children regardless of whether they are biological parents. Different communes have different interests and different emphases on meals, gardens, study, and commune membership varies as people's dispositions and tastes change. But there is no notion of people as property: women, children, and men are all free to choose and change their places of residence. Within communes monogamy is generally neither required nor disallowed. It is but one desirable form of sexual interrelation, for others there will be multiple sexual relations. Heterosexuality, homosexuality, and bisexuality are all likely to be common. And perhaps increasingly common would be sexuality as simply a human activity, androgyny. Though erotica may actually become more popular, certainly sexist pornography and commercial sex will disappear. While ritual and drama within sexuality may increase, sexual exploitation and abuse will disappear.

The whole tone of interpersonal relations will alter. Love will be freed from worry about identity, independence, income, image, and emotional security. Unlike many other "energies," it is not diminished by expression. To love one person does not exhaust a scarce emotional supply which then won't be sufficient to allow expression of love toward someone else. Instead, through multiple expression, our capacities to love will be enhanced. Moreover, by having many "communards" with whom to share tasks, worries, and experiences, no single personal relationship is forced to bear as much weight as is now demanded. Each relationship will benefit as the tensions of daily life are dispersed. Is it too much to think that there will be a time when emotional relations will be so equal and untied to issues of esteem and self-image that both jealousy and unrequited love may disappear? Who knows, but we can envision more than enough changes short of this goal to make the alterations well worthwhile. After all, the processes of loving, procreation, and socialization are now characterized by jealousy, recrimination, suspicion, unfulfilled sexuality, and the general oppression of women and children—psychologically and physically. We have little to lose but our chains.

There is no such thing as particular individuals being "tied to the home" by housekeeping chores or by the requirements of caring for young children. All such responsibilities are shared collectively. Each individual (with the exception of those men who previously took little responsibility at all) has considerably more free time and flexibility. Children are brought up collectively, and are (we suggest) members of a children's collective as well as members of the commune as a whole. Children relate to all adults in whom they are interested, by choice, not strictly in accord with "blood lines."* Their collective provides them with a certain autonomy and ability to voice their own interests and needs, from a perspective that must remain inevitably and existentially different from that of their elders. To the extent their knowledge and experience allow, children

*To the extent that biological ties are important due to the exigencies of birth, genetic endowment, etc., no problem is introduced. Due to their intrinsic qualitative importance, these ties would simply be preserved by free choice. We might also note that some adults might choose to be in a commune without children just as some women might choose communes without men or vice versa, although we personally doubt there would be many of any of these.

manage their own lives and are also responsible, like adults, to the commune for work and study.*

The large membership of the commune provides a base for intellectual, athletic, artistic, and emotional involvement and freedom that is unattainable within a smaller group. Chores can be handled more efficiently. Redundancies of cooking, child care and cleaning are considerably diminished. And there is no loss in privacy —it is more space in which to move and act, not a loss of a room of one's own that socialism offers.

The critical dimension of this description is that while the positive aspects of present-day social ties between relatives are preserved in new forms, the *traditional* "mother," "father," "son," and "daughter" roles are gone. Since "mothering" and "fathering" are now *both* carried out by men and women, the sexism and authoritarianism intrinsic to these roles have no basis in the socialist commune while the love, creative leadership, and emotional security remain. In the commune there is equity, self-management, freedom to come and go. But obviously long-term membership—one could almost say seniority—would have desirable implications that would likely minimize frivolous moving about. There is collectivity *and* privacy, continuity *and* change, in sum an end to the emotional problems traditionally associated with patriarchal marriage, divorce, and aging. We are not suggesting there will be no conflict, pain, or remorse, only that the most extreme forms—those due to oppressive institutions—will be eliminated. Socialism will not change the fact that each individual is the center of his or her own universe no matter how well he or she empathizes with others' situations, nor will it eliminate the related difficulties of communication, conflicting desires, generational conflict and the like. There may well be unrequited love, but not possessiveness. There will be brief physical relations but neither brief nor sustained disrespectful, unequal relations. Children will

*Obviously there will no longer be pressure on women to have children as evidence of their economic worth, nor will men feel the need to sire children as evidence of their masculinity. Within any commune the motivation for childbirth will rest on the collective desire to have the rich addition to life experiences that comes with the "advent" of children, and on particular individuals' personal desires to have and to bring up children—for the pleasure this affords and as a responsibility to the species.

not be adults but neither will they be slaves or clay for adult molding.

While our emphasis has been on the new institution of the socialist commune as the key change in the kinship sphere, this is not to imply that other institutions in the kinship sphere, such as formal education, will remain unaltered. While we cannot provide a thorough discussion of socialist education here, one important point is worth making in passing. The main thing about socialist education is that it has no need to teach us to endure boredom, obey authority, and repress our energies, creativity, and critical spirits. Instead, as it prepares us for a fully-involved and demanding life, socialist education will aim to enlarge our capacities and knowledge to the greatest possible extent. What is most critical is that socialist education contribute to the ability of society to avoid a fixed division between conceptual and executive labor. That is, socialist education must guarantee everybody the opportunity to attain sufficient general knowledge, skill, facility in organization and decision-making, and culture to be able to partake fully and equally in all aspects of social life. This is the fundamental norm of socialist education. Of course the actual institutions for accomplishing this goal will be both more general and more diverse than now. There will be schools for young and old alike. Teachers will also have other social roles. Students will also work. And pedagogy will be aimed toward awakening critical energies rather than stifling them. But we must leave the task of discussing the practical ways in which these aims can be achieved to others and to those who develop them in future practice.

Similarly, our focus on changes in the kinship sphere proper, should not be taken to imply that changes will not take place in the kinship moments of other spheres. Just as patriarchy today is not limited to the kinship sphere but simply "rooted" there, the development of socialist kinship relations must extend to the elimination of sexist role demarcations in all spheres. In the economy, for example, job roles will no longer embody sexist presuppositions about the interests, talents, and dispositions of men and women. In the polity women will become as actively involved, and exercise as much leadership as men. In general, the elimination of patriarchy will contribute to the dimunition of aggressiveness and competitive modes of behavior throughout socialist society, just as the transformation of other spheres will contribute toward achieving socialist kinship goals. In other words, a totalist approach presumes that the possibility of creating socialist communes such as those we have described hinges in part on the success of transformations in other spheres, just as the practicality of socialist relations in other spheres will depend on the creation of socialist patterns of procreation and upbringing.

What a socialist revolution in living forms would mean for the quality of interpersonal relations and accomplishment is already intimated in the discussions above. Women are no longer subordinate. The talents and intelligence of half the species is free at last, and men will also be free to be nurturant. Childhood is a time of play and increasing responsibility, but not of fear. Loneliness does not grip as a vice whose handle turns as each year passes. The sharing and collective approach to daily life decisions makes living a social process, a kind of art which we finally appreciate as such and reclaim from the realm of habit and necessity. We can only guess—extrapolating from our own most human experiences—at the liberation of sexuality and emotions that will accompany the end of patriarchy. Similarly, there will be a great release of creative energy and intelligence and a development of rich human relations alongside the expansion of communal living forms.*

But is all this possible? Is the vision we have outlined humanly possible, or is it contradicted by some aspects of human nature? If men have an innate, biological need and disposition to dominate women, or are biologically incapable of being nurturant, then to break the sexual division of labor would require continual restraints upon some aspects of men's nature. Or, if women were naturally passive and incapable of assertiveness, then again, to break the current division of labor would require institutional pressure,

---

*Although we focus throughout this section on the "bright side" of socialist kinship relations, an interesting passage from Gayle Rubin gives indication of what *might be* an on-going cause of difficulty. "Human sexual life will always be subject to convention and human intervention. It will never be completely 'natural' if only because our species is social, cultural, and articulate. The wild profusion of infantile sexuality will always be tamed. The confrontation between immature and helpless infants and the developed social life of their elders will probably always leave some residue of disturbance." (Gayle Rubin, "The Traffic in Women," in Rayna Reiter, *Toward an Anthropology of Women,* Monthly Review Press, N.Y.).

enforcing otherwise recessive human tendencies. In this case the "free" development of the kin relations we described above would not be "free" at all, and the resulting tensions would be ever-present.

But if human beings have no basic needs incompatible with the goals and values we have outlined, our vision *is* possible. If men and women both have potentials to be nurturant *and* innovative, if fragmented "father"/"mother" personalities, dispositions, and skills are social products of alienated, patriarchal kinship relations, then our vision is not only desirable but a necessary step to fulfillment of our species' potential as well. Then interpersonal possessiveness, non-biological male/female role differentiation, and innumerable insufficiencies of human personality, sexual consciousness and practice, and emotional awareness, are all products of a contingent and oppressive solution to the problems of kinship in what has, till now, been a hostile social setting. What will make socialist kinship relations a realizable goal, in our view, is our human potential for sociality, and the reinforcement provided by the rest of socialist society including the requirements this environment will place on procreation, socialization, and interpersonal relations.

### Kinship Transition

The general structure of problems associated with transition in the kinship sphere is akin to that in politics and economics, though the specific content is of course very different. Like the interface between workers and coordinators, here too it is necessary for people on both sides of a divide to change their ways. But the specific contours of the necessary changes are quite different for kinship and they are textured by a very different set of interactions between the two groups.

Men under patriarchy develop ways of perceiving, thinking, talking, walking and emoting that are "male." And women, likewise, develop "female" modes of being. The task of transition is not to have each adopt some of the aspects of the other's personality. It is rather to have each become something new, a socialist adult, a person who has certain traits akin to those called "male" and "female" but some entirely different traits as well. In other words, a socialist human being—of either sex—is not simply the sum of patriarchal male and female personality traits.

This alteration of personality is going to be very difficult and will likely take two or more generations. Nonetheless, the personality changes that can be achieved even by adults at the time of socialist transition will be substantial. The struggle over enactment of these changes represents the first main problem of kinship transition. The other three we would like to highlight here are the need to address imbalances of power between men and women in all spheres of society, the problem of evolving new institutional forms, particularly for childcare and "cleaning," and the problem of the relation between people of different ages.

Socialism will be impossible without a major reduction in the objectification of women by men. Sexuality will have to be redefined. The equal rights and capacities of women will have to be recognized. Men will have to see themselves and women differently, and women will have to see themselves as whole beings entitled to full participation in all aspects of life. Both men and women will have to develop all sides of their emotional and cognitive beings and become comfortable in certain modes of thought and activity unfamiliar to them at present. The struggle to carry out these and other redefinitions will be exceptionally difficult.

The assault on some of the more visible physical and psychological abuses of women will no doubt be more immediately successful. Women's groups and caucuses will lead efforts to eliminate wife beating, physical harrassment of women on the job and in the streets, and blatant sexism in media, literature, and all role definitions. We would expect many of the campaigns to merely continue from the period before victory over into the period of transition with the primary difference the fact that after a socialist revolution and during the transition period such efforts will be given every means of public support rather than being harrassed by public authorities and mass media alike.

But there will be a subtle underside to the more visible efforts to eliminate blatant obstacles to womens' advance. For a socialist transition in kinship entails inclusion of women at all levels of social activity and influence, and equal participation of men in the work of clean-up, order keeping, and especially nurturance of children. And it is important to realize that these latter changes are both ends in themselves as well as necessary means for the transformation of womens' position in society.

One of the simplest and to date most powerful means for structurally countering imbalances of participation is the use of quotas and we feel strongly that quotas will be one important tool of socialist transition. That is, there will be quotas for minimum participation of women in areas of decision-making and skillful participation in public life, formerly "male activity," and for men in nurturing, cleaning, and other formerly "female activity." Perhaps such quotas won't in all cases immediately be 50 percent due to a lack of trained or otherwise suited men or women, but they will certainly accelerate toward 50 percent very quickly. The price to be paid in training women and also men (who wants incompetent, callous daycare workers or nurses?) and in general dislocation and sometimes under utilization of prior learning of women and men who shift from accustomed fields to new ones, will be respected as a necessary concomitant of combating sexism. Most important, contrary to superficial appearances, it will be recognized that as always the main burden of continuing injustice due to still unresolved imbalances will fall on the oppressed women, not men. Yes, quotas will cause men certain losses (and gains) relative to their accustomed situation. However, until real equity is achieved, such losses are only relative. They diminish the absolute gap between male advantage and female denial. They do not impose an unjust hardship on men but justly diminish their sexist privilege. Indeed, it is the patience of women not men that will be tested by any slacking in movement toward parity of participation in all sides of social life. When women are introduced into positions of skillful work and creative decision-making throughout society, male complaints about a failing of quality due to the women's lack of experience will *not* be cause to delay or slow up the "entry process" but instead to accelerate and enrich it. Two reasons are paramount. First, the claim itself, while likely having some basis in fact will nonetheless be one-sided and therefore spurious. For while it may be true that women lacking years of experience will have some problems dong "good work" in certain tasks, it is also true that they will be *less* saddled by habits of work formed in "oppressive experiences in the past," and especially—and this is of course the point that men are least likely to admit—that they will not have built up nearly so many attachments to sexist modes of operation and will therefore be infinitely more open to their elimination. When the male worries that female participation will mean a loss of efficiency and quality *he* is using the words "efficiency" and "quality"—at least in part—in a myopic way which ignores the human and social cost of sexism. At the same time, to the extent women entering new positions will have gaps in their skills and training, rather than reason for exclusion or slow down, this is simply cause for elaboration of new and liberating training programs. But just to be sure we aren't misunderstanding, the period of transition to socialism will involve an immense redefinition of social roles in all areas of activity. The idea that women will have more to learn, harder things to learn, or a harder time learning new things, seems to us very unlikely so long as there is no compromise on the aim that new conditions not only be socialist in economics, politics, and community but also—and the rest is dependent upon it, as vice versa—in kinship. This means that when the highly skilled male takes a turn cleaning or keeping records, and complains "society is losing because my great skills and experience are being underutilized," assuming care is being taken in all sides of the transition process, he is simply wrong. A) his skills and knowlege are actually quite suspect so long as he does no rote work and, more important, maintains a mindset content to allow others to do his rote work for him. And B) his participation in rote tasks part of the time contributes to developing the talents of others for use to benefit all, an obvious and necessary gain for society. Not to mention that sexism is being overcome—a precondition for all peoples' fullest development. The other main structural basis for the enhancement of women's power in all spheres of social activity is the on-going maintanence of autonomous women's movements, councils, caucuses, etc., and their ultimate authority regarding disputes about kinship issues, but we discussed this dynamic earlier in the chapter on economics and therefore won't repeat here.

But the problems that will likely accompany a serious effort to enlist men in cleaning activity and in child nurturance and daycare, the flip side of women's entry into other spheres, are going to be substantial. The development of a commune structure won't alone accomplish these ends as a survey of hippie experience in the 1960s in the U.S. would clearly show. Obviously, whatever their intellectual acceptance of the need for change might be, many men will balk at the time and effort needed to keep things tidy, and particularly at the mindset and attention that such work requires to be done effectively and without someone else having to come along and repeat it immediately—that someone generally being a woman.

Furthermore, men's habits of expecting things to be cleaned for them, their meals to be prepared, and order to be kept, will get in the way. This is an instance where a group of people are going to have to learn new skills not for obvious personal gain, which is often difficult and disruptive enough, but primarily to allow another group fair participation in all sides of life. In time, men's participation in cleaning and cooking will positively affect male personalities and help in the reconstruction of male identity in a socialist way. But this is not likely to be an effect readily perceived and therefore welcomed by men. Rather, men will see participation in housework, cooking, and keeping order as an infringement of the time available for other kinds of activity. What kinds of social pressure will be brought to bear upon men to compel anti-sexism is hard to say. Obviously, one does not want to establish public institutions which will progressively insinuate themselves in all sides of social life eliminating any prospect for privacy and personal experimentation. And at the same time, the fact that women and men can love each other even while they have an unequal relationship, means that there will be much ambivalence and fear of loss associated with these struggles. Often neither party will want immediate uninvited intrusion by outsiders to mediate sex role inequities or other largely personal interrelations. Yet such sexual asymmetries are not purely personal. Every couple or other group of individuals in which women are saddled, by whatever agreement, with disproportionate responsibility for cleaning and cooking impedes the elimination of sexual imbalances in other more public institutions. A family with sexist role definitions is also a place in which the next generation will be raised without a "socialist model" of non-sexist social relations between adults. And this *is* a public problem but one which must be addressed in a manner which is consistent with all socialist values, including those of privacy.

The issue of men participating in nurturance and child raising will likely be even more complex. In the first place, here there are benefits for men and potential losses for women, as well as the reverse. Men will enter a realm which has its own emotional rewards. Women will be disenfranchised from their prior monopoly not only on these emotional involvements, likely a good thing even in the short run, but also on the power that accrues and the self-respect that accompanies doing a good job with the kids. One need only imagine a situation in which a woman in a contemporary household is partially displaced from having sole responsibility for the children by a husband whose job has very liberal hourly requirements but who is unable to get an interesting job in the economy as a result, to see the complications. Sexism is only being undermined in part. When you add a recognition that the woman may well retain the ultimate responsibility, if not the benefits associated with child-rearing, it is easy to see that the transition may be fraught with tension. There is also the problem of women being loathe to let men make errors. And of course, least justifiably, many men will remain reluctant both due to their own personalities and lack of taste for engaging in nurturant playful behavior, and due to stinginess over how their non-workplace time will be spent. The point is that many of the intricate problems associated with housecleaning alterations will be repeated with regard to childcare, and that here there will be other complicating factors as well. At the same time, progress with respect to men participating in childcare is absolutely critical to an ultimately successful transition. Another means of furthering this participation, therefore, will be the institution of quotas guaranteeing male participation in daycare centers, nursing, and all other previously "woman dominated" social roles.

The last particularly difficult aspect of kinship transition we will address concerns relations between people of different ages. During the early stages of transition there are inevitable problems in making changes that have different effects for different age groups. "They don't have to go through what I went through." "I don't get the benefits I would have had." These attitudes will influence how parents regard young children, and how "grown children" regard their elderly parents. Jealousy and competition do not disappear over night. Under socialism we envision a set of relationships which recognize the impact of age upon social role, but which do not deny people freedom and fulfillment due to age. Thus, we expect young people to have room to develop and make decisions while still being subject to adult authority when it is necessary for either the well-being of the young or of the community as a whole. Likewise, we see elderly people becoming respected members of the community, participants in work and play, and revered for their many experiences and insights. These are far from commonplace attitudes toward young and old, and again, the initiation of communal structures and other institutions of socialist kinship will not automatically guarantee a rapid alteration of perceptions. Rather, to attain such changes, substantial education and effort will be necessary. Exactly what kinds of social programs and struggles will allow both the young and the elderly to express themselves and attain their rightful place in society during the transition, we don't know. But the dislocation that will be caused by these efforts is a small price to pay in order to avoid backsliding into more familiar patterns, especially since the young can be so easily kept in check.

# 9
# SOCIALIST COMMUNITY

> When Marxists speak of socialism to the Negro, they leave
> many young Negro social rebels unimpressed. Many
> concrete questions remain unanswered. What guarantee do
> Negroes have that socialism means racial equality any
> more than does capitalist democracy? Would socialism
> mean the assimilation of the Negro into the dominant
> racial group? Although this would be "racial democracy" of
> a kind, the Negro would wield no political power as a
> minority. If [the Negro] desired to exert political power as
> a racial minority...even under socialism [the Negro] might
> be accused of being "nationalistic."
>
> Harold Cruse

In this chapter we try to describe community relations as they
might exist in a socialist future. As we have seen already, the goal
most often espoused by orthodox Marxists, what we have called
community homogenization, is horribly flawed: it ignores the value
of cultural diversity while simultaneously underestimating the
complexity and profundity of cultural creation in general. The
vision of humanity climbing into one, shared cultural
playpen—with the ideal culture a product of scientific construction,
no less, rather than of the wisdom of countless human acts—is just
not the stuff dreams are made of. Rather such a cultural melting pot
is actually part of a nightmare, no matter how gentle the flame
beneath might be.

Socialist realism, the mode of artistic expression that evolves
from the orthodox approach, reduces art to mere propaganda.
Where art appeals to people as species beings and historical agents,
reflective technique does only the latter. Where art is open, and
constantly addressing the tension between what is and what
might be, socialist realism is closed and blind to what does not yet
exist. In place of touching a timeless aesthetic potential, socialist
realism offers monotony in bright colors.

347

Similarly, even if it could be accomplished, community homo-genization only eliminates the problem of intercommunity relations at the expense of any possibility of diversity. It ignores the need to form a cohesive yet diverse community of communities. It fails to meet two socialist criteria: it is obviously destructive of the development of variety in human social relations, and it also damages the development of self-management since it precludes people from participating in the collective synthesis of their own ways of dealing with life, death, and the place of human beings in the universe. As in the orthodox approaches to political, economic, and kin relations, with respect to community too the chosen palliative all too often creates new problems of its own. There is a tendency for the individual to be subordinated to the whole socialist culture which is beyond the individual's choice or reach. The individual must submit to the given culture to gain even the most minimal social solidarity with others. Real diversity is sacrificed to achieve solidarity, but only a forced solidarity of imposed uniformity. True solidarity that comes with mutual respect and growth is obstructed.

Certainly one reason why the orthodox school of "socialist analysis" has gravitated toward a homogenization approach has to do with the compatibility of homogenization with coordinator eco-nomic aims, authoritarian political premises, and patriarchal kin-ship norms. It is, for example, the culture of the political elite and coordinator class that becomes the basis of "socialist culture" in the new society, and this culture preserves patriarchal norms as well. Further, the idea of a single right culture is quite compatible with the idea of but one elite capable of finding the sole correct solution to all political problems. But there is also a praiseworthy impetus behind the orthodox drift toward cultural homogeneity as a community aim.

Much of the world's misery has always had its roots in hostile community divisions. War, genocide, slavery, colonialism, neo-colonialism, racism, discrimination, bigotry are but some of the oppressive forms that inter-community relations have taken histori-cally. Furthermore, as orthodox Marxists point out, community divisions have often prevented people from resolving other causes of misery. It isn't hard to see why one might lean toward sim-ply eliminating differences among cultures as a way to avoid all this strife and difficulty. But in fact this is neither possible, nor, if it were, would it be an optimal solution. For whatever damning faults they have embodied, ethnic, religious, national, and other community formations have also afforded people the possibility of synthesizing diverse language forms, living styles, and shared customs suited to the infinite variety of ways people can come together to accomplish the necessary task of forming community. And this much is to the good. Moreover, oppressive inter-group relations have developed in large part because each type of community has seen itself in opposition to all others, in constant danger of subordination, cooptation, or even elimination. In a competitive, hostile environment is it any wonder that religious, racial, ethnic, and national communities have felt the need to "be superior," to view others as "inferior," and to develop a fixed, internally cohesive and unyielding cultural definition? At the extreme, each community develops into a sectarian camp, concerned first and foremost with defending itself and willing to wage war on others to do so. The task is not to homogenize these separate sectarian units —an impossible task short of ethnocide in any case—but to overcome the stagnation of each while preserving the variety of experimentation provided by the development of many community groups.

So the problem for socialists is to elaborate an approach to culture and community which encourages community diversity yet overcomes racism, bigotry, and national chauvinism. Instead of pretending the problems will vanish because the differences between communities will eventually disappear, and retreating to paternalistic tolerance in the interim, we must welcome community diversity and make it positive rather than divisive. The magnitude of the problem should not be underestimated. The difficulties of even understanding what a culture is, and how and why communities form are severe enough. But there is also the practical reality that negative stereotypes, bigoted attitudes, and aggressive community modes of thinking and acting *have* become deeply ingrained in the human personality. Yet at the same time, in the U.S. at least, until socialists can speak more clearly not only about racism, but about the *preservation and extension* of Native American, Latin, Black and other minority cultures and the means by which they will attain a position of respect within society as a whole, there will be no unified movement in any form whatever. The debate between orthodox Marxism and nationalism, between integration and separation, has been long and tortured. What is needed now is a vision combining the insights of each while deleting the debilitating dogma of both. Others might call this a dialectical synthesis of opposites. Manning Marable says we need "full cultural diversity in which Blacks as a group have an independent and interdependent status with whites."[1] We call it "socialist intercommunalism:" many nested cultures whose whole is greater than the simple sum of its parts.*

### The Initiation and Definition of Socialist Intercommunalism

Under socialism we will not magically wake up as new people. We will not be reborn free of our past and lacking knowledge of our roots. On the contrary, historical memory, our sensitivity to social process, and our knowledge of history will all be enhanced. To our way of thinking, socialism involves an attitude in which people see themselves as part of a long chain of human development.[2] We will come to understand our place in that chain, know where we have come from, and how we are trying to move forward. Cultural dispositions, language forms, and approaches to celebration and community will not be forgotten nor gradually reduced to a least common denominator, but further explored and enriched. In other words, not only should socialism bring a heightened appreciation of the historical contributions of our different communities, but also provide greater means for their further development and diversification.

The idea is that for individuals there is no single "best" solution to the problem of community identification. For the species, however, there is a single "best" solution, the inter-communal elaboration of many diverse solutions for different subgroups, each solution respecting and respected by the others. Not only does each culture possess some particular knowledge or wisdom that is a unique product of its own historical experience, but the interaction of different cultures can enhance the internal characteristics of each and provide a richness which no single-minded approach could ever hope to attain. As a result, single solutions chosen for whole societies will generally be less worthy than any of the diverse solutions settled upon in a culturally "pluralist"

*To the best of our knowledge the first person to use this term in a way similar to its use here, was Huey Newton, leader of the Black Panther Party, in the late 1960s.

approach—assuming that negative inter-community relations can be replaced by positive ones.

But how can the difficult task of replacing negative inter-community relations with positive ones be achieved? First, the guiding principle of socialist intercommunalism is exactly the opposite of cultural homogenization. Whereas cultural homogenization is the ultimate threat to all distinct communities, socialist intercommunalism takes the view that diverse communities, cultures, and "collective human solutions" are to be encouraged. The most important practical application of the principle is that existing communities must be guaranteed access to all the necessary means for reproducing and developing their particular cultural forms and expressions free from unwarranted outside interference. The most important operational rule to be applied when agreement and mutual understanding between communities are temporarily unachievable is that the larger and/or more powerful community—the community whose very existence is not realistically threatened by the other—bears the greater repsonsibility for making the necessary concessions to avoid an open conflict. Of course, applying these principles in practice is no easy matter.

The goal is to create an environment in which no community will feel threatened and therefore each will feel free to learn from and share with others. Given the historical legacy of negative inter-community relations, this is not a solution that can be simply declared overnight. Furthermore, the relative lack of communication between communities to date, and the multitude of institutions which define community formations—a distinctive feature of the community sphere of daily life—complicate the problem of creating socialist intercommunalism. More so than in the case of any other socialist forms we can think of, intercommunalist relations will have to be painstakingly constructed in a step-by-step process of social practice which will gradually establish a different historical legacy and set of behavioral expectations.

Of course the principle of mutual respect for the integrity of every community must be made meaningful beyond verbal guarantees, however important such guarantees may be. Unless a "suspicious" community—and what community cannot find sufficient reason for concern over its own survival in some aspect of history—is guaranteed the means to produce its own culture, high sounding principles will be no more than hypocrisy.

But what are "necessary means" of cultural reproduction, and what are "warranted outside interferences" to the definition of a community's own relations? It is not our purpose to pretend that these questions won't be the basis for heated dispute, expecially in the early years of socialist construction, any more than we would pretend to solve any particular cases here. But it is important to flesh out our idea of how practical applications of the principle would be handled. Adequate means for reproducing and developing Black and Native American culture—to take two minority communities in the U.S.—would entail both material and communication components. How many Black radio shows, theatre and dance groups? How many Native American musical ensembles and T.V. stations? Supplemented Black and Native American history course, revision of the "regular" history sequence in the schools, or both? Native American reservations and Black neighborhoods, or integrated living and working conditions with cultural safeguards? These and many similar questions will be decided in the future, often differently in different circumstances. All that we can reasonably say now is that the criterion for judging opposing views will be that every community should be guaranteed sufficient material and communication means to self-define and to develop its own culture and represent that culture to all other communities in the context of limited aggregate means and equal right to those means for all.

And when we say communities must be free to develop their own cultural forms without "unwarranted outside interference," what is warranted and what is unwarranted? Again, our point will be not to decide particulars, but to clarify criteria. Just as particular political, economic, and kinship activity and institutions can embody and promote self-management, variety, and solidarity to varying degrees, so can intra-community definitions and cultural practices. We would argue that different communities should examine their own intra-community institutions from a socialist perspective, and we would not consider it an unwarranted intrusion in a community's affairs for people from outside to express an opinion that some aspect of the community's intra-community relations was destructive of socialist goals. For example, atheists might argue that godly religions tended to produce fetishistic consciousness and were therefore destructive of their practitioners' self-management potentials. A debate would likely ensue. Nor would we consider it unwarranted for anti-authoritarians to criticize what they believed to be a hierarchical community institution, or feminists to criticize what they believed to be a sexist aspect of a particular community culture—even should the anti-authoritarians and/or feminists come from outside the community they are criticizing. But it would be unwarranted, in our view, to carry the criticisms beyond the point of voicing one's honest opinions to asserting that outsiders have the right to legislate in the community affairs of others. First, we do not believe in such infringement because we believe it immediately opens the door to inter-community hostility and struggle based upon the insecurity of minority communities who practice beliefs contrary to those of majority communities. Second, we think such interference will not prove necessary to engender change in any case, even if interference could be carried out without not only not engendering positive change but in fact creating negative repercussions beyond the initiating difficulties. First, under socialism communities will exist in a context of relative security which promotes the constant enrichment of community norms via both internal development and the incorporation of lessons from without. Second, members of communities will function within the broader economic, political, and kinship spheres. They will therefore be constantly required to recognize the importance of solidarity, variety, and self-management in these spheres of their daily lives. Whatever the views of outsiders may be, it is unlikely that people with such sensibilities regarding three spheres of life would attach themselves to grossly sexist, or racist, or otherwise inhumane norms in their community life. Thus, in many instances, the outside criticism may be as much a matter of misunderstanding as of correct perception, at least once a socialist society is well established. Finally, the freedom of community groups to make "cultural mistakes" that are not totally within the contours of socialist development is not a *carte blanche* for the oppression of community members against their wills. For people are free to move and live where they like, to choose community affiliations as they desire, and this is a right that no community will be allowed to abrogate for its members. One will not be born Jewish, Black, Latin, or Catholic as much as one will choose to participate in a particular cultural heritage. In a real sense no one will be trapped in any particular community under socialism—any more than anyone is trapped into any religion today. While we expect that over time sexist and authoritarian residues in cultural formations would disappear, in the interim they may certainly prevail for a time. If women found a particular religious movement too sexist to struggle within, they would presumably not join, or leave if they were already members. We are not suggesting there will be no intense problems or conflicts. Instead we are simply arguing that the policy of outside interference within a community's cultural life is neither a likely agency for positive change, nor a tool that is consistent with creating an environment of security for all communities, a condition essential to socialist intercommunalism.

Finally, what should be done when disputes over the interpretation of "adequate means" and "warranted interference" prove intractable? In the early stages of building the new environment of security and respect, it would be naive to assume that this will not occur. It is for this reason, and because of the incredible costs of failure to arrive at agreements, that we propose the rule of placing the ultimate burden of concession on the least threatened party. For example, within the United States in disputes concerning the inter-relations or the intra-relations of either the Black or "white" community, if Blacks felt that racist dynamics were at play and a disagreement ensued as a result, their postion would be considered the more "existentially tenuous" and their perceptions therefore given priority in practice. Likewise, in the international arena, in disputes between nations which concerned a community dimension, again the nation that was more in jeopardy would be the one whose claims had higher priority. An example that is relevant even though not only community factors are at work, is the dynamic of struggles and even war between China and Vietnam and Vietnam and Cambodia. In each couplet it is the latter country which had the greater reason to fear for its existence and the former which should therefore have been willing to make greater concessions.

## The Character and Interrelations of Socialist Communities

It seems most likely that most of the communities that exist today will continue under socialism, though their forms and interrelations will certainly alter. For example, Black people in the United States will certainly continue to form a distinct community, though "Black is Beautiful" will become a statement of fact, not a demand for equality. Further, the Black community will actually no longer be Black in pigmentation. Race is not a community distinction. It is socially manufactured. As we pointed out earlier, the human species has a multitude of distinct characteristics each of which vary from person to person, but the human species is a continuum and such distinctions are arbitrary. What makes a subset of the species a community is their sharing of a specific set of solutions to the problems of human interaction, identity, celebration, and mourning. There is a historical diversity of such solutions, but to this point this diversity has only engendered hostile we-versus-they community dynamics. As this sort of antagonistic identification diminishes and finally ceases, communities will be differentiated solely by their alternative solutions, not by physical or other supposedly innate attributes. An adherent of a different solution is not genetically "different," but simply has a different history, different cultural views and practices. He or she has simply made a different choice in confronting certain of life's options.

Though it will evolve from a defensive means of survival to an assertion of cultural achievement, certainly the culture Blacks have elaborated over years of struggle will persist. A Black community will provide continuity, identity, and self-definition—but in socialism it will not exist in opposition to other communities. It will not define itself as the only natural way or the only right way to live. Community identification will normally provide one good way of living, adaptable and able to be continually enriched by human insight and experience. No longer having a "racial" or "biological" basis, Black community will evolve as an historical human product.

Different life conditions yield different cultural solutions. and the interaction of diverse cultures can provide a richness otherwise unattainable. The continuation and further enrichment of Native American culture in the U.S. will likely lead to a long overdue dialogue which will enrich the cultural consciousness of all members of society. Perhaps even more than with any other single community, Native Americans have a set of practices and beliefs, a long history of ideas and means of celebration and communication which are so different from what is common to most other cultures within the U.S. that mutual respectful communication will lead to much learning by all parties. At present such communication is rendered impossible on three counts. Native Americans feel too threatened to enter into any substantial dialogue for fear of commercialized popularization and oversimplification of their beliefs. Whites hold deep-seated racist suppositions about the country's first citizens which foreclose respectfully studying their cultural solutions. And, with reason, Native Americans are too hostile toward what they see as the "cultural diseases" of the white man to feel any desire to learn from this foreign cultural formation. Obviously, only whites can remove these obstacles to fruitful cultural interchange with Native Americans.

So at this point, tentative as our recommendations may be, we have the beginnings of a socialist community vision wherein diverse communities provide social fulfillments, but adherence to any particular cultural norms is by free choice. We have a vision of cultural pluralism without heretics where those different from ourselves are respected rather than feared and hated.

But will there be religion? It depends upon what we mean by "religion." Contrary to myth and usual conjecture it seems likely that under socialism people will have *increased* concern for broad issues of "life and death," "ultimate causes," "the place of the species in the natural order," and "ethical norms." But again answers will be alternative solutions, not right or wrong. However, if we mean by religion, organized patriarchal churches abetting ruling hierarchies in society, of course these will disappear.[4] Further, religion will not adhere to idle beliefs that are easily proved false, nor will it consign people to positions of subservience to cosmic forces beyond their ken.[5] The contrast between certain religious missionaries in countries like Peru and Bolivia, intent upon ethnocide and genocide against indigenous Indian populations and obviously in service to U.S. client governments and U.S. multinationals,[6] and, on the other hand, other "religious leaders" who are avowedly revolutionary, courageous in their lifestyle, and free in their thinking, in Colombia and Salvador[7] gives some indication of the direction of development we are talking about. Although they will address certain basic needs, we see the evolution of "religions" as embodiments of wisdom, shared beliefs, and cultural solutions to certain problems of life, not as catechisms or indoctrination centers where true believers are told what to think.

We can see the embryonic development of such an evolution in certain developments that took place in the U.S. (as well as in Latin

America) in the 1960s. During those years, the Black church in the southern U.S. began to take on new textures and leave behind inflexibilities while retaining many valid cultural forms. Of course, it was not a perfect process, unflawed or generalized in all churches, but it did occur in many places and could have kept progressing had the movement continued to develop as well. As one example, the church hymns began to subtly alter in content to celebrate Black collective struggle and fulfillment. No longer the Lord, but now the people united were the powerful force to be reckoned with. But at the same time, traditional Black choral forms which were themselves already an artistic embodiment of Black struggle and history were preserved. This simultaneous preservation and alteration is what we expect to see happen on a larger and more sustained scale, for all community norms.

A socialist program must therefore be sensitive to the real human needs and potentials that community affiliations address— yet not be so opportunist as to leave uncriticized the religious and national forms which are debilitating to human potentials. Thus dialogue between Catholics, Protestants, atheists, and Jews; between Blacks, whites, Hispanics, and Native Americans; must focus on identifying both the aspects of existing cultures that are anti-socialist and anti-developmental as well as those which are creative responses to human aspirations.

The situation is similar to other spheres, though there is a new feature too. With community, as with economics, for example, there are old institutional relations which must be criticized and overcome, yet the needs these old institutions partially met must be met anew by socialist forms. And as with kinship struggles, divisions between people must be overcome. But here there is an important difference. Neither male nor female norms as we now know them will be preserved as the central traits adopted by men or women under socialism. Rather, all socialist people will have new kin attributes superseding those we now know—overcoming weaknesses and preserving strengths. With communities, on the other hand, while boundaries will become more porous and no longer associated with biology, they will still exist. It is precisely the idea of "merging diverse cultures into one" that we are opposing.

In coordinator societies, at best there is tolerance of religion, national cultures, and ethnic groups while these are also "urged" to voluntarily assimilate into a new "unity." At worst, and this is the likely outcome, there are various forms of coercion to enforce homogenization, ranging from manipulation of social conflict, to political repression, to genocide.

But under socialism we envision an evolution of community forms that will respect diversity as the basis of a rich cultural environment. Racism is ultimately gone. In the end, race itself is no longer a human concept. After a period no community regards itself as superior or inferior—such a position is foreign to the whole concept of life and culture. The fear to diverge from community norms, the fear of being different and an outcast finally disappears to be replaced by an abiding curiosity about all life's options and a respect for the value of experimentation. Within communities, cultural norms and styles are chosen; they are not blindly adhered to as a means to "belong."

Even beyond the redefinition of community relations per se there will also be a general disruption of the we-versus-they mentality. For example, instead of the clash of sports teams replicating the clash of hostile communities where the goal is solely to win or dominate and internal cohesion is a function of shared opposition to a foe and not of real camaraderie and shared feeling and understanding—sports will replicate socialist inter-communal relations. The aim becomes human fulfillment and advance, teams admire and learn from one another. They appreciate and applaud each other's achievements and take pleasure in each other's accomplishments. It is the quality of the whole athletic process that counts, not the final score. Each actor plays hard and determined but the event is more like a symphony than a war. Each person contributes to advance the whole. Sometimes this means struggling to score or defend; sometimes to propel a teammate *or opponent* to a new height of execution. Some sports will disappear; other new ones will be born. We will continue to admire athletic artistry and accomplishment just as we admire excellent painting, music, or other cultural creation, but we will all contribute as well. Of course, this description is hypothesis, but it is based upon the logic of social development as we understand it, and also the experiences of movement activism in the United States.

And why is such a harmonious redefinition of all human community relations possible? Humans need identity, self-respect, friendship, and knowledge—but we do not need universal cultural norms. Neither the pursuit of superiority and dominance over others nor even the more general we-versus-they approach to others are necessary for human well-being. These are not pursued according to some innate injunction, but rather as a result of social conditions which make them "solutions" to certain life problems, even while they create new difficulties. With a totalist change in social relations, these negative tendencies become counter-productive. Their reason for being disappears even while the possibility of desirable community relations is enhanced.

## Community Transition

We would like to bring three particular kinds of transition problems into focus. First, there is the obvious difficulty of the stubborness of racist perspectives and of the different ways this might be manifest and confronted. Next, there is considerable liklihood of confrontation and difficulty between religious and atheistic people, and perhaps between people of different religions as well. This problem however, is structurally akin to that over race. Last, there is the difficulty of elaborating an anti-imperialist and internationalist attitude among the populace.

Racism directed by whites toward Blacks, Spanish speaking communities, and other minorities is not going to disappear over night. Certainly any movement for socialism in a country like the United States is going to be consciously anti-racist, have autonomous community movements, and enlighten its membership and the society at large to the importance of revolutionizing community relations. Yet, nonetheless, racism runs very deep as do the feelings of inferiority and deference that accompany being a subordinate community in a racist society. As a result, two forms of racism will likely continue to be actively expressed during the transition period. First, there will be more overt expressions like denying minority rights, relatively easily countered by victims and supporters they will have among members of the majority community. More difficult to cope with will be a prevalent paternalism from whites toward minorities. "Of course we will help you, of course we will give you room to move, etc., but you don't really think you're ready to do all that, do you?" Beyond what we said in earlier discussions in the economics and community sections asserting the on-going centrality of minority community movements, councils, and caucuses, the additional tactic of quotas will be necessary during the transition period. Just as racism cannot be eliminated immediately by revolutionary fiat, nor will it disappear without special organizational structures that propel changes in consciousness and attitudes. Quotas are precisely the guarantors and propellants needed for transformation of community relations plagued by a long racist legacy. So just as we argued for the usefulness and necessity of male and female quotas, we would expect quotas during the transition period setting minimum standards for participation of minorities in skillful and decision-making roles. Indeed the entire argument from last chapter carries over. Again the tactic must be employed carefully to bring the previously disenfranchised group to a position of full equity in society. Again dislocation of others, in this case privileged whites, is only a relative discomfort, not one imposing an oppression but one diminishing an unjust privilege only too slowly. Again, claims that neophytes from minorities will do lower quality work due to lack of training should be viewed only as arguments for whatever training is necessary, and discounted for any racism in their assessment of all the costs and benefits quotas bring. In sum, the issues are similar to those we discussed in the previous chapter—where men must develop female facilities as well as overcome their sexism, whites must learn the cultural and community skills they lack, in addition to overcoming their racism—and therefore we need not belabor them here.

But to gain insight into the complexity of possible problems we should consider struggles that may arise over religion. In our earlier assessment of socialist community relations we argued that contemporary religions and cultures would evolve, retaining their accumulated aesthetic and emotional contributions and wisdom but jettisoning features that contradict the integrity of groups of people, self-management, social solidarity, etc. This will obviously not be an overnight phenomenon. It will take time to even assess which rituals and beliefs are contrary to broader socialist aims, to understand the contradictions, and to redress them. Two kinds of potential dispute immediately present themselves. Members of a particular community are going to be looking at their own culture through different eyes than outsiders. Where critics from another culture may see an abhorrent practice, insiders may see something quite mundane or positive. The tension and recrimination that could result as outsiders pursue criticisms and insiders become defensive worrying about the integrity of their community, can be easily envisioned. We have set out some guiding principles in our earlier discussion of socialist community forms. The point is that the application of these principles will be difficult even in a well established socialist society. During a tumultuous transition period, the problems will be that much more profound. What mechanisms will exist both to ensure the integrity of existing communities, and yet to push those communities to seriously confront contradictions between their own practices and the requirements of self-management, solidarity, and variety, we just don't know. But that specifically transitional forms to augment on-going autonomous community movements will be necessary seems likely to us.

Finally, the problem of internationalism for citizens of the United States is straightforward. Consciousness is not like a child's castle built from blocks, each block quite independent of the others except for the fact of their being stacked together. Rather, the building blocks of consciousness become entwined, each affecting the contours of the others and each capable of engendering changes or restorations in the others. The United States has been at the center of an empire almost since its birth. The subtle manner in which imperial attitudes have become enmeshed with racist, sexist, authoritarian and classist conceptions is sometimes hard to perceive, but always present. If a socialist movement in the United States were to pay insufficient attention to the role of the U.S. in the world, nationalistic imperial ventures catering to reactionary attitudes in the populace would destroy its temporary achievements in other areas. Likewise, after victory, should people begin to view their country as a citadel, all the "old rot" would resurface. Thus, an essential part of socialist transition will be hammering out a workable set of international policies: how will we extricate ourselves from our position of economic dominance over the lives of many nations? How will we provide aid with no strings in a manner that won't hinder other countries efforts at development? How will we relate to coordinator societies should any still exist? This is not the place to pursue answers to these questions. We mean only to make perfectly clear their critical importance and therefore the centrality of an anti-imperialist focus to any movement for socialism in the United States.

## Totalist Socialism

At this point we have completed our discussion of socialist politics, economics, kinship, and community. We have initiated an
original argument whose main contours we would like to summarize
in a holistic fashion. Within capitalist societies, non-capitalist but
also non-socialist societies, and envisioned socialist societies there are
four spheres of social life whose institutional networks interactively
define social possibilities via the elaboration of core characteristics at
the level of both center and boundary. In most and perhaps even all
societies the core characteristics elaborated in each sphere are
reproductive of one another's continuing existence. In capitalism as
we know it in the United States, patriarchy furthers class division
which in turn furthers racism which fosters bourgeois political
behavior, and so on around and around in a virtually seamless circle
of reproduction. Yet at the same time the historical motion of each
sphere can lead to disruptions within its own social relations or
between itself and the dynamics elaborated by another sphere, and
these disruptions or contradictions can cause social struggle amongst
groups like classes, communities, kin groups, or political agencies.
These will in turn affect the history of society and may, under
certain circumstances, lead to revolutionary changes.

As we have seen , first in the Soviet Union and now most
recently in China, one possibility is the transition from feudal/
dependent/capitalistic formations to bureaucratic/coordinator
formations in which patriarchy and racism persist, though in
altered forms. Another possibility is a transition from parliamentary advanced capitalism to an electoral/coordinator formation
along the lines proposed by Social Democrats and Eurocommunists, as we will discuss in our concluding chapter. Still another
path is the one we have been urging, leading to totalist socialism
without passing through the purgatory of bureaucratic/coordina-
torism. But just as the requisites of social relations in all four
spheres from a totality that bathes all social interaction in a
holistic light in oppressive societies, we expect the same degree of
inter-relatedness between the four spheres will hold in totalist
socialism.

We believe that neither our community , kinship, political, or
economic visions can stand alone. We don't see how it would be
possible to move from a society like the one we endure in the
United States to the goals we have outlined in one or two of these

spheres alone. We are not going to overcome class division while preserving a sexual division of labor and a kinship process generating shattered personalities. Nor will we attain participatory democracy while pursuing homogenization of different cultural heritages.

The historical condition we find ourselves in is complex. It is pointless to argue that women and men, Blacks and whites, workers of different kinds, people of different political persuasion and position should simply ignore all their differences and merge into a single fighting force against oppression. At the same time, it is equally hopeless to continue to foster the isolation of each oppressed group from every other. What is essential is to build simultaneous solidarity and autonomy, and this must occur at the level of theory and of organization and practice. But for solidarity in context of autonomy to be possible, historical agents like women, workers, young people, rebels within bureaucracies, and national minorities must each begin to perceive that their own freedom requires a revolution in *all* spheres of daily life—a totalist revolution in which they play a central role in one part of the process while supporting and participating in all other aspects of the struggle as well.

This is the kind of picture that emerges from our discussion of theory, the historical lessons of the Soviet Union, China, and Cuba, and the prospects for socialism in the United States. As the kinds of human traits which socialist kinship activity generates provide a basis for economic self-management, and as economic self-management propels participatory politics, and as participatory politics helps instill attitudes necessary for communities to learn from and appreciate one another, so the reverse is true as well. Failure to address male supremacy will consign even the best efforts to eliminate class divisions to failure. An authoritarian approach to politics will prevent the development of economic self-management and cultural pluralism. Community hostility and on-going racism will interfere with struggles against class and sexual stereotypes. In short, the core characteristics of oppression are mutually reproductive. Where they now reign it is necessary to substitute a new totality, new institutions and personalities attuned to self-management, solidarity, and variety. These are the core characteristics we have attempted to embody in our vision of totalist socialism—that is, in each of its spheres, in the interfaces between them, and in the social formation as a whole. They are also the core characteristics we think necessary for the creation of a powerful movement for socialism that can coalesce broad support among all potentially revolutionary sectors of our society.

Just as socialism must be a continuation of socialist transition, the roots of the transition reside in the strategies of socialist struggle against the old society. The problem of being an effective socialist is to carefully assess contemporary relations and future goals, and to develop and enact programs of struggle that can bridge the gap between them. Obviously, in practice many errors of analysis and prognosis will be discovered requiring continual realignment of aims and methods. Viewed in this way, however, socialist transition is simply a continuation of the struggle for socialism against oppressive core relations under altered circumstances. During socialist transition, it is the agents of socialist change who are in dominant positions to build a new hegemony. Before the overthrow of the old regime, it is the agents of reaction who wield the critical levers to maintain their oppressive hegemony. This said, our argument about socialism and socialist transition takes us directly to the immediate problem: strategies for creating a socialist movement suited to contemporary conditions. And that will be the subject of our next and last chapter.

# 10
# NEITHER LENINISM
# NOR SOCIAL DEMOCRACY

> What are these ceremonies and why should we take part in them? What are these professions and why should we make money out of them? Where, in short, is it leading us, the procession of the sons of well educated men?
>
> Virginia Woolf

> Now is the time of the furnace,
> and only the light should be seen.
>
> Jose Marti

The general contours of Bolshevik strategy are unchanging: a democratic centralist party becomes vanguard of the working class. In a complex struggle it seizes state power, nationalizes the economy, and institutes central planning. These acts strengthen the Bolshevik political elite and prepare for the coordinator class's eventual ascension to economic power. The new regime is under way. But as we have seen this process does not offer a truly liberatory alternative. The polity becomes authoritarian, the economy class divided, kinship patriarchal, and community relations remain oppressive as well. The evolving society's new complexity stems from three sources: 1) the vague implications of the Bolshevik scenario for kinship and community; 2) the dual subordination of economic decision-making first to the party as leading political element, and second to the emerging coordinator class as the dominant economic agent, and 3) the possibility of on-going struggle for real socialist alternatives in all spheres of social life.

In this book we have argued that the failure of the Russian revolution to achieve socialism was insured early, and that the Soviet Union is now a culturally homogenized, patriarchal, bureaucratic, coordinator society. In China, however, we showed that the struggle between the coordinator and socialist road was more protracted. The revolutionary dynamic included complex kin, community, political, and economic struggles occuring largely in synchronization throughout the country. The principle limitation of these struggles was their dependence on factions in the leading party. The absence of extra-party democratic political organizations, or independent workers' institutions in the economy, and of autonomous womens' and community movements crippled efforts to combat bureaucracy and class division and to ensure progress in the kin and community spheres. It seems most likely that China too has now stabilized as a homogenized, bureaucratic, patriarchal, and coordinator society.

In evaluating the Cuban experience, however, we have been more reserved about final judgements. While recent economic developments largely counter socialist aims, there is room for optimism about politics and perhaps kinship and community. The lack of correspondence between spheres in Cuba shows that their revolution is unfinished. Our judgments are thus tentative pending further alterations particularly in the employment of "poder popular" to create non-party centers of influence over Cuba's development.

Though they have failed to create socialism, the success of these revolutions in overthrowing capitalism has rested on a number of factors, particularly peasant rebellion, support from intellectuals, and sufficiently muted political, kin, and community concerns so that weaknesses of leading revolutionary organizations in these areas weren't enough to dangerously erode their mass base of popular support.

Yet none of these conditions exist in industrialized countries. In the United States, for example, the peasantry doesn't exist; the coordinator class is too strong to cede leadership to a political elite; and racial, political, and sexual tensions are great enough—as well as the democratic tradition strong enough—so that only a movement sufficiently pluralist to respect autonomous women's and third world organizing and sufficiently democratic to be respected by a populace tired of big government domination will have a chance to attain enough legitimacy to make a leftist run for power.

In this context, an outmoded Bolshevism is challenged on two fronts—by Social Democracy and Eurocommunism on the one hand, and by new totalist movements on the other. The Social Democrats seek a pluralist movement centering on the coordinator class and middle strata. The totalists instead appeal to women, minorities, and workers around issues related to all spheres of daily life, including, most recently, ecology.

The contours of Social Democracy (and Eurocommunism) are predictable: bourgeois democracy is to be preserved as a counter to the emergence of a dangerous political elite; technocratic rationality, science, central planning, economic growth, and nationalization are to be expanded in the interest of the coordinator class and middle strata; vanguard politics and democratic centralism must be disavowed as a hedge against the dangers of bureaucracy and in search of opportunist alliances with women and minorities. With the false rhetoric of proletarian dictatorship gone, these movements will certainly be more attractive to middle elements. Yet the almost desperate need to reach these elements will often attenuate appeals to workers, and particularly to minorities and transients. Given these parameters, whether Social Democratic movements can be receptive enough to racial and sexual struggle, appealing enough to workers despite their coordinator definition, and effective enough in opposing capitalist hegemony to win power, is unknown—yet it is certainly within the realm of possibility. And if Social Democrats (or Eurocommunists) were to win power, there would be every reason to anticipate formation of an electoral coordinator, patriarchal, and racist social formation. No doubt this would be a substantial improvement over crumbling capitalism, but nonetheless not the victory of socialism.

We don't mean to suggest that Social Democratic or Eurocommunist efforts in Europe (or their populist counterparts in the United States) are crassly opportunist nor that their followers have been misled, manipulated, or otherwise dumbfounded. Rather these movements represent a progressive attack on both capitalist profitism and Stalinist authoritarianism. These movements are not self-consciously manipulated by coordinators but rather emerge as an evolving response to changing circumstances. They are often founded and led by committed socialists, however incomplete their understanding may be. What we suggest, however, is that these movements have ideology, programs, and structures reflecting the perspective of coordinators, middle elements, "professional activists," men, and majority communities—and that this perspective will yield non-socialist outcomes despite the progressive insights of many social democrats, and even against the sincere aims of many people at all levels of involvement in these movements.

But what opposes Eurocommunism, Social Democracy, and Populism on the left? On the one hand, there is Western Maoism, Trotskyism in myriad forms, and "old line" Communism in a host of guises—all Leninist. No matter the insights, courage, or conviction of many participants, this is a hopeless pantheon with little to offer. On the other hand, there are countless community organizing projects, anti-nuclear organizations, women's centers, clinics, rank and file labor movements of diverse types, Chicano, Black, Native American and other third world movements and community organizations, and other local organizations and institutions as well as a few national organizations or movements—the ecology party in France, Big Flame in England, NAM in the United States, a variety of formations like Autonomia in Italy, etc. Though in no way a united left, can these elements play a significant role in the coming decade?

Obviously, compared to the United States, the European situation is well advanced, yet it is also confused by the prevalence of orthodox Marxist habits which have never caught on among a broad populace here. In the United States, therefore, there may be a relatively clear road toward a broad anti-capitalist but not yet socialist movement. Our tentative hypothesis is that the potential ideological leadership for this is now forming in the Democratic Socialist Organizing Committee, the California Campaign for Economic Democracy, the farmworkers movement, the Black political caucus and Black party formations, populist groups like ACORN, the Ohio Public Interest Campaign and perhaps Massachusetts Fair Share, in NOW, and in certain trade union formations as well. With the Democratic Party in disarray a desirable scenario is that these elements gain a foothold in mass politics, elaborating a social democratic alternative within the Democratic Party itself. Appeals would be made to women and Blacks, but these would focus around economic equity only minimally challenging the basic dynamics of patriarchy and racism. Appeals would be made to the broad electorate concerning an extension of democracy and end to big government domination, yet this would embody no new definitions of political freedom and participation. Within the economy, the program would call for rationalization, reindustrialization, economic redistribution, and economic democracy, but without a socialist presence these themes would come to mean coordinator leadership; a diminishing piece of pie for capital with the gains that are taken off their plates shared between coordinators, middle elements, and labor; and perhaps a little more freedom at the workplace for workers but mostly more participation in economic planning for coodinator and middle element union bureaucrats. The democratic convention and campaign of 1980 demonstrated the Democratic Party's lack of inspiring vision. In this context, a new vision clustered around the points mentioned above might well gain a hearing from the party. In this positive scenario, the new democratic coalition that could result would start out as a national minority but struggle for political office during the 80s, perhaps gaining the White House by decade's end. Those who move right in the early 80s in response to Reaganism, will be discredited. Those who battle Reagan and develop a new vision will win control of the rejuvenated party.

But then what of socialists, feminists, and nationalists committed to fully restructuring our society's institutions? Obviously the temptation to join in mainstream work will be great, and this is reasonable. Socialists who avoid contact with a broad audience out of ideological purism or out of fear of the people are doomed to irrelevance and stupidity. But particularly at this time, to attain a position of visibility and influence by severely compromising one's politics would be a regrettable error. It would misuse an important opening about to appear in the U.S. political theatre. Rather than entering the fray to push social democratic movements left while simultaneously beginning to create a *viable socialist alternative*, it would mean only adding oneself to an already more than sufficient number of capable people arguing an anti-capitalist but not socialist position. Perhaps individuals or organizations (in the U.S., NAM?), could more easily gain acceptance in large scale politics by such means, but the ensuing loss of a socialist pole would not only delay the development of a socialist movement but, by destroying its left-wing, even weaken the resolve and insight of the on-going progressive fight against the right.

So assuming a scenario such as outlined here, the real question is whether left elements in each sphere will a) melt back into the broad social democratic left, b) become an irrelevant fringe (by moral posturing, avoiding the public, or being Leninist), or c) develop a totalist socialist alternative and movement and take it to the new democratic coalition and the public as a whole. For ecology, womens', third world, rank-and-file, community, and other local and national movements to coalesce into a new socialist left, we will need a theory and program which talks in a clear, committed manner. We will have to recognize the defining importance of four social spheres and legitimacy of autonomous movements and programs within socialist solidarity. We will need to understand complex class alignments to create a workers' movement for participatory planning rather than a coordinator movement which glorifies workers while obscuring their most profound interests. And finally we will have to clearly enunciate a feminist, intercommunalist, democratic, and participatory socialist vision and practice. What strategy can meet these requirements?

Leninism (and Social Democracy) are revolutionary approaches well-suited to creating a class-divided, politically authoritarian, culturally repressed, and patriarchal society. That the transition envisioned within these approaches embodies varying levels of repression, austerity, and dictatorship should come as no surprise. Upon victory, the oppressed who expect their dignity and freedom, must be put back in their proper place. If a Social Democratic movement emerges in the United States without a parallel and eventually superior socialist movement by its side will it be anti-imperialist? Will it be anti-authoritarian? Will it embody the norms of feminism and anti-racism? Will it address the most crying needs of workers especially for power over their lives in the shops? We think not. Though the emergence of Social Democracy would be a large step forward requiring immense efforts on the part of many progressive people, it would not be enough. Moreover, lacking a totalist commitment or vision all its gains would be tenuous. With the victory of Leninists in the third world or of Eurocommunist social democratic movements in the industrialized countries, after the revolution the key problem is not regression to the old form of society but disciplining the mass movements which, in the course of struggle against the old society, have come to desire *more* than the Leninists and/or social democrats are prepared to deliver. It is the dynamics of this "disciplining process" coupled with the intrinsic attributes of the institutional forms these movements establish which together not only preclude socialist outcomes, but engender results far worse even than what was anticipated by these movements' own leaders. In transition to the type of socialist society we propose the population is not going to find itself facing a new society different from what they had taken risks to create and therefore will not need to be coercively re-socialized. Rather, what will be necessary is rapid establishment of socialist institutions and of a socialist political process for addressing conflicts of interest, not the establishment of repressive institutions which yield non-socialist outcomes.

As the constituency for a left social democratic program grows in the eighties, it will certainly move left, developing new political skills and sophistication. But if the trend is to reach fruition in socialist progress, there will have to be a totalist socialist vision and movement constructed alongside the social democratic project. For without this, as women, minorities, and workers become frustrated with the limits of social democracy, they will have no place to go but out of the left. On the other hand, with a clear and viable socialist movement to enlarge and command, the left trend of this constituency will be able to continue toward socialism.

Assuming the above scenario, socialists must accomplish certain tasks in the coming decade. We must elaborate our vision as a real alternative to social democracy for all four spheres of daily life. We need to forge a cooperative yet principled interface with the social democrats to build a mass anti-capitalist movement that fosters rather than impedes later socialist developments. We need to develop an organizational form capable of embodying solidarity and autonomy, develop practical programs addressing four spheres of social life and employ that organization and program in popular struggles of all sorts in all kinds of institutions and forums, to make known our politics and vision to the broadest possible audience. Can we hope to accomplish these ends while clinging to *any* version of Marxism Leninism?

Enter a steel plant, an auto plant, or a box factory and watch, especially in the industrial heartland of the midwest, and no doubt you will shortly suspect some folks of being "political." Spend more time and you'll know: that woman, that fellow, him, her, those guys over there—they are the "communists," the members of Communist Workers Organization 'A', 'B', or 'C'. And do they have a vision of how the plant should be altered? Do they understand what a sexual and a racial division of labor and culture in the workplace is? Do they learn from their workmates' ideas about how things could be rearranged if the workers could have their own way? Is there an understanding of the division of roles according to

conceptual and executionary tasks? No, at least insofar as these
individuals are good Leninist cadre, these questions are not their
priority. And yet this is the sphere of activity where they organize
and apply their "science" most diligently. Their understanding of
the ghetto, of the family, of the state, of schools, sexuality,
churches, movies, and consumerism are weaker still. Indeed, to the
extent that it is able to escape rhetoric and communicate outside its
own circle of cadre, the main business of the Leninist left is at best to
fight vigorously and with great courage in daily battles over work
conditions, job security, wages, and sometimes prices or rents, and
then to return to the committed fold to argue with one another over
who has the correct (handed down) interpretation of recent
international events and their practical implications. The
elaboration of a philosophy, moral perspective, inspiring vision, and
way of understanding and of intervening to change the world that
addresses the situation now (not 60 years ago) and here (not in one
or another homeland) is not on their agenda. Serious sensitivity to
all the issues that concern people in their daily life—work
conditions, fear, racism, war, ecology, religion, diet, sports, crime,
alienation, love, unemployment, homosexuality, family relations,
sexism, drugs, bureaucracy, prices, art, food, religion, sexuality,
friendship, loneliness, energy, competition, boredom, health—is
beyond the capacity of these groups. And then these people view
efforts to elaborate a socialist vision as "utopian" and
"unscientific." And it is true, such efforts do "look into the
future" and "elaborate an ideal." Moreover, they are hardly
scientific like physics or math. Yet *these are not weaknesses but
strengths*. Moreover, these Leninists claim we shouldn't give up
models that great revolutionaries have created for us to emulate. But
what are these models: societies in which workers have little power
over their lives, in which there is dictatorship, patriarchy, and
community oppression. Fidel Castro describes the situation
confronted by socialists in the United States quite vividly:

> There are times when political documents called Marxist
> give the impression that you go to the archives and ask for
> a form: form fourteen, form thirteen, form twelve, they
> are all alike, with the same empty words, which logically is
> a language incapable of expressing real situations. And
> many times the documents are divorced from real life.
> And many people are told this is Marxism...and in what

way is this different from catechism, and in what way is it different from a litany, from a rosary?

And everyone that poses as a Marxist feels almost obliged to go around looking for this or that manifesto. And you read the twenty five manifestos of twenty five different organizations, and they are all alike, copied from the same standard; no one is convinced by any of them.

We can no longer be bound by "a language incapable of expressing real situations." The litany that the Soviet Union, China, Cuba or the Eastern Bloc countries are socialist societies is a lie. The rosary of revolution—we kneel before the altar of Marx and Lenin to recite prayers to save the revolutionary homeland—is a form with counter-revolutionary content. In its class-catechism it precludes the dynamics of kinship, community, and politics implicitly supporting the elites who dominate each of these spheres. In its class-allegiance it actually sacrifices the interests of workers for those of a coordinator elite.

To be for workers on the line, women battered, Blacks, Latinos, Native Americans, and Asians decultured; to be for drunks, addicts, the young and old, those on welfare, mad or sad; to be for those in Salvador, Paraguay, South Africa, and Thailand, death-squadded and starved; and to be against Somoza, the Pinochets, Rockefeller, owners, rapists, and mind molesters—all this requires an unequivocal break with sacraments and rose tinted histories.

Enough is enough. The trajectory of our country and of world relations evinces both danger and possibility. There are those who still consult Stalin's writings for insights on questions of organization, the "woman question," or the "national question." These people mistake barbarism for socialism. Their programs and ideas are not those of the left and do not represent socialism. There is no longer time nor reason to be baited into making believe such people deserve loyal support in their acts of sectarian suicide.

But it is not only the most extreme, the folks who have their hands in their suspenders ridiculously emulating Lenin or Trotsky or some other long-dead, deified potentate who are traveling a path to nowhere. In addition, all those with serious commitment who are sincerely trying to make this world a better place but are either still in the orthodox temple's corridors or, though out of the temple, are still nonetheless tied to its rhetoric and vision, are horribly handicapped in their political efforts. For if we define the situation of ourselves, women, children, parents, sisters, brothers, lovers, and lonely to be the "woman question," an adjunct to the real problems of the economy, we are lost. And even if we see beyond this patriarchal formulation but continue to employ the theoretical categories its forebears have given us, again we are only reciting form fourteen, and the language we are using is insufficient to our circumstances. If we define the situations of ourselves, Catholics, Jews, Chicanos, Irish, Southerners, Asians, Italians, Appalachians, New Yorkers, Protestants, Whites and Blacks as the "national question," an adjunct to the real problems of the economy, we are lost. And even if we transcend this racist formulation but continue to employ its categories, again we will be out of touch with reality. If we can speak of dictatorships of any kind in positive terms or even if we "merely" urge that while democracy is the aim hierarchy is the best means, we are hopelessly behind the common sense of our own country. If we bow down to endless productive growth, worship centralization as a panacea, and promote central planning but ignore the potential of workers to redesign and redefine the workplaces of our society, and deny the importance of consumption thereby ignoring many social movements and the most obvious and crying signals of the environment we live in—then as individuals committed to changing history we become little more than fools.

Leninism and Social Democracy are often arrayed along a single evaluative axis. At the left is Leninism, to the right Social Democracy. They are compared with regard to a cluster of characteristics centering on their strategic conceptions about the role of reform, electoral tactics, coalition building, and other factors. The Social Democrats say that the Leninists are more left, indeed ultra-left, and thus out of touch with the contours of what is possible and desirable. The Leninists in turn say the Social Democrats are to the right, so far right as to be essentially bourgeois and incapable of leading a revolution. Within the disagreement however, there is general agreement about how to draw the scale and place the two alternative approaches along it:

Leninism                    Social Democracy

Much of the debate over strategy asks whether we should choose one of the two orientations or develop a new one either further left than Leninism, further right than Social Democracy, or someplace in between. To the right people propose, for example, electoral participation in the democratic party with no mention nor allegiance to socialism. To the left of Leninism people propose syndicalist and anarchist formulations.

But in our opinion placing totalist socialism anywhere along this axis is simply an improper way to compare it to Leninism and Social Democracy. For it only makes sense to be compared this way if all major differences are to be found by looking at the specific cluster of characteristics that this scale measures. And with regard to evaluating totalist socialism, this is not the case. Rather, this new orientation differs in basic methodology, in focus, in its conceptual apparatus, in its vision of socialism, and in its ideas of organization, discipline and structure. The following graph is more to the point:

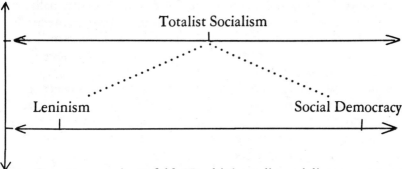

Our argument is twofold. We think totalist socialism represents a close approximation to the kind of revolutionary orientation best suited to achieving socialist ends in a country like the United States, and that adaptations of it would prove useful in many other kinds of society as well. However, should this prove incorrect, should our effort to make explicit certain theoretical, visionary, and strategic principles that have been evolving in leftist practice over the past few decades be significantly in error, we feel confident another recognition *will be* preserved. A better solution will not emerge by returning to the old axis of choices. Rather, new formulations will evolve along the new axis (through the totalist socialist corner of the triangle in the graph) thus sharing more in common with totalist socialism than with either of the other two formulations. This is what we mean when we say "neither Leninism nor Social Democracy." For in fact, along an axis which measures changes in the cluster of attributes held in common by Leninism and Social Democracy, the two perspectives collapse to occupy the same position and totalist socialism is "to their left." This is the axis along which we see need for irrevocable movement.

Totalist socialism as a goal and theoretical orientation emphasizes four spheres of daily life and seeks to understand their independent and entwined dynamics. It is an attempt to evolve a new orientation suited to both our current situation and our socialist aims. To change our society, this view points to a new kind of movement which can combine solidarity and autonomy. But even if many aspects of our formulation were to prove incorrect, socialists will face some hard choices in coming years. While drawing many lessons from the history of countries that have had anti-capitalist revolutions and many insights from theories of the leaders of those revolutions, we are nevertheless going to have to make a clean break and move forward along a new scale of evaluation. Minimally, it would bode well if we could finally learn to distinguish between the two poles of the famous dichotomy, "socialism or barbarism," and to project only the former as our goal. It would generate hope if we could learn to address our country's population clearly and without rhetoric and connect socialist programs with their needs and passions. It would spur our own commitment if we could accurately situate ourselves as part of a vast human undertaking, while neither exaggerating nor demeaning our own contributions.

As we complete this book, Ronald Reagan has proposed a new economic plan and is also, simultaneously, pursuing something of an altered international policy. The mystification has been dropped. With regard to the economy the aim is simple. Redistribute from those at the bottom of the income lists to those at the top by way of massive gifts to the high tech and especially military sectors of the economy. With respect to the international arena, again one must admit the man is succinct and forward. Intervention is justified whenever "our needs" or even "our desires" are threatened, anywhere. Moreover, it would appear that intervention may also be justified in Reagan's mind even if neither economic needs nor ideological desires are threatened, so long as the creation of an accompanying war hysteria would suit his domestic aims by distracting attention from his economic boondoggles for the rich or the coming failures of his "supply-side" miracle cures.

One of the countries we have discussed in this volume, Cuba, is a possible target for Reagan's visionary new policies, as are El Salvador and Nicaragua in Latin America and Iran in the Mideast, among others. The time of political strife and struggle is likely upon us in the U.S. again and it may well attain a scale, very rapidly exceeding anything we have known since the sixties, and even what transpired then. It is a time of very serious danger for all people and thus a time that calls for a most concerted movement to forestall Reaganite catastrophes. But it is also a time of possibility. It is more than conceivable that a left could evolve in defense against Reaganism and then "come out the other side" not only having helped prevent a nuclear holocaust, international interventions, and the dissolution of the U.S. economy at the expense of working people and the poor, but also having created a new movement that will then move to a more aggressive posture seeking positive new gains in the decades ahead. Moreover, the situation we face currently almost compels this new movement not to narrow its aims to any single focus. Reaganism embodies an attack upon the daily life conditions of people in our society not solely through the economy or threat of war, but also via its moral incursions against feminism and by its promotion of racist activities throughout the country. Any effort to fight Reagan's domestic economic plan is going to require that working people not buy the idea that our country must prepare for military hostilities. Any effort to thwart militarism, on the other hand, will fail without support from organized labor, and that will not be forthcoming unless the anti-war movement shows itself sensitive to the situation of working people. Likewise, Reaganism is more than willing to employ the most barbarous racist ideology and hate mongering to divide any efforts at thwarting its aims. And similarly, as we have already seen, the strongest impulse of the conservative drive may well reside in the "social issues" where the leaders of the moral majority feast upon the widespread confusion over the relations between feminism, the family, pornography, sex, and violence.

We are at a time that both calls for and propels creation of a coalition of all types of existing organizations which are currently fighting around issues of class, race, sex, power within society, and imperialism. Whatever the ulitimate theory and strategy to guide a socialist movement in the U.S. will be, the formation of such a coalition and respectful experimentation with working together around all these issues can't help but be an important school for the socialist movement at the same time that it will be an indispensible tool for defense against Reagan's manic assault upon human rights and dignity throughout the world.

Every day socialism is delayed is another day of unnecessary pain and hardship etched into the lifeline of our species. The starvation of Calcutta and of the barrios of Santiago, the boredom and powerlessness of work in the auto plants of Detroit and steel foundaries of Leningrad, the ignorance of media mystification in New York and Peking, the degradation of homosexuals in Manchester, Moscow, and Matanzas, the racism of Boston, the Bantustans, and Belgrade, the cultural regimentation of China and Russia or the cultural depravity of the United States, and the political repression of a new HUAC in Washington or the old spectre of Stalinist show trials emerging in China—all this must be undone before it undoes our species. To define our struggle as anything less is to define our struggle away.

# Brief Bibliographic Comments
# for
# Socialism In Theory and Practice

At the close of Volume One, *Marxism and Socialist Theory*, we included an extensive bibliography by author. Here, rather than repeating that list, we thought it more useful to include some commentary on a brief selection of titles from among all those listed earlier. We do not mean to imply that these are somehow the best, nor that they most closely reflect our views. They are, however, all excellent volumes we have used extensively in preparing this work. With a few exceptions the titles we have listed can be gotten in paperback editions at quality paperback bookstores and certainly at left bookstores and major libraries. Our comments follow the chapter sequence of the two volumes, *Socialism in Theory and Practice*, quite closely.

Methodology: The simplest most straightforward introduction to issues of science, scientific thought, and rationality is Bertrand Russell's *The Art of Philosophy*, a delightful and invaluable short book that describes the canons of philosophical and logical reasoning. Perhaps the first place to turn to pursue a still deeper understanding of the philosophy of science and intellectual theorizing is T.S. Kuhn's *The Structure of Scientific Revolutions*. It has become a classic as a result of its treatment of the concept "paradigm" and though it is often redundant and no longer fully accepted, even by its author, it represents a fulcrum about which much modern discussion pivots. Indeed, to pursue some of that discussion, the best collection of articles extending and debating Kuhn's approach is probably *Criticism and the Growth of Knowledge* edited by Imre Lakatos and Robert Musgrave. An anarchist epistemology is found in the work of Paul Feyerabend, *Against Method*, but in our opinion perhaps the most compelling volume in this area is the recently released collection of essays by Imre Lakatos, *The Methodology of Scientific Research Programmes*. It is difficult reading, but the ease with which Lakatos treats issues of the history *and* philosophy of science and beautifully argued positions he develops are well worth the effort. It is from Lakatos, indeed, that we have taken the idea of "research programmes" and much else as well. Finally, there are a great many volumes of Marxist epistemology and of debate by Marxists over whether Marxism is or is not a science, but, to be honest, we find most of these too abstruse and obscure, too mired in exegesis ("quoting the masters"), and too ignorant of Marxism as other than dry economistic ideology and science in any form at all, to be useful for critical readers. Two exceptions, however, are obvious first choices for further reading (and also themselves contain further bibliographic suggestions): Bertell Ollman's *Alienation* is excellent and readable on problems of epistemology and especially important for his development of the method of "internal relations"; and Alvin Gouldner's *The Two Marxisms* has a great deal to say about Marxism and how it is and is not a science. Also relevant is E.P. Thompson's *The Poverty of Theory*, which addresses the question of Marxism as science or intellectual heritage.

Marxist Social Theory in General: With respect to Marxist theory in general, it is difficult to single out specific volumes. Our own efforts *What Is To Be Undone* and *Unorthodox Marxism* are useful both as supplementary and more extensive readings on many of the topics addressed in this chapter of Volume One. The former, in particular, situates some of our ideas with respect to other schools of thought and includes a more extensive treatment of orthodox Marxist theory, especially, historical materialism. The latter includes an extensive critique of orthodox Marxist economic theory, introduces our fourfold totalist approach, and applies it to problems of understanding the U.S. Gouldner's book, mentioned above, is also good in this category, as is Thompson's, but by and large the best way to get a general overview of contemporary Marxist theory may be to use a collection or survey work. An excellent collection addressing the work of many creative Marxist intellectuals is Dick Howard and Karl Klare's *The*

*Unknown Dimension,* regrettably very difficult to get because Basic Books has not undertaken a paperback edition. Arthur Hirsh has provided a much more accessible (South End Press) volume surveying the ideas of Sartre, de Beauvoir, Castoriadis, Gorz and other French "neo-Marxists" all analyzed in context of the events of May '68 seen as a kind of watershed in contemporary revolutionary thought and practice. Likewise, *The Origin of Modern Leftism* by Richard Gombin provides an important and succinct summary of "libertarian" or what Gombin calls left Marxist tradition and thought. Helmut Fleischer's *Marxism and History* gives a comprehensive but succinct and readable overview of different interpretations of Marx's approach to history and the meaning of "historical materialism." Finally, the writings of Herbert Marcuse have been especially important to our own intellectual development, particularly *One Dimensional Man, Essay on Liberation* and *Aesthetic Dimension.*

Political Theory: Two volumes that are particularly well known and useful for getting a grip on Marxist theory of the state are Ralph Miliband's *The State in Capitalist Society,* and Nicos Poulantzas' *State, Power, and Socialism.* The former is more readable, but the latter which is more recent is also perhaps theoretically richer. The journal *Kapitalistate* regularly includes articles on theory and analysis of state relations which are excellent and one of the frequent contributors in particular, Alan Wolfe, has done a number of provocative pieces. Carole Pateman's *Participation and Democratic Theory* deals with broader questions of democracy and participatory power in a very readable and rich fashion that bears not only on understanding the state under capitalism, but also the problems of state structure under socialism as well. Similarly, Mihaly Vajda's recent volume, *The State and Socialism* is quite interesting regarding the structure of "existing socialist" states and state theory in general, and the title essay is especially good and relevant to our thesis that the state, like the other three primary spheres of social activity, must be understood both autonomously and in interaction within a whole social formation. Anarchists have contributed significantly regarding our understanding of the ills of authoritarianism in state relations and society as a whole and a good survey volume is Daniel Guerin's *Anarchism,* while the works of Bakunin—for example the collection, edited by G.P. Maximov, *Bakunin*—are very indicative of the main trends of anarchist theory as well. Finally, a concrete discussion of how to understand the modern capitalist state and policy formation is found in Paul Joseph's South End Press volume, *Cracks in the Empire*, which uses the period of the Vietnam War and U.S. policy making for it as a case study for understanding state operations in general.

Kinship Theory: Two collections published by Monthly Review, Zillah Eisenstein's *Capitalist Patriarchy and Socialist Feminism* and Rayna Reiter's *Toward an Anthropology of Women*, have become contemporary classics as sources for socialist feminist theory and analysis. Particularly important, from our perspective, is the contribution by Gayle Rubin in the latter volume and the overall effort in both volumes to make a compelling case for the need to address patriarchy and sexism centrally but also in context of other social relations as well. A new South End Press collection edited by Lydia Sargent, *Women and Revolution*, takes the trend set in these two volumes still a step further by engaging in a clear debate over the importance of patriarchy in history, the dynamics and impact of sexism, the role of women as agents of social change, and the relation between feminist and Marxist analysis at all levels. Another South End Press work, *The Curious Courtship of Women's Liberation and Socialism*, by Batya Weinbaum, includes both a critique of Marxism's failings as a result of its not having conceptual categories capable of understanding the relations of the sexes, and a theoretical proposal for what such categories might look like. A volume that was particularly important in giving a framework to radical feminist thought was Shulamith Firestone's *The Dialectics of Sex*, though the more recent work of Mary Daly, *Gynecology*, is now having a greater impact. Her volume is unique not only for its scope and scholarship, but also for the style of writing Daly employs in her effort to counter not only "male language" but even "male thinking." Two important books which are post Gayle Rubin's essay and which focus on the importance of family relations and especially the dynamics of "mothering" for the determination of kinship relations are Dorothy Dinnerstein's *The Mermaid and the Minotaur* and Nancy Chodorow's *The Reproduction of Mothering*. Dinnerstein's book is more popularly written and accessible, but the difficulty of Chodorow's is worth the effort for those who are interested in psychology and pursuing the issues to great depth. Finally, Barbara Ehrenreich and Deirdre English's *For Her Own*

*Good* is an example of theory in use rather than theory for theory's sake.

Community Theory: The writings of Amilcar Cabral recently made available by Monthly Review are an excellent source for understanding the importance of cultural and community concerns and their relation to problems of social change in the Third World. Harold Cruse's *Rebellion and Revolution* offers both a critique of orthodox Marxist and Leninist approaches to community issues and many viable alternative insights as well. It is an exceptionally important but regrettably not widely enough read volume. Likewise, Robert Allen's two works, *Black Awakening in Capitalist America* and *Reluctant Reformers*, also provide criticism of accepted socialist norms for addressing these issues and insights into alternative viewpoints, but in this book the approach is more historical than theoretical. The focus is on an historical account and the theory and analysis is woven into the texture of that. There are many collections and volumes devoted to treatment of nationalist perspectives, but perhaps the fastest route to a working understanding is to be had by reading the *Autobiography of Malcolm X* and his collected speeches and essays. The work of Frantz Fanon, especially *The Wretched of the Earth* and *Toward an African Revolution* is especially important to coming to an understanding of the psychological dimensions of racism and colonialism. James Boggs' *The American Revolution* is an important work on race and class in capitalist society and, finally, the more recent South End Press volume by Manning Marable, *From the Grassroots,* takes up the same issues anew attempting as well to broaden the Marxist approach to encompass a serious concern for community relations.

Economic Theory: For the most part what is available regarding left economic theory is a host of different treatments of Marxist economic theory, in particular, focusing upon the Labor Theory of Value and its applications. In our opinion the best of these works is still Paul Sweezy's *The Theory of Capitalist Development,* for its clarity and conciseness, unless the reader has the time and energy to pursue Marx's *Capital,* especially Volume One. On class analysis, two volumes are particularly useful in light of the discussion that we have engaged in here: Pat Walker's South End Press collection, *Between Labor and Capital* is a dialogue by a number of different leftists revolving around Barbara and John Ehrenreich's essay on the "professional and managerial class," and Alvin Gouldner's *The Future of Intellectuals and the Rise of the New Class* is a succinct volume which includes important material bearing on the same question. Walker's volume includes diverse views, often critical of the lead essay, in a debate format. Our own contribution, "A Ticket to Ride: New Locations on the Class Map," contains an argument concerning the definition and importance of the concept "coordinator class." Gouldner's work argues the central role of the "new class," whatever their other failings, in all socialist programs for change. Our own approach to economic theory is presented in *Unorthodox Marxism* and also a forthcoming volume on economic welfare theory. Of immense importance to the development of our approach, and infrequently cited by others, is the creative work of Cornelius Castoriadis, for example, the Solidarity pamphlet "Crisis in Modern Society," which includes a powerful critique of orthodox Marxism. Another valuable critique of Marxist economic theory is Joan Robinson's essay *On Marxian Economics,* and a number of feminist and community studies to be referenced below also include relevant critiques. Regarding the economics of capitalism, beyond general theory, Steve Marglin's "What Do Bosses Do?" Harry Braverman's *Labor and Monopoly Capital,* and diverse articles in RRPE—especially those by Herb Gintis and Sam Bowles on the economics of the capitalist firm—as well as our own work referenced above, give a good overview of criticism in tune with the analysis in these two volumes. Concerning socialist economics, on the other hand, few books have an approach like ours but Lange's *Problems of the Political Economy of Socialism,* Sweezy and Bettleheim's *Transition to Socialism,* Bertram Silverman's collection *Man and Socialism in Cuba,* and especially Cornelius Castoriadis' *Councils and the Economics of a Self-Managed Society,* all provide important reading about problems of workers' control, socialist workplace relations, and socialist allocation and incentives.

Soviet Union: The literature available on the Soviet Union is virtually endless. Maurice Dobb's *Soviet Economic Development* and E.H. Carr's multi-volume, *The Bolshevik Revolution* are two classic histories rich in detail and information though neither shares our interpretation of the history. Maurice Brinton's *The*

*Bolsheviks and Workers' Control* provides a particularistic summary of information relevant to the development of economic centralization and authoritarianism which is indispensable as an aid to understanding the Soviet experience. In *What Is To Be Undone* Albert discusses the Soviet revolution in context of a critique of Marxism Leninism attempting to trace historical failings back to strategic and theoretical roots. A volume that is very revealing concerning the situation of women in the Soviet Union and also in the Eastern bloc countries is Alena Heitlinger's *Women and State Socialism,* and her analysis was very useful in our treatment of the same issue. Likewise, the two Volume set by Horace Davis on *Marxism and Nationalism* was useful concerning the situation of minorities in the Soviet Union.

China: MacFarlane and Wheelwright's *Chinese Road to Socialism* provides an excellent overview of Chinese economic and political history through the Cultural Revolution. For understanding the period of the Cultural Revolution itself, however, we found K.S. Karol's volume, *The Second Chinese Revolution* exceptionally insightful. It is journalistic in tone and yet operates within a very sophisticated analytic framework. However, for one book that covers the whole expanse of the Chinese experience with sensitivity and critical insight, and for an analysis that dovetails with our own at many points, see the regrettably not too widely known *Mao's China,* by Maurice Meisner. William Hinton's *Fanshen* remains the single most compelling description of life before the revolution and of the intricacies of the revolution itself. Albert's *What Is To Be Undone* has a chapter evaluating Maoism in context of a critique of Leninism and orthodox Marxist theory and is a good supplement to our discussion here. Two important volumes on the experience of women in China are Delia Davin's *Women-Work* and Elizabeth Croll's *Feminism and Socialism in China.* Finally, Simon Leys' volume *Chinese Shadows* gives a disturbing account of what may be an all too real underside of life in revolutionary China. Of course, it also pays to read Mao's own writings, especially those in the first volume of his four volume collected works.

Cuba: In our opinion K.S. Karol's *Guerillas in Power* remains the best overview and analytic volume on the Cuban revolution. It is especially revealing regarding relations between Cuba and the

Soviet Union, but does have the major drawback of being somewhat out of date. Indeed, another early volume, Maurice Zeitlin's
*Workers in Cuba*, is also good, and especially worth a look is its
introduction which addresses a number of concerns about workers'
control. The more recent volume by Arthur McEwen fills out
much of the story concerning contemporary political and economic
history, but without the journalistic style that makes Karol's book
so delightful to read. Bertram Silverman's *Man and Socialism in
Cuba* provides an account of the economic debate between Che
and others that was so important to Cuban history and to our own
analysis and evaluation of the Cuban experience. For ourselves,
however, the speeches and collected writings of both Che Guevara
and Fidel Castro have been exceptionally important, not only to
understanding the Cuban experience, but also for their more
univeral insights, analyses, compassion, and revolutionary spirit.
Perhaps the best volume of Che's works is *Che* by Gervasi, and
M.I.T. press is currently assembling a multi-volume collection of
all of Castro's speeches, writings, etc. Finally, one can maintain a
good familiarity with the comings and goings of Cuban policy by
keeping up with *Granma*, the major Cuban newspaper.

Socialist Vision:  Paul Sweezy and Charles Bettelheim engaged in
a series of debates in Monthly Review which were subsequently
published as *The Transition to Socialism*, and these still constitute
a very important interchange of views about socialist economic
possibilities and forms. A critique, however, of this discussion can
be found in *What Is To Be Undone*, mentioned above. Another
volume bearing on similar economic issues and addressing questions associated with the debate over the merits of planning,
market allocation, and different incentive schemes is Bertram
Silverman's *Man and Socialism in Cuba*, also mentioned above.
Anton Pannekoek's *Workers' Councils* provides an excellent
account of how workers might organize councils and the merits of
such organization for shopfloor self-management, while Cornelius Castoriadis' *Workers' Councils and the Economics of a Self-
Managed Society* is the one work we know of which makes a
serious effort to propose an alternative to both central planning
and markets as means of socialist allocation. While we differ with
Castoriadis at many points, his essay is certainly provocative and
important reading. Regarding socialist visions in the eyes of

Marxists from Eastern Europe, Marc Rakovsky's *Towards an East European Marxism*, and George Konrad and Ivan Szelenyi's *The Intellectuals on the Road to Class Power*, are discussions addressing the nature of the systems in current dominance—both the polity and the economy—and include numerous discussions relevant to developing a viable socialist model. Bahro's and the Konrad/Szelenyi books, in particular, have done much to advance the recognition that a major obstacle to socialist economic successes can be the desire of intellectuals to preserve or extend their own interests as opposed to those of all other workers. Ursula Le Guin's novel, *The Dispossessed*, is infinitely more readable and graphic than any of the other works we have mentioned, and while it focuses on a situation of scarcity, it raises a great many practical questions related to what it means to have participation and self-management within a social formation.

Regarding socialist political possibilities, Bahro's book is again relevant, but particularly useful are some anarchist works, Bakunin's—mentioned earlier—perhaps being the most compelling. Murray Bookchin's writings are relevant to considerations of a revolutionary model regarding not only politics, but also economics, city planning, and especially ecological and social diversity. Perhaps it is best to look at his *Listen Marxist* and *Limits to the City*. In the former, one also finds a scathing polemic aimed at orthodox Marxist Leninists.

The only volume we have found dealing with a socialist vision of kinship relations is *The Humanisation of Socialism* authored jointly by Andras Hegedus, Agnes Heller, Maria Markus, and Mihaly Vajda, each of whom contributed essays. A particularly important article, however, is to be found in Socialist Review, No. 49: "When Women and Men Mother," by Diane Ehrensaft. Regrettably, we don't have familiarity with any volumes on socialist community that are even roughly in tune with the visions we have put forward in this volume.

Strategy: Regarding the problem of strategy, disappointingly leftists in the West, and particularly in the United States, have failed to write many analytic studies of their own recent experiences or serious proposals for strategy for social change. Nonetheless, there are numerous books that address matters related to strategy. For broad concerns a good starting place—in tune, more or less, with many of the ideas we have presented—are certain of the works of Herbert Marcuse and Andre Gorz. Marcuse's *Counter Revolution and Revolt,* for example, not only challenges many Leninist shibboleths, but also offers original thoughts about agents and means of revolution in industrialized countries. Gorz has been perhaps the left's most courageous writer on "what to do" and his *Strategy for Labor* is still a classic volume for explicating how to develop a strategic sense and especially for an analysis of reformism and presentation if Gorz's alternative, non-reformist reforms, a concept of program which is immensely important to socialists who want to base their activity in immediate needs but also address it to long run goals. Gorz's collection of essays, *Socialism and Revolution,* regrettably dropped out of print by Doubleday, is also very important for ideas about who will make a new revolution, revolutionary organization, and reformism. We are not really familiar with new turns in Gorz's thought, but without doubt, they will certainly provide provocative reading. Also accessible and important regarding agents and means of social change other than what Leninism has to offer, are a series of interviews with Jean Paul-Sartre collected in the volume titled, *Between Existentialism and Marxism.* Daniel Singer's book, *Prelude to Revolution,* about May '68 in Paris, provides not only an exciting history of those events, but also a readable discussion of revolutionary strategy. Our own strategic ideas are spelled out in some detail in both *What Is To Be Undone* and *Unorthodox Marxism.* A primarily strategic study that we like very much and that is written in a committed, spirited fashion is Sheila Rowbotham's essay in the volume *Beyond the Fragments.* She not only critiques archaic (but still breathing) Leninist catechism about strategy and socialism, but also begins charting a new approach sensitive to many more sides of social life than other activists generally address. Hers is a socialist feminist approach which not only proposes new aims and stances, but addresses even questions of the tone and lifestyle of the left. Richard Wright's autobiography, *American Hunger,* while not really a book of revolutionary strategy, does recount Wright's experiences with the C.P. and thereby serves as a very provocative study regarding the problems of organizing and weaknesses of many old conceptions about how to do it. Harold Cruse's volume mentioned earlier, and Robert Allen's works as well, criticize

Marxism Leninism as incapable of encompassing the needs of national and racial minorities in strategy and vision and offer both implicit and explicit alternatives. The essays of Wilhelm Reich in *Sex Pol* and particularly "What Is Class Consciousness," are an especially good antidote to simplistic ideas about where consciousness comes from and how it takes root in our psyches, and the meaning such issues have for problems of socialist program and organization. It is a classic work and teaches its readers not only about people and consciousness, but about what strategy and strategic thinking really are. At that level, indeed, it is valuable to look at volumes about strategic thinking in any context—or Lenin's or Mao's strategic essays—not for the concrete content, so much as to develop clarity about what "tactics," "strategy," "aims," long and short term program, and analysis are, and how they interrelate. Even reading someone like Clauswitz or a volume on strategic thinking in some game—chess, football, etc.—can be very useful. Returning to the concrete, however, Dick Cluster's recent South End Press volume *They Should Have Served That Cup Of Coffee* includes a collection of pieces about experience during the 1960s and early 70s compiled in a way designed to not only preserve the history and give it a human reality and depth, but also to draw strategic lessons relevant for the immediate future. Likewise Dan Georgakas and Marvin Surkin's *Detroit: I Do Mind Dying* is perhaps the most readable and revealing account of a recent social movement in the U.S. and provides considerable data and rich history relevant for anyone trying to assess the prospects for social change and the problems which need to be overcome to develop workable organizations and political programs. Of historical studies that readily provide strategic insights a good prospect is Tony Cliff's first volume of his four volume biography of Lenin. Finally, the Ehrenreich's piece on the professional and managerial class in Walker's *Between Labor and Capital* mentioned above, and many other essays included there as well, offer strategic insights, while in general all of Barbara Ehrenreich's work repays a very close reading as she is one of the few leftist writers who not only functions well in the mists of abstract theory, but has the experience and touch to also bring it all down to the real world of breathing, feeling, struggling people. Most recently, for the kind of strategic thinking that will be essential to developing workable programs in the eighties, readers should see her essay, "The Women's Movements: Feminist and Anti-Feminist," in *Radical America* Vol. 15, No. 1/2, a magazine which itself regularly makes important theoretical and strategic conceptions.

# FOOTNOTES

## The Soviet Experience

1. For a discussion that seeks to trace an analysis of the practical Soviet experience to its theoretical roots, see Michael Albert, *What Is To Be Undone*, Porter Sargent Publisher, Boston, 1971, Chapters three and four.
2. Ibid. p. 30-32.
3. Isaac Deutscher, *The Prophet Armed*. London, Oxford Univ. Press, 1954.
4. Maurice Dobb, *Soviet Economic Development Since 1917*, International Publishers, New York, 1968, p. 79.
5. Ibid. p. 92.
6. Ibid. p. 104.
7. Ibid.
8. Ibid. p. 93.
9. Ibid. p. 104.
10. Ibid. p. 105.
11. Daniel Cohn-Bendit, *Obsolete Communism: A Left Wing Alternative*, McGraw Hill, New York, p. 220.
12. Ibid. p. 221.
13. Ibid. p. 222.
14. Albert, op. cit. Chapter five.
15. Paul Avrich, *Kronstadt 1921*, Princeton Univ. Press, p. 29.
16. Ibid. p. 238.
17. Cohn-Bendit, op. cit. p. 236.
18. Ibid. p. 238.
19. Richard Gombin, *The Radical Tradition*, St. Martins, New York, 1979, p. 31.
20. Cohn-Bendit, op. cit. p. 239.
21. Charles Bettleheim, *Class Struggles in the USSR: 1917-1923*, Monthly Review, New York, 1976, p. 365.
22. Leon Trotsky, *Terrorism i Kommunism*, Petersburg, 1920.
23. Bettleheim, op. cit. p. 395.
24. Ibid. p. 399.
25. Ibid.
26. Ibid.
27. Ibid. p. 400.
28. Alvin Gouldner, "STalinism: A Study of Internal Colonialism," *Telos*, No. 34, Winter 1977-'78, p. 5-48.

29. Ibid. p. 12.
30. Ibid. p. 42.
31. Ibid. p. 29.
32. Ibid. p. 30
33. Ibid. p. 35
34. Ibid.
35. Ibid.
36. Ibid. p. 36.
37. Ibid.
38. Ibid. p. 38.
39. See E. P. Thompson, *The Poverty of Theory*, Monthly Review Press, 1980, for a relevant discussion of Althusser's theories.
40. Dobb, op. cit. p. 83.
41. Ibid. p. 90.
42. Ibid.
43. Ibid. p. 87.
44. Ibid. p. 91-92.
45. Ibid. p. 93.
46. Likely Dobb and Bettelheim would take a position of this type.
47. We would support this type of position, largely in the council communist heritage.
48. It seems likely that Maurice Brinton would support a view like this.
49. Dobb, op. cit. p. 110-111.
50. Ibid. p. 110.
51. Ibid. p. 118.
52. Ibid. p. 119.
53. Ibid. p. 128.
54. Ibid.
55. Bettleheim, op. cit. p. 402.
56. Ibid. p. 405.
57. Ibid. p. 406.
58. Ibid. p. 337.
59. Ibid.
60. Ibid. p. 398.
61. Dobb, op. cit. p. 182.
62. Ibid. p. 183.
63. Ibid. p. 181-182.
64. Ibid. p. 182.
65. Ibid. p. 182-183.
66. Ibid. p. 228.
67. For a remarkably clear self-criticism on this matter, see Bettelheim, op. cit. p. 19-29.
68. Dobb, op. cit. p. 259-260.

69. Daniel Singer, "Weaknesses and Potentialities of the Dissident Movement," Il Manifesto, *Power and Opposition in Post-Revolutionary Societies,* Ink Links, 1979, p. 21.

70. Ibid. p. 31.

71. Ibid. p. 23.

72. Ibid. p. 29.

73. Boris Weyl, "Marx and Lenin Read in the Camps," Il Manifesto, op. cit. p. 93-94.

74. Alena Heitlinger, *Women and State Socialism,* MacMillan, London, 1979, contains an excellent discussion and useful bibliography.

75. Kate Millet, *Sexual Politics,* New York, Avon, 1971.

76. Sheila Rowbotham, *Women, Resistance, and Revolution,* Vintage, New York, p. 138.

77. Ibid. p. 139.

78. Viktor Haynes and Olga Semyonova, Eds. *Workers Against the Gulag,* Pluto Press, London, p. 7.

79. Heitlinger, op. cit. p. 100.

80. Ibid. p. 102.

81. Haynes op. cit. p. 7.

82. Heitlinger op. cit. p. 94.

83. Ibid.

84. Ibid. p. 103.

85. Ibid. p. 103, 106.

86. Rowbotham, op. cit. p. 165.

87. Heitlinger op. cit. p. 112.

88. Rowbotham, op. cit. p. 138.

89. Rowbotham, op. cit. Miller, op. cit. and Wilhelm Reich, *Sex Pol,* Vintage, New York, are all relevant references.

90. The writings of Emma Goldman and Alexandra Kollantai as well as biographies of each are readily available and listed in our bibliography.

91. Batya Weinbaum, op. cit. includes a relevant discussion.

92. Rowbotham, op. cit. p. 149.

93. Ibid.

94. Ibid.

95. Ibid. p. 152.

96. Ibid.

97. Weinbaum, op. cit. p. 57.

98. Ibid.

99. Ibid. p. 58.

100. Heitlinger op. cit. p. 21.

101. Ralph Bolton, Washington Post, Jan. 5, 1981.

102. Weinbaum, op. cit.

103. Heitlinger op. cit. p. 51-52.

104. Albert and Hahnel, *Marxism and Socialist Theory,* South End Press, Boston, 1981, Chapter five.
105. Heitlinger op. cit. p. 131.
106. Ibid. p. 203.
107. Horace Davis, *Nationalism and Socialism,* Monthly Review, 1967, and *Toward a Marxist Theory of Nationalism,* Monthly Review, 1978.
108. *Marxist Theory of Nationalism,* op. cit. p. 98.
109. Ibid. p. 106.
110. Ibid. p. 120-121.
111. Ibid.
112. Ibid. p. 117.

## The Chinese Experience

1. William Hinton, *Fanshen,* Monthly Review, New York, 1966.
2. Edgar Snow's discussion in *Red Star Over China,* Grove Press, and Mao's own *Selected Works* are relevant to this point.
3. We have chosen to employ the "old spelling" for names on the simple criterion that they are far more familiar and their use, which is by no means ruled out by the Chinese, makes comprehension of already complex material that much simpler.
4. Maurice Meisner, *Mao's China,* New York, Free Press, 1977 and K.S. Karol, *The Second Chinese Revolution,* Hill and Wang, New York, 1973 have proven to be the most useful references in our work on China.
5. Meisner, op. cit. p. 65-66.
6. Meisner, op. cit. p. 71-72.
7. This self-description can be readily found throughout the works of Mao, for example, even in the excerpts of the *Little Red Book.*
8. Franz Schurman, *Ideology and Organization in Communist China,* Univ. of Calif. Press, includes a detailed analysis of these dynamics.
9. Karol, op. cit. p. 24.
10. Albert, op. cit. p. 221-222.
11. Mao Tse-tung, "On Coalition Government," in *Collected Works,* Peking.
12. Karol, op. cit. p. 15.
13. Moshe Lewin, *Lenin's Last Struggles,* Pluto, London, 1968.
14. Albert, op. cit.
15. Edoarda Masi, "China: The Dialectic of Revolutionary Upsurges and Counterrevolutionary Waves," Il Manifesto, op. cit. p. 73.
16. Meisner, op. cit. p. 387-388.
17. We roughly follow the periodization of Wheelright and MacFarlane *The Chinese Road to Socialism,* Monthly Review, 1970.

18. Hinton, op. cit.
19. MacFarlane op. cit. p. 37.
20. Ibid. p. 43-53.
21. Ibid.
22. Ibid. p. 49.
23. This view is argued by Bill Russell in "Chinese Roads to State Capitalism," in Issue No. 8 of *Root and Branch.*
24. Meisner, op. cit. Chapter 12.
25. Ibid. p. 243.
26. Ibid. p. 245.
27. Ibid. p. 246-247.
28. Ibid.
29. Ibid.
30. Ibid. p. 275.
31. Ibid. p. 279.
32. Ibid.
33. Ibid. p. 280.
34. Ibid.
35. Ibid.
36. Russell, op. cit. p. 24.
37. Ibid.
38. Meisner, op. cit. p. 324.
39. Weinbaum, op. cit. Chapter one.
40. Albert and Hahnel, *Marxism and Socialist Theory, op. cit.*
41. *Rowbotham, op. cit. p. 173.*
42. *Delia Davin, Women-Work,* Oxford, 1973, p. 10.
43. Ibid. p. 11.
44. Judith Stacy, "When Patriarchy Kowtows," *Socialist Patriarchy,* Zillah Eisenstein, Monthly Review Press, p. 300.
45. Rowbotham, op. cit. p. 185.
46. Stacy, op. cit. p. 321.
47. Weinbaum, op. cit. p. 6.
48. Stacy, op. cit. p. 326-327.
49. Davin, op. cit. p. 195.
50. Stacy, op. cit. p. 328.
51. Weinbaum, op. cit. p. 80.
52. Stacy, op. cit. p. 329-330.
53. Ibid.
54. Ibid. p. 328.
55. Ibid. p. 330.
56. Weinbaum and Davin, op. cit., both make this argument.
57. Rowbotham, op. cit. p. 180.
58. Ibid

59. Stacy, op. cit. p. 307.
60. Ibid.
61. Ibid.
62. Ibid. p. 312.
63. Ibid. p. 313.
64. Ibid. p. 314.
65. Ibid.
66. Ibid.
67. Weinbaum, op. cit. p. 140.
68. Stacy, op. cit. p. 316.
69. Elisabeth Croll, *Feminism and Socialism in China*, Schocken, 1978, p. 289.
70. Croll, op. cit. p. 310.
71. Ibid.
72. Ibid. p. 317.
73. Ibid. p. 323-325.
74. Ibid. p. 323.
75. Ibid. p. 328.
76. Steven Butler, *Washington Post*, Oct. 19, 1981.
77. Ibid.
78. Thomas Weiskopf, *Washington Post*, Nov. 12, 1981.
79. Stacy, op. cit. p. 321.
80. Simon Leys, *Chinese Shadows*, London: Penguin, 1974.
81. Ibid.
82. Tamara Deutscher, "A Chinese Journey." *New Left Review*, No. 120-121.
83.    Davin, op. cit. p. 122.
84. Ibid.
85. Stacy, op. cit. p. 311.
86. Robert Orr, *Religion in China*, Friendship Press, New York, 1980, p. 32.
87. Ibid.
88. Ibid. p. 162.
89. Ibid.
90. Ibid. p. 43.
91. Ibid.
92. Ibid. p. 70.
93. Ibid.
94. Ibid. p. 99-100.
95. Ibid. p. 89.
96. Ibid. p. 130.
97. Ibid. p. 35.
98. Mao Tse-tung, *Selected Readings*, "Talks at the Yenan Forum on

Literature and Art," Peking, 1971, p. 251.
99. Ibid. p. 264.


## The Cuban Experience

1. Fidel Castro, "The Duty of the Revolutionary," in Kenner and Petras, *Fidel Speaks*, Evergreen, 1969.
2. K.S. Karol, *Guerrillas in Power*, Hill and Wang, New York, 1970, p. 138.
3. Ibid.
4. Hans Magnus Enzenberger, "Portrait of a Party: Prehistory, Structure, and Ideology of the PCC," in *The New Cuba, Paradoxes and Potentials*, Ronald Radosh, ed. William Morrow and Co., New York, 1976, p. 116.
5. Ibid. p. 117-118.
6. Karol, op. cit. p. 57.
7. Enzenberger, op. cit. p. 119.
8. Ibid.
9. Ibid. p. 122.
10. Karol, op. cit. p. 246.
11. Enzenberger, op. cit. p. 123.
12. Carmelo Mesa-lago, *Cuba in the 1970s: Pragmatism and Institutionalization*, Univ. of New Mexico, Albuquerque, 1978, p. 70-71.
13. Ibid. p.71.
14. Ibid. p. 72.
15. Arthur MacEwen, draft copy of forthcoming work on Cuba, chapter 24. p. 2.
16. Ibid. p. 4-5.
17. Ibid. p. 3-4.
18. Ibid. p. 6-7.
19. Ibid. p. 8.
20. Mesa Lago, op. cit. p. 75.
21. Ibid.
22. Ibid. p. 80.
23. Ibid.
24. MacEwen, op. cit. p. 9.
25. Marta Harnecker, *Cuba: Dictatorship of Democracy?* Lawrence Hill, 1980, p. 78.
26. Ibid. p.83.
27. Kenner, op. cit.
28. Harnecker, op. cit. p. 101.
29. MacEwen, op. cit. p. 7.
30. First Congress of the Communist Party of Cuba, Havana, December 17-22, 1975, Progress Publishers, Moscow, 1976, "Fidel Castro's Report to

the Central Committee," p. 45.
31. Ibid. p. 43.
32. Sam Dolgoff, *The Cuban Revolution: A Critical Perspective*, Black Rose Books, Montreal, 1976, p. 180.
33. Fidel Castro, Speech to First Party Congress, op. cit. p. 49-50.
34. MacEwen, op. cit. chapter seven.
35. Ibid.
36. Ibid. chapter ten.
37. Castro, Speech to First Party Congress, op. cit. p. 65.
38. Karol, op. cit. p. 215.
39. Ibid. p. 216.
40. Ibid.
41. Ibid. p. 220.
42. Ibid. p. 236.
43. Ibid. p. 320-321.
44. Ibid.
45. Ibid. p. 287.
46. See Bertram Silverman's introduction to *Man and Socialism in Cuba*, Bertram Silverman, ed. Atheneum, 1973.
47. Karol, op. cit. p. 327.
48. From a letter to Carlos Quijana, written from Africa in 1965, published in *Economics: Mainstream Readings and Radical Critiques*, David Mermelstein, ed., Random House, 1972, p. 455.
49. Ibid.
50. Karol, op. cit. p. 330.
51. Mesa Lago, op. cit. p. 8.
52. Karol, op. cit. p. 203.
53. Ibid. p. 201, 202.
54. Ibid.
55. Ibid. p. 357.
56. Ibid. p. 361.
57. Ibid.
58. Ibid. p. 363.
59. MacEwen, op. cit. chapter seventeen.
60. Ibid. chapter thirty one.
61. Ibid.
62. Ronald Radosh, "Cuba: A Personal Report," Radosh, op. cit., p. 60.
63. Ibid. p. 55.
64. Ibid. p. 52.
65. MacEwen, op. cit.
66. Radosh, op. cit. p. 62.
67. Ibid.
68. Ibid. p. 55.

69. Ibid. p. 61.
70. Mesa Lago, op. cit. p. 35.
71. Ibid.
72. Ibid. p. 36.
73. Ibid. p. 32.
74. Ibid. p. 10.
75. Ibid. p. 32.
76. MacEwen, op. cit. chapter twenty three.
77. Mesa Lago, op. cit. p. 30-31.
78. Castro, op. cit. p. 114-119.
79. Ibid. p. 123-125.
80. Ibid.
81. Marlise Simons, "Cuba Reviving Market Forces to Lift Economy," *Washington Post*, May 29, 1980.
82. Maurice Zeitlin, *Revolutionary Politics and the Cuban Working Class*, Harper Torchbooks, 1970, p. xv.
83. C. Wright Mills, *Listen Yankee: The Revolution in Cuba*, Ballantine, N.Y., 1960, p. 15.
84. Rowbotham, op. cit. p. 221.
85. Oscar Lewis, *Four Women*, Univ. of Illinois, 1977, p. xvi.
86. Ibid. p. xv.
87. Carollee Bengelsdorf and Alice Hageman, "Emerging from Underdevelopment: Women and Work in Cuba," in Eisenstein, op. cit. p. 277.
88. Ibid.
89. Lewis, op. cit. p. xviii.
90. Bengelsdorf, op. cit. p. 278.
91. Ibid. p. 278-279.
92. Lewis, op. cit. p. xxvi.
93. Bengelsdorf, op. cit. p. 279.
94. Ibid. p. 279.
95. Benglesdorf and Hageman, "Women and Work," *Cuba Review*, Vol. 4, No. 2, p. 8.
96. Ibid.
97. Lewis, op. cit. p. 20.
98. Bengelsdorf in Eisenstein, op. cit. p. 283.
99. Ibid. p. 279.
100. Ibid.
101. Margarita Matias, "The Cuban Family," *Cuba Review*, Vol. 2, No. 4, p. 6-12.
102. Ibid.
103. Ibid.
104. Heidi Steffens, "A Woman's Place," *Cuba Review*, Vol. 4, No. 2, p. 30.
105. Ibid.

106. Margaret Randal, "Introducing the Family Code," *Cuba Review*, Vol 4, No. 2, p. 32.
107. Bengelsdorf in Eisenstein, op. cit. p. 290.
108. Rowbotham, op. cit. p. 231.
109. Matias, op. cit. p. 11-12.
110. Ibid.
111. Ibid.
112. Bengelsdorf in Eisenstein, op. cit. p. 292.
113. Ibid. p. 272.
114. Rowbotham, op. cit. p. 233.
115. Karol, op. cit. p. 238-239.
116. Ibid.
117. Ibid. p.240.
118. Ibid.
119. Ibid.
120. Ibid. p. 241.
121. Ibid.
122. Maurice Halperin, in Radosh, op. cit. p. 199-200.
123. Ibid.
124. Karol, op. cit. p. 246.
125. Halperin, op. cit. p. 201.
126. Karol, op. cit. p. 395.
127. Halperin, op. cit. p. 203.
128. Ibid. p. 204.
129. Retamar, Robert Fernandez, "Caliban: Note Toward a Discussion of Culture in Our America," Mass. Review, Vol. XV, No. 1/2, p. 66-67.
130. Halperin, op. cit. p. 193.
131. Ibid. p. 208.
132. *N.Y. Times*, May 22, 1971.
133. *Granma, Weekly Review*, May 9, 1971.
134. Ibid.
135. Phyl Garland, "Cuban Music," *Black Scholar*, Summer 1977.
136. Bernice Reagan, "Impressions of Cuban Culture by an Afro-American Artist," *Black Scholar*, Summer, 1977, p. 55.
137. Ibid. p. 56.
138. Ibid.

## Prospects for Socialism

1. Daniel Singer, *The Road to Gdansk*, Monthly Review, 1981, p. 221.
2. Ibid. p. 235.
3. Ibid.

4. Ibid.
5. Abraham Blumberg, "Poland: The Revolt of the Workers," *Dissent,* Winter, 1981, p. 25-26.
6. Ibid. p. 26.
7. Jacek Kuron, "What Next In Poland?" *Dissent,* op. cit. p. 34.
8. Ibid.

## Kinship Vision

1. Weinbaum, op. cit. p. 12.
2. Hegedus, Heller, Markus, Vajda, *The Humanization of Socialism* Allison and Busby, 1966.
3. Diane Ehrensaft, "When Women and Men Mother," *Socialist Review,* No. 49.

# Index

403